The Bibles of the Far Right

The Bibles of the Far Right

HANNAH M. STRØMMEN

OXFORD
UNIVERSITY PRESS

Oxford University Press is a department of the University of Oxford. It furthers
the University's objective of excellence in research, scholarship, and education
by publishing worldwide. Oxford is a registered trade mark of Oxford University
Press in the UK and certain other countries.

Published in the United States of America by Oxford University Press
198 Madison Avenue, New York, NY 10016, United States of America.

© Oxford University Press 2024

All rights reserved. No part of this publication may be reproduced, stored in
a retrieval system, or transmitted, in any form or by any means, without the
prior permission in writing of Oxford University Press, or as expressly permitted
by law, by license, or under terms agreed with the appropriate reproduction
rights organization. Inquiries concerning reproduction outside the scope of the
above should be sent to the Rights Department, Oxford University Press, at the
address above.

You must not circulate this work in any other form
and you must impose this same condition on any acquirer.

CIP data is on file at the Library of Congress

ISBN 978–0–19–778989–6

DOI: 10.1093/oso/9780197789896.001.0001

Printed by Sheridan Books, Inc., United States of America

Contents

Preface vii

1. The European Far Right — 1
2. Mapping Biblical Assemblages — 39
3. Biblical Assemblages in Breivik's Manifesto — 82
4. Biblical Connections and Continuities — 113
5. The War Bible — 141
6. The Civilisation Bible — 176
7. The Problem of Biblical Violence — 209
8. Deterritorialising Biblical Assemblages — 243
9. Biblical Lines of Flight — 287

Bibliography — 313
Index — 329
Biblical References — 333

Preface

"We had three days of fun before the nightmare began. I had already made new friends but a few of these friendships wouldn't last long, in fact, they would be the shortest I ever had".[1] These are the words of Tonje, who was nineteen years old in 2011, when the terror attacks in Norway struck. On 22 July 2011, a far-right terrorist set off a bomb in the government quarter in Oslo. He then drove to Utøya, an island nearly forty kilometres from Oslo, where Norway's Labour Party youth organisation (AUF) held its annual summer camp. Disguised as a police man, he made it onto the island. It did not take long before he dropped his cover and started to shoot at the participants of the summer camp and those working there. In her account of that day at Utøya, Tonje remembers hiding from the perpetrator, hearing his footsteps nearby:

> In my head I said goodbye to everyone I knew, to my mum, to my little brother, to my dad, I was ready to die. I was ready to get up, take the shots standing, not lie in fear, I was ready to die. I was just about to get up when I couldn't hear the steps anymore, he had passed by, he hadn't seen me. Just afterwards, he shot about ten teenagers.[2]

Tonje survived. Seventy-seven people did not survive. Many more were badly injured.

At the time of my writing this book, just over ten years have passed since that day. But the far-right worldview that the perpetrator was inspired by, and contributed to, continues to be propagated in extreme and more mainstream forms across Europe and beyond. Biblical texts and Bibles are part of this worldview. This study examines how bits of Bible and invocations of Bibles function in the far-right worldview of which the 22 July perpetrator is a part. In particular, it elucidates how Bibles are used to negotiate claims

---

[1] Tonje S, 'Mitt Utøya', Testimony published on the 22 July Centre website: https://www.22julis enteret.no/aktuelt/artikler/tonje-s. (Last accessed December 2022). My translation.
[2] Ibid.

about European identity. There are textures to this worldview that are yet to be examined regarding the forms Bibles take in contemporary far-right circles, their connections and continuities with past Bible-use, as well as the directions these Bibles might take in the future.

I began thinking about the questions that animate this book back in 2011. Generative conversations with Yvonne Sherwood, Ward Blanton, and Fatima Tofighi spurred on my interest in Bible, politics, and Islam. When I started working at the University of Chichester in 2015, colleagues supported me in sitting down to write this book, though it took many more years before I got to the point of it becoming anything resembling a book. I am hugely grateful to colleagues at Chichester for their support during this time, particularly Hugo Frey, Ruth Mantin, Stephen Roberts, and Graeme Smith. Mark Mason and Tommy Lynch are intellectual companions—and friends—I couldn't imagine being without. The Chichester Inn was a perfect spot for ruminating past working hours. Hannah Lynch's company made this time feel well spent. Early career funding from Chichester was highly appreciated. I particularly thank my students at Chichester for thinking with me about the themes that arise in this book. Much of my inspiration came from them.

My time at the Centre of Theological Inquiry (CTI) in Princeton was invaluable. I am particularly grateful to Will Storrar for his leadership, as well as to Joshua Mauldin, Ephraim Meir, Ed Noort, Wolfgang Palaver, Antti Pentikainen, Louise Du Toit, David Tombs, and Lisa le Roux. Thanks to CTI, I was invited to share parts of this book at a United Nations symposium in New York in 2019. This was followed by a UN consultation in Geneva on religion, hate crime, and migration, where I was helped through the ropes by Bonnie Evans-Hills. Many colleagues in biblical studies and beyond have invited me to present work in progress. I am particularly grateful to James Crossley, Marianne Bjelland Kartzow, Mikael Larsson, Ole-Jakob Løland, Mia Lövheim, Peter-Ben Smit, and Ian Wilson. The Worthing Theological Society invited me twice to talk about my research, and on both occasions offered a hospitable and stimulating environment. Friends in the International Network for Experimental Philosophy and Theology have put up with draft versions of practically all the chapters in this book and have, seemingly, never tired of offering invaluable feedback. I am grateful to the two anonymous peer reviewers for constructive comments on the manuscript. I thank Steve A. Wiggins at Oxford University Press for his interest in the book and encouragement along the way, and Brent Matheny for his support in the publication process. I couldn't have asked for a better copy editor than Rick Delaney. (Any remaining errors and inconsistencies are my own.)

I finished this book at Lund University. I am grateful to the Knut and Alice Wallenberg Foundation as well as colleagues at the Centre for Theology and Religious Studies in Lund, who have provided funding and a new institutional home. Thanks go especially to Johanna Gustafsson Lundberg and Jayne Svenungsson, as well as to Aaron Goldman, Samuel Byrskog, Joel Kuhlin, Alexander Maurits, and Blaženka Scheuer. Einar, Mary, and Sigrid Strømmen, Amy, Kristian, and Freya Beckenstrøm have offered encouragement, joy, and perspective. Finally, I dedicate this book to Ulrich Schmiedel, without whom I probably would never have finished this book or enjoyed the time not working on it so much.

1
The European Far Right

This book has two aims. The first aim is to uncover patterns in contemporary far-right Bible-use. This includes demonstrating the way this Bible-use functions, and showcase the significance it has for claims about European identity. I set out to do this by examining a case of far-right terrorism in Norway, in which seventy-seven people were killed in Oslo and Utøya on 22 July 2011. Focusing on this case allows me a concrete starting point. But this is not a book that is straightforwardly about the terror attacks in Norway more than ten years ago. Rather, I use this case to map the trends and tendencies of Bible-use that are crucial to the Islamophobia that is so rife across Europe, particularly in far-right circles, but that takes mainstream as well as extreme forms. In this sense, I begin with a very concrete case of far-right terror, before I gradually—chapter by chapter—move further outwards, from the manifesto the perpetrator produced, to the sources he was inspired by, to the thinkers on whom these sources in turn drew, to historical forms of Bible-use that are being activated today.

My second aim is to propose a way of doing biblical reception that maps how Bibles operate in the world, not always as central actors, but as elements that function with particular groups, in specific versions, alongside theories and conspiracies, with different dispositions, attachments, and feelings, imagined according to assumptions and attitudes, and used to serve interests and achieve ends. Part of this aim is a call for biblical scholars to take seriously diverse and complex forms of Bible-use as a subject to study. This, I contend, cannot be done only from a descriptive vantage point, as if biblical scholars sit above the messy fray of politics. There is also a normative edge to this work, though not as if biblical scholars have all the right answers and can simply proclaim them, top-down, in neat prescriptions. Towards the end of the book, I broaden out from a discussion of far-right Bibles, to the problem of violent Bible-use more generally. I evaluate responses to biblical violence from biblical scholars and put forward my own response, based on the analysis in earlier chapters of the way Bibles can be put to use to do harm to those who are not deemed "native" in "Christian" Europe.

If you tell people that you are a biblical scholar researching the far right, most people assume you are working on such phenomena in the United States. At least, that has been my experience. Although the rise, and threat, of the far right has been heralded in media outlets and by police commissions, security experts, and, at times, politicians across Europe, the idea that the far right—and certainly the religious right—is primarily a problem in the United States has stuck. One reason why I insist on writing about Europe in this book, then, is to push back against this pervasive idea. This book is not straightforwardly about Europe, though. For one, "Europe" itself is an unruly term. It is too big a term: meaningful claims about Europe in general will rarely be persuasive. It is simultaneously too small a term: transnational and transcontinental networks of communication operate globally, particularly through the internet. Political ideas and practices are not confined by borders. In that sense, I have ended up writing a book that is about the way particular constructions of sacred scripture operate in Norway, Europe, the United States, and in a more amorphous network that operates through the spread of texts, online communication, ideological affiliations, and bizarre blends and borrowings of conspiracies on blogs, web pages, and manifestos.

What the material I examine has in common is the anti-immigration rhetoric that has intensified in recent decades in Europe and the United States, and particularly the Islamophobia that has become so central in Europe. I argue that particular understandings and uses of the Bible are part of this Islamophobic worldview. It is not enough to explain how this Bible works or where it comes from, though I hope to elucidate both of those questions. It is, in my view, imperative also to challenge this Bible-use. Islamophobia is of course not the only characteristic of European far-right milieus. Antisemitism is on the rise.[1] Antifeminism is also rife.[2] My concentration in this book is on the way Bibles specifically get caught up in claims about Europe that relate to Islamophobic campaigns. But as I will go on to discuss, although not my main focus, the way Judaism gets drawn into such campaigns,[3]

---

[1] See for instance James Renton and Ben Gidley, *Antisemitism and Islamophobia in Europe: A Shared Story?* (London: Palgrave Macmillan, 2017) and Christine Achinger and Robert Fine, eds., *Antisemitism, Racism and Islamophobia: Distorted Faces of Modernity* (Abingdon: Routledge, 2015).

[2] See for instance Michaela Köttig, Renate Bitzan, Andrea Pető, eds., *Gender and Far Right Politics in Europe* (London: Palgrave Macmillan, 2017); Roman Kuhar and David Paternotte, eds., *Anti-Gender Campaigns: Mobilizing against Equality in Europe* (London: Rowman and Littlefield, 2017).

[3] This is particularly through problematic allusions to the "Judeo-Christian" heritage of Europe. See Emmanuel Nathan and Anya Topolski, eds., *Is There a Judeo-Christian Tradition? A European Perspective* (Berlin: De Gruyter, 2016). I discuss this further in chapter 3.

and the way issues of gender become part of this Bible-use, cannot be ignored.[4]

This introductory chapter has a threefold focus. First, I discuss the 22 July case in some more detail, situate it in a broader political context, and outline what I mean by the far right. Second, I make a case for why I think it is important to analyse the role Christianity, and more particularly Christian scripture, plays in contemporary far-right circles. Third, I outline briefly how I proceed, indicating the way my analysis unfolds in the next eight chapters, and why I suggest it is crucial to study far-right Bible-use not as an aberration from the norm but as part of norms that become unquestioned.

Far-right Terror in Norway

The acts of terror on 22 July 2011 have been called Norway's 9/11.[5] Despite initial assumptions broadcast on traditional and social media as the attacks unfolded in Oslo and on Utøya, Islamist extremists were not the perpetrators.[6] When it comes to extremism and fanaticism, as Alberto Toscano notes, there has been a "tendentious focus on religious and especially Islamic fundamentalism",[7] particularly since the terror attacks in the United States on 11 September 2001.[8] Terror attacks in Europe that are associated with Islamic organisations such as al-Qaeda and ISIS have fuelled fears and intensified public debate on the dangers of Islam. The image of the "spooky" brown man of Middle Eastern descent has come to dominate the public imaginary.[9]

However, the perpetrator of the 22 July terrorism in Norway, Anders Behring Breivik, was a white Norwegian man in his early thirties who was

---

[4] Especially relevant, as I go on to discuss, are fantasies of masculinity.
[5] Ole Jakob Løland, 'The Norwegian 9/11: In the Church without a Bible', *Political Theology* 18, no. 7 (2017): pp. 628–642.
[6] This reaction is effectively presented in one of the permanent exhibitions in the 22 July Centre in Oslo, where one of the walls shows the media reactions and speculations minute by minute (particularly on social media sites such as Twitter) as the violent attacks were reported in national and international media.
[7] Alberto Toscano, *Fanaticism: On the Uses of an Idea* (London: Verso, 2010), p. 23.
[8] See for instance Jocelyne Cesari, *Muslims in the West after 9/11: Religion, Politics and Laws* (London: Routledge, 2009); Peter Morey and Amina Yaqin, *Framing Muslims: Stereotyping and Representation after 9/11* (Cambridge, MA: Harvard University Press, 2011); Halim Rane, Jacqui Ewart, and John Martinkus, *Media Framing of the Muslim World: Conflicts, Crises and Contexts* (Basingstoke: Palgrave Macmillan, 2014).
[9] Mehdi Semati, 'Islamophobia, Culture and Race in the Age of Empire', *Cultural Studies*, 24, no. 2 (2010), p. 257.

inspired by far-right ideology. In the 1990s, the Norwegian political scientist Tore Bjørgo warned that terrorism and political violence have "gravitated increasingly towards the extreme right, in the direction of racism and extreme nationalism, and adopting slogans like 'ethnic cleaning' and 'race war'".[10] But in 2011 the idea of a white Norwegian far-right terrorist[11] seemed to be almost unimaginable in public consciousness.[12] Norwegian and International media were, as Andrew Elliott puts it, "scarcely able to mask their surprise at revelations that the gunman was a white, blond Norwegian".[13] Once that became known, the question of the perpetrator's political and religious affiliation largely disappeared from debate.[14] Mattias Gardell notes a "remarkable shift in attitude" after it became clear the perpetrator was not a Muslim, as if the phrase "terror attack" was so dependent on the term "Islamic" that all of a sudden it was not so clear that Breivik's acts of terror should be labelled as

[10] Tore Bjørgo, 'Introduction', in *Terror from the Extreme Right*, edited by Tore Bjørgo (London: Frank Cass, 1995), p. 1. Jacob Aasland Ravndal points out that while right-wing terrorism and militancy in the Nordic countries were well researched during the 1990s, scholarly attention decreased in the 2000s and 2010s. Jacob Aasland Ravndal, 'Right-wing Terrorism and Militancy in the Nordic Countries: A Comparative Case Study', *Terrorism and Political Violence* 30, no. 5 (2018): p. 772.

[11] The labels "terrorism" and "terrorist" are contentious, particularly as they have been increasingly used in securitisation measures and in counter-terrorism practices. I use "terrorism" here in the sense Mark Jurgensmeyer describes it, to refer to "public acts of destruction, committed without a clear military objective, that arouse a widespread sense of fear", though I note the very criticisms of the term that Jurgensmeyer raises about the problems in distinguishing organisers of terrorist attacks from those who support these attacks, directly and indirectly, as well as issues around terrorism as a subjective judgement about the legitimacy of violent acts. Mark Jurgensmeyer, *Terror in the Mind of God: The Global Rise of Religious Violence*, 3rd ed. (Berkeley: University of California Press, 2003), pp. 5, 7, 9. For a further discussion of problems in definitions of terrorism and uses of the label "terrorist", see for instance Ben Saul, *Defining Terrorism in International Law* (Oxford: Oxford University Press, 2008); Seumas Miller, Adam Henschke, and Jonas Feltes, eds., *Counter-Terrorism: The Ethical Issues* (Cheltenham: Edgar Elgar, 2021).

[12] Sindre Bangstad has written about how the Norwegian police security services, PST (Politiets Sikkerhetstjeneste), predicted in 2010 and 2011 that it was mainly "extreme Islamists" who posed a terror threat to Norway. Sindre Bangstad, *Anders Breivik and the Rise of Islamophobia* (London: Zed Books, 2014), p. 2. As he puts it, it "was therefore not surprising that both national and international news media throughout the evening and long into the night of 22/7 featured 'terror experts' engaging in wild speculation about the identity of the perpetrators and the motives for the terror attacks, ascribing them to al-Qaeda or affiliated radical Islamist groups according to well-established media scripts" (Bangstad, *Anders Breivik and the Rise of Islamophobia*, p. 2). For further discussion and critique of the unpreparedness of the Norwegian secret service, see Bangstad's discussion of the 22/7 Commission report. He calls the report "a damning indictment of a series of institutional as well as individual failures ahead of and during the events of 22/7" (Bangstad, *Anders Breivik and the Rise of Islamophobia*, p. 13).

[13] Andrew B. R. Elliott, *Medievalism, Politics and Mass Media: Appropriating the Middle Ages in the Twenty-First Century* (Cambridge: DS Brewer, 2017), p. 134.

[14] Ida Marie Høeg has discussed the way Norwegian Muslims and immigrants with dark skin reported feeling vulnerable at this time and that their loyalty to Norway was questioned. When it turned out the terrorist was not a Muslim, they were in some ways relieved. Ida Marie Høeg, 'Silent Actions: Emotion and Mass Mourning Rituals after the Terrorist Attacks in Norway on 22 July 2011', *Mortality* 20, no. 3 (2015): pp. 197–214.

terror or as politically motivated.[15] The focus on the psychology of the perpetrator became paramount. As Tom Egil Hverven commented in his book on the trial, the first psychiatric reports of Breivik did not take account of his political or ideological context.[16] Breivik's background, including his family circumstances, was scrutinised.[17] Mia Eriksson suggests that the fact that Breivik was continuously framed as a deviation from the norm was made possible by the fact that as a white, Norwegian, adult man, he embodied, and was expected to inhabit, the norm.[18]

But both Breivik's trial and his over 1,500-page manifesto point clearly to the perpetrator's ideological affiliations and political commitments. It is crucial to analyse the far-right terror attacks in Norway as part of wider and ongoing ideological trends and political practices in Europe. To understand the case of 22 July and the wider landscape it is a part of, it is necessary to grapple with the sources that influenced the perpetrator's thinking and the more mainstream forms it takes—both before 2011 and since then. Breivik called his acts of terror "horrible" but "necessary" to gain a platform for his "political project".[19] When he walked into the courtroom for his trial in the spring of 2012, he raised his hand in a far-right salute.[20] As social anthropologist Sindre Bangstad shows in his study of the Breivik case, although the manifesto is a messy cut-and-paste document, it nonetheless displays an ideology that locates itself recognisably on the extreme right of the political spectrum.[21] What the manifesto also makes clear—although it has been far less discussed—is that Christianity and Christian scripture play a role in Breivik's worldview.

The perpetrator's political commitments became particularly clear in the trial that followed the terror attacks and from the manifesto he distributed online to people he thought would be sympathetic to his views,

---

[15] Mattias Gardell, 'Crusader Dreams: Oslo 22/7, Islamophobia, and the Quest for a Monocultural Europe', *Terrorism and Political Violence* 26 (2014): p. 130.
[16] Tom Egil Hverven (text) and Sverre Malling (drawings), *Terrorens ansikt: skisser fra 22.juli-rettsaken* (Oslo: Flamme Forlag, 2013), pp. 42, 149.
[17] Hverven, *Terrorens ansikt*, pp. 36, 163–164. Hverven points out that important books on Breivik that came out in the first years after 2011, such as Aage Borchgrevinck's *En Norsk Tragedie (A Norwegian Tragedy)*, focused more on the perpetrator's childhood than on right-wing extremism.
[18] Mia Erikson, 'Breivik and I: Affective Encounters with "Failed" Masculinity in Stories about Right-wing Terrorism', *International Journal for Masculinity Studies*, 13, no. 3–4 (2018): p. 269.
[19] Geir Lippestad, *Det Kan Vi Stå For* (Oslo: Aschehaug, 2014), pp. 45, 47, 102.
[20] Ginny Whitehouse has written about the way this salute was characterised in the media and the coverage it got during and after the trial. Ginny Whitehouse, 'The Murderer's Salute: News Images of Breivik's Defiance after Killing 77 in Oslo', *Journal of Mass Media Ethics* 28, no. 1 (2013): pp. 57–59.
[21] Bangstad, *Anders Breivik and the Rise of Islamophobia*, 78.

shortly before the terror attacks. In his commentary on the trial, Hverven recounts the way Breivik portrayed himself as a "saviour" figure, fighting for a future Europe, where Christian culture can be saved from the purportedly unclean, impure Muslim culture.[22] The terror actions of 22 July were directed at Norway's governing party at the time, the social-democratic Labour party (Arbeiderpartiet), and their youth wing, AUF (Arbeidernes ungdomsfylking), because they were seen as "deconstructing" what Breivik called "the Norwegian ethnic group".[23] Norway's so-called inner enemy was seen as acute, namely those who Breivik deemed a threat to Christian Europe and who would open the West to so-called Muslim colonisation.[24] In court, the perpetrator made claims about how the Norwegian version of Christianity, and Norwegian culture and identity, are threatened.[25] Breivik's manifesto proclaims that an "Islamic Imperialism" is taking hold in Europe and is supported by the political elites. It is purportedly compiled for all "European patriots",[26] to "prevent the annihilation of our identities, our cultures and traditions and our nation states".[27] The ultimate aim outlined in the manifesto is to stop the spread of Islam. The hope is that "a monocultural Christian Europe"[28] will "once again be governed by patriots".[29] In the manifesto, Breivik describes himself as a crusader and calls for Europe to return to the Latin Bible, the Vulgate, to aid the revival of Europe and resist the detrimental effects of politically correct modern Bible versions.[30] He cites Psalms 18:34 to confirm the idea of God's support for battle: "he teaches my hands to make war".[31]

---

[22] Hverven, *Terrorens ansikt*, pp. 43–44.
[23] Ibid., p. 50. As Jorunn Økland points out, the previous prime minister of Norway, Gro Harlem Brundtland, was a primary target for Breivik. She had given a speech at Utøya a few hours before Breivik arrived. Gro Harlem Brundtland was Norway's first female prime minister and one of the longest to serve in that office in Norway. For Breivik she represented everything he hated about modern Norway: feminism, cultural Marxism, and multiculturalism. Jorunn Økland, 'Feminismen, tradisjonen og forventning', in *Akademiske Perspektiver På 22. Juli*, edited by Anders Ravik Jupskås (Bergen: Fagbokforlaget, 2012), p. 118.
[24] Gardell, 'Crusader Dreams', p. 148.
[25] Hverven, *Terrorens ansikt*, p. 50.
[26] Manifesto, p. 13. When I cite the manifesto, I refer to the page numbers on the PDF version which was made available on various webpages following the terror attacks, but which has since been taken down from many sites. It can still be readily found online on, for instance, the Internet Archive webpage.
[27] Ibid.
[28] Ibid., p. 1404.
[29] Ibid., p. 1413.
[30] Ibid., p. 1140.
[31] Ibid., p. 1331. There is a danger in my summary to present a too coherent picture of the manifesto's many claims. As I discuss later on, and in more detail in chapter 3, the manifesto is disparate and diverse in its claims, drawing on, and copying from, an array of sources. In many ways, the manifesto is marked by contradictions and inconsistencies. But as I go on to discuss, once it is

The tenth anniversary of the 22 July attacks, in 2021, sparked renewed debate in Norway around the way it was dealt with. Much critique centred on the fact that the political dimension of the terror attacks had not been adequately understood or confronted. This critique came from journalists, scholars, and survivors of the terror. Axel Geard Nygaard, for instance, commented in the socialist national newspaper, *Klassekampen*, that although the lack of attention to the politics of 22 July in the ensuing years was problematic, it is perhaps only now that the wounds from the events have been healed enough to face up to terror as a political event.[32] Now more than ever, he urged, it is necessary to confront the politics of 22 July and its wider resonances in Europe.[33] Other national newspapers published similar reflections that highlighted the fact that the hate that inspired Breivik had strengthened in the ten years since the attacks.[34] A Norwegian scholar of religion, Iselin Frydenlund, called for the Islamophobic elements that motivated the attacks in Norway to be given more serious and sustained attention.[35] Ten years after the attacks, Breivik's defence lawyer, Geir Lippestad, cautioned against a battle over values, where individuals are stamped as Breivik sympathisers.[36] He contended that knowledge is the best remedy against radicalisation and the best confrontation we as a society can take with far-right attitudes.[37]

In her reflection on the ten years since Breivik's attacks, the Utøya survivor Elin L'Estrange urged for more attention to the fact that extremism arguably has a greater place in society today than in 2011, with an explosion of hate on the internet, and new politically motivated terror attacks in Norway.[38] Other survivors and their families made similar points, such as Randi Johansen Perreau, the mother of one of the victims, Rolf Christopher Johansen Perreau,

---

contextualised within wider far-right trends and tendencies, there are patterns that can be identified, particularly when it comes to the references to Islam, Christianity, and Europe.

[32] Axel Geard Nygaard, 'Ti år', *Klassekampen*, 22 July 2021.
[33] In a special issue in the journal *Terrorism and Political Violence*, editors Leena Malkki, Mats Fridlund, and Daniel Sallamaa discuss in turn the relatively scarce attention in academic publications to political terror in the Nordic countries and seek to address this gap. Leena Malkki, Mats Fridlund, and Daniel Sallamaa, 'Terrorism and Political Violence in the Nordic Countries', *Terrorism and Political Violence* 30, no. 5 (2018): pp. 761–771.
[34] Kato Nykvist, 'Ti år etter terroren er vi flere som bør reflektere litt', *Adresseavisen*, 22 July 2011.
[35] Iselin Frydenlund, 'Global Islamofobi', *Klassekampen*, 22 July 2021.
[36] Geir Lippestad, 'Vi skal ikke etterlyse en verdikamp med 22. juli som utgangspunkt', *Aftenposten*, 8 June 2021.
[37] Lippestad, "Vi skal ikke etterlyse en verdikamp med 22. juli som utgangspunkt".
[38] Elin L'Estrange, 'Det vanskelige hatet', *Klassekampen*, 22 July 2021. On 10 August 2019, another young Norwegian man instigated a terrorist attack in Norway, killing his step-sister and attacking Muslims at the Al-Noor Islamic Centre in Bærum, Norway.

who was one of the first to be shot on Utøya. Randi Johansen Perreau reflects that it is important that we "as a society have enough information about what happened", which includes, vitally, "which thoughts and ideas lay behind the events".[39] Critiques were voiced in Norway about the way figures on the far right were given ample airtime in Norway after 22 July, while survivors who called for a critical engagement with the rhetoric and ideology that inspired the terror were silenced.[40] Concerns with protecting free speech took precedence over concerns with the rise of the far right.

The far-right terror of 22 July in Norway has been likened to 9/11 in its impact on Norway. Although of course the attacks sparked debate, in-depth and sustained discussions about the perpetrator's politics were elided, perhaps particularly in relation to the far-right Islamophobia espoused by the perpetrator. To deal with the impact and implications of the 22 July terror, though, it is crucial to understand Breivik as more than a so-called lone wolf terrorist.

A Lone Wolf?

At first glance, Breivik looks like a lone wolf terrorist. In other words, he appeared to act alone with no accomplices or leader telling him what to do. The label "lone wolf", however, is problematic. The perpetrator clearly saw himself as part of a far-right network. He sought allies on- and offline for his increasingly extreme views in the years before 2011. The manifesto Breivik composed before his acts of terror was emailed to at least one thousand email contacts in Europe and Israel whom he considered potential allies. Bangstad notes that the number of recipients suggests that even if Breivik was alone in his actions, he did not conceive of himself as alone in his worldview.[41] After years on far-right blogs and web pages such as Gates of Vienna and Stormfront, where Breivik expressed his anti-Muslim views, these views were expanded and extended to views about forced deportation of Muslims and blame directed at the political establishment in Norway.[42]

As many have pointed out, the manifesto was not straightforwardly authored by Breivik. It is a cut-and-paste-style text made up of multiple texts

---

[39] Randi Johansen Perreau, 'Vi fikk sorgen og gleden rett i fanget', *Addresseavisen*, 22 July 2011.
[40] Nykvist, 'Ti år etter terroren er vi flere som bør reflektere litt'.
[41] Bangstad, *Anders Breivik and the Rise of Islamophobia*, p. 108.
[42] Linn Stalsberg, 'Det enkle er ofte det verste', *Agenda*, 21 July 2021.

and citations.[43] A lot of it, then, is not written by Breivik himself. Jorunn Økland has argued that if we want to understand the manifesto, it is necessary to ask what it is about Breivik's modern context that led him to reference different anecdotes and traditions, to examine which sources are selected and cited, what new connections are construed, and how the hybrid text he created reshapes the material gathered together in the so-called manifesto.[44] The composite nature of the manifesto points to the fact that Breivik was drawing on a discourse already operating and circulating on- and offline prior to the attacks. Importantly, this is also a discourse that has continued to be spread and cited since 2011, both in conjunction with violent terror attacks as well as in more politically mainstream settings. To mention a particularly lethal example, Brenton Tarrant killed fifty-nine people in a terrorist attack in Christchurch, New Zealand, on 15 March 2019, when he targeted two mosques during Friday prayer. Tarrant cited Breivik as an inspiration.[45]

The patchwork manifesto Breivik cobbled together from the writings of prominent and not-so-prominent far-right figures is a testament to the network of which he considered himself a part. Breivik could be seen as a "cybermilitant", drawing from Islamophobic texts on the internet, using them to frame his terrorist attacks.[46] He is a representative of what Jean-Yves Camus and Nicolas Lebourg call the "'far right 2.0', which primarily operates through forums, websites, and social networks".[47] The sharing of ideas across borders, particularly via online forums, creates what Franco 'Bifo' Berardi has called "digital tribes".[48] Individuals such as Breivik become part of "amorphous, slightly structured social entities, or associative and cooperative

---

[43] Jorunn Økland discusses the genre of the "manifesto" in a fascinating comparison with the Book of Revelation and Valerie Solana's SCUM manifesto. Jorunn Økland, 'Manifestos, Gender, Self-Canonization, and Violence', in *The Bible and Feminism: Remapping the Field*, edited by Yvonne Sherwood, with the assistance of Anna Fisk (Oxford: Oxford University Press, 2017), pp. 15–44.
[44] Økland, 'Feminismen, tradisjonen og forventning', p. 121.
[45] Graham Macklin and Tore Bjørgo discuss Breivik's impact in the ten years since his acts of terror on extreme-right lone actor terrorists by exploring thirty cases where Breivik is mentioned by name as an inspiration. They are critical of sweeping assertions and sensationalist headlines that assume an influence in cases such as the 2019 Christchurch shootings. While in the Christchurch shootings, as they suggest, there is ample evidence that Breivik's influence was substantial, the influence is often more indirect. They argue that, overall, Breivik's tactical influence has been limited. They are not, however, evaluating the extent to which the ideas Breivik was drawing on, and spreading, have been limited in their reach. Graham Macklin and Tore Bjørgo, 'Breivik's Long Shadow? The Impact of the July 22, 2011 Attacks on the *Modus Operandi* of Extreme-right Lone Actor Terrorists', *Perspectives on Terrorism* 15, no. 3 (2021): pp. 14–36.
[46] Jean-Yves Camus and Nicolas Lebourg, *Far-Right Politics in Europe*, translated by Jane Marie Todd (Cambridge, MA: Belknap Press, 2017), p. 113.
[47] Ibid.
[48] Franco 'Bifo' Berardi, *Heroes: Mass Murder and Suicide* (London: Verso, 2015), p. 118.

networks of individual and collective actors".[49] This is in many ways not a new phenomenon. In his study from the late 1990s, *Inside Terrorism*, Bruce Hoffman elucidates this type of terrorist "organisation", suggesting that although there may be a leadership of sorts in these networks, the role of such leadership is not necessarily that of direct command and control and rather has an inspirational and motivational function.[50] Contemporary far-right networks frequently "communicate, coordinate, and conduct their campaigns in an internetted manner".[51]

The notions of "lone wolf" and "leaderless resistance" are in any case not neutral descriptors but are themselves political strategies.[52] Camus and Lebourg explain how the American neo-Nazi Joseph Tommasi put forward the lone wolf idea as a method already in the mid-1970s.[53] Together with William Pierce, Tomassi founded the National Socialist Liberation Front in 1969. In 1971, Pierce became leader of the National Alliance, and in 1978, he published *The Turner Diaries*. This book became a global bestseller in the neo-Nazi movement. Thomas Grumke calls it the "right-wing extremist bible".[54] It narrates a white supremacist uprising against Zionist power and a final race struggle, as well as providing instructions on bomb making. *The Turner Diaries* influenced Timothy McVeigh, the far-right militant who committed the 1995 Oklahoma City attack, as well as others—including Breivik. The popularity of the book and the further movements it spawned were supplemented in 1983 by the idea of "leaderless resistance", put forward by American white supremacist Louis Beam of Aryan Nation.[55] The idea that you could create terrorist cells that were linked by a common objective and a strategy but with no clear leader or formal connections could protect individuals from detection. Largely due to the internet, the strategies of the lone wolf and leaderless resistance can also be observed in Europe.[56]

---

[49] Ralf Wiederer, 'Mapping the Right-Wing Extremist Movement on the Internet—Structural Patterns 2006–2011', in *In the Tracks of Breivik: Far Right Networks in Northern and Eastern Europe*, edited by Mats Deland, Michael Minkenberg, and Christin Mays (Münster: Lit Verlag, 2013), p. 20.

[50] Bruce Hoffman, *Inside Terrorism* (London: Victor Gollianz, 1998), p. 39.

[51] Ibid.

[52] Mattias Gardell writes about the way the lone wolf strategy worked as a strategy for the Swedish racist serial shooter, Peter Mangs, who targeted and killed non-white people for many years before being caught by police. Mattias Gardell, 'Urban Terror: The Case of Lone Wolf Peter Mangs', *Terrorism and Political Violence* 30, no. 5 (2018): pp. 793–811.

[53] Camus and Lebourg, *Far-Right Politics in Europe*, p. 111.

[54] Thomas Grumke, 'Globalized Anti-Globalists—The Ideological Basis of the Internationalization of Right-Wing Extremism', in *The Extreme Right in Europe: Current Trends and Perspectives*, edited by Uwe Backes and Patrick Moreau (Göttingen: Vandenhoeck & Ruprecht, 2012), p. 326.

[55] Camus and Lebourg, *Far-Right Politics in Europe*, p. 111.

[56] Ibid.

Gardell has argued that as white racist violence has intensified in the West, it is crucial that the threat from far-right and ultranationalist milieus are taken seriously, especially those lone actors who operate according to the tactics of leaderless resistance.[57]

The 22 July attacks in Norway, then, have to be seen in a larger context and the perpetrator himself as a figure who identifies with a network that does not constitute an official group or formal movement but that communicates particularly through online channels, mutual influence, and shared texts. The "lone wolf" idea might be correct in one sense, in that Breivik was not following orders and was not part of a formalised group, but it arguably obscures more than it elucidates. As Camus and Lebourg unequivocally put it: "the lone wolf belongs to a milieu".[58]

22 July in Context

Attention to Breivik's manifesto demonstrates that the two major features of the far-right milieu that he was influenced by are the so-called Eurabia conspiracy and counterjihadism. Øyvind Strømmen elucidates key features in Breivik's worldview.[59] The Eurabia theory, if one can call it that, consists of the view that political leaders in Europe, especially the European Union, are part of a conspiracy to turn Europe into an Islamic colony. The most important aspect of the Eurabia theory is that the "Islamization" of Europe through immigration is taking place as a conscious plan, aided and abetted by European governments, academics, journalists, banks, and religious leaders.[60] Counterjihadism is characterised by the view that Islam and the West are at war, that Islam is not a religion but a totalitarian political ideology. The duty of counterjihadists is to stop a supposed "Islamization", contain Islam in countries that already have a Muslim majority, and establish an anti-multicultural political network to replace the current political classes that enable the purported Islamic imperialism.[61] Proponents of these

---

[57] Gardell, 'Urban Terror: The Case of Lone Wolf Peter Mangs', p. 807.
[58] Camus and Lebourg, *Far-Right Politics in Europe*, p. 110.
[59] Øyvind Strømmen, *Det Mørke Nettet: Om Høyreekstremisme, kontrajihadisme og terror i Europa* (Oslo: Cappelen Damm, 2012). See also Øyvind Strømmen, *I Hatets Fotspor* (Oslo: Cappelen Damm, 2014).
[60] Strømmen, *Det Mørke Nettet*, p. 50.
[61] Strømmen, *I Hatets Fotspor*, pp. 102–103.

pernicious views take different forms, and versions vary, from the extreme to more subtle forms of fearmongering about Islam.

In the aftermath of the 22 July attacks, several public figures expressed their support for Breivik's ideas as an icon and defender of the West against Muslim invasion.[62] As Strømmen shows in his discussion of Breivik's views, if you look away from the will and capacity to put the ideology into action, Breivik is far less untypical than might be thought.[63] The ideas he reproduces and the texts he cites in his manifesto resonate with street movements as well as parliamentary politics, from extra-parliamentary grassroots activism to party politics. Far-right street-based groups have been on the rise across Europe, with asylum facilities being attacked and set fire to, and migrants being shot at with air rifles.[64] Street-based organisations such as Pegida (Patriotic Europeans against the Islamisation of Europe), the Identitarian movement, and the English Defence League (EDL), all champion similar anti-Islamic views to Breivik and call for the defence of Christian Europe. The EDL, for instance, propagates the idea that Islam challenges an English, Christian way of life. With a significant online presence, EDL has sought to mobilise supporters in protests and demonstrations around the perceived Islamic threat.[65] Non-Muslims are portrayed as victims, and although Muslims are deemed to be cultural outsiders, racist language is frequently used.[66] Western culture is viewed as tolerant and progressive, while Muslim culture is seen as intolerant and backward.[67] Concerns about national identity and religion lead to "hostility, scapegoating and stereotyping about the perception of Muslims".[68] Breivik alluded to connections to the EDL in his manifesto.[69] As Elliott explains, "in Breivik's view, the EDL represents part

---

[62] Bangstad, *Anders Breivik and the Rise of Islamophobia*, p. 8. Bangstad mentions a member of the French Front National, Jacques Coutela, the Italian MP Mario Borghezio, and Arne Tumyr of the Norwegian far-right organisation Stop the Islamization of Norway (SIAN) (Bangstad, *Anders Breivik and the Rise of Islamophobia*, p. 8).
[63] Strømmen, *Det Mørke Nettet*, p. 48.
[64] Pietro Castelli Gattinara and Andrea L. P. Pirro, 'The Far Right as Social Movement', *European Societies* 21, no. 4 (2019): pp. 448–449.
[65] Jamie Cleland, Chris Anderson, and Jack Aldridge-Deacon, 'Islamophobia, War and Non-Muslims as Victims: An Analysis of Online Discourse on an English Defence League Message Board', *Ethnic and Racial Studies* 41, no. 9 (2018): p. 1542. Cleland, Anderson, and Aldridge-Deacon analysed active users on an EDL message board between September 2013 and October 2013, to examine how EDL activists construe and advance their racial prejudice in a digital environment.
[66] Ibid., p. 1548.
[67] Ibid., p. 1550.
[68] Ibid., p. 1551.
[69] Manifesto, pp. 1236, 1240–41, 1253, 1263, 1282. Further, in the police questioning of Breivik after the attacks, he claimed that he was part of the Knights Templar, a network he linked to an "English mentor" whom he calls in his manifesto Richard the Lionhearted. This person was later identified with Paul Ray, a British expatriate who hosted a far-right blog and was affiliated with

of the same counterjihad movement to which he sought to belong, leading him to defend the EDL as a patriotic organisation of 'knights' devoted to fighting jihadists and so-called cultural Marxists".[70] The leader of EDL at the time, Tommy Robinson, made an appearance on British TV to distance his movement from Breivik.[71] All the same, connections continued to appear, including one threat from an EDL member to carry out an "Oslo-style" attack.[72]

Counterjihadist groups have managed to garner popular support by propagating everyday forms of racism and xenophobia, directed at Muslims in particular, in the service of patriotic defence of the nation.[73] This kind of rhetoric can be found in multiple local, regional, and national grassroots movements such as the EDL and other "Defence Leagues" across the world, as well as in groups such as Germany's Pegida and Pamela Geller's Stop the Islamisation of America and its European and national versions.[74] Farid Hafez has discussed the way a militant, racist, and Islamophobic news outlet, *White Media*, which expressed sympathy for Breivik, has supported Czech and Slovak activists.[75] In 2016, the Czech Martin Konvička Initiative (Iniciativa Martina Konvicky) organised several street spectacles, including the burning of a Qur'an in front of a mosque, alongside people drinking beer and eating pork goulash and promenading women dressed in bathing suits.[76] Examining Poland, the Czech Republic, Slovakia, and Hungary, Hafez argues that attention to street-level Islamophobic groups is not enough, "because mainstream political parties have co-opted the issue so effectively that popular mobilization is not required".[77] This argument raises a wider point that is important to stress, namely that Breivik's thinking does not belong only in the extreme echo chambers of the web or in far-right street-level protest movements.

---

the English Defence League. Andrew Elliott discusses these connections in his chapters 'Anders Behring Breivik and the Templar Knights' and '"God bless the EDL, the new Templar Knights": The EDL, the Far Right and the Crusaders', in Andrew B. R. Elliott, *Medievalism, Politics and Mass Media: Appropriating the Middle Ages in the Twenty-First Century* (Cambridge: DS Brewer, 2017), pp. 132–154, 155–182.

[70] Elliott, *Medievalism, Politics and Mass Media*, p. 155.
[71] 'EDL Denies Links to Norway Gunman', *BBC*, 25 July 2011.
[72] See Elliott, *Medievalism, Politics and Mass Media*, p. 156.
[73] Ibid., p. 157.
[74] Ibid.
[75] Farid Hafez, 'Street-level and Government-level Islamophobia in the Visegrád Four Countries', *Patterns of Prejudice* 52, no. 5 (2018): p. 441.
[76] Ibid., p. 441.
[77] Ibid., p. 436.

Many of the views that appear in Breivik's manifesto have been repeated by populist right-wing party politicians across Europe over the last years, including in Breivik's home country, Norway. Some scholars have argued that little has been done to examine the intersections of extreme right-wing discourse and more populist right-wing politics in Norway. Bangstad, for instance, has drawn attention to the way the Norwegian right-wing populist Progress Party (*Fremskrittspartiet*) consistently cast Muslims in Norway as a threat during the twenty-five years prior to 22 July. In the years leading up to Breivik's attacks, the Progress Party propagated, in his words, an "increasingly vitriolic political discourse on Islam and Muslims".[78] The term "Islamization by stealth" (*snikislamisering*) was frequently used in Norwegian political discourse by prominent Progress Party members. It is hardly surprising, Bangstad writes, that Breivik was attracted to the party in his late teenage years and was a party member for a short time.[79] Bangstad suggests that "extreme and populist right-wing discourses on Islam and Muslims form part of a continuum, rather than political discourses in complete isolation from one another".[80] In addition to the Progress Party, think tanks such as Human Rights Service, more radical organisations such as Norwegian Defence League and Stop the Islamization of Norway, web pages such as *Document. no* and *Honestthinking.org* all pedal anti-Islamic positions, varying from the more moderate to the more extreme.[81] Breivik endorsed and was affiliated with many of these movements and web pages.[82]

But the ideas propagated by Breivik have resonances also in North American and European political circles more broadly. The US think tank the Center for Security Policy, for instance, fosters counterjihadist claims, stating that the United States is being taken over by "creeping shariah" and

---

[78] Bangstad, *Anders Breivik and the Rise of Islamophobia*, p. 112.

[79] Nykvist made similar points in his newspaper article near the ten-year anniversary around the language-use of the Progress Party, particularly terms such as "stealth Islamism", "crusade", and "cultural betrayal". Nykvist, 'Ti år etter terroren er vi flere som bør reflektere litt'.

[80] Bangstad, *Anders Breivik and the Rise of Islamophobia*, p. 111. Lars Erik Berntzen and Sveinung Sandberg, too, have discussed the need to frame Breivik's actions in a wider anti-Islam movement in Norway. In their study from 2014, they relate that 40 percent of Norwegians consider immigration to be a serious threat to Norwegian values, and 50 percent consider Islamic values to be generally or completely incompatible with Norwegian ones. Although this data should be treated with care, as they put it, "there is no doubt that many Norwegians consider Muslim 'values' and immigration from Muslim countries to be problematic, and several organizations and political parties appeal to these opinions and segments of the population". Lars Eric Berntzen and Sveinung Sandberg, 'The Collective Nature of Lone Wolf Terrorism: Anders Behring Breivik and the Anti-Islamic Social Movement, Terrorism and Political Violence', *Terrorism and Political Violence* 26, no. 5 (2014): p. 761.

[81] Berntzen and Sandberg, 'The Collective Nature of Lone Wolf Terrorism', p. 762.

[82] Ibid.

that a "civilization jihad" is going on.[83] While the think tank could be labelled as a fringe movement, scholars have demonstrated the way it acts as a primary source for Islamophobic discourse that is used by right-wing politicians and pundits and conservative movements more broadly.[84] In Europe, right-wing populism has become an increasingly utilised category to describe the far-right groups that have emerged since the 1980s.[85] Cas Mudde defines populism as "an ideology that considers society to be ultimately separated into two homogenous and antagonistic groups, 'the pure people' versus 'the corrupt elite', and which argues that politics should be an expression of the *volonté générale* (general will) of the people".[86] Blame is put on supposedly elitist democratic governments that fail to reflect the will of the people. The elites and "others" more generally are not considered to be part of "the people", and to solve the situation "the people must be given back their role as rightful sovereign before it is too late".[87] As Nadia Marzouki and Duncan McDonnell elucidate, populist far-right parties also tend to identify an "other" from below that threatens the homogenous "people", increasingly since 9/11: Muslims.[88]

These tendencies can be seen for instance in the German federal elections of 2017, where the far-right party the Alternative for Germany (Alternative für Deutschland) won a major breakthrough, becoming the third party in the Bundestag. Although they did not do as well in the 2021 federal elections, they remain a strong political force particularly in East Germany. Marine Le Pen, of the longstanding far-right party National Rally (Rassemblement National, previously Front National), came second in the first rounds of the French presidential elections in 2017 and 2022. While in the UK elections of 2017, the votes for the populist right-wing party UKIP (United Kingdom Independence Party) fell significantly, the previous leader of UKIP, Nigel Farage, played a significant part in the successful "Leave the EU" campaign in 2016, along with other far-right parties Britain First and the British

---

[83] S. Jonathan O'Donnell, 'Islamophobic Conspiracism and Neoliberal Subjectivity: The Inassimilable Society', *Patterns of Prejudice* 52, no. 1 (2019): p. 3.
[84] Ibid., p. 5.
[85] Gabriella Lazaridis, Giovanna Campani, and Anne Benveniste, 'Introduction', in *The Rise of the Far Right in Europe: Populist Shifts and "Othering"*, edited by Gabriella Lazaridis, Giovanna Campani, and Anne Benveniste (New York: Palgrave Macmillan, 2016), pp. 3–4.
[86] Cas Mudde, 'The Populist Zeitgeist', Government and Opposition 39, no. 4 (2004): p. 544.
[87] Lazaridis, Campani, and Benveniste, 'Introduction', p. 3.
[88] Marzouki and McDonnell, 'Populism and Religion', p. 3. See also Ulrich Schmiedel, 'Introduction: Political Theology in the Spirit of Populism—Methods and Metaphors', in *The Spirit of Populism: Political Theologies in Polarized Times*, edited by Ulrich Schmiedel and Joshua Ralston (Leiden: Brill, 2021), pp. 1–22.

National Party, where the issues of immigration, Islam, and notions of exclusive national identity were central. Hungary's prime minister, Viktor Orbán, had a razor fence erected along the country's borders to keep Muslim migrants out, alleging that in doing so he was stopping "invaders" who "represent a radically different culture".[89] A defence of Christianity was a key part of Orbán's vision. Many other examples of far-right politics in Europe could be mentioned.

In his study of the relationship between the media and the far right, Antonis Ellinas argues that far-right figures and movements have "reshaped the contours of legitimate political discourse, injecting it with xenophobia, racism, and anti-Semitism".[90] Ellinas argues that in many ways it is mainstream political parties in Europe that have sowed the seeds from which far-right parties reaped the fruits.[91] Ivan Kalmar has emphasised the "cross-border connections" that spread and mainstreamed Islamophobia.[92] There is an "international dialectic" to the far right as a political phenomenon,[93] whereby overlapping issues around immigration, multiculturalism, and perceived social change are highlighted and intensified in public debates and media across the political spectrum. "The Islamophobic theme taking hold among the general public and the spasms of the ostracised fringes are not disconnected phenomena".[94]

The events of 22 July, then, and the "making" of Breivik as a terrorist, need to be understood within larger trends in Europe and beyond, before and after the attacks in Norway. Demonisations of Islam, complaints about the loss of European culture, and blame laid on the so-called elite proponents of multiculturalism that are so prevalent in street-based and populist right-wing party programmes lie at the heart of the worldview that he sketches in his manifesto. As I will go on to discuss in more detail, both Islam and Christianity play key parts in this worldview. Before that, however, I will sketch my use of the term "far right".

---

[89] Ivan Kalmar, '"The Battlefield Is in Brussels": Islamophobia in the Visegrád Four in its Global Context', *Patterns of Prejudice* 52, no. 5 (2018): p. 406.
[90] Antonis A. Ellinas, *The Media and the Far Right in Western Europe* (Cambridge: Cambridge University Press, 2010), p. 5.
[91] Ellinas, *The Media and the Far Right in Western Europe*, p. 27.
[92] Kalmar, '"The Battlefield Is in Brussels"', p. 417.
[93] Camus and Lebourg, *Far-Right Politics in Europe*, p. 114.
[94] Ibid.

The Far Right

I have used the term "far right" several times, explicitly in outlining the worldview Breivik subscribed to, but also indicating that this far-right worldview is shared by a diverse array of actors, from street-level movements to think tanks and populist right-wing parties. But definitions of the "far right" are complex as well as contested. As I explained at the beginning of this chapter, the far-right worldview I discuss in this book is in some ways highly specific in relation to the Breivik case. In important ways, though, it is indicative of far-right trends and tendencies in Western Europe, as well as Europe more generally.[95] Yet the far-right material that I go on to discuss is also part and product of transnational and transcontinental trends, spread through online networks, despite geographical distances and social differences.

Contemporary far-right politics in Europe is a "variegated milieu".[96] Gabriella Lazaridis, Giovanna Campani, and Anne Benveniste rightly ask whether it makes sense to compare figures as diverse as gay-rights supporter Geert Wilders, the Catholic conservative Timo Soini, and the neo-Nazi Michaloliakos, or to associate Cinque Stelle with the anti-immigration Dansk Folkeparti under the headline "far right".[97] There are, however, some notable trends and tendencies amongst individuals and groups labelled "far right" in recent decades in Europe. Forms of nativism and strong nationalism are often highlighted. The "far right" can be used to refer to "the broader galaxy of nativist actors including extreme and radical organisations", as Pietro Gatinarra and Andrea Pirro put it.[98] Nativism is "a radical and exclusionary form of nationalism" and represents the ideological common ground for far-right parties and movements.[99] Antonis Ellinas speaks of an "ethnocentric conception of politics",[100] where the state is equated with the nation, citizenship with ethnicity, and the demos with the ethnos.[101] "This emphasis on a nationalist conception of politics—or 'ethnocracy'—is what sets the Far Right apart".[102] But while forms of nativist nationalism are prevalent, Andrew

---

[95] With Ulrich Schmiedel, I similarly discuss such trends and tendencies in Hannah Strømmen and Ulrich Schmiedel, *The Claim to Christianity: Responding to the Far Right* (London: SCM Press, 2021), see particularly chapter 2, pp. 15–37.
[96] Gattinara and Pirro, 'The Far Right as Social Movement', p. 449.
[97] Lazaridis, Campani, and Benveniste, 'Introduction', p. 2.
[98] Gattinara and Pirro, 'The Far Right as Social Movement', p. 450.
[99] Cas Mudde, *Populist Radical Right Parties in Europe* (Cambridge: Cambridge University Press, 2007), p. 19.
[100] Ellinas, *The Media and the Far Right in Western Europe*, p. 10.
[101] Ibid., p. 1.
[102] Ibid., p. 10.

Mammone, Emmanuel Godin, and Brian Jenkins highlight the way far-right movements from the extreme to the more moderate also tend to insist on the primacy of European civilisation and culture.[103] As I will come back to in the next section, Christianity has become a defining feature of these calls to defend and uphold European civilisation and culture. I have already indicated that this is the case with Breivik's claims, too.

European civilisation and culture are seen as under threat, particularly from immigration. The purported threat of immigration is a shared anxiety and source of enmity for most far-right groups, particularly, the idea of migrants from non-Western countries challenging the "values", "traditions", and "cultures" of the host country.[104] In Mammone, Godin, and Jenkins's words, the focus on migrants reflects "the usual extreme-right obsession with the decline of homogenous pan-European or Western identities", where explicit racism is avoided.[105] As I have already highlighted in relation to the Breivik case, Islam has increasingly become perceived as the paramount problem in this respect. Many scholars have pointed out the way Islamophobia has become "the new xenophobic flag of the far right throughout Europe".[106] A deliberate process of "Islamisation" as "invasion, infiltration, contagion, conspiracy, replacement and impending irreversible crisis" is presented in the far-right imaginary as the fate—and doom—of Western democracies.[107] Conspiracy theories are frequently propagated, where events are described in apocalyptic terms as a cosmic drama between good and evil.[108] Invoking a conflict with Islam has provided not only common values among activists across Europe and beyond, but also "opportunities to further their cooperation across borders, via Internet sites, music festivals, sporting events and other rallies".[109] Michael Minkenberg, Mats Deland, and Christin Mays emphasise the effective dissemination of "cross-national historical legacies" and "the building of action networks across national or regional borders" by agents on the extreme right, spreading and reinforcing overlapping

---

[103] Andrew Mammone, Emmanuel Godin, and Brian Jenkins, 'Introduction: Mapping the "right of the mainstream right" in Contemporary Europe', in *Mapping the Extreme Right in Contemporary Europe*, edited by Andrea Mammone, Emmanuel Godin, and Brian Jenkins (London: Routledge, 2012), p. 4.
[104] Ibid., p. 6.
[105] Ibid.
[106] Ibid. This is not to say that Islamophobia always plays a role in European far-right politics.
[107] Nadia Marzouki and Duncan McDonnell, 'Populism and Religion', in *Saving the People: How Populists Hijack Religion*, edited by Nadia Marzouki, Duncan McDonnell, and Olivier Roy (London: Hurst & Co, 2016), p. 5.
[108] Bjørgo, 'Introduction', p. 3.
[109] Mammone, Godin and Jenkins, 'Introduction', p. 6.

xenophobic messages.[110] Farid Hafez talks about "tendencies and special lineages" when it comes to different actors on the far right.[111] Islamophobia provides not only common values among activists, thus characterising such tendencies and lineages in important ways, but also provides "opportunities to further their cooperation across borders".[112]

Islamophobia as a contemporary phenomenon is often connected to the Runnymede Trust, set up in 1968 in Britain. Its report from 1997, *Islamophobia: A Challenge for Us All*, was intended to inform British government policies as well as awaken awareness of anti-Islamic sentiments more broadly in society. As Raymond Taras explains, the Runnymede Trust characterised Islamophobia as unfounded hostility towards Islam and listed a number of negative characterisations of Islam, such as viewing Islam as monolithic, other, irrational, primitive, and inferior to the West.[113] But as Taras emphasises, Islamophobia draws crucially also from a historical anti-Muslimness that merges with twentieth-century racist ideologies.[114] The perceived incompatibility of European and Islamic values has been, and still is, central to the rise of Islamophobia, and is central to most far-right campaigns.

Violence does not necessarily follow from a far-right worldview as I have described it. Groups and individuals would need to go through a radicalisation process whereby the named enemies are increasingly dehumanised and the described threat is perceived to be acute.[115] Particular social and psychological conditions in relation to Islamophobia are necessary.[116] With peer pressure, group coherence, propaganda, dehumanisation of the other, the exaggeration of differences between groups, and racial stereotyping, violence can be condoned and conducted.[117] The term "far right", then, might be used as an umbrella concept; some actors who fall

---

[110] Michael Minkenberg, Mats Deland, and Christin Mays, 'Introduction', in *In the Tracks of Breivik: Far Right Networks in Northern and Eastern Europe*, edited by Mats Deland, Michael Minkenberg, and Christin Mays (Münster: Lit Verlag, 2013), p. 14.
[111] Farid Hafez, 'Shifting Borders: Islamophobia as Common Ground for Building Pan-European Right-wing Unity', *Patterns of Prejudice*, 48, no. 5 (2014): p. 480.
[112] Mammone, Godin, and Jenkins, 'Introduction', p. 6.
[113] Raymond Taras, '"Islamophobia never stands still": Race, Religion, and Culture', in *Racialization and Religion: Race, Culture and Difference in the Study of Antisemitism and Islamophobia*, edited by Nasar Meer (London: Routledge, 2014), p. 34.
[114] Ibid., p. 35.
[115] Bjørgo, 'Introduction', p. 4.
[116] James G. Crossley, *Jesus in an Age of Terror, Scholarly Projects for a New American Century* (London: Equinox, 2008), p. 97.
[117] Ibid., p. 98.

under the heading are explicitly anti-democratic and violent, while others comply with democratic procedures and participate in mainstream politics.[118] I am keen not to limit the category "far right" to one set of fixed characteristics that fit all contexts either globally, in Europe, or in Western Europe. Rather, in this book I set out to track particular ideological trends and political practices that involve forms of Bible-use that support claims about saving and defending Christian culture from Islam.

When I draw connections between different facets and factors in far-right politics in this book, then, it is with an eye for the tendencies to call for a defence of Christian Europe and denunciations of Islam as a threat. More particularly, I am interested in the way Europe is imagined in relation to Christianity and a particular biblical legacy in order to exclude and other Islam. Not all of these imaginings are "far right". Some of the sources that are important in feeding the worldview that Breivik bought into and propagated stem from outside Europe's borders, such as the United States. The far-right thought and practice that I delineate does not adhere to national borders or neatly fit into fixed regions or closed groups. In the next chapter, then, I make a case for how mapping Bible-use can help scholars to understand the concrete connections and constructions that emerge in a particular case and how this Bible-use gains traction through repetition, citation, sharing, as well as more diffuse forms of dissemination. But before turning to the biblical elements that will be the focus of this book, it is necessary to outline further the role religion plays in the worldview of which Breivik is a part.

The Role of Religion

As Pietro Castelli Gattinara discusses, the shift in far-right rhetoric from biological to cultural racism has resulted in less rhetoric around the "other" as inferior, and more rhetoric centred on the culture and religion of the "other" as incompatible with Western values.[119] Religion rather than race becomes the primary boundary marker. But as Hafez shows, this does not mean that the notion of race has disappeared.[120] "The far right's 'differential racism' or 'cultural racism' incorporates notions of religion and culture as by-products

---

[118] Gattinara and Pirro, 'The Far Right as Social Movement', p. 450.
[119] Pietro Castelli Gattinara, 'Framing Exclusion in the Public Sphere: Far-Right Mobilisation and the Debate on Charlie Hebdo in Italy', South European Society and Politics 22, no. 3 (2017): p. 346.
[120] Hafez, 'Shifting Borders', p. 481.

of a biological determinism that merely hides the notion of race that has become taboo in contemporary public discourses".[121] Whether it is by religious or racial markers, or a mixture of the two, an "essentialist framing" of Muslims takes place that fixes all Muslims as dangerous or as "other" to Europe.[122]

Breivik's worldview is indebted to an ethnocentric view of politics, in which immigration and multiculturalism are treated as anathema and where Muslims are essentialised. European civilisation is seen as under threat due to the loss of European values. These positions may be more extreme in Breivik's manifesto, but the refrain is familiar. A "border politics" operates in far-right and populist right-wing movements, in which criteria of belonging and of boundaries are emphasised.[123] If Islam is positioned outside Europe's boundaries, then Christianity is appealed to when it comes to belonging. This trend can be seen across Europe. To contextualise Breivik's own claims to Christianity, I focus here on examples from Western Europe, rather than Europe more broadly, to make clear that the countries that would be expected to be more secularised—such as Norway, France, Austria, Germany, the Netherlands, or the United Kingdom—do in fact contain far-right and populist-right movements with Christian terms, themes, and tropes.

Olivier Roy points out that the Austrian Freedom Party (Freiheitliche Partei Österreichs), the Italian League (Lega), the French National Assembly (Rassemblement National, previously Front National), the Dutch Party for Freedom (Partij voor de Vrijheid), and the United Kingdom Independence Party (UKIP) "have all claimed that the Christian identity of European nations is being threatened by a potentially deadly combination of pro-globalisation national/supranational liberal elites on the one hand, and, on the other, by an aggressive process of Islamisation".[124] In 2011, the same year of the Utøya and Oslo attacks, the leader of the Dutch Freedom Party, Geert Wilders, gave a speech in Rome in which he spoke of immigration as a dangerous threat to the West. Appealing to a common European culture, he stated that the West shares the same Judeo-Christian culture and that this

---

[121] Ibid.
[122] Taras, '"Islamophobia never stands still"', p. 422.
[123] Ruth Wodak, *The Politics of Fear: What Right-Wing Populist Discourses Mean* (London: Sage, 2015), p. 35.
[124] Olivier Roy, 'Beyond Populism: The Conservative Right, the Courts, the Churches and the Concept of a Christian Europe', in *Saving the People*, edited by Marzouki, McDonnell, and Roy, p. 186.

culture is superior.[125] Previous UKIP leader Nigel Farage wrote in UKIP's 2015 "Christian manifesto" that there is need for "a much more muscular defence of our Christian heritage and our Christian Constitution"; "ours is fundamentally a Christian nation" and, sadly, "UKIP is the only major political party left in Britain that still cherishes our Judaeo-Christian heritage".[126]

Even Marine Le Pen has emphasised French *laïcité* as key to France along with France's "Christian roots".[127] In Austria, both the Austrian Freedom Party and movements such as the Viennese Citizenship Initiative have spoken of Christianity as a criterion of inclusion into the Austrian people.[128] Christianity is treated as a "natural" common ground, in contrast to the alleged "natural" difference of Muslims.[129] For the German far-right organisation Pegida, crosses are carried and hymns are sung on the weekly marches through Dresden.[130] Along with a proclamation of the dangers of Islam across these parties and movements, then, there is often a claim to Christian heritage and identity. The idea of a Christian Europe at risk of Islamic colonisation, and the fears stoked about the degradation of purportedly "Christian values" at the heart of Europe, are invoked to posit a "clash of civilizations"—a theme I will come back to later in this book.[131] Globalisation, immigration, and multiculturalism are blamed for causing a loss of identity for particular nations and for Europe as a whole. Increased globalisation and the changes globalising processes bring have caused fear and unease.[132] Therefore, according to Marzouki and McDonnell, a cultural re-awakening and re-conquest of an idyllic past is part of the carrion-call of many far-right movements.[133]

---

[125] Wodak, *The Politics of Fear*, pp. 55–57. Wilders's proclamation that a Judeo-Christian Western culture will be lost if it is not protected against immigration has been echoed by leaders of the far right across Europe. See Birgit Sauer and Edma Ajanovic, 'Hegemonic Discourses of Difference and Inequality: Right-Wing Organisations in Austria', in *The Rise of the Far Right in Europe: Populist Shifts and "Othering"*, edited by Gabriella Lazaridis, Giovanna Campani, and Anne Benveniste (New York: Palgrave Macmillan, 2016), p. 94.

[126] The manifesto has since been taken down, but is discussed by Carey Lodge on *Christian Today*, at, https://www.christiantoday.com/article/nigel-farage-promises-muscular-defence-of-christianity-in-christian-manifesto/52937.htm.

[127] Olivier Roy, 'The French National Front: From Christian Identity to Laïcité', in *Saving the People*, edited by Marzouki, McDonnell, and Roy, p. 91.

[128] Sauer and Ajanovic, 'Hegemonic Discourses of Difference and Inequality', pp. 81–108.

[129] Ibid., p. 94.

[130] See Ulrich Schmiedel, '"We Can Do This!" Tackling the Political Theology of Populism', in *Religion in the European Refugee Crisis*, edited by Ulrich Schmiedel and Graeme Smith (New York: Palgrave Macmillan, 2018), pp. 205–224.

[131] Samuel P. Huntington, 'The Clash of Civilizations?', *Foreign Affairs* (1993), pp. 22–49. I will discuss the clash of civilisations thesis further in chapters 3, 5, and 6.

[132] Thomas Grumke, 'Globalized Anti-Globalists', pp. 323, 327–328.

[133] Marzouki and McDonnell, 'Populism and Religion', p. 4.

These ideas about the past are often connected to the defence of native religious identities and symbols that are presented as under threat.[134] The need to re-assert these identities and symbols is emphasised to stop the undermining of "native identity" that is seen to be eroding due to the forces of secularism, immigration, and multiculturalism.[135] Culture is understood as an identifiable set of symbols or codes of behaviour (such as the crucifix[136]) that can determine who is in and who is out.[137] Far-right movements and parties in Europe have engaged in campaigns against the building of mosques and minarets. These campaigns are a way of signalling that mosques and minarets do not "belong" in the idea of a "pure" native territory, as well as of stoking fears about breeding grounds for terrorism.[138] What is often called for, then, is a re-nationalised, racial order, with an ethnically defined national volkish community.[139] Frequently, this order and community is characterised at least vaguely by Christian culture versus an Islamic other.

As I have stressed, far-right groups and figures across Europe simultaneously function as a "transnational network" with, Thomas Grumke explains, "a collective identity and an internationally compatible ideology".[140] Grumke calls it "an international of nationalists".[141] The collective identity is grounded in notions of a (white) Western culture.[142] Fixating on a common enemy, "networking has become tighter, contacts abroad have intensified, and communication channels have improved, altogether making for a permanent exchange of information and lively event tourism".[143] The common enemy is religiously defined, just as the collective identity is religiously described.

---

[134] Ibid.
[135] Ibid.
[136] For a discussion of the way the crucifix is understood in this way, see Ulrich Schmiedel, '"Take Up Your Cross": Public Theology between Populism and Pluralism in the Post-Migrant Context', *International Journal of Public Theology* 13, no. 2 (2019): pp. 140–162.
[137] Marzouki and McDonnell, 'Populism and Religion', p. 4.
[138] Ibid., pp. 4–5.
[139] Grumke, 'Globalized Anti-Globalists', p. 327. One aspect alluded to several times by now, and written about extensively, is of course the role of religious nationalism. In this book, though, I deliberately focus on the way "Europe" is constructed through transnational trends and networks. For an excellent introduction and intervention into debates about religious nationalism, see Atalia Omer and Jason A. Springs, *Religious Nationalism* (Santa Barbara, CA: ABC-CLIO, 2013), or more recently J. Christopher Soper and Joel S. Fetzer, *Religion and Nationalism in Global Perspective* (Cambridge: Cambridge University Press, 2018). Atalia Omer and Joshua Lupo's *Religion, Populism, and Modernity: Confronting White Christian Nationalism and Racism* has as its focus the way constructions of nation and peoplehood are key for exclusionary right-wing populisms.
[140] Ibid., p. 329.
[141] Ibid.
[142] Ibid. The word "white" is in brackets, because the racial aspect is often left tacit.
[143] Ibid., p. 330.

As in Breivik's worldview, it is a matter of Christian Europe against Islam. As I will go on to elucidate in this book, notions of Christian scripture are part of this allegedly ineluctable conflict between Christian Europe and Islam. But it is necessary to argue a little more for why these claims to Christianity need to be taken seriously in academic scholarship, both in the case of Breivik and for far-right movements in Western Europe more broadly.

"Real" Religion?

While ample attention is given to the fact that Christianity is invoked by far-right figures and right-wing populists, there has been a noticeable reluctance to treat this as a sign of "real" religiosity or "Christianity" per se amongst some scholars. In the introduction to *Saving the People: How Populists Hijack Religion*, for instance, Marzouki and McDonnell write that the use of religion in populist far-right movements in Europe:

> is much more about 'belonging' than 'belief' and revolves around two main notions: 'restoration' and 'battle'. What has to be restored is usually described as the importance afforded within society to a particular native religious identity or set of traditions and symbols rather than a theological doctrine with rules and precepts. This restoration, however, requires battling two groups of 'enemies of the people': the elites who disregard the importance of the people's religious heritage, and the 'others' who seek to impose their religious values and laws upon the native population.[144]

Traditions and symbols are associated with far-right populist notions of religion, while theological doctrines with rules and precepts are associated with a different kind of religion. Belonging is part of the former camp; belief is part of the latter. In the final chapter of the volume, Olivier Roy emphasises the way religion is conceived as "identity" for far-right populist parties: Christendom is placed above Christianity.[145] These parties are "Christian largely to the extent that they reject Islam".[146] The far right uses religion as a set of symbols, a marker of tradition and identity.[147] The Christianity of these far-right

---

[144] Marzouki and McDonnell, 'Populism and Religion', p. 2.
[145] Roy, 'Beyond Populism'.
[146] Ibid., p. 186.
[147] Ibid.

parties, then, is not really Christianity. "Christianity" is even set aside as the proper term, in favour of "Christendom". Religion, proper, is taken to be synonymous with a set of beliefs, theological doctrine, and adherence to rules and precepts. The improper religion of the populists is concerned with tradition, symbols, and belonging.

There has been a similar reluctance to recognise the religious aspects of Breivik's ideology. In a *Guardian* article written two days after the attacks in Oslo and Utøya, Andrew Brown dismissed any relationship between Christianity and Breivik, as his title makes clear: "Breivik Is Not a Christian but Anti-Islam".[148] Brown stated that Breivik's views "had nothing to do with Christianity but was based on an atavistic horror of Muslims and a loathing of 'Marxists'".[149] Bangstad admits that Breivik self-identifies as a conservative Christian, but seems to agree with Brown when he goes on to write: "However, as was amply illustrated by his deeds and in his tract, he was not in any respects a practising Christian".[150] Here the distinction between proper and improper religion is drawn between those practicing and those non-practicing.[151] Rasmus Fleischer outlines different types of fascism in order to attempt to categorise far-right trends in Europe. Breivik roughly falls into what Fleischer calls "mono-fascism". According to Fleischer, "[m]ono-fascism does indeed insist on a 'Christian' identity, but this identity is cultural rather than religious", lacking "theology".[152] Culture and religion are here sliced cleanly apart, and it is the lack of theology that is taken to prove the non-religious aspect of Breivik's worldview. Øyvind Strømmen refers to Breivik's "Christian identity" as one of the characteristics of his ideological proclivities but does not discuss this aspect in much detail.[153] In Amos N. Guiora's account of the Breivik case, he compares the absolute convictions that underpin extremism, whether they are of a secular or a religious kind.

---

[148] Andrew Brown, 'Breivik Is Mot a Christian but Anti-Islam', *The Guardian*, 24 July 2011.
[149] Ibid.
[150] Bangstad, *Anders Breivik and the Rise of Islamophobia*, p. 3.
[151] Spurred on by the ten-year anniversary of the 22 July terror attacks, Bangstad himself points out the lack of engagement with the religious elements in the Breivik case and calls for further analysis of invocations of white Christianity and Judeo-Christian civilisation. Sindre Bangstad, 'Which Populism, Which Christianity?', in *Religion, Populism, and Modernity: Confronting White Christian Nationalism and Racism*, edited by Atalia Omer and Joshua Lupo (Notre Dame, IN: University of Notre Dame Press, 2023), pp. 228–229.
[152] Rasmus Fleischer, 'Two Fascisms in Contemporary Europe? Understanding the Ideological Split of the Radical Right', In *In the Tracks of Breivik: Far Right Networks in Northern and Eastern Europe*, edited by Mats Deland, Michael Minkenberg, and Christin Mays (Münster: Lit Verlag, 2013), p. 60.
[153] See for instance his reference to Christian identity in *Det Mørke Nettet*, p. 23.

He discusses Osama bin Laden and compares him to Timothy McVeigh and Anders Behring Breivik. McVeigh and Breivik, he claims, both operated with an "extreme secular worldview".[154] "Although McVeigh and Breivik were not motivated by religion, their convictions and beliefs were no less absolute and violent than Bin Laden".[155] Here it is simply taken for granted that Breivik was in no way motivated by religion.[156]

Admittedly, Breivik describes himself as not an "excessively religious man".[157] His manifesto is a messy text full of references to paganism and Hinduism as well as to Christianity and the Bible.[158] Aage Borchgrevink points to the Norse mythology Breivik brings in to name his weapons, as well as mixing together ideas from Orthodox, Catholic, and Protestant traditions.[159] Did Breivik, then, as Borchgrevink suggests, get lost in the religion department?[160] In the manifesto, Breivik calls himself "a supporter of a monocultural Christian Europe".[161] A "we" is conjured up who "believe in Christianity as a cultural, social, identity and moral platform".[162] He insists: "This makes us Christian".[163] Through his actions and manifesto, Breivik was trying to build a network for Christian, militant nationalists in Europe.[164] In court in April 2012, Breivik said that he wanted to build a platform and a bridge between national socialists, national conservatives, and true-believing Christians.[165] Hans Rustad, the editor of the Norwegian

---

[154] Amos N. Guiora, *Tolerating Intolerance: The Price of Protecting Extremism* (Oxford: Oxford University Press, 2014), p. 6.
[155] Ibid., p. 6.
[156] An exception to the tendency to dismiss the Christianity of Breivik's ideology is a publication produced by academics in Norway (in translation, *Academic Perspectives on 22. July*), from 2012, which I will come back to. Specifically, the chapters that are relevant are by Jone Salomonsen on paganism, misogyny, and Christianity in Breivik's ideology; by Øystein Sørensen on Breivik's vision of the church; and by Jorunn Økland on feminism and Christian tradition. Jone Salomonsen, 'Kristendom, paganisme og kvinnefiendskap', in *Akademiske Perspektiver På 22. Juli*, edited by Anders Ravik Jupskås (Bergen: Fagbokforlaget, 2012), pp. 74–89; Øystein Sørensen, 'En totalitær mentalitet: det ideologiske tankegodset i Anders Behring Breiviks manifest', in *Akademiske Perspektiver På 22. Juli*, pp. 103–114; Jorunn Økland, 'Feminismen, tradisjonen og forventning', in *Akademiske Perspektiver På 22. Juli*, pp. 115–127.
[157] Manifesto, p. 1404.
[158] I will discuss the pagan and Christian references in more detail later in this book. See Praveen Swami for a brief overview of Breivik's references to Hinduism: Praveen Swami, "Norwegian Mass Killer's Manifesto Hails Hindutva", *The Hindu*, 26 July 2011.
[159] Aage Borchgrevink, *A Norwegian Tragedy: Anders Behring Breivik and the Massacre at Utøya*, translated by Guy Puzey (Cambridge: Polity Press, 2013), pp. 174–175.
[160] Ibid., p. 175.
[161] Manifesto, p. 1404.
[162] Ibid., p. 1308.
[163] Ibid.
[164] Hverven, *Terrorens ansikt*, p. 57.
[165] Ibid. The term used in Norwegian is "rettroende kristne".

far-right webpage document.no—one of the websites Breivik was most active on before 2011—wrote openly in several articles around the beginning of the court case about himself as a conservative Christian.[166] Hverven writes that the longer the court case went on, the more convinced he was that it would "be useful to go further into theology to shed light on some of the dilemmas that have come up in court about Breivik's self-representation".[167]

Jorunn Økland discusses the way Breivik comes across as a product of the secularisation he derides: "he does not come across as someone who has a clear idea of how to approach the Bible other than in slogans and stereotypes".[168] "He wants the aura of authority that the Bible conveys".[169] Discussions such as Økland's are correct. But the question stands: What happens if we still take seriously the way biblical slogans and stereotypes function inside and outside the manifesto? As I will go on to discuss, Breivik is tapping into a biblical register and forms of Bible-use that resonate not just among contemporary far-right groups in Europe and the United States, but also historically. I will analyse the biblical elements of Breivik's manifesto in chapter 3. The manifesto contains numerous references to Christianity.[170] The crusades are a central topic.[171] Stories about the persecution of Christians are prevalent (and is mostly blamed on Muslims).[172] Modern anti-Christian sentiments are decried.[173] The pros and cons of Christianity and the Church are discussed.[174] The future and reform of Christianity is part of the plan for a restored Europe.[175] A Christian justification of the struggle altogether is included.[176] My point is not that Breivik himself must be a Christian. My point is rather that he cannot be dismissed as having nothing to do with Christianity when references to Christianity and the Bible form a part of his worldview. Whether or not Breivik is a believing or practicing Christian is not my concern. My concern is that Christianity and Christian scripture are part of the discourse that he encountered and propagated on- and offline.

---

[166] Ibid., p. 54.
[167] Ibid., p. 130.
[168] Økland, 'Manifestos, Gender, Self-Canonization, and Violence', p. 35.
[169] Ibid., p. 35.
[170] This has been increasingly observed by scholars writing on Breivik, although it is not usually the focus of attention. See for instance Berntzen and Sandberg, 'The Collective Nature of Lone Wolf Terrorism', pp. 759–779; Gardell, 'Crusader Dreams', pp. 129–155.
[171] Manifesto sections: 1.11–1.14; 1.22
[172] Manifesto sections: 1.19; 2.31–2.34; 3.146.
[173] Manifesto section: 2.84.
[174] Manifesto sections: 2.82; 2.83.
[175] Manifesto sections: 2.85; 3.80; 3.81.
[176] Manifesto sections: 3.148–3.152.

As my overview of the debate about the role of religion on the far right has made clear, assessments about far-right uses of religion are mired in assumptions about what religion—or more specifically Christianity—is or ought to be: a special domain that can be singled out from other aspects such as politics and culture.[177] It is assumed that Christianity is first and foremost a matter of belief,[178] and that the beliefs tied to Christianity will be demonstrated in a particular set of practices. Presumably because far-right figures such as Breivik do not look familiar according to this understanding of Christianity, the Christianity of the far right is not treated as *real* religion. It is seen instead as politically expedient or as really about culture and identity. "Mere" reference to Christian symbols, snippets of scripture, and identity claims based on Christian tradition and culture are not taken seriously. There is little critical engagement with the complex and fraught concept of "religion" in these discussions, or with the various and varying manifestations of "Christianity" throughout history. There is neither attention to the way Christianity might always have taken forms that are entangled in complex and ambiguous ways in culture and politics, nor to the way Christianity might be adapted to modern conditions in ways that might alter perceptions and practices of religion.[179] The metaphor of religion being "hijacked" is pervasive and problematic. As Ulrich Schmiedel points out, this metaphor "presupposes that religion is a category that can be controlled, either by its legitimate or its illegitimate owners".[180]

One of the most cited scholars to suggest that the return of religion in Western European populist right-wing rhetoric is not really a return to *religion* is Rogers Brubaker. He argues that the Christianity in far-right and populist-right politics is "not a substantive Christianity".[181] Brubaker invokes

---

[177] Ulrich Schmiedel and I problematised the way Christianity is dismissed in far-right and populist-right politics in *The Claim to Christianity: Responding to the Far Right* (London: SCM Press, 2020).

[178] The assumption that religion is centred on belief has been widely critiqued as an assumption based on Protestant forms of religiosity. See for instance Tomoko Masusawa, *The Invention of World Religions: Or, How European Universalism Was Preserved in the Language of Pluralism* (Chicago: University of Chicago Press, 2005).

[179] Hector Avalos has critiqued a lack of communication between disciplines when it comes to the topic of religious violence. Working with "views of religion that are outdated, inaccurate, or not sufficiently cognizant of debates within the field of religious studies" leads to unexamined assumptions and therefore questionable conclusions. Hector Avalos, 'Explaining Religious Violence: Retrospects and Prospects', in *The Blackwell Companion to Religion and Violence*, edited by Andrew Murphy (London: Blackwell, 2011) p. 145.

[180] Schmiedel, 'Introduction: Political Theology in the Spirit of Populism—Methods and Metaphors', p. 3.

[181] Rogers Brubaker, 'Between Nationalism and Civilizationism: The European Populist Moment in Comparative Perspective', *Ethnic and Racial Studies* 40, no. 8 (2017): p. 1199.

the term "Christianism" to describe this non-substantive Christianity. Ulrich Schmiedel has critiqued the easy distinction between proper and improper Christianity that underlies Brubaker's category of "Christianism" as it is applied to right-wing populism in Europe.[182] Schmiedel demonstrates that Brubaker is drawing a normative distinction between different kinds of Christianity that is neither acknowledged nor assessed. What "Christianism" denotes for Brubaker, as Schmiedel shows, is "secularized"[183] references to the Christian faith, which treat Christianity as cultural and civilisational rather than religious or theological. Belonging rather than believing is emphasised. Christianity is treated as a means to an end. "Christianity" proper, as Brubaker seems to understand it, denotes non-secularised references to the Christian faith, where believing rather than belonging is emphasised. As Schmiedel puts it: "Christianism is nondoctrinal, nonorganizational, and without ritual, while Christianity is doctrinal, organizational, and with ritual".[184] Schmiedel makes the point that a number of assumptions about "proper" religion and Christianity are at play here. The strong contrasts between Christianism and Christianity may be nice and neat for scholarly purposes, but fail to take account of the more complex and messy phenomena of lived Christianity—past and present.[185]

Belief versus belonging, proper theology against deficient theology, practicing or non-practising—these distinctions are not as easy to make as they might seem if scholars actually confront the ambiguous, messy, and complex manifestations of lived religion. Belonging as a key facet of Christianity is not the invention or exclusive characteristic of the far right. What counts as Christianity is not only what is of ancient pedigree, doctrinally described, or peer-reviewed. Attempting to disentangle different features of religion—belief from belonging, practice from non-practice—is potentially to misrepresent the way Christianity is lived. To neatly slice off some forms of religious commitment from others by appealing to neat categories of belief versus

---

[182] Ulrich Schmiedel, 'The Cracks in the Category of Christianism: A Call for Ambiguity in the Conceptualization of Christianity', in *Contemporary Christian-Cultural Values: Migration Encounters in the Nordic Region*, edited by Cecilia Nahnfeldt and Kaia S. Rønsdal (London: Routledge, 2021), pp. 164–182, and Schmiedel 'Introduction: Political Theology in the Spirit of Populism—Methods and Metaphors', pp. 1–22. The main article of Brubaker's that Schmiedel engages with is: Brubaker, 'Between Nationalism and Civilizationism', pp. 1191–1226. See also Rogers Brubaker's post, 'A New "Christianist" Secularism in Europe', available on *The Immanent Frame*: https://tif.ssrc.org/2016/10/11/a-new-christianist-secularism-in-europe/.
[183] Schmiedel, 'Introduction: Political Theology in the Spirit of Populism—Methods and Metaphors', p. 12.
[184] Schmiedel, 'The Cracks in the Category of Christianism', p. 167.
[185] Ibid., p. 171.

belonging will obscure the textured ways in which religion works. Attention to lived religion can help show how secularised versions of Christianity and Christian versions of secularism might play out in ambiguous, complex, and contested ways.[186]

Lived Scripture

The problem with focusing too narrowly on particular notions of religion as belief and particular kinds of practice is that all sorts of religious textures and theological material are lost from sight. What Bryan Turner has called "post-institutional, hybrid and post-orthodox religiosity"[187] becomes invisible. Robert Orsi has urged scholars to move beyond simplistic judgements of *good* versus *bad* religion, to the ambiguous and ambivalent relations and practices that constitute religion.[188] He asks about what relationships are formed between humans and holy figures and what consequences these relationships have in the everyday lives of women, men, and children.[189] He calls religion, then, a "network of relationships between heaven and earth involving humans of all ages and many different sacred figures together".[190] Drawing on Orsi, Elizabeth Shakman Hurd calls for greater scholarly attention to "the improvised, situational practices that often take place outside of churches, synagogues, and mosques".[191] Secularisation processes have undoubtedly left their mark on European conceptions and practices of religion. But secularisation is a process, and not a smooth and straightforward one. It also entails what Turner speaks of as "the transformation (metamorphosis) of religion as it adjusts to new conditions".[192] In *Formations of the Secular*, Talal Asad notes that if the secularisation thesis seems increasingly

---

[186] Johanna Gustafsson Lundberg discusses a particularly interesting example of these interconnections between the secular and the Christian in a case in Sweden, namely the so-called #mycross campaign. Johanna Gustafsson Lundberg, 'Christianity in a Post-Christian Context: Immigration, Church Identity, and the Role of Religion in Public Debates', in *Religion in the European Refugee Crisis*, edited by Ulrich Schmiedel and Graeme Smith (London: Palgrave Macmillan, 2018), pp. 123–143.
[187] Bryan S. Turner, *Religion and Modern Society: Citizenship, Secularisation and the State* (Cambridge: Cambridge University Press, 2011), p. ix.
[188] Robert A. Orsi, *Between Heaven and Earth: The Religious Worlds People Make and the Scholars Who Study Them* (Princeton, NJ: Princeton University Press, 2005), p. 2.
[189] Ibid.
[190] Ibid.
[191] Elizabeth Shakman Hurd, *Beyond Religious Freedom: The New Global Politics of Religion* (Princeton, NJ: Princeton University Press, 2015), p. 15.
[192] Turner, *Religion and Modern Society*, p. 11.

implausible, this is not only due to the vibrant role religion seemingly plays on the various screens broadcasting world events.[193] What we might call "religion", he suggests, was "*always* involved in the world of power".[194] Asad argues:

> objects, sites, practices, words, representations—even the minds and bodies of worshipers—cannot be confined within the exclusive space of what secularists *name* 'religion'. They have their own ways of being. The historical elements of what come to be conceptualized as religion have disparate trajectories.[195]

Critical of all-too-neat categorisations of religion, many scholars have by now examined the way religious motifs "do not always signal a belief in certain articles of faith, let alone obedience to some ecclesial or scriptural authority", but are lodged in the very fabric of discourse and structures of politics, traditions, habits, and culture.[196] This recognition has sparked renewed interest in religions and religiosity, also outside the field of theology and religious studies.[197] As Hent de Vries remarked about the so-called turn to religion in the humanities in the late 1990s, this turn is indebted to the recognition of ingrained theological motifs and structures in philosophy, culture, and politics, but also to the "resurfacing of religion as a highly ambiguous force on the contemporary geopolitical stage".[198]

In the Norwegian publication *Academic Perspectives on 22. July*, published a year after the terror attacks, attention to the religious aspects of Breivik's worldview show its salience and its strangeness. In her discussion of the role that tradition and antifeminism plays in Breivik's ideology, Økland discusses the way Breivik emphasises the biblical and the Catholic Christian traditions as instruments to preserve European patriarchal culture.[199] Jone Salomonsen demonstrates how Breivik mixes allusions to Christianity and paganism.[200] The Maltese cross on the front of Breivik's manifesto alludes both to the

---

[193] Talal Asad, *Formations of the Secular: Christianity, Islam, Modernity* (Stanford, CA: Stanford University Press, 2003), p. 200.
[194] Ibid.
[195] Ibid., p. 201.
[196] Hent de Vries, *Philosophy and the Turn to Religion* (Baltimore, MD: Johns Hopkins University Press, 1999), p. 5.
[197] Ibid.
[198] Ibid., p. 6.
[199] Økland, 'Feminismen, tradisjonen og forventning', p. 123.
[200] Salomonsen, 'Kristendom, paganisme og kvinnefiendskap', pp. 74–89.

Christian crusades and to pagan symbolism.[201] These discussions add to other recent calls to make sense of the appearance of religious symbols and artefacts in public debates in societies that are considered highly secular, such as Johanna Gustafsson Lundberg's discussion of a campaign to wear crosses in Sweden.[202] What is at stake in these discussions is precisely how the private versus the public, the personal versus the political, is played out when statements about religion are made, or when religious clothing and symbols are brandished in places where secularisation is considered the norm.

Hence, in the dismissals of far-right references to Christianity, there is a failure to seriously probe, and critically examine, the forms religion might take in the contemporary world and how these forms sustain themselves, draw on past models, and re-invent themselves to suit the circumstances of the followers, users, claimants to, and makers of a religious tradition. As Hurd argues, religious sentiments, language-use, and practice "unfold amid and are entangled in all domains of human life, forms of belonging, work, play, governance, violence, and exchange".[203] "Religion cannot be singled out from these other aspects of human experience, and yet also cannot simply be identified with these either".[204] Figures on the far right such as Breivik might not be regular churchgoers. They might not adhere to classic Christian doctrines. But nor do many who would still class themselves as Christian. Figures such as Breivik certainly operate with a number of beliefs as to what Christianity signifies, notions of salvation and martyrdom, and how to be a "Christian".

Why does Breivik liken himself to David fighting Goliath? Why does Alternative für Deutschland write about the Good Samaritan in party literature? Why do the members of Pegida carry a cross on their demonstrations? Why is the image of a sword-bearing Jesus embraced from Jean-Marie Le Pen to Oriana Fallaci? Simply stating that these are superficial allusions that do not have anything to do with *real* religion—whatever that is—is to operate with a number of unexamined normative assumptions about what religion is and who can and who cannot lay claim to Christianity and its scripture.

---

[201] Ibid., p. 84.
[202] Lundberg, 'Christianity in a Post-Christian Context', pp. 123–143.
[203] Hurd, *Beyond Religious Freedom*, p. 7.
[204] Ibid. The idea that "religion" is a unique domain that can be separated from law, sociality, culture, and politics, has recently been troubled by what Cécile Laborde has summarised as the Semantic critique, the Protestant critique, and the Realist critique. These critiques have been articulated in debates that have come to the fore recently in the work of scholars such as Hurd, as well as Talal Asad and Saba Mahmood, amongst others. Cécile Laborde, *Liberalism's Religion* (Cambridge, MA: Harvard University Press, 2017).

I have already mentioned that Breivik referenced biblical texts in his manifesto. I have made clear that this study seeks to tease out where this Bible-use comes from and how it functions in broader far-right trends. Invocations of "the Bible" and references to biblical texts are an overlooked aspect of the contemporary far right in Western Europe. This may be in part because such references appear sporadic and superficial, and in part because those who research biblical texts—biblical scholars—are mostly not concerned with contemporary political Bible-use. Much of the blindness specifically to political Bible-use might stem from a secularisation narrative in which the decline of biblical literacy is a key part. But as the contributors to Katie Edwards's *Rethinking Biblical Literacy* show, that narrative depends very much on what we mean by biblical literacy and biblical knowledge.[205]

If what is expected is what James Crossley calls a quasi-Protestant notion of biblical literacy[206]—individual knowledge of biblical texts, chapter-and-verse citations, or the sort of rote learning that indelibly imprints on the mind the list of biblical books in the correct order—then we might see a decline in biblical literacy. But perceptions of "the Bible" persist, and biblical motifs, stories, characters, and tropes are told and retold with impressive plasticity.[207] Bits of Bible are, in Jonneke Bekkenkamp and Yvonne Sherwood's words, "recycled, appealed to, exploited, banalized, as they circulate as part of ongoing vocabularies".[208] Alastair Hunter points to the fact that the cultural influence of the Bible, even in a highly secularised Europe, means that processes in which Bibles are invoked entail an authority that is difficult to challenge and easy to exploit.[209] I want to emphasise that attention to how Bibles are used—and what we could call lived scripture—is crucial. Particularly, it is important to investigate how political scripture

---

[205] Katie Edwards, ed., *Rethinking Biblical Literacy* (London: Bloomsbury, 2015).

[206] James G. Crossley, *Harnessing Chaos: The Bible in English Political Discourse since 1968*, revised edition (London: Bloomsbury T&T Clark, 2016), p. xvi.

[207] Numerous reception history studies show this. To mention only a few particularly good examples, see for instance James Crossley, *Cults, Martyrs and Good Samaritans: Religion in Contemporary English Discourse* (London: Pluto Press, 2018); Yvonne Sherwood, *Biblical Blaspheming: Trials of the Sacred for a Secular Age* (Cambridge: Cambridge University Press, 2012); Erin Runions, *The Babylon Complex: Theopolitical Fantasies of War, Sex and Sovereignty* (New York: Fordham University Press, 2014); Jennifer L. Koosed and Robert Seesengood, *Jesse's Lineage: The Legendary Lives of David, Jesus and Jesse James* (London: Bloomsbury, 2013).

[208] Yvonne Sherwood and Jonneke Bekkenkamp, 'Introduction: The Thin Blade of Difference Between Real Swords and Words about "Sharp-edged Iron Things"—Reflections on How People Use the Word', in *Sanctified Aggression: Legacies of Biblical and Post-Biblical Vocabularies of Violence*, edited by Jonneke Bekkenkamp and Yvonne Sherwood (London: T&T Clark, 2003), p. 3.

[209] Alastair G. Hunter, '(De)Nominating Amalek: Racist Stereotyping in the Bible and the Justification of Discrimination', in *Sanctified Aggression*, edited by Bekkenkamp and Sherwood, p. 98.

practices function in order to shed light on a variety of modes, registers, and contested practices when it comes to claims to Christianity.[210] At the same time, Atalia Omer and Joshua Lupo are right to point to the "theological poverty" of much far-right and populist-right use of religion.[211] That is why it is key to maintain that the far-right Bibles I go on to analyse are not somehow natural, inevitable, or necessary. Louder, "more masculine and militant interpretaters of religion do not have a monopoly on what counts as religious knowledge".[212]

What is known as "biblical reception history" is dedicated to engaging with exactly these uses and influences of the Bible. I will discuss this approach in more detail in the next chapter. As Crossley argues, reception history is about bringing diverse questions about "how and why biblical texts got to the multiple places where they are today, how and why people have felt the need to engage with biblical texts, and how and why there is loathing, despising and indifference".[213] In asking these questions, the field of biblical studies can provide a significant contribution to our understanding of history and society.[214] What knowledge of Bibles is operant, or what level of biblical literacy might be evident, will differ from case to case. Knowledge and literacy might in any case not be the main issue or the most interesting question when it comes to political and public use of Bibles. The use-value, effects, and affects of Bibles, bits of Bible as mottos and memes or as tracts and sermons, as adverts and puns or tweets and films may prompt far more interesting questions about the plasticity of Bibles and biblical texts. Rather than boorishly lament a decline in biblical literacy, it might be more important and interesting for biblical scholars to map the different uses of Bibles and ask how and why certain references to "the Bible" are operative, how they work, and where they gain traction or fall flat. This is what I aim to do here.

---

[210] I have discussed lived scripture and political scripture practices in Hannah Strømmen, 'Scripts and Scriptures of Populism: On Populist Reading Practices', in *The Spirit of Populism: Political Theologies in Polarized Times*, edited by Ulrich Schmiedel and Joshua Ralston (Leiden: Brill, 2022), pp. 85–100.
[211] Atalia Omer and Joshua Lupo, 'Introduction: The Cultural Logic of White Christian Nationalisms', in *Religion, Populism, and Modernity*, edited by Omer and Lupo, p. 6.
[212] Omer and Lupo, 'Introduction: The Cultural Logic of White Christian Nationalisms', p. 6.
[213] James G. Crossley, 'The End of Reception History, a Grand Narrative for Biblical Studies and the Neoliberal Bible', in *Reception History and Biblical Studies: Theory and Practice*, edited by Emma England and John Lyons (London: Bloomsbury T&T Clark, 2015), p. 47.
[214] Ibid.

Far-Right Bibles

The central claim of this book is that a particular understanding and use of "the Bible" plays a key, if sometimes subtle and supple, role in strands of the contemporary European far right, specifically the milieu in which far-right Anders Behring Breivik is a part. I have put "the Bible" in scare quotes, because part of my argument is that conceptions and constructions of what "the" Bible *is* are precisely what is at stake. I refer to Bibles in the plural rather than *the* Bible, because part of my point in this study is that there is not only one Bible. There are only specific copies of Bibles and concrete biblical texts, and there are multiple claims to "the Bible" that operate according to different understandings of what is included in this collection of texts as well as what its status, authority, and significance is beyond the textual. Bibles are by no means central to all or even most far-right movements, practices, and ideologies in Western Europe or beyond. But as I will go on to show, Bibles and biblical texts function as components that play parts in the worldview espoused and propagated by prominent far-right figures.

I will make my argument by analysing Breivik's manifesto and the far-right milieu that informed him. By mapping the forms Bibles take in strands of the far right that inspired the 22 July terror, I will explore patterns emerging and claims multiplying regarding Bibles and their role in relation to far-right concerns with identity and otherness. To do so, though, it is necessary to outline in some detail how I approach this thing we call "the Bible". Following on from this first introductory chapter, the second chapter provides an outline for mapping Bible-use in far-right milieus. I situate this study within biblical reception history, though I believe—or hope—that it can be relevant also for other fields. For my approach, I draw on Gilles Deleuze and Félix Guattari's *A Thousand Plateaus: Capitalism and Schizophrenia*, particularly their concept of "assemblage". Bibles are always, I will argue, contingent constructions that operate in concrete ways and under concrete conditions. Bibles never operate alone or solely as textual artefacts. Bibles and biblical texts always operate with other texts, ideas, institutions, interpreters, technologies, practices, histories, and materials. Mapping biblical assemblages involves identifying what constructions of Bible operate in a milieu and what non-biblical and non-textual elements stick to a Bible to make it what it is.

In the third chapter, I ask what Bibles are at work in Breivik's manifesto. I set out to map the concrete biblical assemblages operating in the worldview of Breivik. I examine which biblical texts are alluded to and how "the Bible" is construed in the manifesto. I will argue that two biblical assemblages are at work in Breivik's manifesto, namely what I will call the War Bible and the Civilisation Bible. These Bibles are not only made up of biblical references and allusions to "the Bible", but are also connected to key parts of the manifesto, such as stories about Muslim violence against Christians, conspiracies about European decline, and civilisational claims.

In the fourth chapter, I ask: Where do Breivik's biblical assemblages come from? The Bible-use that can be identified in Breivik's manifesto does not emerge out of nowhere, and it cannot be seen as an isolated phenomenon. The Bibles invoked in the manifesto form assemblages with a number of far-right texts, theories, and ideologues in Europe and beyond. Examining key figures in the counterjihad milieu that Breivik cited and was inspired by, I examine the Bible-use that operates more broadly by those who propagate the Eurabia conspiracy. Far-right figures Breivik was inspired by, such as Robert Spencer, Bat Ye'or, "Fjordman", Bruce Bawer, and Oriana Fallaci, complain about the decline of the West and of the threat of Islam to European countries and culture, and they see the loss of a particular Bible as part of this decline.

In chapters 5 and 6 I will examine the War Bible and Civilisation Bible assemblages in more detail. In the fifth chapter, I demonstrate the connections between the War Bible in Breivik's manifesto and American online and published sources, such as Joseph Farah's Tea Party Manifesto.[215] To indicate what might be useful about a War Bible, I explore the way this War Bible is an activation of past Bibles used to legitimate violence, particularly Bible-use in the medieval crusades and the First World War. But I also explore the way non-biblical components are key for Breivik's War Bible, particularly histories of the crusades and performances of masculinity. Chapter 6 focuses on the Civilisation Bible. Here, I discuss philosophical thinkers who are drawn into Breivik's far-right worldview as inspirational sources, particularly the way thinkers such as Roger Scruton and Rémi Brague become part of the emergence and acceleration of a Civilisation Bible. I highlight the way the Civilisation Bible is an activation of past Bibles used particularly in early modern Europe and the colonial era. Non-biblical components stick to this Bible, too, in crucial ways, such as the clash of civilisations thesis.

---

[215] Joseph Farah, *The Tea Party Manifesto: A Vision for an American Rebirth* (Washington, DC: WND Books, 2010).

After my analysis of the War Bible and the Civilisation Bible, I switch gears in the seventh chapter in order to question how biblical scholars might respond to the kind of Bible-use I have identified. I summarise four trends: historicising biblical texts; battling selectivity; challenging biblical authority; and resistant reading. I evaluate their efficacy in relation to my material and my approach to biblical assemblages. Building on this discussion, I reflect in chapter 8 on the way the concept of biblical assemblages can provide a way forward for understanding the trends, workings, and directions of Bibles. Biblical scholars, I propose, can map biblical assemblages as they form and reform—or, to use Deleuze and Guattari's terminology, as they territorialise and deterritorialise. Following Deleuze and Guattari, I argue that mapping biblical assemblages is not only a descriptive task, but always has a normative edge as well. Finally, in chapter 9, I summarise my main argument and reflect on the implications of this book for biblical scholarship.

From the Extreme to the Mainstream

I began this chapter by explaining the case of 22 July in some more detail, particularly the way the perpetrator's political motivations were understood—or not understood. I contextualised this case of far-right terror by pointing to continuities and connections with far-right movements in Europe in the last decades. I made the case that although Western European countries might be deemed the most secular in Europe, religion plays a significant if not always central role in the programmes, proclamations, and practices of far-right figures and movements.

The Islamophobia that is so central across the contemporary European far right is frequently accompanied by claims to Christianity. I argued for why it is crucial to pay attention to these claims, particularly to the Bible-use that is part of far-right ideology and practice. Although the "far right" is a broad and baggy term, I highlighted the tendency to emphasise the decline of Christian Europe and the threat of Islam as my focus. The Bible-use that is part of these far-right movements, I proposed, should be taken seriously and studied closely to tease out the mechanisms whereby religious traditions and texts become crucial components for propagating Islamophobia. This is the case also in Western European countries that are perceived to be highly secularised and where references to Christianity are often treated by scholars as purely instrumental.

Overall, then, this is not a book about the person who killed seventy-seven people in Norway. Nor is it about the devastating details of the attacks on 22 July 2011. It is about a far-right worldview that has taken hold in contemporary Europe, and the role particular Bibles have come to play in this worldview. It begins with the far-right discourse that Breivik propagated in his manifesto, and then moves towards an examination of the material that Breivik was inspired by. However, this book is not primarily an attempt to understand the extreme political margins as an aberration or exception to the norm. Many of the core ideas about Islam and Christian Europe that are espoused by Breivik and the figures he was inspired by are shared and reproduced by more mainstream thinkers and groups. It is not my intention to collapse the margins and the mainstream, or suggest that the ideas about Islam that are propagated by more mainstream actors in some simplistic way *cause* acts of terror such as Breivik's. But there are connections between the extreme manifestations of the far right and its more mainstream incarnations that are crucial to expose, not least when it comes to Bible-use.

2
Mapping Biblical Assemblages

In far-right demonstrations across Europe in recent years, Qur'ans have been central, mostly as objects to be scorned and destroyed. The Danish far-right party Stram Kurs, for instance, has thrown Qur'ans to the ground and burnt Islam's sacred scripture in Muslim-majority neighbourhoods. The leader of the party, Rasmus Paludan, was filmed in 2019 dousing a Qur'an in what he said was the semen of Christian men, before burning it.[1] He had allegedly previously wrapped a Qur'an in bacon.[2] But Bibles—or bits of Bibles—have also made appearances in European far-right circles in the last decades. In the United Kingdom, for instance, the far-right British National Party (BNP) produced an election poster in 2009 that featured a picture of Jesus, including words from the Gospel of John 15:20: "If they have persecuted me, they will also persecute you".[3] The biblical verse is followed by the question: "What would Jesus do?" The answer was presumably to vote BNP in the European elections that year. In 2014, the far-right organisation Britain First invaded mosques across the United Kingdom, presenting Muslims with army-issued Bibles.[4] The German far-right party Alternative für Deutschland has made use of the Good Samaritan story from the Gospel of Luke (10:25–37) to promote its anti-immigration agenda, strange as that may seem.[5] For Rassemblement National in France, Joan of Arc is an iconic religious-nationalist figure whose annual celebration day has been a trademark for the

---

[1] Rachael Kennedy, 'Denmark's Quran-burning Politician Gathering Support for Election Candidacy', *Euronews*, 25 April 2019, https://www.euronews.com/2019/04/25/denmark-s-quran-burning-politician-gathering-support-for-election-candidacy (last accessed August 20, 2020).

[2] Florian Elabdi, 'Dane Who Wants to Deport Muslims, Ban Islam to Run in Election', *Aljazeera*, 16 May 2019, https://www.aljazeera.com/indepth/features/rasmus-paludan-danish-islamophobe-rises-political-stardom-190516090301567.html (last accessed August 20, 2020).

[3] Timothy Peace, 'Religion and Populism in Britain: An Infertile Breeding Ground?' in *Saving the People: How Populists Hijack Religion*, edited by Nadia Marzouki, Duncan McDonnell, and Olivier Roy (London: Hurst & Co, 2016), p. 107.

[4] Helen Pidd and Declan Lloyd, 'Police Investigate Far Right "invasions" of Bradford and Glasgow Mosques', *The Guardian*, 13 May 2014, https://www.theguardian.com/world/2014/may/13/police-far-right-invasions-bradford-glasgow-mosques-britain-first (last accessed November 2022).

[5] Beatrix von Storch, 'Grußwort', in *Warum Christen AfD wählen*, edited by Joachim Kuhs (Eßbach: Arnshaugh Verlag, 2018), pp. 11–13. See Hannah Strømmen and Ulrich Schmiedel, *The Claim to Christianity: Responding to the Far Right* (London: SCM press, 2020), pp. 76–77.

party since 1978.[6] The founder of the party, Jean-Marie Le Pen, folded the legendary figure of Joan of Arc into the Jesus of the Gospels and the party's antagonistic politics when, quoting the Gospel of Matthew (10:34), he stated that she did not come to bring peace but a sword.[7]

As I have already indicated, biblical texts also play a role in the Islamophobic worldview espoused by the perpetrator of the 22 July violence. In the previous chapter I briefly referred to Breivik's call for Europe to turn away from modern, politically correct Bible versions and return to the Latin Vulgate of Europe's Middle Ages. Particularly in part three of his manifesto he cites a number of biblical texts, primarily related to fighting, violence, and war. In this chapter I outline my approach. I then go on to use this approach to analyse references to "the Bible" and specific biblical texts, examining where they come from, how they are echoed and amplified in other sources, and what past Bible-use is being activated in these contemporary far-right circles. Reception history of the Bible is by no means uncharted territory, but there is no one agreed way to go about doing it.

To map the role Bibles and bits of Bible play in contemporary far-right milieus, I draw on Gilles Deleuze and Félix Guattari's concept of assemblage, from their work *A Thousand Plateaus: Capitalism and Schizophrenia*, originally published in 1980.[8] I propose that their concept of assemblage helps to make visible constructions of "the Bible" and the function of biblical texts

---

[6] Olivier Roy, 'The French National Front: From Christian Identity to Laïcité', in *Saving the People: How Populists Hijack Religion*, edited by Nadia Marzouki, Duncan McDonnell, and Olivier Roy (London: Hurst & Co, 2016), p. 86.

[7] Ibid.

[8] Gilles Deleuze and Félix Guattari, *A Thousand Plateaus: Capitalism and Schizophrenia*, trans. Brian Massumi (London: Bloomsbury, 2013), originally published in 1980 in French as *Mille plateaux: capitalisme et schizophrénie*. An enormous amount has been published on Deleuze and Guattari's writings. The concept of assemblage has been taken up in many different disciplines. Within biblical studies, less attention has been paid to their work, though a handful of recent publications may indicate increasing interest, at least from New Testament studies. See Stephen D. Moore's *The Bible after Deleuze: Affects, Assemblages, Bodies without Organs* (Oxford: Oxford University Press, 2022); Bradley Hudson McLean's *Deleuze, Guattari and the Machine in Early Christianity: Schizoanalysis, Affect and Multiplicity* (London: Bloomsbury, 2022); Robert Paul Seesengood, 'Bespoke Words: The Bible, Fashion, and the Mechanism(s) of Things', *The Bible and Critical Theory* 16, no. 2 (2020): pp. 50–58; Eric C. Smith, 'The Affordances of *bible* and the Agency of Material in Assemblage', *The Bible and Critical Theory* 18, no. 1 (2022): pp. 1–13; Joel Kuhlin, *A Beautiful Failure: The Event of Death and Rhetorical Disorder in the Gospel According to Mark* (Lund: Mediatryck, 2024). *Moore* in particular sets out an ambitious programme, asking what it might mean to read the Bible with and after Deleuze. The first chapter of Moore's book provides an extensive and in-depth introduction to Deleuze; the following chapters deal with questions of text, body, sex, race, and politics. Contributors to the special issue on New Materialism in *The Bible and Critical Theory* journal from 2020 also draw on Deleuze and Guattari, though not as a central focus; see for instance SuJung Shin, 'A "Vital Materiality" of the Ark in its Relativity to the Body of David in 2 Sam 6', *The Bible and Critical Theory* 16, no. 2 (2020): pp. 7–22.

in contemporary far-right circles. More generally, however, the argument of this chapter is that thinking in terms of *biblical assemblages* demonstrates the multiple components that are needed to make any Bible-use work and clarifies tendencies towards change and stabilisation in the emergence of Bibles.[9] The assemblage concept is useful, then, for the case of biblical reception at the centre of this study, but the approach I outline can be generative for biblical reception in all kinds of areas. I therefore discuss my suggested approach more generally in this chapter, before bringing the focus back to the far-right uses of Bibles that I go on to discuss in the following chapters.

Following Brent Adkins's description of *A Thousand Plateaus* as an "open-ended field guide",[10] I aim to draw out the aspects of this "nearly endlessly provocative" book,[11] that enable me to demonstrate the biblical components in far-right material, indicate how these components work, and explore possibilities for critiquing and combating the use of Bibles and biblical texts to demonise Muslims. Deleuze and Guattari, I contend, have much to offer for understanding Bible-use. As will already have become clear, I emphasise Bible-*use* here rather than *readings* of biblical texts to indicate something broader than *readings* and *interpretations* of biblical texts. In this too I am inspired by Deleuze and Guattari's *A Thousand Plateaus*. Emphasising Bible-use signals that I am not only discussing *texts*, but Bible as material object, as symbolic capital, and as an idea. My approach is not founded on a close exegesis of *A Thousand Plateaus* as a whole, though, or an attempt to put Deleuze and Guattari's many concepts, terms, and ideas to work on Bibles in any straightforward way. My argument is based on what the assemblage concept helps to make visible and what it affords in terms of a particular mode of critical analysis. As this and future chapters make clear, the way I build on the concept is informed by the work of a number of other key thinkers, some more inspired by Deleuze and Guattari than others, such as Brian Massumi, Sara Ahmed, Bruno Latour, and Rita Felski.

I begin by discussing reception history. I put forward my critique of what I call "bibliocentrism"—the idea that the Bible or a biblical text is the privileged centre or protagonist for biblical reception history. Bible-use is not

---

[9] Eric C. Smith has argued for thinking about Bible and assemblage; I engage with Smith's argument later on in my discussion, illuminating how my argument both draws on, and differs from, his conception of Bible. Smith, 'The Affordances of *bible* and the Agency of Material in Assemblage'.

[10] Brent Adkins, *Deleuze and Guattari's* A Thousand Plateaus: *A Critical Introduction and Guide* (Edinburgh: Edinburgh University Press, 2015), p. 250.

[11] Robert Paul Seesengood and Andrew Wilson, 'Biblical Stuff: (Re)reading the Bible as/with/through/by Materiality', *The Bible and Critical Theory* 16, no. 2 (2020): p. 2.

at the centre of the forms of the contemporary far right that I discuss in the ensuing chapters. At the same time, I make the case that although the Bible-use I analyse could be accused of being banal, with very little interpretation of biblical texts to study, it is nonetheless crucial to pay attention to. I then turn to a brief exposition of Deleuze and Guattari's concept of the assemblage, before discussing in some detail what I mean by "biblical assemblages" and the mapping of biblical assemblages. Part of this elaboration of biblical assemblages and what it means to map them involves addressing questions of agency, affect, and materiality.

Biblical Reception

Historically, biblical scholars have more often than not been concerned with origins. The attempt to "discern the proper identity of the original text" and "discover the meaning those original texts would have held in their contexts of production" has been at the centre of modern biblical criticism.[12] As John Barton points out in *The Nature of Biblical Criticism*, for many if not most scholars it is "axiomatic" that traditional biblical criticism is dominated by historical questions.[13] "Both those who attack biblical criticism and those who defend it generally do so by emphasizing its essentially historical character".[14] History in biblical studies is normally ancient history. Biblical reception, however, is more interested in the interpretation, impact, and influence of biblical texts.[15] Biblical reception scholars ask: How have biblical motifs, characters, and stories been understood and interpreted? In what ways are different interpretations of Bibles at work in films, literature, art?[16] There

---

[12] Brennan Breed, 'What Can a Text Do? Reception History as an Ethology of the Biblical Text', in *Reception History and Biblical Studies: Theory and Practice*, edited by Emma England and Willian John Lyons (London: Bloomsbury T&T Clark, 2015), p. 96.

[13] John Barton, *The Nature of Biblical Criticism* (Louisville, KY: Westminster John Knox Press, 2007), p. 31.

[14] Ibid., p. 32.

[15] The study of reception is not confined to *biblical* reception. For a helpful overview of different approaches to reception more generally, see Ika Willis, *Reception* (London: Routledge, 2017).

[16] It is not my intention to discuss in detail here the term "reception history". Hans-Georg Gadamer and his concept of *Wirkungsgeschichte* from *Truth and Method* in 1989 is often credited as a key figure for biblical reception, in reflecting critically on the history of influence or history of effects. As Mark Knight explains in his discussion of Gadamer's contribution to biblical reception history, Gadamer's outline of *Wirkungsgeschichte* is characterised by a sustained awareness that interpretation always occurs within historical contexts and does not originate with some notion of "an autonomous author or a timeless, interpreting subject". It is about the stories we can tell about how a text has been used and understood throughout history. Mark Knight, '*Wirkungsgeschichte*, Reception History, Reception Theory', *Journal for the Study of the New Testament* 33, no. 2 (2010): p. 138. The

has been an increased interest in biblical reception over the last years.[17] Sometimes this interest is closely related to the focus on antiquity that has traditionally marked biblical studies, by examining ancient reception.[18] Much interest has been focused on Bible and film.[19] Yvonne Sherwood comments that "excurses into literature, film, art and 'culture'" have been popular in biblical reception. Less attention has been given to "the territory of law and politics".[20] While attention to biblical reception in US politics has been ample,[21] there has been less sustained analysis of biblical reception in Europe from the discipline of biblical studies.

How to go about tracing and tracking understandings and uses of biblical texts is not straightforward. An important intervention into the theory of biblical reception is Brennan Breed's *Nomadic Text: A Theory of Biblical Reception History*, in which Breed draws on the French philosopher Gilles Deleuze (as I too will do, though taking a different direction).[22] Breed argues

---

term "reception history", or *Rezeptionsgeschichte*, was in turn coined by one of Gadamer's protégés, Hans Robert Jauss. In *Towards an Aesthetic of Reception* from 1982, Jauss outlines seven theses that make up a method for studying reception. Gadamer and Jauss have been important for the study of biblical reception. For a discussion of how New Testament scholars have in turn received Gadamer and Jauss, see Knight, '*Wirkungsgeschichte*, Reception History, Reception Theory', pp. 137–146.

[17] In *Reception History and Biblical Studies: Theory and Practice*, Emma England and William John Lyons marked the intensified need for, and interest in, studies that foreground the role the Bible and biblical texts have played in society. Emma England and William John Lyons, 'Explorations in the Reception of the Bible', in *Reception History and Biblical Studies: Theory and Practice*, edited by Emma England and William John Lyons (London: Bloomsbury T&T Clark, 2015), pp. 3–13. This increased interest can be seen in the increase of journals and publications such as the *Journal of the Bible and its Reception*, the SBL book series "Bible and its Reception", research groups on biblical reception at the European Association of Biblical Studies (e.g., "The Politization of Bibles and the Biblization of Politics in the Twenty-First Century") and the Society of Biblical Literature (e.g., "The Use, Influence and Impact of the Bible") conferences, and ambitious projects such as the *Encyclopaedia of the Bible and its Reception* (De Gruyter).

[18] Such as the three volumes entitled *The Reception of Jesus in the First Three Centuries*, edited by Chris Keith, Helen Bond, Christine Jacobi, and Jens Schröter (London: Bloomsbury, 2019).

[19] See for instance, Richard Walsh, *Reading the Gospels in the Dark: Portrayals of Jesus in Film* (San Antonio, TX: Trinity Press, 2003); Adele Reinhartz, *Bible and Cinema: An Introduction* (London: Routledge, 2013); Rhonda Burnette-Bletsch, *The Bible in Motion* (Berlin: De Gruyter, 2016); Richard Walsh (ed.), *T&T Clark Companion to the Bible and Film* (London: T&T Clark, 2018); Matthew S. Rindge, *Bible and Film: The Basics* (Abingdon: Routledge, 2022).

[20] Yvonne Sherwood, *Biblical Blaspheming: Trials of the Sacred for a Secular Age* (Cambridge: Cambridge University Press, 2012), p. 321.

[21] See for instance, Jacques Berlinerblau, *Thumpin' It: The Use and Abuse of the Bible in Today's Presidential Politics* (Louisville, KY: John Knox Press, 2007); Erin Runions, *The Babylon Complex: Theopolitical Fantasies of War, Sex and Sovereignty* (New York: Fordham University Press, 2014); F. Flannery and R. Werline, *The Bible in Political Debate* (London: Bloomsbury, 2016); Nyasha Junior and Jeremy Schipper, *Black Sampson: The Untold Story of an American Icon* (Oxford: Oxford University Press, 2020); James P. Byrd, *A Holy Baptism of Fire and Blood: The Bible and the American Civil War* (Oxford: Oxford University Press, 2021).

[22] Brennan Breed, *Nomadic Text: A Theory of Biblical Reception History* (Bloomington: Indiana University Press, 2014).

that biblical texts are always already a series of processes whose nature it is to change and be changeable, underdetermined and undeterminable also in their so-called original context. Biblical texts are from the "very moment of their initial inscription, already sedimented with various semantic, literary, and historical contexts".[23] For instance, the book of Daniel in the Hebrew Bible is hugely complex when it comes to its formation and transmission. Its contents have been altered over the course of time by many different hands and traditions. Breed asks:

> Where along these diverse historical lineages can one pick a point that is ontologically pristine? And how could one know, with objective epistemological certainty, that this point was "it", that any changes that occurred afterward were secondary and that they thus belonged to the history of reception instead of the history of composition?[24]

Rather than maintain a hierarchy between a text's original state and later interpretations, biblical scholars should recognise, Breed argues, that a first context is not inherently more important or determined than any stage of a text's signification and significance. Biblical texts must be studied as things "for which movement and variation is a necessary quality".[25] How can biblical scholars account for this movement and variation? Breed suggests that reception scholars can organise and make sense of "the history of a text's unfolding capacities".[26] Reception inquiries would provide a survey of "the text's ever-expanding potentials".[27]

To exemplify his model for reception, Breed takes Job 19:25–27 as his text case. Beginning with this short biblical text, Breed examines different receptions of it. He notices that readings of the text can be divided into three thematic concerns, or "semantic nodes" as he calls them, namely justice, survival, and presence.[28] Mapping these semantic nodes demonstrates the "diverse readerly actualizations" of the text.[29] It shows the potentials of Job 19:25–27 and the actual readings that have arisen from these potentials. He then goes on to show how the semantic node of survival is actualised

---

[23] Ibid., p. 204.
[24] Ibid., p. 33.
[25] Ibid., pp. 116–117.
[26] Ibid., p. 142.
[27] Ibid., p. 142.
[28] Ibid., p. 150.
[29] Ibid., p. 161.

throughout history. Even if, as he says, he can only hope to scratch the surface of "the interpretive trajectory of survival", he is able to demonstrate the varying capacities of the text in different contexts that are oriented around the theme of survival.[30]

What Breed demonstrates is the fact that biblical texts are, as he puts it, never quite at home.[31] They change throughout history. In light of this fact, he suggests that biblical texts should be seen as nomads. Nomads have no origin and no endpoint. They are always on the move. They cannot be consigned to a proper home.[32] Drawing on Deleuze, Breed argues that biblical scholars need to take into account the virtual and actual dimensions of a text. Texts have actually been used in certain ways—or they have been *actualised*—but there are also other ways texts might be used. In other words, they have virtual possibilities, potentially yet to come. Breed argues that a nomadic reception history "tells the story of the text's development by portraying the text as the protagonist".[33] It involves examining the text's variation over time.[34] Reception scholars can posit semantic nodes as "heuristic devises that aid in the sorting of materials" and "reflect general determinations of a text's problematic structure".[35] The question, for Breed—following Deleuze—is ultimately: What can this text do?[36]

Breed's question about the capacities of a text, his concern with its actualisations in readings, and the potentials of a text that have perhaps never or rarely been actualised are instructive and illuminating. He is able to show just how many potentials lie in a small biblical text like Job 19:25-27. But biblical texts are not always at the centre of their receptions. These texts and their receptions always exist in relation and combination with other elements. This is what the assemblage concept helps to illuminate.

Bibliocentrism

The potential problem lies in Breed's starting point: the biblical text. The semantic nodes he maps orbit around this biblical text as if the text is the

---

[30] Ibid., p. 189.
[31] Ibid., p. 202.
[32] Ibid., p. 203.
[33] Ibid., p. 205.
[34] Ibid.
[35] Ibid., p. 206.
[36] Ibid.

gravitational, and therefore privileged, centre. This model for reception history works well for surveying the trajectory of individual biblical texts such as Breed's example of Job 19:25–27. It also works for tracking the different activations of biblical characters, such as in Sara Koenig's work of reception, *Bathsheba Survives*.[37] Koenig follows the biblical character of Bathsheba from the biblical texts, through Rabbinic literature, the Patristic period, the Middle Ages, the Reformation, the Enlightenment, and finally to our contemporary times.

The model works less well, however, for invocations of "the Bible" or cases in which several biblical texts are invoked as components in a worldview where other elements—ideologies, symbols, practices, rituals, texts, artefacts—are a part. This is the case with the far-right material I examine in this book. It is not clear that any one biblical text, or any one conception of "the Bible", is operative in the far-right worldview that Breivik propagates. While there *are* elements of Bibles in the manifesto and the sources Breivik was inspired by, this fact is difficult if not impossible to make sense of without identifying the bits of Bible and invocations of "the Bible" as components of a larger connective web. In other words, there is not much substantial biblical interpretation or reception that could be extricated from the diatribes against Muslims, the conspiracies about so-called stealth Islamisation, fantasies about Western civilisation, misogynistic attitudes, and allusions to Norse mythology. As Økland puts it, Breivik "does not come across as someone who has a clear idea of how to approach the Bible other than in slogans and stereotypes".[38] And yet, my hunch is that the biblical elements fulfil a function that is key to elucidate. One reason why such references might be missed is precisely because scholars usually look for *interpretations* of biblical texts. Bible-use that takes more diffuse and seemingly superficial forms might easily, then, be overlooked. This kind of use is only diffuse and superficial, though, when judged by particular standards of relating to Bibles that assume close reading and clear-cut interpretation of texts.

Although the inextricability of Bible with non-biblical elements is particularly marked in the case of this study, Bibles or biblical texts are arguably always understood and used in conjunction with other elements. Sometimes, the biblical component in a worldview might be quite minor. A person may hold a positive view of immigration and campaign or vote accordingly, where

---

[37] Sara M. Koenig, *Bathsheba Survives* (London: SCM Press, 2019).
[38] Økland, 'Manifestos, Gender, Self-Canonization, and Violence', p. 35.

their reasons for holding this view may be based on experience, background, political ideologies, history, and, in a fairly minor way, also their Christian upbringing and stories of people's movement in the Bible. This person may not connect their view on immigration to any particular biblical text, but more vaguely to a number of partially known biblical texts. Starting with a particular biblical text comes naturally to biblical scholars. There is nothing inherently wrong with it, but it is bibliocentric. As Breed puts it, the biblical text is the protagonist. But often the Bible plays a bit part.[39] Sometimes a Bible acts as a doorstop or a prop, such as Donald Trump's brandishing of a Bible in front of St. John's Episcopal Church in Washington, DC, in June 2020.[40] The Bible was a key prop in this situation. But the function of this Bible can only be understood as one element among many. Bibles never act alone.

It is perhaps unfair to accuse biblical scholars of bibliocentrism. If they cannot be bibliocentric, who can? There are, however, ways of explaining the way particular Bible versions, biblical stories, or characters function in milieus without making the *texts* central and without highlighting the biblical aspects at the expense of other crucial contextual components. Even if an example of Bible-use is made central for the sake of shedding light on this use, it is possible to make clear that this centrality is strategic, heuristic, or pedagogical. Reception studies—though they may not call themselves that—that foreground the way bits of Bible and implicit or minimal uses of Bibles play out in diverse contexts have been undertaken in sometimes brilliant ways by non-biblical scholars. Vincent Wimbush and the contributors to his edited volume *African Americans and the Bible: Sacred Texts and Social Textures,* published over twenty years ago, is one example.[41] Some, like Wimbush himself, are biblical scholars, but most of the over sixty contributors are from other areas in the humanities.[42] The contributors present an ambitious challenge to biblical studies, while simultaneously modelling the kind of work they call for. One of the main calls is for more sustained attention to "the

---

[39] Even a protagonist is only intelligible in relation to the other actors, the scenography, the storyline, and the economic and social capital invested in the story.
[40] Martin Pengelly, 'A Photo Op as Protests Swirled: How Trump Came to Walk to the Church', *The Guardian*, 2 June 2020, https://www.theguardian.com/us-news/2020/jun/02/trump-washington-walk-to-the-church-photo-op (last accessed November 2022).
[41] Vincent Wimbush, ed., *African Americans and the Bible: Sacred Texts and Social Textures* (Eugene, OR: Wipf & Stock, 2000).
[42] In his response to the volume, Efrain Agosto comments on the fact that only a handful of the contributors are actually trained in biblical studies. Efrain Agosto, in Wimbush, ed., *African Americans and the Bible*, p. 823.

problematics of sacred texts in the present".[43] The volume showcases major and minor ways Bibles function, in music and art, on clothing, as a physical object, an icon, a symbol, and an idea. The contributors do not assume bibliocentrism. Instead, bits of Bible and implicit and explicit Bible-use are explored in illuminating ways. The slowness with which this volume has been emulated or cited in the European context is striking and disappointing.[44]

The anthropologist James Bielo similarly calls for more attention to what he terms "the social life of the Bible".[45] In *The Social Life of Scriptures*, contributors pay explicit attention to "the theological, political, historical, and otherwise social processes that underwrite and legitimate the social life of scripture".[46] Again, the contributors come from a variety of disciplinary perspectives—anthropology, law, linguistics, comparative religion, history, theology, religious studies—but none seemingly from biblical studies.[47] Bielo sets out the kinds of questions the volume asks:

> [W]here do we find Bibles physically present and absent in different Christian communities? How are Bibles situated in these places, and how do they work to signify? How do Christians recreate biblical texts in other material forms, and what are the semiotic connections between the two? How do the Bible's material significations coexist with its position as an interpretive and discursive text? What institutions encourage Christians to reproduce, reflect on, and contest these functions of materiality?[48]

Bielo is interested in posing questions about "how actual people, in actual social encounters, amid actual institutional conditions interact with their sacred texts".[49] It is about taking seriously the way Bibles are invoked due

---

[43] Vincent Wimbush, 'Introduction: Reading Darkness, Reading Scriptures', in Wimbush, ed., *African Americans and the Bible*, p. 13.

[44] Though I have not come across many direct citations of the Wimbush volume from 2000, emerging work in reception in Europe will hopefully provide good platforms to build on. See for instance, Annemarie Foppen, Anne-Mareike Schol-Wetter, Peter-Ben Smit, and Eva van Urk-Coster, 'The Most Significant Book of the Netherlands—And its Ordinary Readers', *Journal of the Bible and its Reception* 8, no. 1 (2021): pp. 107–133, and Marianne Bjelland Kartzow, Outi Lehtipuu, and Kasper Bro Larsen's edited volume *The Nordic Bible: Bible Reception in Contemporary Nordic Societies* (Berlin: De Gruyter, 2023). I maintain that much can be learnt from the Wimbush volume, however, also in Europe.

[45] James S. Bielo, 'Introduction: Encountering Biblicism', in *The Social Life of Scriptures: Cross-Cultural Perspectives on Biblicism*, edited by James S. Bielo (New Brunswick, NJ: Rutgers University Press, 2009), p. 7.

[46] Ibid.

[47] Bielo's volume is in the Signifying (On) Scriptures series, led by Vincent Wimbush.

[48] Bielo, 'Introduction: Encountering Biblicism', p. 7.

[49] Ibid., p. 5.

to their "intense cultural capital",[50] and the way Bibles are not just textual objects of discourse but also material objects of use and signification.[51] What Bielo does not mention, however, is that Bibles do not play important roles only for Christian communities, but also for groups, movements, and people who are not so easily recognisable as "Christian".

Studies like these make clear that, as I have suggested, bibliocentrism can be a problem in biblical reception studies. A Bible or biblical text is not necessarily in the centre, functioning as a protagonist. Bible-use and biblical interpretations need to be seen as relational,[52] part of "social life", and may be implicit or explicit. To take account of the multiple elements that make up the use and understanding of a Bible or biblical text and the way this use and understanding may be major or minor in terms of reach and longevity, Deleuze and Guattari's concept of "assemblage" is useful.[53] At this stage, though, I want to come back to the question of banality. After all, it could be suggested that, as I myself admit, Bibles play only bit parts in European far-right circles, I am making much ado about not very much.

Banal Bibles

The examples of Bible-use that I mentioned at the start of this chapter are banal. What is there to study and understand? As Andrew Elliott's work on modern-day "medievalisms" in the media demonstrates, however, what is banal might in fact operate effectively in communicating political messages and meanings.

In *Medievalism, Politics and Mass Media: Appropriating the Middle Ages in the Twenty-First Century*, Elliott focuses on "the excision and remediation

---

[50] Ibid., p. 6.
[51] Ibid.
[52] Velma Love, 'The Bible and Contemporary African American Culture I: Hermeneutical Forays, Observations, and Impressions', in Wimbush, ed., *African Americans and the Bible*, p. 50; Barbara A. Holdrege, 'Beyond the Guild: Liberating Biblical Studies', in Wimbush, ed., *African Americans and the Bible*, p. 140.
[53] The concept of assemblage has been considered useful by numerous scholars over the years, in academic disciplines as diverse as education, governance, and architecture. See for instance, Gareth Abrahams, 'The Building as a Deleuzoguattarian Strata/Machinic Assemblage', *Architectural Theory Review* 23, no. 3 (2019): pp. 363–379; Sung-Jae Moon and Kyeong-Hwa Lee, 'Deleuzian Actualizations of the Multiplicative Concept: A Study of Perceptual Flows and the Transformation of Learning Assemblages', *Educational Studies in Mathematics* 104 (2020): pp. 221–237; Helen Briassoulis, 'Governance as Multiplicity: The Assemblage Thinking Perspective', *Policy Sciences* 52 (2019): pp. 419–450.

of medieval ideas and practices in a post-medieval era", particularly the political uses of the medieval past in online networks.[54] Elliott discusses the Middle Ages as a contested period. He argues that each

> reading of the Middle Ages, from the moment that they "officially" came to an end, has thus been precisely that: a *reading*. That is to say, each attempt to offer a kind of renewal of the period has looked into the past and taken up those elements which suited present concerns, or which a given movement wished, nostalgically, to reinvent. In banal medievalism it is not the period itself which is summoned up by the signifier but *the dominant reading* of that period.[55]

Elliott is not interested in complaining about the reuse and remediation of the Middle Ages in different forms, or in berating inaccuracies. Rather, he examines how and why ideas, events, facts, and concepts tied to the Middle Ages are reused, why they might be seen as useful, and to what purpose they are used.[56] As he puts it, the "rhetorical strategies of medievalism merit analysis".[57] Elliott analyses the way mediated medievalisms do not belong only to high culture or to cultural gatekeepers with privileged positions in culture and education. Instead,

> a march to a statue, the launch of an anti-Muslim blog or the creation of a medieval meme all represent a participatory form of popular culture which has been fundamentally—and powerfully—democratised, created and promulgated by anyone with the basic software, capacity and skills to do so.[58]

Elliott coins the term "banal medievalism" to make sense of the references to the Middle Ages he identifies across different media platforms, from more traditional newspapers to social media sites. References to the Middle Ages chop and change, depending on their use-value.[59] Banal medievalism signifies the way the weight of multiple deployments of medieval

---

[54] Andrew B. R. Elliott, *Medievalism, Politics and Mass Media* (Woodbridge: Boydell and Brewer, 2017), p. 5.
[55] Ibid., p. 32.
[56] Ibid., p. 5.
[57] Ibid., p. 24.
[58] Ibid., p. 7.
[59] Ibid., p. 37.

symbols, imagery, snippets of text, and bits of history have caused particular associations and meanings attached to the Middle Ages. These deployments might be uninformed by the standards of academic scholarship. They may be ignorant of historical details. But the "power of banal medievalism lies not in its correspondence with any historical precedent but in its suitability to be retransmitted, and it is at its most powerful precisely when there is no expertise or historical knowledge required to decode it".[60] It is, therefore, "a question of function, not of accuracy".[61] Insisting on the accuracy or lack of accuracy misses the point. "What matters is its functional capacity of indexically pointing to the medieval past as a means of legitimising itself".[62] He argues that it is important to map how these media mechanisms work.[63] The spreadability and stickiness of tropes in the media lie in their ability "to be reported widely across a range of mass media and filtered through to a wider public while flattening the details as little as possible".[64] Calling these medievalisms banal is not for Elliott a means of dismissing them as unimportant or silly. Drawing from Hannah Arendt, Elliott points to the way the seemingly banal "can in fact mask politically sensitive, ideologically perverse or odious ideas under the guise of an ostensibly innocuous banality".[65] The most toxic and extreme ideas can be "rendered banal" by being shrouded within medievalism.[66] The same can be said for invocations of the Bible and banal uses of biblical texts.[67]

It would be easy to point to inaccuracies and banalities when it comes to the use of bits of the Bible in the public and political arenas. When the British Conservative politician and previous prime minister, Boris Johnson, called for negotiations over the United Kingdom's exit from the European Union (EU) to channel "the spirit of Moses in Exodus and say to Pharaoh in Brussels—LET MY PEOPLE GO", the biblical reference could easily be mocked as an unfortunate choice. As anyone who has read a bit more of the Exodus story knows, the Israelite flight from Egypt was followed by

---

[60] Ibid., p. 23.
[61] Ibid., p. 37.
[62] Ibid., p. 18.
[63] Ibid., p. 10.
[64] Ibid., p. 8.
[65] Ibid., p. 17.
[66] Ibid.
[67] See also Elayne Oliphant, *The Privilege of Being Banal: Art, Secularism and Catholicism in Paris* (Chicago: University of Chicago Press, 2021) for a discussion of the disguised significance of what looks on the surface to be banal forms of religiosity, and Mia Lövheim and Linnea Jensdotter, 'Banal Religion and National Identity in Hybrid Media: 'Heating' the Debate on Values and Veiling in Sweden', *Nordic Journal of Religion and Society* 36 no. 2: pp. 95–108.

many tough years in the wilderness—a point which Johnson was presumably not wanting to convey, even if it turns out to be accurate. Johnson's biblical reference could certainly be accused of banality.[68] Sylvi Listhaug, of the Norwegian populist right-wing Progress Party, has written about her political visions and values, and in the same book reminisces about the Bible she read in Sunday school, in a way that might seem banal. "So we got to hear about the lost sheep, Moses leading his people out of Egypt, and not least the baby Jesus, who was born in a manger in Bethlehem. Every time we were there, we got a star-sticker".[69] But following Elliott, it is worth lingering on the effects of Bibles and bits of Bibles being deployed in political programmes, public statements, publications, films, memes, adverts, art, and protests. Why might a banal Bible actually function quite effectively in a particular context? What ideological forces and political affects are masked by the banality of a Bible? As I will go on to show with the Breivik case, banal invocations of "the Bible" and "biblical values" resonate with the narratives told and retold about Europe and Islam, forming and informing the practices and performances of protest against migrants and Muslims across Europe.

Elliott's notion of banal medievalism is instructive for biblical studies. What is not taken up by Elliott is the way different elements stick together to make for effective discursive and material practices. Here the concept of "assemblage" pushes further the idea that bits of history, periods of the past, and parts of sacred scriptures are deployed and redeployed in a number of ways that never work in isolation. It is possible for Elliott's medievalisms to work without a Bible, but as I will go on to show, often a Bible is tagged on to an understanding of the Middle Ages in online and offline political culture. To understand the complex, composite, and variously textured ways references to Bibles and biblical texts work, the concept of assemblage is helpful.

Of course, it could be pointed out at this stage that all I am saying is that *context* is needed to understand the biblical references in any given scene or situation. Such a call for context is hardly contested. However, the call for "context" implies that there is a need for some background to be sketched in order for the role of a Bible to come clearly into view. The concept of

---

[68] For a discussion that goes beyond this sort of accusation, see James G. Crossley, 'Boris Johnson and the Divisive Bible', *The Institutem Blog*, St. Mary's University Twickenham, March 2019.

[69] Sylvi Listhaug, *Der andre tier* (Oslo: Kagge Forlag, 2018), p. 143. I have analysed these biblical references and their relation to far-right politics in Hannah Strømmen, 'A Nordic Far Right Bible? Right-wing Biblical Assemblages and the Role of Reception History', in *The Nordic Bible: Bible Reception in Contemporary Nordic Societies*, edited by Marianne Bjelland Kartzow, Outi Lehtipuu, and Kasper Bro Larsen (Berlin: De Gruyter, 2023), pp. 39–59.

assemblage, however, as I will go on to discuss, flattens out the terrain to show that a Bible (or biblical text) does not come to the forefront as a focal point, and cannot be isolated as its own stand-alone item. Rather, the very way a biblical text or invocation of "the Bible" works is relational and connective, or "sticky", to use Sara Ahmed's term, which I will return to later in this chapter. I therefore turn now to the assemblage concept in order to foreground the relationality and connectivity of Bibles in a flat terrain where "the Bible" is not necessarily at the forefront and where context is not simply background.

Biblical Assemblages

The French philosopher Gilles Deleuze (1925–1995) and French psychoanalyst and activist Félix Guattari (1930–1992) sought to move away from notions of essence and identity.[70] For my purposes, I draw on them to emphasise precisely process over essence. Their attention to how a thing *works* or is *put to use*, rather than what something *is* or *means*, is what I hold to be most generative for biblical reception. Their focus on process and use over essence allows for ways of studying biblical texts that open up beyond what a text means. What Deleuze and Guattari inspire is a jolt away from Bibles as *textual things to be interpreted,* and rather to see them as the result of processes that are given to both stabilisation and flux, and that involve all sorts of components that are not normally recognised as biblical. Searching for meaning easily falls into abstraction; mapping different kinds of use (such as the use of Bibles and biblical texts in reception) allows for analysis of the complex machinery of concepts, texts, behaviours, and practices.

During their lifetime, Deleuze and Guattari co-authored several publications. *A Thousand Plateaus: Capitalism and Schnizophrenia,* originally published as *Mille plateaux: capitalisme et schizophrénie* in 1980, is arguably their most famous and influential work. Rather than asking what something *is,* they are interested in how things work and their use. Their philosophy calls for a conception of the world that is characterised by dynamic

---

[70] This is not the place for a lengthy introduction to their lives and writings. For an introduction to their writings, see for instance Phillip Goodchild, *Deleuze and Guattari: An Introduction to the Politics of Desire* (London: Sage, 1996). The introductory chapter to Stephen D. Moore's *The Bible after Deleuze: Affects, Assemblages, Bodies without Organs* (Oxford: Oxford University Press, 2022), provides a detailed and helpful introduction from a biblical scholar.

processes, capacities, and potential activities, rather than static essences. Questions such as "What is?" are questions about essence, about what does not change. They are questions about the intelligible as distinct from the sensible.[71] "What is a table?" is a question that presupposes an idea of a table, rather than the specific table at which I am sitting and working. Deleuze and Guattari are more interested in asking: Which one? Focusing on change rather than essence involves reflecting on the capacities and affects of a thing. As Brent Adkins puts it: "What can a body do? What is a thing capable of? What are the forces that compose it and decompose it? These are questions of becoming in which essence is not seen as the ground but the temporary result of a continuous process".[72] At what point might my table no longer be considered a table but rather wood to fuel a bonfire? And what are the processes that lead to such a becoming-fuel?

The concept of assemblage is at the heart of *A Thousand Plateaus*. Assemblage can be thought of as Deleuze and Guattari's answer to the question "What is a thing?"[73] Deleuze and Guattari posit that assemblages are comprised of two segments, content and expression.[74] There is the part of the assemblage which Deleuze and Guattari speak of as the "machinic assemblage", that is, an "intermingling of bodies reacting to one another".[75] But assemblages are also marked by what they call a *"collective assemblage of enunciation"*, made up of acts and statements.[76] There are both territorial sides which stabilise the assemblage and cutting edges of deterritorialisation that destabilise an assemblage.[77] An example that Deleuze and Guattari discuss is the "feudal assemblage".[78] For the feudal assemblage we have to consider "the interminglings of bodies defining feudalism: the body of the earth and the social body; the body of the overlord, vassal, and serf; the body of the knight and the horse and their new relation to the stirrup; the weapons and tools assuring a symbiosis of bodies—a whole machinic assemblage".[79] But it is just as important to take account of "statements, expressions, the juridical regime of heraldry, all of the incorporeal transformations, in

---

[71] Adkins, *Deleuze and Guattari's* A Thousand Plateaus, p. 3
[72] Ibid., p. 4.
[73] Ibid., p. 10.
[74] Deleuze and Guattari, *A Thousand Plateaus*, p. 102.
[75] Ibid.
[76] Ibid., p. 103. Emphasis in original.
[77] Ibid.
[78] Ibid.
[79] Ibid.

particular, oaths and their variables", the "collective assemblage of enunciation".[80] Interminglings are key for assemblages. No individual object such as a tool exists without the interminglings with other things and bodies that make it possible. "The stirrup entails a new man-horse symbiosis that at the same time entails new weapons and new instruments".[81] Finally, we would then need to consider the "feudal territorialities and reterritorializations, and at the same time the line of deterritorialization that carries away both the knight and his mount, statement and acts".[82] I will come back to the notions of territorialisation and deterritorialisation in chapter 8, but essentially these terms are about the tendencies of any assemblage towards stability and change.

Assemblages, then, are "concrete collections of heterogeneous materials that display tendencies toward both stability and change".[83] An assemblage is a "temporary coagulation of intensive processes into a stable state".[84] Assemblages have differing temporal and spatial scales: "The intensities of tectonic movement that stabilize into mountain ranges exist on a vastly different temporal and spatial scale compared to the intensities that stabilize into a person's mood".[85] What matters for Deleuze and Guattari is attention to the "processes that create the mountain range and the processes that result in a particular mood" without resorting to notions of universal or eternal properties.[86] We could ask in this vein: What can a Bible do? Which Bibles have emerged in different settings? How, for instance, did a Bible become part of justifications for slavery and thus a tool for oppression? How did a Bible become part of campaigns to abolish slavery? Which Bibles were at work? Which texts of the Bible were emphasised, and which non-textual elements were crucial in making the slavery or anti-slavery Bible legible and effective? Deleuze and Guattari's concept of "assemblage" draws attention to the connections and continuities of things.

Manuel De Landa explains that assemblage is "a term that refers to the action of matching or fitting together a set of components (*agencer*), as well as to the result of such an action: an ensemble of parts that mesh together well".[87] An assemblage for Deleuze and Guattari is not a unified gathering

---

[80] Ibid.
[81] Ibid., p. 105.
[82] Ibid., pp. 103–104.
[83] Adkins, *Deleuze and Guattari's A Thousand Plateaus*, p. 14.
[84] Ibid., p. 15.
[85] Ibid.
[86] Ibid.
[87] Manuel De Landa, *Assemblage Theory* (Edinburgh: Edinburgh University Press, 2016), p. 1.

but made up of heterogeneous elements.[88] A unity is made up of the intrinsic relations that different parts have to the whole. We could think about an organic whole such as the organs of the human body.[89] As Thomas Nail points out, in contrast to organic unities, "assemblages are more like machines, defined solely by their external relations of composition, mixture, and aggregation".[90] An assemblage is not a part or a whole but a multiplicity. It is a case of potentially quite diverse things brought together, such as a series of things unearthed in an archaeological dig (bowls, cups, bones, figurines) that come to express a particular character such as "Etruscanness".[91] Assemblages are not only or primarily material, though. They are caught up in semiotic signs and systems, such as discourses, words, meanings, and non-corporal relations that connect signifiers with effects.[92]

In his study, *Assemblage Theory and Method*, Ian Buchanan critiques the reception of Deleuze and Guattari's concept of assemblage in scholarship. Almost "any and every kind of *collection of things* has in recent times been called an assemblage".[93] According to Buchanan, scholars have strayed too far from the concept as it was conceived by Deleuze and Guattari. In that straying, important facets of the concept have been lost from view—facets that, he believes, are what make the concept valuable.[94] While I am not particularly keen to jump on a loyalist or purist return to Deleuze and Guattari as if they provide all the answers, I am sympathetic to Buchanan's critique of the term "assemblage" being used simply to stick a label on a collection of things we already know about. He argues that the value of talking about assemblages should lie in bringing about a new way of seeing and understanding something. He notes that the term "assemblage" comes from the French word "agencement", and so assemblages are about arranging, laying out, or piecing together, rather than joining, gathering, assembling.[95] Another translation could be "arrangement", as long as such an arrangement is conceived as a process.[96]

---

[88] Thomas Nail, 'What Is an Assemblage?', *SubStance* 46, no. 1 (2017): p. 22.
[89] Ibid.
[90] Ibid., p. 23.
[91] J. Macgregor Wise, 'Assemblage', in *Giles Deleuze: Key Concepts*, edited by Charles J. Stivale (Montreal: McGill-Queen's University Press, 2005), p. 78.
[92] Ibid., p. 80.
[93] Ian Buchanan, *Assemblage Theory and Method* (London: Bloomsbury, 2021), p. 3. Emphasis in original.
[94] Ibid., pp. 4–5.
[95] Ibid., pp. 19–20.
[96] Ibid., p. 20.

According to Buchanan, it is crucial to be attentive to *how* different components come together in an assemblage, how these components interact in a given arrangement, and what form these components take at a given time. This is a key task for analysing a polyphonic text like Breivik's manifesto. Fredrik Wilhelmsen has warned against seeking a logic in the manifesto, with its vast array of material, multiple sources, and many contradictions.[97] But thinking about the assemblages that are formed in and by such a manifesto helps to show how seemingly contradictory and divergent elements can be brought together and arranged in such a way that they fulfil a function. Buchanan's call is for scholars to stop thinking of the concept of the assemblage as a way of describing a thing or situation and instead see it for what it was always intended to be: a way of *analysing* a thing or situation. "Faced with an apparent assemblage we should ask, what holds it together? What are its limits (internal and external) and what function does it fulfil?"[98] He critiques "the tendency to treat the assemblage as a physical entity cobbled together from random bits of material like a potluck dinner or a patchwork quilt".[99] Buchanan urges us to ask instead: How were these elements selected? What power of selection was in operation? What brought these elements together? How did they interact? What caused them to interact the way they did?[100]

As Buchanan points out, an important aspect of Deleuze and Guattari's outlook is that history is profoundly contingent. They write about strata and stratification to draw attention to "the relations of dependency that exist between various moments in history that taken together produce the present as we know it".[101] When it comes to geology, stratification refers to the different layers in a rock formation that delineate the changing forms these sedimentary rocks have taken over time. The value of thinking in terms of stratification lies in enabling "us to see and think about a certain type of process" rather than some fixed and finished notion of the end result: the rock.[102] How have we come to be as we are? How has a particular situation arisen?

---

[97] Silje J. Eggestad, 'Gullalder, korstog og apokalypse: Forskeren om høyreekstremismens historieforståelse', *Filter Nyheter*, 10 July 2021, https://filternyheter.no/gullalder-korstog-og-apokalypse-forskeren-om-hoyreekstremistenes-historieforstaelse/ (last accessed April 2024).
[98] Buchanan, *Assemblage Theory and Method*, p. 132.
[99] Ibid., p. 113.
[100] Ibid., p. 116.
[101] Ibid., p. 26.
[102] Ibid., p. 27.

Our present is the "sum of both the paths taken and the paths not taken", as Buchanan puts it.[103]

To follow Deleuze and Guattari's thinking of assemblage, then, is to problematise the appearances of any situation, particularly of any thinking that assumes that things are somehow naturally as they are and could not have been otherwise. Thinking about the "stratification" of things, in other words about the processes that lead to a given state, is about "transforming that which seems to have been given by either god or nature into something that is the product of multiple processes and forces over time".[104] It is about the processes and relations that emerge between different periods and moments in history that altogether produce the present as it is today.[105] The point is not that contemporary society in some way resembles geological formations. Rather, as Buchanan argues, to analyse contemporary society we need to see society as a problematic field.[106] We need to "wonder how it is that our world is populated" by "inexplicable phenomena".[107] Bibles might be seen as assemblages. A logic of essence and identity would state: the Bible *is* this or that. Rejecting this logic of essence, I follow Deleuze and Guattari in pursuing a logic of "and" and "with": The Bible is X *and* Y *and* Z. It functions *with* A and *with* B and *with* C.[108] Bibles are the result of processes that are not automatic or given. What processes have led to the state of a particular Bible, or the use of a particular biblical character or story?

In a recent article published in *The Bible and Critical Theory*, Eric Smith has made a good case for why seeing Bibles as assemblages draws attention to the material and relational aspects of Bibles or bits of Bible that are beyond the textual.[109] "A passage on a t-shirt, a roadside sign, a necklace, or a greeting card might not be *a bible,* but is *bible* in the sense that it is an example of *bible* acting in an assemblage".[110] Smith takes the example of biblical stories represented in a fourth-century piece of gold glass exhibited in a museum in Rome. The biblical story depicted in the gold glass is not a textual thing, it is part of an assemblage that is made up of glass and gold but also a number of other shifting elements that are part of the ancient object this gold glass

---

[103] Ibid., p. 26.
[104] Ibid.
[105] Ibid.
[106] Ibid., p. 27.
[107] Ibid.
[108] Deleuze and Guattari, *A Thousand Plateaus*, p. 26.
[109] Smith, 'The Affordances of *bible* and the Agency of Material in Assemblage', pp. 1–13.
[110] Ibid., p. 9.

was part of, as well as contemporary museum policies, to mention only a few examples.[111] In this way, Smith illuminates the way bits of Bible function that go far beyond acts of reading and interpretation. Smith helpfully shows how notions of "Bible" need to be diversified to encompass bits of text as they feature on or with material objects. The idea of Bible-as-assemblage can be pushed much further, though, and expanded for the theorisation and practice of biblical reception. In particular, I would like to push further how different biblical assemblages emerge in ways that make visible how invocations of "the Bible" work, and how such invocations demonstrate the way Bibles always function as assemblages. This is a matter of paying attention to how different biblical verses or stories might be arranged, as well as how a claim to "the Bible" is connected to other statements and materials. Focusing on how biblical verses feature on and in material artefacts can be one aspect of Bible-as-assemblage. But the very idea of what a Bible is—as a collection of books, as symbolic capital, as sacred object, as a set of manuscripts, as an outdated artefact, as pedagogical resource, as cultural heritage, as literary history—would be better deflected to questions of what Bibles *do*, and how Bibles *become*.

As Deleuze and Guattari argue, understanding texts is not a matter of the inside, the interior, of reading and interpreting content, rather, a "book is a little machine".[112] It works in conjunction with other things.[113] Books transmit intensities or fail to transmit intensities.[114] Intensities here might mean the way particular books function not only as texts to be read but as objects of desire: objects that are marketed, gain traction, get talked about, or indeed, are ignored and forgotten. Seen through the eyes of Deleuze and Guattari, then, "the Bible" is a changing entity made up of different and shifting parts—some of which are textual, and some of which are not. It is better, then, to speak of Bibles in the plural, then, or as biblical assemblages. Bibles are made up of different, heterogeneous matters brought together temporarily to form particular assemblages. "Assemblages select elements from the milieus (the surroundings, the context, the mediums in which the assemblages work) and bring them together in a particular way".[115] Different types of multiplicities "coexist, interpenetrate, and change places—machines,

---

[111] Ibid. Smith lists many more but to make the point that this list can only touch a fraction of the assemblage.
[112] Deleuze and Guattari, *A Thousand Plateaus*, p. 2.
[113] Ibid., p. 3.
[114] Ibid., p. 3.
[115] Wise, 'Assemblage', p. 78.

cogs, motors, and elements that are set in motion at a given moment, forming an assemblage productive of statements",[116] such as the much-(ab)used statement that begins "the Bible says . . .". Stephen Moore emphasises Deleuze's resistance to the *interpretation* of texts—what is dubbed "Interpretosis"—despite his long-standing interest in literature.[117] Instead of interpretation, we should address the use of things, not their meaning. As Deleuze and Guattari comment early on in *A Thousand Plateaus*, they will not ask what a book *means*, they will instead ask "what it functions with", what connections it has to other things, what it plugs into to work.[118]

Thinking about Bibles as assemblages is useful because it moves away from the misleading singularity in the term "the Bible". Talking about biblical assemblages enables a focus on the changeability and variability of "the Bible", rather than the supposed essence to a singular entity. Different Bibles emerge at different times, and Bibles take different forms. The Bible is very obviously not singular or straightforward in the sense that what people might mean by "the Bible" depends on their religious affiliation, their geographical location, their language capacities, and their aesthetic preferences. Canons differ. Bibles come in different languages, are made up of different words, different texts, and different textures. The particular texts that make up a Bible can be fitted together in different ways—producing different biblical assemblages. Bibles are machines made of multiple parts, as Robert Paul Seesengood writes, "for creation of other meanings, other machines".[119]

Doing biblical reception through attention to the way different bits of Bible get stuck to other things and work in particular constellations is close to Timothy Beal's vision for biblical studies from a cultural history point of view.[120] He posits that this is a form of research that "explores how biblical words, images, things, and ideas (including ideas of 'the Bible') take particular meaningful forms in particular cultural contexts".[121] Such an approach starts with the fact that there is no *one* Bible and there are no fixed biblical

---

[116] Deleuze and Guattari, *A Thousand Plateaus*, p. 41.
[117] Moore, 'A Bible That Expresses Everything While Communicating Nothing: Deleuze and Guattari's Cure for Interpretosis', pp. 108–125. See also Moore's subsection, 'Interpretosis: Symptoms and Treatment', in Moore, *The Bible after Deleuze*, pp. 19–24.
[118] Deleuze and Guattari, *A Thousand Plateaus*, p. 4.
[119] Seesengood, 'Bespoke Words: The Bible, Fashion, and the Mechanism(s) of Things', pp. 50–58, 56.
[120] Timothy Beal, 'Reception History and Beyond: Toward the Cultural History of Scriptures', *Biblical Interpretation* 19 (2011): pp. 357–371; Timothy Beal, *The Book of Revelation: A Biography* (Princeton, NJ: Princeton University Press, 2018), p. 5.
[121] Ibid.

texts simply waiting to be received throughout history. Instead, "there are multiple, often competing, symbolic, and material productions of the Bible—that is, biblical media—that are generated and generative in different cultural contexts".[122]

The idea of an unstable Bible might be thought of as a historical point, in the formative years of Judaism and Christianity, or for the Christianities that emerged during the Reformation. But, as biblical scholars know well, there is no easily attainable singular "original" Bible. Introductions to the Bible make efforts to clarify the difficulty of referring to "the Bible" as a self-evident object.[123] The book people refer to as "the Bible" today is not continuous with some ancient original, stable, and self-contained book, but the result of often fragmented and multiple manuscripts. Most modern English translations of the Old Testament are based on a manuscript copied in 1008 or 1009 CE, the Leningrad Codex, the earliest complete example of the traditional Hebrew Bible. There are other important manuscripts that testify to parts and versions of "the Bible", such as the Aleppo Codex from the end of the tenth century, and the Samaritan Pentateuch, the Samaritan version of the first five books of the Hebrew Bible. There is also the Greek translation of the Hebrew Bible, the Septuagint, which has its own differences in terms of the order of books and which texts it includes. The discovery of the Dead Sea Scrolls from the middle of the twentieth century has yielded copies of biblical texts that date between the third century BCE and the first century CE. But this discovery has not meant that the idea of *the* Bible has been discovered. Rather, it is clear that versions of biblical texts were fluid and multiple already from the start. The New Testament set of texts is similarly complex, and has been based on manuscripts from different times, such as the Codex Sinaiticus and Codex Vaticanus discovered in the late nineteenth century. Since then, earlier manuscripts have been discovered, and the Nestle-Aland critical edition of the New Testament in Koine Greek (currently in its twenty-eighth edition) is mostly used by biblical scholars and for modern translations. This should not cover over the fact that there are thousands of handwritten versions of New Testament texts, though, that contain variations, even if they are often minor.

---

[122] Ibid.
[123] John W. Rogerson's chapter 'What Is the Bible?', in J. W Rogerson, *Introduction to the Bible* (London: Routledge, 2006), pp. 1–18, is nicely illustrative of English language translations in relation to manuscript discoveries and developing trends in biblical scholarship.

There is also, of course, the question of canons—the selection of books decided by religious councils that would count as authoritative or sacred texts. Jews and Christians have different canons, and different Christian groups operate with different canons. For the Christian Bible, as Einar Thomassen discusses, the idea of a list of accepted books emerges with Irenaeus in the 180s, but it is not until after the fifth century that the Christian canon reaches a stability that is hardly questioned seriously in subsequent centuries.[124] But Bibles have continued to be volatile, despite the idea of fixed canons. In practice, churches and religious communities do not relate to biblical canons in simple or slavish ways. Rather, canons-within-canons are formed, informally and formally, through lectionaries, or through the theological preferences of particular groups and leading figures, as well as due to historical contingencies. What Tarald Rasmussen calls a "hierarchical logic" is applied to a canon, demonstrating that authority is not simply conferred on the whole canon in the same way.[125] This was explicitly acknowledged by figures such as Martin Luther, as Rasmussen points out. In Luther's eyes it was not that every book in the Bible had equal status: some texts were more important and valuable than others, such as Paul's letters in the New Testament and the Psalms and Genesis in the Old Testament.[126] Religious teachings about what biblical texts mean change as theologies are revised, updated, or corrected, and as academic commentaries evaluating the meaning of texts also alter according to shifting methodologies, trends, and discoveries. Even if the biblical canons of Jewish, Orthodox, Roman Catholic, and Protestant communities are seen as relatively fixed, their *words* have not been fixed, as scholars have evaluated and re-evaluated manuscripts and translations.[127]

Assemblages, Deleuze and Guattari write, stake out a territory.[128] "The territory makes the assemblage".[129] Such territories can be national, cultural,

[124] Einar Thomassen, 'Some Notes on the Development of Christian Ideas about a Canon', in *Canon and Canonicity: The Formation and Use of Scripture*, edited by Einar Thomassen (Copenhagen: Museum Tusculanum Press, 2010), p. 19. Thomassen notes the "force of tradition" as the reason for this, since especially the rise of modern critical biblical scholarship punctured the idea of apostolic authenticity that had been the justification for canonical status for many texts in the first place. Thomassen, 'Some Notes on the Development of Christian Ideas about a Canon', p. 24.
[125] Tarald Rasmussen, 'The Biblical Canon of the Lutheran Reformation', in *Canon and Canonicity: The Formation and Use of Scripture*, edited by Einar Thomassen (Copenhagen: Museum Tusculanum Press, 2010), p. 149.
[126] Rasmussen, 'The Biblical Canon of the Lutheran Reformation', pp. 147–149.
[127] R. Glenn Wooden, 'The Role of "the Septuagint" in the Formation of the Biblical Canon', in *Exploring the Origins of the Bible: Canon Formation in Historical, Literary, and Theological Perspective*, edited by Craig A. Evans and Emmanuel Tov (Grand Rapids, MI: Baker Academic, 2008), p. 136.
[128] Deleuze and Guattari, *A Thousand Plateaus*, p. 586.
[129] Ibid.

political, economic, social, geological, theological—and a particular assemblage is staked out in and across these different domains. The Luther Bible, for instance, is a biblical assemblage that occupies a particular national territory, is connected to a formative moment in time, but continues to operate as a key assemblage in German language and literature. Because biblical assemblages are more than recognisably "biblical" components, though, Bibles are also territorialised through the traction a particular interpretation gains. A Hollywood film about Noah as an environmental champion is a territorialisation of the Genesis flood story.[130] It is an assemblage that is made up of the commercial machines of Hollywood glitz and glamour as much as it is made up of "biblical" elements—that is, elements that have been recognisably part of Bibles in the past. The first versions of biblical texts stake out a particular territory, but as Breed has so effectively shown, there is no reason to suppose such "original" or early versions are more stable, or that they ought to be more privileged, than later versions. Biblical assemblages also stake out territories through translations, through the inclusion or exclusion of certain texts, histories of interpretation, decisions about production and distribution, and what additions are part of it, such as marginal notes or scholarly citations.

Bible-as-assemblage draws attention to the material processes involved in producing and transmitting Bibles. A white-and-gold embossed King James Bible given as a baptismal gift is a different Bible from the Nestle-Aland Novum Testamentum Graece studied by scholars in libraries and seminar rooms. New Materialist approaches to religion have recently been taken up also in biblical studies.[131] Robert Paul Seesengood and Andrew Wilson write in their introduction to the special issue on New Materialism in the journal *The Bible and Critical Theory*, that the issue sets in motion conversations about "new ways to think about not just what is 'in' a Bible, but how actual, material Bibles in/and other parts of the material world engage with us as readers and interpreters".[132] The most obvious example of the way material

---

[130] See the film *Noah* (2014), directed by Darren Aronofsky; Sewell Chan, 'Darren Aronofsky on the Environmental Message of Noah', *New York Times*, 30 November 2015, (https://www.nytimes.com/interactive/projects/cp/climate/2015-paris-climate-talks/darren-aronofsky-on-the-environmental-message-of-noah) (last accessed November 2022). For an analysis of the film from biblical scholars viewing it from a reception studies perspective, see Rhonda Burnette-Bletsch and Jon Morgan, eds., *Noah as Anti-Hero* (New York: Routledge, 2017).

[131] See Robert Paul Seesengood and Andrew Wilson's special issue on New Materialism in *The Bible and Critical Theory* 16, no. 2 (2020): https://www.bibleandcriticaltheory.com/issues/vol-16-no-2-2020-bible-and-critical-theory/.

[132] Robert Paul Seesengood and Andrew Wilson, 'Biblical Stuff: (Re)reading the Bible as/with/through/by Materiality', *The Bible and Critical Theory* 16, no. 2 (2020): p. 4.

conditions hugely alter what Bibles look like and how they are related to is of course the invention of the printing press in the fifteenth century. The age of the printed book in Europe was kick-started by the Gutenberg Bible, the first major book to be printed using the new printing technology. But before that, the shift from the scroll to the codex was hugely significant for the production of Christian texts, and particularly the very idea and possibility of such a thing as a canon.[133] George Aichele explains how the "different technologies of codex and scroll entail different types of reading".[134] By binding together multiple texts, a sequence is needed to order the texts, which indicates a particular order and organisation.[135]

In the modern world, since the advancements of print culture, the Bible has become a book amongst many other books bought and sold in competitive marketplaces embroiled in the mass phenomenon of printed text.[136] Sara Moslener has analysed "girl-bibles" to show how American evangelicals negotiate notions of sacred scripture through publication and adaptation of material Bibles for teenage girls.[137] Examining the contemporary purity movement, she highlights the production of Bibles such as *The True Love Waits Study Bible* and *The Abstinence Study Bible*. As Moslener argues, research into the "impact of gender ideologies on the material development of the Bible alongside the impact of the material Bible on gender ideologies" is necessary before we can fully comprehend this trend.[138] Cheryl Tonsend Gilkes writes about the Masonic Bible, which has visual depictions of Jesus as well as King Solomon, Hiram, king of Tyre, and Hiram Abi conferring during the building of the Jerusalem Temple, but also an index of scriptural references for nearly every term that is significant in Freemasonry.[139] Another

---

[133] See, e.g., Eric G. Turner, *Typology of the Early Codex* (Philadelphia: University of Pennsylvania Press, 1977); Colin H. Roberts and T.C. Skeat, *The Birth of the Codex* (London: Oxford University Press, 1987); Harry Y. Gamble, *Books and Readers in the Early Church: A History of Early Christian Texts* (New Haven, CT: Yale University Press, 1995); Larry W. Hurtado, 'The Early Christian Preference for the Codex', in Larry W. Hurtado, *The Earliest Christian Artefacts: Manuscripts and Christian Origins* (Grand Rapids, MI: Eerdmans, 2006), pp. 43–93.

[134] George Aichele, 'Canon, Ideology, and the Emergence of an Imperial Church', in *Canon and Canonicity: The Formation and Use of Scripture*, edited by Einar Thomassen (Copenhagen: Museum Tusculanum Press, 2010), p. 52.

[135] Ibid.

[136] Ibid., pp. 52–53.

[137] Sara Moslener, 'Material World: Gender and the Bible in Evangelical Purity Culture', in *The Bible and Feminism: Remapping the Field*, edited by Yvonne Sherwood with the assistance of Anna Fisk (Oxford: Oxford University Press, 2017), pp. 608–621.

[138] Ibid., p. 615.

[139] Cheryl Townsend Gilkes, 'The Virtues of Brotherhood and Sisterhood: African American Fraternal Organizations and their Bibles', in *African Americans and the Bible: Sacred Texts and Social Textures*, edited by Vincent Wimbush (Eugene, OR: Wipf & Stock, 2000), p. 398.

example is the Norwegian Bible that was published in 2015, a few years after Breivik's attacks in Norway, called *Fattigdoms- og rettferdighetsbibelen*. The Poverty and Justice Bible, as it can be translated, was produced by Norway's Bible Society. In it, three thousand verses about poverty and justice are highlighted in colour.[140] The biblical texts are accompanied by twenty-five reflections by a variety of people who interpret the highlighted passages for the present.

But Bibles are material in other ways, too, as Velma Love explains when examining the way that Bibles are engaged amongst contemporary African Americans in the United States. Love writes about identifying the iconic status of Bibles as it can be found "on clothing, jewellery, tables, walls, windows, and doors".[141] Today, the digital revolution is radically changing forms of communication, the spread of information, and practices of reading. It is also changing what Bibles look like, how they are used, and how they feel. As Jeffrey Siker shows in his study, *Liquid Scripture: The Bible in a Digital World*, the way Bibles exist on screens—smartphones, tablets, laptops—alter the engagement with, and experience of, "the Bible", particularly in relation to the Bible-as-a-book.[142] In Beal's words: "if there is one thing the material history of Bibles makes extremely clear, it is that there is no such thing as the Bible, and there never has been".[143] The way Bibles are produced, the apparatus around Bibles determining how they are related to and read, the cultures that form and reform Bibles, do not only need to be taken into account as secondary features to some platonic idea of "the Bible", but are primary features in mapping receptions of Bibles.[144]

The point I want to make about Bibles as assemblages is not only about either different canons or the physical medium of a Bible. Rather, I am arguing that it is necessary to push the point further, to take account of the many non-biblical elements that are connected with Bibles to make them what they are. It is necessary to take into account the elements that are part of how Bibles come into being and why, how they are mediated, packaged, marketed, and how they are given authority, status, and currency. Beal makes

---

[140] *Fattigdoms- og rettferdighetsbibelen* (Oslo: Verbum, 2015).
[141] Velma Love, 'The Bible and Contemporary African American Culture I: Hermeneutical Forays, Observations, and Impressions', in *African Americans and the Bible*, p. 50.
[142] Jeffrey S. Siker, *Liquid Scripture: The Bible in a Digital World* (Minneapolis, MN: Fortress Press, 2017).
[143] Beal, 'Reception History and Beyond: Toward the Cultural History of Scriptures', p. 368.
[144] Beal critiques biblical reception history for conceiving of biblical texts "primarily, if not exclusively, in terms of literary content, that is, as immaterial, disembodied words". Ibid., p. 365.

this point when he calls for attention not only to the materiality of Bibles, but also to "the economic aspects of scriptural production, marketing, and consumption, and to the way those processes trade in various unstable forms of social, cultural, financial, and sacred capital".[145] In a slightly different vein, but similarly close to my own approach to reception, Terje Stordalen writes of canonical ecologies.[146] Stordalen highlights the "multimedial" character of collections of texts that are charged with authority.[147] Scriptural canons are enveloped in webs of institutions, practices, and ideologies.[148] Canonical collections are "embedded in a canonical ecology of agents, institutions, commentaries, ideologies, media, practices, habits, and memory".[149] Few texts, as Moore writes, have "been so extended, so overextended, as the biblical texts, becoming huge, constantly whirring cogs in extratextual practices that themselves constitute continent-spanning social machines".[150]

It is not only, then, that the King James Bible and the Nestle-Aland Novum Testamentum Graece look and feel different, with different texts, fonts, sizes, smells, prices, textures, and qualities of paper. They are assemblages made up of all sorts of non-biblical components less obviously connected to the production of the text. The first is connected to church rites, to family celebrations, to traditions of gift-giving, to national histories, to habits of ownership and use (or non-use) of Bibles-as-ornaments. The second is made up in conjunction with academic institutions, scholars, practices of translation, manuscripts, philological examinations, and text-critical analysis, to particular authorities in the guild, and a scholarly apparatus of reading and relating to ancient texts. To understand these connections better, the concept of assemblage is useful. Bibles always operate *with* non-biblical components.

---

[145] Ibid., p. 366.
[146] See Terje Stordalen, 'Canon and Canonical Commentary: Comparative Perspectives on Canonical Ecologies', in *The Formative Past and the Formation of the Future: Collective Remembering and Identity Formation*, edited by Terje Stordalen and Saphinaz Naguib (Oslo: Novus, 2015), pp. 133–160; Terje Stordalen and Saphinaz Naguib, 'Time, Media, Space: Perspectives on the Ecology of Collective Remembering', in *The Formative Past and the Formation of the Future: Collective Remembering and Identity Formation*, edited by Terje Stordalen and Saphinaz Naguib (Oslo: Novus, 2015), pp. 17–37; Terje Stordalen, 'The Production of Authority in Levantine Scriptural Ecologies: An Example of Accumulative Cultural Production', in *Levantine Entanglements: Cultural Productions, Long-Term Changes and Globalizations in the Eastern Mediterranean*, edited by Terje Stordalen and Øystein S. LaBianca (Sheffield: Equinox, 2021), pp. 322–372.
[147] Stordalen, 'The Production of Authority in Levantine Scriptural Ecologies: An Example of Accumulative Cultural Production', p. 325.
[148] Ibid., p. 324.
[149] Ibid., p. 324.
[150] Moore, *The Bible after Deleuze*, p. 31. Stordalen highlights how this is the case for many canonical collections. Stordalen, 'The Production of Authority in Levantine Scriptural Ecologies: An Example of Accumulative Cultural Production'.

Communities, traditions, customs, cultures, and reading practices form assemblages with Bibles. Coming back to the issue of different Bibles due to differing canons, it is not just a matter of sharing some texts and not sharing others. Robert Carroll points to the common but erroneous conception that the difference between the Bibles of Jews, Catholics, and Protestants is "merely a matter of degree".[151] Perhaps more important than what particular books are shared in some form between Jews and Christians is the matter of reading practices and modes of interpretation: "How a Jew relates to the Hebrew Bible and reads it are very different modes of perception and practice from how Christians might relate to it or its equivalent".[152] The resemblance of books between Jews and Christians are "radically altered when the interpretive frameworks are changed and the life situations in which the translated texts are read are different".[153] In other words, part of any biblical assemblage are the material cultures, theological practices, local traditions, and historical conditions that form how a Bible is used and understood.

Bibles are not only found and formed amongst religious communities or in the academy, however, but also in culture. Biblical assemblages are formed in and with high and popular culture. Robert Myles describes how biblical texts presented in popular culture "typically remove the text from canonical control altogether, enabling different meaning and reality effects to emerge".[154] The story of Noah's ark is formed and reformed in children's stories, commercial artefacts, adverts, films, and artwork. Different biblical assemblages have formed in high and popular culture through particular biblical stories and characters being repeatedly reproduced in and through cultural production. The images of Jesus on the cross and of Mary holding the baby Jesus in her arms are familiar from films and art galleries across Europe. These stories and images transmit a selective familiarity with parts of the Bible, but this familiarity is always formed as an assemblage with the elements that become joined to this cultural Bible, such as school nativity plays, children's books, art galleries, and films. It is not that different canons are formed in these settings. Rather, biblical assemblages are formed,

---

[151] Robert P. Carroll, *Wolf in the Sheepfold: The Bible as Problematic for Theology* (London: SCM Press, 1997), p. 14.
[152] Ibid., p. 15.
[153] Ibid., p. 18.
[154] Robert Myles, 'Biblical Literacy and *The Simpsons*', in *Rethinking Biblical Literacy*, edited by Katie Edwards (London: Bloomsbury T&T Clark, 2015), p. 146. Myles takes *The Simpsons* as a case study to show that this hugely popular cartoon mediates particular ideas about the Bible to a large audience, often satirically with regard to the authority of scripture in American political and cultural life.

wherein some biblical stories, motifs, and characters are invoked as "biblical" and enjoy cultural currency, while others do not.

In *The Book of Revelation: A Biography*, Beal attends precisely to the way the last book of Christian scripture is "not a book, not even narrowly a text, but an ever expanding and contracting multimedia constellation".[155] This multimedia constellation "of images, stories, and story-shaped images" "expands and contracts, with parts of it attaching to and detaching from other cultural artifacts within different media ecologies throughout history".[156] He even puts forward the idea of the book of Revelation as an "othering machine".[157] I very much follow Beal's approach, as I do Stordalen and Naguib's in their concept of canonical ecologies. But I propose that the use of "assemblage" as a concept for the formation and reformation of Bibles brings something new and instructive to the understanding of how Bible-use works. Assemblage is used not only to describe a number of different things brought together. Rather, as I already discussed—drawing on Buchanan—it is also a mode of analysis that allows something new to be *seen*. Further, as becomes clear later on in my analysis, the assemblage concept opens up for specific understandings of change and power that operate in different kinds of Bible-use.

When it comes to understanding the role Bibles play in far-right environments, then, it is not enough to only look at which biblical texts might be used by figures and movements on the far right and analyse *interpretations* of biblical texts. Biblical scholars are understandably focused on the interpretation of biblical texts, so, in a way, suffer from what Deleuze has dubbed "interpretosis".[158] I would not go so far as to turn the focus on interpretation into a disease! Building on Deleuze and Guattari, though, I stress that for many if not most Bible-users, it is about—precisely—use, and about the way a Bible, or a biblical text, fits together with other non-biblical components: political affiliations, group identification, cultural rites and practices, and material conditions. Use can of course include more or less

---

[155] Beal, *The Book of Revelation*, p. 199.
[156] Ibid., p. 6.
[157] Ibid., p. 54
[158] Gilles Deleuze and Claire Parnet, *Dialogues* (New York: Columbia University Press, 1987), p. 47. See also, Stephen D. Moore, 'A Bible That Expresses Everything While Communicating Nothing: Deleuze and Guattari's Cure for Interpretosis', in *Biblical Exegesis without Authorial Intention? Interdisciplinary Approaches to Authorship and Meaning*, edited by Clarissa Breu (Leiden: Brill, 2019), pp. 108–125.

explicit and conscious forms of interpretation. Use, then, is intended here as much broader than acts of reading and interpretation.

In Breivik's far-right counterjihad milieu, there is no sole or central Bible that is interpreted at length or in depth. As Tom Egil Hverven remarks from his observations of Breivik in court, "Breivik's thought-world is syncretic; he mixes different religious and political perspectives. A secular, cultural understanding of Christianity is mixed with elements in a neo-heathen Odin-faith".[159] The concept of assemblage can help to make sense of this mixture. For the contemporary far right, it is necessary to ask which Bible is at work and to examine which non-biblical elements enable their Bible to *become* and to *work* as a component of a broader set of ideas and contexts. Where did this Bible come from? In which direction is it going? How fast? Along with what else? What can become of it?[160]

All Bibles, then, function as assemblages. Bibles are made up of many different parts, some of which are material and others that are made up of statements and expressions. Some of these parts are recognisably "biblical" in the sense of texts that have been canonised by a community for use in worship, for memory, or in other practices. Other parts are institutional and ideological, linguistic and cultural, material and symbolic. We might talk about a Luther Bible as a particular kind of assemblage, made up of specific translation processes, moments in history, and particular people, and picking up complexities in the history of use since its first emergence in the sixteenth century. But we could also talk about a Slavery Bible, which might refer to a specific set of texts in the Christian canon that are emphasised and elevated beyond others, as well as a number of practices, historical circumstances, and material conditions, coming together to form a Bible that could be used to sanction slavery.

I have talked a lot about Bible-use but have so far not focused much on Bible-*users*. Rather than emphasise *human* interpreters as the main agents, I have—following Deleuze and Guattari—sought to draw attention to the multiple elements that constitute biblical assemblages. Some of these are human, some are not. The question of agency, and particularly the agency of Bibles, is necessary to address, before sketching my approach of mapping biblical assemblages.

---

[159] Hverven, *Terrorens ansikt*, p. 171.
[160] Holland, *Deleuze and Guattari's A Thousand Plateaus*, p. 35.

What Bibles Can and Cannot Do

Earlier in the chapter, in my discussion of Breed's theorisation of biblical reception, I mentioned that he asks what a Bible can do. I have repeated this question myself as a key concern that draws from Deleuze and Guattari, who in turn draw on Baruch Spinoza, who famously stated that "no one has yet determined what the body can do".[161] Phrased in terms of the body, it is perhaps not so strange to ask about capacities. Asking about what a book can "do", however, might seem strange. Surely a Bible does not *do* anything. People do stuff to a Bible or with a Bible. Bibles are inert objects, not subjects endowed with agency.

But the agency, or vitality, of objects has been explored and emphasised for some time.[162] I build on Bruno Latour's prompt to take objects seriously as agents, or, to use Latour's terminology, as actors. According to Latour, "*any thing* that does modify a state of affairs by making a difference is an actor".[163] An actor, in Latour's sense, "is not the source of an action but the moving target of a vast array of entities swarming toward it".[164] As Latour points out, bringing objects and actions together is part of our daily language: "kettles 'boil' water, knifes 'cut' meat, baskets 'hold' provisions, hammers 'hit' nails on the head, rails 'keep' kids from falling away, schedules 'list' class sessions, price tags 'help' people calculating".[165] This does not mean that we think kettles *cause* water to boil or that knives *cause* the meat to be cut, or that these objects alone *determine* actions. Rather, as Latour writes, "it means that there might exist many metaphysical shades between full causality and sheer inexistence".[166] Things *do* in the sense that they might "authorize, allow, afford, encourage, permit, suggest, influence, block, render possible, forbid".[167]

In his discussion of Bible-as-assemblage, Smith, too, focuses on the issue of agency. Drawing on Jane Bennett, he emphasises the way Bibles are "entangled with human agency, but not defined or limited by it".[168] Bibles are "entangled

---

[161] Baruch Spinoza, *Ethics* (London: Penguin, 1994), p. 71.
[162] See for instance, Jane Bennett, *Vibrant Matter: A Political Ecology of Things* (Durham, NC: Duke University Press, 2010) and Karen Barad, *Meeting the Universe Halfway: Quantum Physics and the Entanglement of Matter and Meaning* (Durham, NC: Duke University Press, 2007).
[163] Bruno Latour, *Reassembling the Social: An Introduction to Actor-Network-Theory* (Oxford: Oxford University Press, 2005), p. 71.
[164] Ibid., p. 46.
[165] Ibid., p. 72.
[166] Ibid., p. 72.
[167] Ibid.
[168] Smith, 'The Affordances of *bible* and the Agency of Material in Assemblage', p. 9.

with material agency or the agency of assemblages", they are "funded by and constituted by those agencies more than humans often suppose".[169] As Rita Felski puts it in her discussion of the capacities of art works, *things* make a difference.[170] She asks: "What do works of art do? What do they set in motion? And to what are they linked or tied?"[171] When she reflects on why art works matter, she begins with the fact that they create, or co-create, enduring ties—between people and between people and objects.[172] Art works are not, for her, magical entities that spark these ties. They must be activated to exist and to matter.[173] Nonetheless, she posits: "Novels and music and paintings do things; they intervene in the world; they inspire and energize, seduce or repel".[174] Meanings of works of art are remediated and translated and, as this occurs, "new realities come into view" and "new attachments" are forged.[175] This is also the case with Bibles. As interpretations and uses of Bibles come into existence, are shared and reshared, or pass into oblivion, as Bible-uses and readings gain traction or lose popularity, new realities emerge.

Drawing on Latour's actor network theory, Felski writes about distributed agency.[176] In other words, she reflects on how attachments to works of art "are the result not of a single all-powerful cause steering things behind the scenes but of different things coming together in ways that are often hard to pin down".[177] I am not, then, endowing some fully-fledged notion of agency, or responsibility, to *things*, such as a Bible on a shelf or biblical texts as they are arranged on a webpage. But it is a matter of probing the difference a thing makes. It entails identifying the productive relations between different things that enable particular capacities and prompt potentials. Like Felski, I take Latour's attention to things seriously and consider "anything whose existence makes a difference" as an actor.[178] For this minimal understanding of an actor, the interesting question is not, then, really what counts

---

[169] Ibid., p. 9.
[170] Rita Felski, *Hooked: Art and Attachment* (Chicago: University of Chicago Press, 2020).
[171] Ibid., p. viii.
[172] Ibid., p. 1.
[173] Ibid., p. 7.
[174] Ibid., p. 42.
[175] Ibid., p. 48.
[176] Jane Bennett, too, talks about distributive agency, developing a theory for agentic assemblages, as she calls them. Bennett writes about a power blackout in North America in 2003 to convey the way multiple human and non-human agencies work together in an assemblage. Jane Bennett, 'The Agency of Assemblages', in Jane Bennett, *Vibrant Matter: A Political Ecology of Things* (Durham, NC: Duke University Press, 2010), pp. 20–38.
[177] Felski, *Hooked*, p. 9.
[178] Ibid., p. 21.

as an actor, as almost anything could count. Rather, the interesting question lies in examining in what ways things do or do not actually make a difference in particular situations and milieus.

With Felski, I want to think of this as an attention to different networks. Things exist only in and via relations, but these relations take hugely variant forms. Different groups of actors work together, "whether persons, things, plants, animals, machines, texts, or competences", and have "no necessary size, shape, or scale".[179] An assemblage could be described as a kind of network. An assemblage is only an assemblage so long as particular elements have come together to form a set of relations, such as the knight with his stirrup and horse. Everything functions in particular relations and these relations are changeable. Each element in these relations makes some difference to the others. As Jane Bennett sees it, each part of an assemblage has a certain vital force but "there is also an effectivity proper to the grouping as such: an agency *of* the assemblage".[180]

Bibles, then, are not only about "textuality", about how people read and interpret the texts of a Bible. In *The Cultural Politics of Emotion*, Sara Ahmed discusses the way texts generate effects.[181] Texts, particularly classics and canonical texts, are stuck to histories of association. The way these associations orbit a text and make it thick with what Ahmed calls "affective value" is often concealed.[182] Ahmed talks about the effects of repetition, but also of the concealment of the work of this repetition.[183] What sticks, she asks?[184] Bibles are thick with association. But association does not adequately denote the materiality of Bibles as they become stuck to a lectern, held up in the hands of a priest, kissed by a congregant, or gather dust on a shelf. The associations attached to Bibles as authoritative, holy, antiquated, quaint, judgemental, boring, beloved, are all related to the way physical Bibles are treated. But associations also become thick from the kinds of ideas, histories, and affects that have accumulated from practices and debates about what "the Bible" is and what its texts signify. Some historical Bible-use is stickier than others. Bibles have been used and understood in multiple, varied ways. Some of these uses and ways have been more stubborn than others. Some have grown

---

[179] Ibid., p. 22.
[180] Bennett, *Vibrant Matter*, p. 24.
[181] Sara Ahmed, *The Cultural Politics of Emotion*, 2nd ed. (Edinburgh: Edinburgh University Press, 2014), p. 13.
[182] Ibid., pp. 11, 13.
[183] Ibid., p. 12.
[184] Ibid., p. 11.

dominant and mainstream. Some are hard to forget or fully move past, even as the contexts in which these Bibles emerged have slipped into new and other contexts. Some Bibles, on the other hand, are and remain minor assemblages, never gaining much traction outside niche uses.

Partly, the things that stick, stick because there is a vested interest in propagating particular structures and their effects. A Bible that propagates patriarchal structures in society, for instance, will be perpetuated according to patriarchal interests, perspectives, and practices. This Patriarchal Bible will be invested in as part of a programme (which could be explicit or implicit, conscious or unconscious) to perpetuate patriarchy. Other non-Patriarchal Bibles are in play, too, at the same time as the Patriarchal Bible. A Feminist or Queer Bible may gain traction or fail to gain traction; they may gain speed in particular circles, just as the Patriarchal Bible, too, has its own milieus and props to keep it going. Ahmed's attention to emotions and stickiness in relation to politics is about asking why some societal structures are so persistent, even when they have been met with resistance. Why is change so hard? Her answer is that the accumulated affective value of a practice or position may override thoughtful and evidence-based rebuttals of these practices and positions. Emotional investments in particular ways of life structure the very way the world is encountered and experienced. Undoing emotional entanglements is not a matter of saying, "Stop feeling like that".

As I have already discussed, Deleuze and Guattari's *A Thousand Plateaus* prompts a turn away from text, interpretation, and ideology to affect. The surge of interest in the writings of Deleuze and Guattari in recent years has marked what some have called an affective turn in the humanities.[185] Affect "is the name we give to those forces—visceral forces beneath, alongside, or generally *other than* conscious knowing, vital forces insisting beyond emotion—that can serve to drive us toward movement, toward thought and extension".[186] Affect is about "the capacities to act and be acted upon", to follow Spinoza's influential understanding.[187] In Spinoza's words, it

---

[185] Though affect is not only or always traced back to Deleuze and Guattari. See for instance Patricia Ticineto Clough, with Jean Halley, eds., *The Affective Turn: Theorizing the Social* (Durham, NC: Duke University Press, 2007). In her introduction to the volume, Ticineto Clough articulates the affective turn as "a new configuration of bodies, technology, and matter instigating a shift in thought in critical theory". It is about disciplines in the humanities focusing on bodily capacities, affective capacities, to attend, to feel. Patricia Ticineto Clough, 'Introduction', in *The Affective Turn*, p. 29.

[186] Melissa Gregg and Gregory J. Seigworth, 'In Inventory of Shimmers', in *The Affect Theory Reader*, edited by Melissa Gregg Durham and Gregory J. Seigworth (London: Duke University Press, 2010), p. 1.

[187] Spinoza, *Ethics*.

is about the "affections of the body by which the body's power of acting is increased or diminished, aided or restrained, and at the same time, the ideas of these affections".[188] As Fiona Black and Jennifer Koosed argue, thinking about affect is to explore "encounters that move, stick, and slide, probing the meanings that manifest in the spaces between the words, tracing the circulation of power".[189] Karen Bray and Stephen Moore call for "the critical exploration both of what types of acts, knowledge, bodies, and worlds are produced in the capacious, intensely charged spaces of in-betweenness, beneathness, and alongsideness *and* of how we might better attend to affect's roles in such productions".[190] It is about relationality. But it is also about moving beyond what a text seems to "say" or what it "means". "Instead of asking what a scriptural text, a doctrinal document, or missionary tract *means*, we might ask how the sensory encounter with it *felt* to particular bodies in particular places in particular moments of history".[191] I will come back to the way affect is an important aspect of biblical assemblages in my discussion of far-right Bibles. For now, however, it is a matter of reflecting on the way affect—understood as both emotion and as force or potency—is part of the way biblical assemblages work.[192] Some Bibles might make us feel good. Others will make us shudder or cringe. What affects are produced by what Bible will of course depend on our affective investments, on our beliefs, commitments, contexts, and experiences. As Ahmed puts it: emotions accumulate over time as "a form of affective value".[193]

To sum up so far, I have posited that Bibles as assemblages do different kinds of work—they have differing functions and varied effects. I have wanted to pick up on ways of thinking—particularly Latour's actors and distributed agency—that probe the kinds of difference a thing makes, exploring the effects and affects of a particular arrangement. I have spoken of Bibles as thick with association and as accumulating affective value. By drawing

---

[188] Ibid., p. 70.
[189] Fiona C. Black and Jennifer L. Koosed, 'Introduction: Some ways to Read with Feeling', in *Reading with Feeling: Affect Theory and the Bible*, edited by Fiona C. Black and Jennifer L. Koosed (Atlanta, GA: SBL Press, 2019), p. 9.
[190] Karen Bray and Stephen D. Moore, 'Introduction: Mappings and Crossings', in *Religion, Emotion, Sensation: Affect Theories and Theologies,* edited by Karen Bray and Stephen D. Moore (New York: Fordham University Press, 2020), p. 2.
[191] Ibid., p. 7.
[192] The way emotions are invested in particular Bibles and biblical texts will become important in my discussion of how to respond to harmful Bible-use. There are other understandings of affect, though, that differ from affect as emotion and feeling. I return to these other notions of affect, particularly Brian Massumi's understanding of affect as potency, in chapter 8.
[193] Ahmed, *The Cultural Politics of Emotion*, p. 11.

attention to affect in relation to biblical assemblages I have aimed at pointing to both affect as emotion but also as force, capacity, or potency. The way affect can be thought in relation to the capacity to act and be acted on is something I will come back to, particularly when addressing the territorialisation and deterritorialisation of biblical assemblages.

Mapping Biblical Assemblages

If Bibles are assemblages, then biblical scholars can map these assemblages. Any assemblage has a history of formation and a finite life span: it emerges, gains and loses intensity, and becomes something else—another assemblage.[194] Eugene Holland explains that for Deleuze and Guattari, the aim of mapping is not to represent the world as it is "but to survey and map its tendencies or becomings, for better and for worse".[195] In other words, mapping biblical assemblages is about analysing their emergence, identify the way particular uses of a Bible are stabilised, and probe where tendencies to change might lie. I return to the task of mapping as it relates to the question of change in chapter 8, but for now I will focus on the analysis part of mapping the emergence and stabilisation of assemblages.

Part of the point about assemblages is that they are all about process and use, rather than fixity and essence. In my proposal for thinking about biblical assemblages, it is necessary to undertake reception history without knowing in advance what "the Bible" is, or what a biblical text looks like. Here I follow Latour's call to follow the actors—or in my case, the Bible-users—to see what Bibles emerge in a milieu and how they are put to work.[196] There is no pristine and platonic Bible already in existence, to which uses, misuses, and abuses of Bibles can be compared. There are only biblical assemblages. There is only the emergence of Bibles in their use. To look for "the Bible" or a biblical text in society naturally necessitates starting off with some idea of what the Bible or the biblical text is. But the starting point is heuristic, and the practice is experimental. "The Bible" does not point to an essence. Rather, based on *use*, we know that there are Bibles that have looked certain ways

---

[194] Bennett, *Vibrant Matter*, p. 24.
[195] Holland, *Deleuze and Guattari's* A Thousand Plateaus, p. 37.
[196] Latour, *Reassembling the Social*, p. 36.

and Bibles that are used in more and less stable text-formations with more and less stability as to trends in usage.

The way I go about mapping biblical assemblages in this book, then, involves asking questions relating to what is recognisably "biblical" and then seeing what kind of biblical assemblage emerges and how it is made up of recognisably biblical and non-biblical components. In other words, I will examine what bits of biblical texts are cited first of all in Breivik's manifesto, then in the sources he was influenced by. The easiest way to do this is to look for biblical texts that are "canonical". It quickly becomes clear, as I go on to detail in the next chapter, that Breivik, and the far-right milieu he drew on, mostly assume a Christian Bible—that is, bits of text from the so-called Old Testament and the New Testament canons. Further, I look for references to "the Bible" more broadly. As I detail in the chapters that follow, it is necessary to ask what a Bible plugs into. With what else does it work? What other components are closely connected to the particular Bible-use that makes it legible or useful? This may be material components or statements and stories. It may be particular authorities in Breivik's far-right worldview and it may be particular histories of Bible-use. Part of mapping, then, is also to probe what connections and continuities there are to previous forms of Bible-use. What sticks to the far-right Bible-use I identify? Then I can ask: What difference does a Bible or bit of Bible make in any given situation?

In this chapter, I have varied between writing about "Bibles" and "bits of Bibles". This is deliberate, to indicate that my understanding of mapping biblical assemblages includes both biblical texts—short or long—and invocations of "the Bible" as a collection of books. In other words, a tattoo of John 3:16 is a particular kind of biblical assemblage that involves text, skin, ink, electromagnetic coils, trends in fashion, neighbourhoods, economic conditions, theologies, traditions, and communities. An NRSV Bible is a different kind of assemblage that is also made up of texts, but additionally a number of other components, such as institutions, translators, another set of communities, buildings, trends, and traditions. In the chapters that follow, I go on to name Bibles. The names for these Bibles are not like the New Revised Standard Version or John 3:16, but are intended to name a particular biblical assemblage. I do not do so to name an essence in the world, but a process or a phenomenon that becomes visible through the act of naming. I could myself be accused of bibliocentrism in naming biblical assemblages things like "War Bible" and "Civilization Bible", as I go on to do. By putting the emphasis on the parts of an assemblage that might be seen as biblical, though, I am aiming to make the emergence and use of particular Bibles and bits of Bible visible, not point to their natural or privileged centrality. In mapping biblical assemblages, then, I seek to make clear how the arrangement of a number of biblical verses functions in a particular way or how a claim to "the Bible" functions. But these elements of the analysis are balanced out by clarifying what other components are crucial for the Bible-use to be legible, effective, and affective.

I emphasised previously in my discussion that there is no singular Bible. This does not mean there is not continuity, however. If a mountain range can be seen as an assemblage that has involved particular processes of formation, then it becomes clear that some processes have stabilised an assemblage in fairly major ways. A mood or a melody, on the other hand, might involve a very brief period of stabilisation before it transforms into a different kind of assemblage. I return to tendencies to change and stabilisation later in the book, but for now, it is crucial to point out that part of my mapping involves examining precisely continuities and connections in the way Bible-use unfolds. This would hold for both the example of the tattoo of John 3:16 and an NRSV Bible. They are both the result of different kinds of processes. Some of these processes are established and dominant; other processes are given to flux and flexibility.

There is no given territory that is fixed in advance as the territory to be mapped. All I can do is to look for where a Bible seems to matter and to make a difference, whether that is in a minor or a major way. In this study, a lot of my focus is on how biblical assemblages are stabilised in texts. In this sense, I am concerned with textual territories in which bits of Bible and references to "the Bible" are operative. In mapping historical connections and continuities in Bible-use, I pay attention to precisely the *use* of Bibles over interpretation. I examine historical moments and intensive periods where particular Bibles are activated and which are in turn reactivated in contemporary right-wing circles.

Although I hope it is by now clear that I do not want to treat biblical assemblages as only or primarily *material*, it is worth pointing out that doing so would miss important aspects of how assemblages work. As Buchanan indicates, although Deleuze and Guattari conceive of their work as a form of materialism, that does not mean they privilege material objects as the main focus of analysis.[197] "*Assemblages are not collections of things.* In many cases

---

[197] Buchanan, *Assemblage Theory and Method*, p. 58.

the physical things assemblages draw into themselves are completely incidental, just so many props needed to actualize a particular *arrangement of desire*".[198] The texts I analyse demonstrate the way far-right environments have become stuck to notions of Christianity and Islam that are repeated and propagated on mainstream and more extreme platforms. Although as Brian Massumi writes, "no situation is ever fully predetermined by ideological structures or codings", and any analysis that pays exclusive attention to such structures is incomplete",[199] texts can be important indicators of the stabilisation of ideas, structures of thought, and the attempt to produce and reproduce feelings such as hate, fear, and nostalgia through written communication.

I agree with the view that ideology alone cannot explain why movements emerge or why particular people do what they do. In other words, I do not think that it was simply a matter of Breivik reading far-right ideology, being convinced by it, and then acting upon it. The worldview he repeats and propagates in his manifesto is in many ways incoherent as a set of views, and yet might operate effectively—virally—when it comes to tapping into powerful affects of fear, nostalgia, and hatred. Texts do not operate alone or only according to content and meaning. They always operate in relation to other texts, they become effective in light of activities, events, behaviours, or as components that work well with non-textual elements such as protests, symbolic artefacts, and violence. Mapping biblical assemblages necessarily entails analysis of the kinds of non-textual and non-biblical elements that stick to Bibles to make them work, and evaluating the kind of affective value a biblical assemblage might have in a given situation.

Mapping biblical assemblages, then, is about analysing components at work in a milieu that are recognisably "biblical" and then seeing what kind of biblical assemblage emerges and how it is made up of recognisably biblical and non-biblical components, textual and non-textual elements. Mapping cannot be exhaustive, but it can hope to identify particular assemblages that are stabilised for a time, indicating the way such assemblages work. In this sense, I am looking for the way Bibles and bits of Bible stick to other things, how they gain traction, stabilise in a milieu, and take on a particular function.

My aim in introducing the idea of biblical assemblages in this study is to bring about a new way of seeing the far-right milieu of which Breivik was a

---

[198] Ibid., p. 65. Emphasis in original.
[199] Brian Massumi, *Politics of Affect* (Cambridge: Polity Press, 2015), p. 58.

part, where a Bible is one component amongst others in this milieu. By focusing on biblical assemblages, the aim is to see contemporary far-right ideas and practices in a way that helps us to better understand a worldview that is shared by many more than the perpetrator of the terrorism in Norway in 2011. The point is not only that without particular understandings and uses of a Bible, this worldview would not have looked as it does. But also, that by understanding the formation of a particular Bible and its workings, such a Bible can be problematised when it comes to future uses. More broadly, though, I propose that thinking in terms of biblical assemblages can help studies in biblical reception in all sorts of areas. What this approach makes visible is the way Bibles are never self-evident things, but the result of certain processes. No Bible-use can be understood without examining the components that are stuck to invocations of "the Bible" or to the use of a biblical story, verse, motif, or character. These components are crucial for understanding how any kind of Bible-use works effectively or falls flat. It moves biblical scholars away from narrow notions of *reading* and *interpretation*, as well as from imagining there is some singular or original version of Bibles and biblical texts against which receptions are measured.

Made and Unmade Bibles

There were and are no platonic and pristine biblical texts waiting to be "received" by groups and individuals. All we have are Bibles that are made and unmade in different times and places, put together with different components, and working in varying ways. There are trends in Bible-use that have become dominant, versions of Bibles that are prevalent, and understandings of biblical texts that are traditional and that have even become mainstream. But these too are the result of processes of emergence and stabilisation of particular biblical assemblages rather than reflecting some biblical essence. Rather than blandly invoking "the Bible", the concept of biblical assemblages can, I have argued in this chapter, help to shed light on the way a particular Bible comes into being as an effective and affective component in a situation or milieu, such as the focus of this study, in the contemporary European far-right. "The Bible" is a changing entity made up of different and shifting parts—some of which are textual, and some of which are not. This does not only reflect *interpretations* of the Bible since its inception, but the very nature of the Bible and its texts from the beginning. It is a matter of examining how biblical assemblages establish "connections between semiotic chains, organizations of power, and circumstances relative to the arts, sciences, and social struggles".[200]

By analysing the way Bibles are used, biblical scholars can map the shifting forms of biblical texts and the terrains such texts occupy. There is not a "root" original Bible from which secondary interpretations spring. There are only Bibles, and no Bible operates alone; there are, in other words, only biblical assemblages. To take the use of Bibles seriously, then, I have made the case for why I aim to map biblical assemblages in the far-right milieu that can be found in the Breivik case and beyond. To map such assemblages, it is crucial not to assume we know in advance what a Bible will look like and how it is used. Bibles or bits of Bible may not be central or operate as protagonists. That does not mean they do not potentially play a key function, though. Some Bible-use might look banal, because *interpretation* or *exegesis* is sparse, but it is crucial to pay attention to the way Bibles are fundamentally relational and operate on a number of levels. They are not only texts to be read but also function as material, symbolic, and, crucially, relational, objects. Speaking of Bibles and bits of Bible emerging as assemblages draws attention to this relationality with other non-biblical components, from the materials that constitute Bibles as books or textual artefacts to institutions, movements, and practices that operate with a Bible or biblical text. Bibles do not have agency, exactly, but they do make a difference in ways that are not only tied to human use or to conscious control. In this sense, what a Bible "does" can be a good starting question in order to examine the role a Bible or bit of Bible makes as part of an assemblage.

The approach I have outlined can help biblical reception studies, because it vastly opens up the field of inquiry, far beyond reception as the description or analysis of different kinds of *interpretation* of biblical texts. Rather, it opens up for the mapping of processes whereby Bibles and bits of Bible take on particular forms, stabilising and destabilising according to a number of material and non-material elements. Admittedly, I find it hard to move beyond Bible-as-text. In doing biblical reception it seems natural to look out for people *interpreting* biblical texts and dismissing what looks like more mundane, material, and muddled forms of Bible-use. It is hard, also, I find, to avoid slipping back into the language of "the Bible", however much I know there is no singular Bible. What I try to do, however, in what follows, is to

---

[200] Deleuze and Guattari, *A Thousand Plateaus*, p. 6.

resist falling back into notions of Bible purely as text and of Bible as a singular thing. Maintaining an emphasis on Bibles as assemblages is and remains, however, an experiment. The main gain, as I see it, is that analysing Bibles as assemblages allows me to see something new in the way bits of Bible and claims to "the Bible" operate in a milieu where there is not obviously much biblical interpretation present but where Bibles are operating in some way. It is this vague "some way" I set out to make more concrete.

Mapping biblical assemblages in this study involves identifying what concrete Bible-use looks like in the far-right milieu of which 22 July is a part. It involves asking about what biblical assemblages emerge and stabilise in this milieu, how they work, and with what they work with. No biblical assemblage appears out of nowhere. There are long and sticky histories of Bible-use that mean there are always connections and continuities in the emergence and stabilisation of biblical assemblages, as well as disruptions and disconnection. I will come back to this issue of change, but for now, I turn to the far-right material I introduced in the previous chapter, and the bits of Bible that are part of far-right obsessions with the decline of Europe and the threat of Islam.

3
Biblical Assemblages in Breivik's Manifesto

Between 2003 and 2010, serial shooter Peter Mangs targeted and killed those he saw as not belonging in Sweden—Black, Muslim, and Roma people.[1] The neo-Nazi terror group National-Sozialistischer Untergrund killed nine immigrants of Turkish, Kurdish, and Greek descent in Germany in the first decade of the 2000s. A sympathiser of the extreme right Casa Pound organisation killed two Senegalese men in Florence in 2011. In Norway, another far-right-inspired attack followed the 22 July attacks in 2011. Eight years later, on August 10, 2019, a gunman shot his stepsister and attacked the Al-Noor Islamic Centre in Bærum, opening fire just after the prayers in the mosque had ended. These lethal occurrences are only a selective sample of far-right violence in contemporary Europe.[2] Nonetheless, it is perhaps easy to denounce extreme views and explicit violence of this kind as exceptional. In his analysis of the interlinking of far-right networks across the United States and Europe, however, Ralf Wiederer cautions that "the problem of hate groups and hate propaganda is ultimately rooted in mainstream society".[3]

This chapter focuses on the manifesto of the perpetrator of the 22 July violence. Is it problematic to essentially reproduce Breivik's far-right worldview here? Elizabeth Pearson confronts this question in her work on far-right groups.[4] Among others, Pearson argues that there is a need for "close-up" research of the often distasteful and dangerous individuals and groups who spread hate and, as in Breivik's case, commit acts of violence.[5] My aim in this

---

[1] See Mattias Gardell for a detailed analysis of Mangs. Mattias Gardell, 'Urban Terror: The Case of Lone Wolf Peter Mangs', *Terrorism and Political Violence* 30, no. 5 (2018): pp. 793–811.
[2] Michael Minkenberg, Mats Deland, and Christin Mays, 'Introduction', in *In the Tracks of Breivik: Far Right Networks in Northern and Eastern Europe*, edited by Mats Deland, Michael Minkenberg, and Christin Mays (Münster: Lit Verlag, 2013), p. 9.
[3] Ralf Wiederer, 'Mapping the Right-Wing Extremist Movement on the Internet—Structural Patterns 2006–2011', in *In the Tracks of Breivik,* edited by Deland, Minkenberg, and Mays, p. 51.
[4] Elizabeth Pearson, 'Extremism and Toxic Masculinity: The Man Question Re-posed', *International Affairs* 95, no. 6 (2019): pp. 1252–1253.
[5] Ibid., pp. 1252–1254. See also Kathleen M. Blee, 'Ethnographies of the Far Right', *Journal of Contemporary Ethnography* 36, no. 2 (2007): pp. 119–128; Johanna Esseveld and Ron Eyerman,

chapter is to analyse the way a Bible is invoked and constructed in Breivik's manifesto. But the more overarching purpose of the analysis is to shed light on the constructions of "the Bible" in the manifesto in the hope that it will be easier, as Wiederer puts it, to "identify widespread but subtle discrimination and marginalization of minorities in everyday life".[6] Examining the way hate is produced and reproduced in a text such as Breivik's manifesto is about doing the work of exposure that George Yancy argues is absolutely necessary before questions can be asked about how we move forward to counter racism.[7] It is about staying in the "unfinished present", as he puts it, in order "to recognise the complexity and weight of the current existence of white racism", to attempt to understand the ways in which racism is perpetuated, and "to begin to think about the incredible difficulty involved in undoing it".[8]

In my analysis in this chapter, I treat the manifesto as a "text" and focus on what connections and constructions are created in this text when it comes to Bibles, and what biblical assemblages emerge through these connections and constructions.[9] What Bible(s) emerge in Breivik's manifesto? What biblical assemblages are at work? How do the biblical assemblages that form in the text work? With what other elements are they connected? By paying attention to the ways biblical references are arranged and what notion of Bible they constitute, it becomes possible to identify how assemblages are stabilised in Breivik's worldview. To anticipate my argument, two biblical assemblages in particular can be identified in the manifesto. The first I will call the Civilisation Bible, and the second I will call the War Bible. These assemblages are not only made from biblical components—that is, biblical texts or allusions to "the Bible". The Civilisation Bible and the War Bible emerge in the manifesto through references to biblical texts and "the Bible" *along with* non-biblical elements in and connected to the manifesto.

'Which Side Are You On? Reflections on Methodological Issues in the Study of "distasteful" Social movements', in *Studying Collective Action*, edited by Mario Diani and Ron Eyerman (London: Sage, 1992), pp. 217–218.

[6] Wiederer, 'Mapping the Right-Wing Extremist Movement on the Internet', p. 51.
[7] George Yancy, *Look, a White! Philosophical Essays on Whiteness* (Philadelphia: Temple University Press, 2012).
[8] Ibid., p. 158.
[9] In this chapter I am developing further a previous analysis I have undertaken on the biblical references in the manifesto. See Hannah M. Strømmen, 'Christian Terror in Europe? The Bible in Anders Behring Breivik's Manifesto', *The Journal of the Bible and its Reception* 4, no. 1 (2017): pp. 147–169.

The chapter begins with an overview of Breivik's so-called manifesto. I then briefly sketch the Christian counterjihadism presented in the manifesto and the biblical references that are part of the conspiracies pedaled by Breivik, before outlining in more detail the way the Bible-use in the manifesto could be understood as both a War Bible assemblage and a Civilisation Bible assemblage.

The Manifesto

The manifesto Breivik composed and distributed online runs to over 1,500 pages. It is titled *2083, A European Declaration of Independence* and is in English. The author's name is given as Andrew Berwick, an anglicised form of Anders Breivik. Shortly before his attacks, Breivik attempted to email the manifesto to at least one thousand would-be sympathisers.[10] The manifesto has been circulated widely on anti-Muslim websites and by anti-Muslim activists.[11] The title of the manifesto refers to the year Breivik imagined his political vision to be achieved, a vision of "a monocultural, patriarchal Europe without Muslims, Marxists, multiculturalists, or feminists", as Mattias Gardell has summarised it.[12]

A "cut-and-paste, hybrid document",[13] the manifesto is a messy and mixed PDF file that can be found on the web. It is not exactly a carefully crafted political treatise. Sindre Bangstad describes it as "an ideological tract and a detailed instruction manual for potential future solo terrorists".[14] According to his self-presentations in court, Breivik did not see his main act as the infamous killings on 22 July, but the compiling of his manifesto. As Jone Salomonsen articulates it: "Blood had to be shed so that we would read it".[15] But as I have already discussed, even if no blood had been shed in Norway that July, the positions propagated in the manifesto on multiculturalism, immigration, and Islam would have existed. They might have continued to

---

[10] Jacob Aasland Ravndal, 'Anders Behring Breivik's Use of the Internet and Social Media', *Journal Exit-Deutschland. Zeitschrift für Deradikalisierung Und Demokratische Kultur* 2 (2013): p. 182. Some scholars say "thousands" and others a more modest "thousand".

[11] Gardell, 'Crusader Dreams: Oslo 22/7, Islamophobia, and the Quest for a Monocultural Europe', p. 131.

[12] Ibid.

[13] Bangstad, *Anders Breivik and the Rise of Islamophobia*, p. 78.

[14] Ibid., p. 71.

[15] Jone Salomonsen, 'Graced Life After All? Terrorism and Theology on July 22, 2011', *Dialog: A Journal of Theology* 54, no. 3 (2015): p. 251.

operate below the radar in Norway,[16] but these positions would nonetheless be connecting and disconnecting figures, movements, and parties across Europe.

Andrew Elliott suggests that what is immediately clear from the manifesto is Breivik's narcissism and his insecurity, clear from "his determination to be remembered as an expert and an intellectual", keen to preserve the "purity" of his "philosophy" from the contamination of formal education.[17] In reality, Elliott goes on, this philosophy is "a kind of pseudo-scholarly analysis of international relations" which attempts to mask itself as "serious attempts at political theory".[18] As Breivik admitted in his trial, the manifesto was made up mostly of internet sources, of which he had composed about one third.[19] In his book about Breivik, the writer Aage Borchgrevink, too, comments on the way the far-right terrorist is not an "ideologue or a fundamental thinker. He shops around".[20] Even so, scholars such as Bangstad have argued that while the manifesto is "full of personal fabrications, statistical manipulation and partly unattributed uses of other people's texts", "the underlying ideological logic expressed in it is clear and terrifying enough".[21] Breivik's manifesto can be situated on the extreme right of the ideological spectrum.[22] Lars Erik Berntzen and Sveinung Sandberg, too, state that despite the fragmented and multivocal nature of the manifesto, "it is nonetheless the work of a single 'author'", and it can be taken as "indicative of Breivik's worldview and motives for the terrorist attacks".[23]

In any case, outlining trends in the manifesto is not about identifying "the author's unique thoughts or articulations", as Økland posits, but is rather about paying attention to what is "selected or discarded, elaborated or criticized amongst the included sources".[24] In her study of the text, Økland

---

[16] Although, as some scholars have argued, to some extent, refrains about Islam found in Breivik's manifesto are in fact at the very centre of Norwegian political life. Sindre Bangstad has discussed the connections between Breivik and Norway's right-wing populist party, Fremskrittspartiet. Bangstad, *Anders Breivik and the Rise of Islamophobia*, pp. 25–31.
[17] Elliott, *Medievalism, Politics and Mass Media*, p. 136.
[18] Ibid.
[19] See the discussion by Bojan Pancevski, 'Loser Who Lived with His Mum: The Pathetic Life of Mass Killer Anders Breivik', *The Sunday Times*, 22 April 2012, https://www.thetimes.co.uk/article/loser-who-lived-with-his-mum-g7d3sm8w50d.
[20] Borchgrevink, *A Norwegian Tragedy: Anders Behring Breivik and the Massacre at Utøya*, p. 171.
[21] Bangstad, *Anders Breivik and the Rise of Islamophobia*, p. 73.
[22] Ibid., p. 78.
[23] Lars Eric Berntzen and Sveinung Sandberg, 'The Collective Nature of Lone Wolf Terrorism: Anders Behring Breivik and the Anti-Islamic Social Movmement, Terrorism and Political Violence', *Terrorism and Political Violence* 26, no. 5 (2014): p. 763.
[24] Økland, 'Feminismen, Tradisjonen og Forventning', p. 121. My translation.

likens the manifesto to a hybrid medieval text with multiple layers of text, where parts of the text are added to and commented on.[25] The manifesto is a text that brings together different traditions, ideas, and elements of contemporary far-right ideology that Breivik copied and propagated with his manifesto and his acts of violence.[26] If we want to understand the manifesto, it is necessary to examine what sort of connections are made, and how material is used and reused. Or, in a more Deleuzoguattarian register, it is important to tease out what assemblages are formed by different material being brought together and stabilised in the text.

2083, A European Declaration of Independence is divided into three "books". The first book contains an account of Europe's historical trajectory towards a crisis point.[27] The second book describes the "European Civil war" taking place from 1950 to 2083, when the war will end and a new Europe will emerge.[28] The third book is the longest, and contains a mixture of diary-style entries, recipes for terrorism, and advice for armed conflict against the forces of "Islamism" and "multiculturalism".[29] Despite its eclecticism, the main themes of the manifesto are clear. Reproducing central tenets of the Eurabia conspiracy and counterjihadism, the manifesto presents a worldview in which a supposed Islamic imperialism is taking hold in Western Europe. This imperialism is said to be supported by a totalitarian political correctness embedded in the dominant forces in European politics, higher education, and media. The manifesto is compiled in the name of a Western European Resistance, for all European patriots, and cultural conservatives,[30] to "prevent the annihilation of our identities, our cultures and traditions and our nation states"[31] and "win the ongoing Western European cultural war".[32] Europe is seen as radically threatened by modern and postmodern attacks on "the bases of Western culture, including Christianity, capitalism, authority, the family, patriarchy, hierarchy, morality, tradition, sexual restraint, loyalty, patriotism, nationalism, heredity, ethnocentrism, convention and conservatism".[33] This has supposedly led to a loss of freedom of

---

[25] Ibid., p. 120.
[26] Ibid.
[27] Borchgrevink, *A Norwegian Tragedy*, p. 162.
[28] Ibid.
[29] Ibid.
[30] Manifesto, p. 13.
[31] Ibid.
[32] Ibid., p. 12.
[33] Ibid., p. 23.

speech and a destruction of the traditional social order.[34] Multiculturalism is presented as profoundly anti-Christian,[35] leading to an Islamic colonisation of Europe through demographic warfare that is facilitated by leading powers in Europe.[36]

The ultimate aim outlined in the manifesto is to repel the spread of Islam along with the cultural Marxist and multiculturalist hegemony in Western Europe. The hope is for a "monocultural Christian Europe"[37] that will "be governed by patriots".[38] In addition to emailing his manifesto to potential sympathisers, Breivik uploaded a video of himself to YouTube, where, as Salomonsen explains, he urged "radical nationalists, extremists and new-right activists in Europe and the United States to 'embrace martyrdom' and join him in defending ethnic rights to homeland, separatism, gender hierarchy, and monoculture for white survival".[39] The YouTube video shows Breivik dressed as a Knights Templar, wielding a large sword, using text blurbs to call for a return to the zeal of the early Christian crusades.

A Christian Counterjihad

As I have already outlined, Breivik was influenced by the Eurabia conspiracy and counterjihad networks. He cites key figures in these milieus extensively in the manifesto. To briefly recount, the idea of Eurabia is that political leaders in Europe, especially the European Union, are part of a conspiracy to turn Europe into an Islamic colony.[40] Europe is allegedly being taken over by Arabs, hence the warning calls over Europe becoming "Eurabia". The "Islamization" of Europe is supposedly taking place, particularly through immigration. This takeover is seen as a conscious plan, aided and abetted by European governments, academics, journalists, banks, and religious leaders.[41] For counterjihadists, Islam and the West are at war. Islam is not a religion but a totalitarian political ideology that is threatening Western culture and people. The duty of counterjihadists is to stop a supposed "Islamization",

---

[34] Ibid., p. 24.
[35] Ibid., p. 692.
[36] Manifesto, p. 16. While America is mentioned and treated somewhat similarly to the fate of Europe in places, the focus is on a particularly European conflict, past, present, and future.
[37] Ibid., p. 1404.
[38] Ibid., p. 1413.
[39] Salomonsen, 'Graced Life After All? Terrorism and Theology on July 22, 2011', p. 250.
[40] See Strømmen, *Det Mørke Nettet* and *I Hatets Fotspor*.
[41] Strømmen, *Det Mørke Nettet*, p. 50.

contain Islam in countries that already have a Muslim majority, and establish an anti-multicultural political network to replace the current political classes that enable the purported Islamic imperialism.[42]

As Gardell has outlined, Breivik was inspired by anti-Muslim news hubs, online journals, and blogs such as *Gates of Vienna, Brussels Journals, Jihad Watch,* and *Front Page Magazine*.[43] He was particularly inspired by, and cited in his manifesto, figures such as Robert Spencer, Pamela Geller, Bruce Bawer, Serge Trifkovic, and Baron Bodissey from the United States, and Geert Wilders, Bat Ye'or, and "Fjordman" (the pseudonym of Peder Nøstvold Jensen) from Europe.[44] Muslims are presented as a timeless and malevolent threat against Christian Europe. As Gardell points out, the "racist logic underlying the figure of the Eternal Muslim is integral to the theory of an Islamic world conspiracy that Breivik promotes".[45]

The worldview in which a Christian West is in conflict with Islam is in many ways indebted to political scientist Samuel P. Huntington's narrative of a clash between civilisations from the 1990s.[46] If a confrontation between global communism and global capitalism played out during the Cold War, then what has followed this confrontation, Huntington argues, is a return of religion to the political stage. Dividing the world into different "civilizations", Huntington claims that civilisations are characterised by the cultural inheritances and cultural identities of a people who share historical, territorial, and linguistic characteristics. Most important, though, is religion.[47] Differences between civilisations are "fundamental", even if they are not always sharp.[48] Huntington focuses particularly on Europe, for which Christianity is the foundation, and Islamic civilisation as clashing civilisations.[49] For Huntington, encounters between different civilisations "enhance the civilization-consciousness of people that, in turn, invigorates differences".[50] These differences sustain animosities that stretch back

---

[42] Strømmen, *I Hatets Fotspor*, pp. 102–103. See also Gardell, 'Crusader Dreams', pp. 133–134.
[43] Gardell, 'Crusader Dreams', p. 134.
[44] Ibid. I follow up on the sources Breivik was inspired by in the next chapter.
[45] Ibid., p. 135.
[46] Samuel P. Huntington, *The Clash of Civilizations and the Remaking of World Order* (New York: Simon and Schuster, 1996). The first to put forward this idea of a clash was Bernard Lewis, 'The Roots of Muslim Rage', *The Atlantic*, September 1990, pp. 47–54. See also Hannah Strømmen and Ulrich Schmiedel, *The Claim to Christianity: Responding to the Far Right* (London: SCM Press), pp. 4–5, 16–18.
[47] Huntington, 'The Clash of Civilizations', pp. 24–25.
[48] Ibid.
[49] Ibid., p. 27.
[50] Ibid., p. 26.

"deep into history".[51] According to Huntington, religion is key for these animosities.[52] Through the demarcation of different peoples and civilisations into religious groups, a political dynamic will arise that brings intensified animosity and increased conflict.[53]

Huntington claims that the "Velvet Curtain of culture" is the single most significant dividing line in Europe.[54] The terror attacks of 9/11 have been taken as evidence for Huntington's concept of a clash of civilisations. The idea of the clash of civilisations has been extensively critiqued.[55] Nonetheless, Huntington's narrative has figured in far-right propaganda, conspiracies, and political commentary. It has been popularised and is repeatedly rehashed as an accepted truth. Far-right forces claim Christianity as the common cultural inheritance and the common cultural identity of Europe, a Europe that must be safeguarded against the invasion of Islam. As I will go on to show in ensuing chapters, this clash of civilisations narrative is operative in the far-right milieu of which Breivik was a part.

Another way of understanding Breivik's worldview is what Rasmus Fleischer has called "Mono-fascism".[56] He distinguishes mono-fascism from multi-fascism. Mono-fascism is explicit in its aim to rid Europe of Muslims; all Muslims are perceived as agents of jihad, and jihad is seen as a project of imperialist expansion.[57] The only way to stop this expansion is for Western civilisation to consolidate itself and engage in a counterjihad.[58] Fleischer's description of mono-fascism to some extent fits Breivik's views as expressed in the manifesto. But when it comes to the mythology and symbolism Fleischer attributes to mono-fascism, it becomes messier. Medieval allusions and a religious inclination towards atheism and Protestantism fit some elements of Breivik's worldview. But Breivik messes up the categories and borrows elements that Fleischer attributes to multi-fascism: Catholic and pagan symbolism and mythology. My point is not to refute Fleischer's categories. They are, after all, ideal types.[59] The point is rather that Breivik's

---

[51] Ibid.
[52] Ibid., p. 27.
[53] Ibid., p. 29.
[54] Ibid., p. 31.
[55] See for instance Chiara Bottici and Benoît Challand, *The Myth of the Clash of Civilizations* (London: Routledge, 2010); Richard W. Bulliet, *The Case for Islamo-Christian Civilization* (New York: Columbia University Press, 2004).
[56] Fleischer, 'Two Fascisms in Contemporary Europe?', p. 53.
[57] Ibid., pp. 56–57.
[58] Ibid., p. 57.
[59] Ibid., p. 56.

worldview benefits from being seen as an assemblage that combines a number of elements that appear to be contradictory.[60] Andreas Önnerfors talks about "ideological fuzziness".[61] The concept of assemblage has the benefit of pointing to the way it is not only about fuzziness but also about different components being brought together to connect in ways that make them effective and affective in some way. In other words, fuzziness is a feature, not a bug.

In many ways, the manifesto itself can be seen as an assemblage. It is quite literally pieced together from different texts. Commentators frequently refer to it as a hybrid or a patchwork compilation.[62] But the manifesto is also inextricably connected to other non-textual textures, to the YouTube video Breivik posted of himself, to the crusader costume he dressed up in, to his courtroom appearance in the spring of 2012 where he sought a platform for the views he expressed in the manifesto. Bits of Bible are a part of this multifaceted arrangement.

Bibles in the Manifesto

The manifesto, as Salomonsen points out, is about the size of the Bible and ends—like the Christian Bible—with an apocalyptic vision of a new heaven and a new earth, including a judgement day, and suffering and death for those who are not chosen.[63] There are at least 62 explicit references to biblical texts in the manifesto and 27 references to "the Bible" more generally. Within the pages of the manifesto snippets of text can be found from Genesis, Exodus, Leviticus, Numbers, Deuteronomy, Judges, 1 Samuel, 2 Kings, 1 Chronicles, 2 Chronicles, Nehemiah, Psalms, Proverbs, Isaiah, Ezekiel, Daniel, Habakkuk, Maccabees, Matthew, Luke, Acts, Romans, 1 Corinthians, 2 Corinthians, Ephesians, James, and Revelation.

The majority of the biblical references in the manifesto can be found in the third and final book, titled "A Declaration of Pre-Emptive War".[64] Øystein

---

[60] For instance, Breivik combines Islamophobia with antisemitism. See Fleischer for a discussion of the way these two expressions of racism and hate are combined: Fleischer, 'Two Fascisms in Contemporary Europe?', pp. 55–56, 59.

[61] Andreas Önnerfors, 'Between Breivik and PEGIDA: The Absence of Ideologues and Leaders on the Contemporary European Far Right', *Patterns of Prejudice* 51, no. 2 (2017): p. 161.

[62] See for instance Bangstad, *Anders Breivik and the Rise of Islamophobia*, p. 78; Økland, 'Feminismen, Tradisjonen og Forventning', p. 120.

[63] Salomonsen, 'Kristendom, paganisme og kvinnefiendskap', p. 84.

[64] Manifesto, p. 776. Øystein Sørensen goes on to compare Breivik's notions of a culturally and politically Christian Europe with the Islamic Republic of Iran. Ironically, Sørensen suggests, Breivik's

Sørensen suggests that it is in the third book that Breivik's totalitarian ideas fully come to the fore.[65] Here, the vision for a new era when the conservative church will uphold the structure of European society is laid out.[66] The citations of biblical verses mostly feature in a section under the heading "The Bible and Self-Defence",[67] which is a sub-heading under the larger section "Christian Justification of the Struggle".[68] But there are also a number of more diffuse references to "the Bible". For instance, the Bible is first in a list of important "text books" for Europe's revival, alongside authors such as Nicolò Machiavelli, Thomas Hobbes, John Locke, Edmund Burke, and William James.[69] Bible versions are also mentioned. The idea that the modern Bible version is perverted is presented, proposing that "we will have to go back to our roots, to the Vulgate, the Versio Vulgata or the original pre-1611 King James Bible".[70]

Regarding references to Christianity and biblical texts in the manifesto, Gardell has pointed out that Breivik draws on American right-wing preachers Michael Bradley, founder of the evangelical Bible-Knowledge Ministries, and Joseph Francis Farah, author of the *Tea Party Manifesto*, as well as editor-in-chief of the conspiracy-peddling *WorldDailyNet* that Breivik frequented.[71] The battle verses Breivik cites from the Bible are compiled by Bradley on a web page called Bible-Knowledge.com.[72] But as I will discuss in the next chapter, the references to Christianity and the constructions of "the Bible" in Breivik's manifesto go beyond these figures that Gardell mentions. And there

---

views on religion mirror those of his worst enemies. Øystein Sørensen, 'En totalitær mentalitet: det ideologiske tankegodset i Anders Behring Breiviks manifest', in *Akademiske Perspektiver På 22. Juli*, pp. 106, 112–113. But there is not, arguably, any irony here; while there is a hatred expressed for Islam and its adherents, there is also perhaps something like an envy and imitation of what is seen as a "Muslim" capacity to take the Islamic religious and cultural heritage seriously, and, indeed, for taking sacred scripture seriously.

[65] Sørensen, 'En totalitær mentalitet', p. 106. Sørensen argues that Breivik's manifesto displays a totalitarian mentality, defined by, among other things, a firm belief in having a recipe for the perfect society; a firm belief in one's own vision of the truth, the insights of which are beholden to a chosen few; and a firm belief in the right to use any means to achieve the aims, including violence and terror, targeting everyone who stands in the way of the aims, as they are considered enemies. Sørensen, 'En totalitær mentalitet', p. 105.
[66] Ibid., 109–110.
[67] Manifesto: section 3.149, pp. 1328–1334.
[68] Ibid., p. 1325.
[69] Ibid., p. 380.
[70] Ibid., p. 1140.
[71] Gardell, 'Crusader Dreams', pp. 145–146.
[72] Ibid., p. 146. See Michael Bradley's page titled 'Battle Verses of the Bible': https://www.bible-knowledge.com/battle-verses-of-the-bible/ (last accessed December 2023).

is more to the Bible citations as well. For now, my aim is to identify what constructions and invocations of "the Bible" are operative in the manifesto.

My aim in the following sections is to demonstrate what biblical assemblages emerge when references to biblical texts and "the Bible" are analysed in this larger manifesto assemblage. The purpose is not so much to ask what the biblical assemblages in the manifesto *mean* or how they should be *interpreted*, but rather to zoom in on their function in the manifesto: What do they do and how do they fit together with other non-biblical components in the manifesto? Økland comments that throughout the manifesto "there are dispersed verses from the Bible, but they do not seem to *mean* very much; they add authority and legitimacy rather than meaning and content".[73] Bits of Bible are present, she argues, to prop up the idea of a static and unified Bible that is invoked as the charter text of the West.[74] But this only makes it all the more necessary to examine the way these bits of Bible work alongside other elements, both in the manifesto and beyond in broader far-right and conservative-right circles. To understand the manifesto, it is not a matter only of its "content" or "meaning". Rather, it is itself a little machine with multiple effects. In my analysis of the biblical references in the manifesto I begin with the multiple citations of biblical verses that are found grouped together in part three of the manifesto. I argue that they constitute a particular kind of Bible-use, namely, Bible-use that stabilises an assemblage I call a War Bible.

The War Bible

As I already mentioned, most of the references to the Bible in the manifesto are in a section under the heading "The Bible and Self-Defence",[75] which is a subheading under the larger section "Christian Justification of the Struggle".[76] The section "Christian Justification of the Struggle" begins with an allusion to Popes Urban II and Innocent III granting favour to "martyrs of the church, those men and women who, by virtue of their suffering, assists in the intercession for all Christians" [*sic*], stating that in the twelfth century such favour was extended beyond crusaders of a particular context, to

---

[73] Jorunn Økland, 'Manifestos, Gender, Self-Canonization, and Violence', in *The Bible and Feminism: Remapping the Field*, edited by Yvonne Sherwood, with the assistance of Anna Fisk (Oxford: Oxford University Press, 2017), p. 34.
[74] Ibid.
[75] Manifesto: Section 3.149, pp. 1328–1334.
[76] Ibid., p. 1325.

all.[77] Moving to modern times and Pope Benedict XVI, the question is raised as to whether he would condone a new crusade. Answered in the negative, Breivik concludes that Christianity in Europe has been abandoned. It is for "the cultural conservatives of Europe" to initiate "coups against the given multiculturalist European regimes and contribute to repell [sic] Islam from Europe".[78] The biblical references that follow, in the section "The Bible and Self-Defence", are situated within the framework of a religiously motivated warfare. As Økland points out, it is where violence is concerned that Breivik makes the greatest effort to assemble biblical references.[79] The assumption seems to be that the Bible can support the violent cause.

The biblical references about violence and war that are cited in "The Bible and Self-Defence" section are prefaced by the statement that many "Christians claim that acts of self-defence are unbiblical, unscriptural and ungodly. However, they are un-doubtfully wrong. The Bible couldn't be clearer on the right, even the duty we have as Christians to self-defence".[80] Already at the outset, then, the idea that the Bible could be seen as warmongering or peace-fostering is present. By assembling particular biblical texts and leaving out others, Breivik opts for a warmongering Bible. He builds a biblical machine fit for his purpose. Of course, Breivik does not treat this as an optional Bible, but as *the* Bible. Nonetheless, the fact that certain biblical references are listed and not others is a testament to the production of a particular Bible.

Multiple verses are cited in the manifesto to show that it "is not a pacifist God we serve".[81] It is stated that over and over again "throughout the Old Testament", God's people are "commanded to fight with the best weapons available to them at that time".[82] Biblical citations are listed one after another in this section, all related to war and violence. Psalms 68, for instance, is one of the first biblical texts to be cited; it calls for the Lord to rise up against his enemies: "Rise up O Lord, and may thy enemies be dispersed and those who hate thee be driven from thy face".[83] 1 Samuel 25:13 follows, which tells of David instructing his men to take up their swords in preparation for a battle.[84] Daniel 11:32 highlights the promise of "great exploits" and strength

---

[77] Ibid., p. 1327.
[78] Ibid.
[79] Økland, 'Manifestos, Gender, Self-Canonization, and Violence', p. 33.
[80] Manifesto, p. 1328.
[81] Ibid.
[82] Ibid.
[83] Ibid.
[84] Ibid.

"for the people who know their God". Psalms 18:34 is cited to confirm the idea of God's support for battle and an affirmation of violent victory: "He teaches my hands to make war", and continues from v.37–39:

> I have pursued my enemies and overtaken them; Neither did I turn back again till they were destroyed. I have wounded them, So that they could not rise; They have fallen under my feet. For You have armed me with strength for the battle; You have subdued under me those who rose up against me.[85]

1 Corinthians 4:20 supplies the claim that "the kingdom of God is not in talk but in power".[86] The comment that follows is that "God can anoint you with His supernatural power to defeat any enemy that may come your way".[87] This is emphatically stated: "All of the above Scripture verses are definitely telling you that God can anoint you with His power whenever that power is going to be needed to take on any kind of enemy or challenge".[88] The need for mental strength and courage is emphasised, in order "to step out with His power to use it to directly engage with your enemy".[89] It is a matter of impetus as much as comfort: "God is telling you that He does not want you to be a wimp".[90] Proverbs 24:10 is cited to back up this point, by showing that "If you faint in the day of adversity, your strength is small".[91] To re-emphasise the divine aid given to warriors of the cause, a reference to Acts 12:23 presents angels as protective beings, "for the purpose of helping you out with something", just as the "angel of the Lord" strikes Herod and he is "eaten by worms and died".[92]

Part of the point of these biblical verses is to present God as above human government and a God who is the lord of war. For the righteous victim, then, what human leaders might say is beside the point. God is on their side. To remove authority from contemporary European leaders who are seen as "traitors", Acts 5:29 is referenced to make the claim that we "must obey God rather than men".[93] In addition to sometimes running "a protective shield around you where nothing can get through to attack you", God is depicted

---

[85] Ibid., p. 1331.
[86] Ibid.
[87] Ibid.
[88] Ibid.
[89] Ibid.
[90] Ibid., p. 1332.
[91] Ibid., p. 1331.
[92] Ibid., p. 1334.
[93] Ibid.

as stepping in himself: "This is where God will literally take your enemy head on and do battle with it".[94] Isaiah 41:13, for example, displays the Lord's help: "For I, the Lord your God, will hold your right hand, Saying to you, 'Fear not, I will help you.'" Other verses such as Exodus 15:3 and 15:6 portray the Lord as a warrior and the Lord shattering the enemy. A reference to Isaiah 42:13 emphasises this point: "The Lord shall go forth like a mighty man; He shall stir up *His* zeal like a man of war. He shall cry out, yes, shout aloud; He shall prevail against His enemies".[95] God is wheeled out as a hyper-masculine, ferocious icon of war, lending fervour and divine credence to the cause. Accordingly, the manifesto makes use of what John J. Collins calls a fashioning of "identity by constructing absolute, incompatible contrasts" that can be gleaned in some biblical texts in regard to self and other.[96] The "absoluteness of the categories is guaranteed by divine revelation and is therefore not subject to negotiation or compromise".[97] In this way, violence is justified, even mandated, by a higher power that cannot be questioned.

But a glorification of violence for its own sake is avoided in the manifesto. Although Luke 22:36 is quoted to show that Jesus commands his disciples to buy a sword, Matthew 26:52-54 is cited directly afterwards, seemingly to demonstrate that Jesus advises Peter to put away his sword: this was not the right time to fight.[98] The function of the select biblical passages is to gloss violence as self-defence as well as a necessary means to an end, the end of a "pure" and "protected" Europe free of Muslims. Exodus 22:2-3, for instance, is cited to show that if a thief breaks into your home, you "have the right to protect your home, your family and your property, the Bible says".[99] The connection between this Bible and the current situation is made explicit:

> In the context of cultural conservative Europeans current war against the cultural Marxist/multiculturalist elites and the ongoing Islamic invasion through Islamic demographic warfare against Europe, every military action against our enemies is considered self-defence. There will be much

---

[94] Ibid., p. 1332.
[95] Ibid.
[96] John J. Collins, 'The Zeal of Phinehas: The Bible and the Legitimation of Violence', *Journal of Biblical Literature* 122 (2003): p. 18.
[97] Ibid.
[98] Manifesto, p. 1329.
[99] Ibid., p. 1328. Recalling Nehemiah building the walls of Jerusalem, Nehemiah 4:17-18 similarly serves to highlight the necessity of defence against the perceived threat of invasion.

suffering and destruction but eventually we will succeed and may be able to start rebuilding.[100]

The implicit message gleaned from what "the Bible" supposedly "says" is that Europe and European culture are like forms of property, property that is being broken into by Muslims coming to Europe, aided by multiculturalists within Europe.

The way these biblical verses are brought together in the manifesto can be called a War Bible assemblage. A selection of biblical verses is assembled in the manifesto and connected to a perceived warfare between Christians and Muslims in contemporary Europe. The biblical verses are selected seemingly because they legitimate violence and they speak of enemies and the necessity of self-defence. These verses can be used to sketch the contours of a Christian warfare against Muslims in Europe today. Other bits of a Christian biblical canon—to do with loving your enemy, for instance (Matt. 5: 43-47), and loving the stranger and foreigner (Deut. 10:19; Lev. 19:34)—are simply ignored. They do not feature in the Bible that is produced in the pages of the manifesto. The War Bible that emerges in this section of the manifesto functions to support the clash of civilisations which Breivik propagates. In Bangstad's words, Breivik has "learned the lessons of the new Huntingtonian identity politics".[101] His War Bible is a clear sign of this commitment to a clash of civilisations. What Breivik's manifesto does, as Arne Johan Vetlesen outlines, is to supply his mission with the martyr's self-righteousness played out in a drama of antithetical forces framed by a larger historical-political situation.[102] The biblical material lends a particularly effective tone of "righteousness"—both a "tradition" to fight for and the terminology to construe a righteous self against the enemy other. While cases where bits of the Bible are selected to justify violence can, as John J. Collins puts it, "be seen as a case of the devil citing Scripture for his purpose, it is also true that the devil does not have to work very hard to find biblical precedents for the legitimation of violence".[103] In this sense, Breivik's War Bible cannot be immediately dismissed as somehow unbiblical, despite the obvious selectivity.

---

[100] Ibid., p. 1329.
[101] Bangstad, *Anders Breivik and the Rise of Islamophobia*, p. 96.
[102] Arne Johan Vetlesen, 'Ondskap som perspektiv på hendelsene 22. juli', in *Akademiske Perspektiver På 22. Juli*, p. 96.
[103] Collins, 'The Zeal of Phinehas', p. 3.

This War Bible could be thought of as a minor assemblage in a large and unruly manifesto, made up of biblical references, selected and listed in a small section of the manifesto on self-defence, tucked away in book three. The assemblage formed that I am calling the War Bible cannot, however, be treated in isolation from the rest of the content of the manifesto. The biblical references that are assembled are part of a much larger arrangement. I want to briefly highlight three key themes in the manifesto that connect to the kind of Bible that appears in book three and that I have called a War Bible.

First, the War Bible I have highlighted plugs straight into the Eurabia and counterjihad conspiracies that are so central to the manifesto. As Bangstad has pointed out, the term "Eurabia" comes up 171 times in the manifesto.[104] Figures connected to the Eurabia and counterjihad milieu also come up frequently. Mattias Ekman has explained the way Breivik's terrorist violence embodied the rationale of the counterjihadist ideology that can be found particularly on internet forums.[105] Ekman discusses the way these conspiracy theories depict Muslim culture and Muslim individuals "as inherently violent, and since there is no distinction between Islam and Islamism, between non-violent and violent Islamism, and so forth, 'moderate Islam' is only presented as violent Islamism".[106] Furthermore, as the "gradual decline of Western societies are perceived as a process orchestrated from the inside, Muslim colonizers are dependent on internal allies",[107] namely European governments, educational institutions, the media, and others deemed part of the European elite. What is needed to stop the violence and imperialism of Muslims, then, is a violent response: war. As Salomonsen points out, Breivik's positions cannot be discussed democratically, because they are framed as a cosmic warfare.[108] Only an extraordinary intervention can make a difference in Breivik's worldview.[109] Breivik sees himself as a warrior, and the manifesto is meant to legitimate his acts of violence and invite its readers to become fellow warriors.[110] The War Bible that emerges in the pages of Breivik's manifesto is part and parcel of this worldview in which Europeans

---

[104] Bangstad, *Anders Breivik and the Rise of Islamophobia*, p. 78.
[105] Mattias Ekman, 'Online Islamophobia and the Politics of Fear: Manufacturing the Green Scare', *Ethnic and Racial Studies* 38, no. 11 (2015): p. 1998.
[106] Ibid., p. 1995.
[107] Ibid., p. 1996.
[108] For further discussion of the idea of a cosmic warfare, see Mark Jurgensmeyer, 'Sacrifice and Cosmic Warfare', *Terrorism and Political Violence* 3, no. 3 (1991): pp. 101–117.
[109] Salomonsen, 'Kristendom, paganisme og kvinnefiendskap', p. 82.
[110] Ibid., p. 84.

are called to defend their culture and civilisation in a situation configured as a "war zone".[111]

The War Bible in the manifesto contributes to the notion of a war as that of innocent, good people fighting an enemy, rather than two equal forces fighting over ideology or territory, or an aggressive majority power fighting a small minority. In *Terror in the Mind of God: The Global Rise of Religious Violence*, Mark Jurgensmeyer points to this common feature amongst groups labelled as terrorist, namely the perception or construction of a position under attack: "their acts are therefore simply response to the violence they have experienced".[112] A choice is given based on biblical verses selected in the manifesto, to *either* "rise up in the power of your Lord and Saviour and learn how to become a true warrior in the Lord, or you can continue to keep your head in the sand".[113] While the possibility of keeping "your head in the sand" is put forward as a choice, the manifesto simultaneously emphasises that *all* are "called to be soldiers of Jesus Christ, not just a select few".[114] Breivik "is expecting each and every one of us to learn how to war against any enemy or challenge that could come our way".[115] This is, as is probably clear by now, a fantasy of rejuvenated masculinity, as I will come back to in later chapters. Breivik's misogyny and antifeminist stance is a recurrent feature in the manifesto,[116] where, as Gardell has shown, feminists are seen by Breivik as traitors to the West not only by neglecting their so-called natural duties, but also by favouring multiculturalism and the marginalised, such as refugees.[117] In Gardell's words: "Breivik sees himself as a heroic knight, but is distressed with the fact that so few women want to be rescued".[118]

Second, the War Bible needs to be read in relation to the theme of the crusades that comes up in the manifesto. The section on "Christian Justification of the Struggle" begins with a reference to the medieval crusades and to the need for a new crusade.[119] I have already mentioned the way Breivik self-presented as a medieval knight. Several sections of the manifesto

---

[111] Manifesto, p. 1330.
[112] Mark Jurgensmeyer, *Terror in the Mind of God: The Global Rise of Religious Violence* (Berkeley: University of California Press, 2000), p. 12.
[113] Ibid.
[114] Manifesto, p. 1332.
[115] Ibid.
[116] See for instance Stephen J. Walton, 'Anti-feminism and Misogyny in Breivik's "Manifesto"', *Nordic Journal of Feminist and Gender Research* 20, no.1 (2012): pp. 4–11.
[117] Gardell, 'Crusader Dreams', p. 140.
[118] Ibid.
[119] Manifesto, p. 1327.

are dedicated to discussions of the medieval crusades. Early on in the manifesto, in Section 1.11–1.14, the chair of St. Louis University's history department, Thomas Madden, is cited to make the claim that the crusaders were a defensive force. The aim of the crusades is stated as a defence of "the holy places in Palestine, especially Jerusalem, and to provide a safe environment for Christian pilgrims".[120] The portrayal of the crusades is one in which the "Christian world" would have "to defend itself or simply succumb to Islamic conquest".[121] According to Breivik's citation of Madden, "the Crusades were a direct and belated response to centuries of Muslim conquests of Christian lands".[122] These views are repeated and reinforced by further citations. Crucially, they are also assembled with bits of Bible. Money and land are denied as motivating factors for crusaders. Rather, atonement of sin and salvation through good works are cited as the key motivating factors. The crusaders were, apparently, "mindful of Christ's exhortation that he who will not take up his cross is not worthy of Christ".[123] They "remembered that 'Greater love hath no man than this, than to lay down his life for his friends'".[124] John 15:13 in the King James Version is cobbled together in the manifesto with the crusades to demonstrate the biblical sanction for sacrificial violence, in other words, the biblical citation underlines the righteousness of the crusader to "sacrifice" himself for his fellow Christians in the face of an enemy.

Other bits of Bible enhance the theme of the crusades as the righteous hero-victim fighting an enemy. After invoking David's rising up against the Goliath of liberal elites and Islam, Breivik states: "ANY Christian European, anywhere in the world, can become a Justiciar Knight for the Knights Templar".[125] The significance of David and Goliath is that David is the archetypal heroic underdog, taking on an enormous and threatening enemy.[126] Ruth Wodak has commented on the tendency in right-wing populist discourse to hanker after a saviour figure, a Robin Hood–type figure who saves the ordinary people on the street but can also appear as a patriarchal heroic

---

[120] Ibid., p. 146.
[121] Ibid., p. 145.
[122] Ibid., p. 148.
[123] Ibid., p. 145.
[124] Ibid., p. 145.
[125] Ibid., p. 1158.
[126] For discussions of David's story as a paradigmatic underdog triumph, see Marti J. Steussy, *David* (Columbia: University of South Carolina Press, 1999), p. 41; Gnana Robinson, *1 and 2 Samuel* (Grand Rapids, MI: W. B. Eerdmans, 1993), p. 102; Walter Brueggemann, *David's Truth in Israel's Imagination and Memory* (Minneapolis, MN: Fortress Press, 1985), p. 19.

male figure.[127] Here, arguably, David fulfils that role. "Spirited by romantic warrior ideals of heroism, bravery, honor, and glory", Gardell writes, Breivik desires a "social order built on what he thinks of as nature's eternal principle of hierarchy, in which the strong rules the weak, white rules black, male rules female, and rich rules poor".[128] But the allusions to David and Goliath in the manifesto also show the way Breivik positions himself as an underdog figure, seemingly weak but righteous and heroic.

Allusions to David and Goliath come up three times in the manifesto.[129] The point of presenting the crusades as a defensive fight for Christian Europe and of invoking David and Goliath is to produce a sense of the righteousness of Breivik's cause, one in which the crusaders/Davids/counterjihaders are righteous victims fighting an unjust enemy. The biblical David—whether Breivik is aware of it or not—bears connotations both of the righteous good young man who kills the enormous enemy, and the man who becomes a king. The myth of the saviour plays into the idea of "us" versus "them", where the "us" need heroic figures to bravely take up the fight.[130] The effect of using the crusades and a Bible in this way is to lend a historical bent to the contemporary far-right agenda: a battle is raging now which is a continuation of biblical and medieval battles, where Christianity and Islam are ancient and eternal enemies. The Bible is used to justify a form of aggressive, militant self-defence that alludes to the allegedly pious heroism of the crusades: "we are now all good soldiers of Jesus Christ".[131] Read with the reconstruction of the crusades also present in the manifesto, it becomes clear that the War Bible is an assemblage that aims to glorify the battle scenario by mobilising the imagery of "knights" of Christ and enhance the righteous courage of those going to battle. The War Bible is connected to the crusader costume and identity Breivik donned in his YouTube video.

Third, the War Bible is arguably also connected to the stories of Christians persecuted by Muslims that feature as a recurring theme in the manifesto. In Sections 2.31–2.34, for instance, stories of Indonesian Christians being persecuted are recounted, before mention is made of murdered Christian

---

[127] Wodak, *The Politics of Fear*, p. 67.
[128] Gardell, 'Crusader Dreams', p. 148.
[129] Manifesto, pp. 33, 1158, 1329. I have discussed these David and Goliath references in more depth in Hannah Strømmen, 'Goliatmyten: Bibelbruk i høyrepopulistiske og høyreekstreme miljøer', in *Populisme og kristendom*, edited by Sturla Stålseth, Kristin Graff Kallevåg, and Sven Thore Kloster (Oslo: Cappelen Damm), pp. 86–101.
[130] Wodak, *The Politics of Fear*, p. 67.
[131] Manifesto, p. 1330.

clergy in Iraq, Coptic Christians victimised in Egypt, Jihadist aggression against Christians in Pakistan, and religious cleansing elsewhere in the Islamic world (Gaza, Sudan, Nigeria, Lebanon, Algeria, Malawi, Libya, Cyprus, and Saudi Arabia).[132] Converts from Islam to Christianity in "the Muslim world" are described as being "hunted".[133] The Qur'an is said to justify the persecution of Christians, and due to central tenets in Islamic scripture and doctrine, there is an "enduring enmity between Muslims and Christians".[134] Like the references to the crusades, the claims about Christian persecution form a substantial part of the manifesto. These stories are effective in their affective capacity to evoke horror and to provide "evidence" that it is necessary to fight back. The War Bible can be seen as a response to these stories, where Christians are called to rise up against the enemy and where God is on the side of Christians. Patricia Anne Simpson has shown that much far-right rhetoric invokes the "position of the persecuted" for themselves in order to gain appeal.[135] Breivik himself self-conceived as the sacrificial heroic underdog who sets out, in lonesome fashion, to "defend" the West through violent terror. As Bernzten and Sandberg point out, the word "martyr" is mentioned two hundred times in the manifesto.[136] This is the "spectacular action with strong symbolic intentions and precise rules of composition and execution" that Franco 'Bifo' Berardo talks about in his book *Heroes: Mass Murder and Suicide*.[137] For the mass murderer, the line between reality and imagination are blurred: "He wants to take part in the spectacle, so that the spectacle may become life, and—ultimately—death".[138]

The War Bible that emerges out of the main themes of the manifesto is connected to Breivik's weaponry and passion for paganism, too. Salomonsen points out that Breivik called his pistol Mjølner, after Thor's magic hammer in Norse mythology, and his gun Gugne, which is the name of Odin's magical spear of eternal return.[139] These names are also carved onto the gun and pistol in Rune letters. In addition, he named his car Sleipner, after Thor's

---

[132] Ibid., Sections 2.31–2.34, pp. 437–461.
[133] Ibid., p. 443.
[134] Ibid., p. 446.
[135] Patricia Anne Simpson, 'Mobilizing Meanings: Translocal Identities of the Far Right Web', *German Politics and Society* 121.34, no. 4 (Winter 2016): p. 38. Simpson is focusing on far-right cases in Germany.
[136] Berntzen and Sandberg, 'The Collective Nature of Lone Wolf Terrorism', p. 771.
[137] Franco 'Bifo' Berardi, *Heroes: Mass Murder and Suicide* (London: Verso, 2015), p. 30.
[138] Ibid., p. 44.
[139] Salomonsen, 'Graced Life After All? Terrorism and Theology on July 22, 2011', p. 251.

wagon.¹⁴⁰ Salomonsen demonstrates the way Breivik's manifesto brings different religious and pagan worldviews together:

> He calls his Christianity cultural, of the medieval, empire-building type. But he is also a cultural Odinist, since he is an ethnic Norwegian and Odin was a Norse god. As a European and a federalist (as opposed to a unionist), Breivik self-identifies with Christianity. As a Norwegian and a nationalist, he self-identifies with paganism.¹⁴¹

It is conceivably the case, as Borchgrevink suggests, that Breivik's religiosity displays a dizzying confusion and palpable contradictions.¹⁴² There is, however, "still a coherence" there in the adamant preference for the "West" in opposition to Islam.¹⁴³ Another way of looking at this mix of religious references is to see the worldview described in the manifesto as an assemblage. The pagan names for his weapons are connected to the biblical verses he lists, in that they all are assembled to fight what is deemed an "other" culture: Islam. The fact that paganism and Christianity would not seem to be natural bedfellows in the cause is not a concern when both can be invoked in such ways that they operate in opposition to Islam, as part of Nordic and European history and mythology, as identity-fixing and as warmongering.

Altogether, then, the first biblical assemblage that is at work in Breivik's manifesto is a War Bible. This assemblage emerges in the number of biblical verses cited that seemingly justify self-defensive violence against the enemy and having God on your side in the fight against this enemy. This Bible produces feelings of righteous victimhood. The righteous victim is confronted with a strong and evil enemy who needs to be fought. The victim can gain strength from the idea of God being on their side against the evil enemy. The War Bible is not only the minor assemblage of biblical verses cited in book three of the manifesto, though. It works because it is connected to key themes in the manifesto. Three components of the manifesto are particularly important as connections to the biblical verses: the Eurabia and counterjihad conspiracy theories, reconstructions of the medieval crusades, and anecdotes about contemporary persecution of Christians by Muslims. Breivik's affection for the Middle Ages and paganism can be seen in

---

[140] Ibid.
[141] Ibid., p. 252.
[142] Borchgrevink, *A Norwegian Tragedy*, p. 175.
[143] Ibid.

connection with the War Bible, in the invocation of a particular (imagined) medieval history to justify violence against what is deemed "other", and in the mixture of knightly costumes and weaponry with pagan-inspired names. When assembled in the manifesto, these biblical verses, conspiracy theories, reconstructions, and anecdotes form a potent assemblage. In the brutal imagery, stark scenarios, and simplistic divisions of "us" versus "them" in this assemblage, feelings of indignation at Muslim violence can be stoked and pity for innocent Christian victims is invoked.

But the War Bible assemblage I have just outlined does not account for all the biblical references and their effects in the manifesto. There are others that escape and slip through the capture of the War Bible. Another construction of "the Bible" can be discerned in Breivik's text that denotes a very different pattern of Bible-use: the Civilisation Bible.

The Civilisation Bible

Not all the biblical references in the manifesto pertain to violence and war. In fact, some references to "the Bible" are vaguer and less concerned with citing specific verses. Further, some references to bits of Bible seem to point in a very different direction than divinely legitimated warfare, the Lord as a warrior, and justifications for violence. It is necessary to analyse this Bible-use, too, to explain the way different biblical assemblages might operate side by side in a text such as the manifesto and—as I will show—in the wider far-right milieu of which Breivik is a part. I suggest that the remaining bits of Bible in the manifesto can best be understood as an assemblage I call a Civilisation Bible. Even more than the War Bible, the Civilisation Bible works *with* other elements. Particularly, as I will highlight, it works with other classic Western literature and culture, the imagined roots of Europe, and a pre-modern period in which Christianity held its ground against Islam.

Early on in book one of the manifesto, one of the proposed aims is to reconfigure the academic discipline of sociology in order to replace dominant Marxist ideological views with "a conservative/anti-Marxist" ideology.[144] Oddly, the Bible features at the top of the list of "text books" for this reconfiguration, followed by authors such as Nicolò Machiavelli, Thomas Hobbes, John Locke, Edmund Burke, and William James.[145] As Gardell explains, for

[144] Manifesto, p. 380.
[145] Ibid.

Breivik, proponents of egalitarianism and multiculturalism have "altered the curriculum at the universities to relativize the Western tradition", thus "systematically ridiculing, silencing, and persecuting" those who "dared insist on the value of traditional learning, absolute truths, the Western literary canon, and Eurocentric history".[146] The function of the Bible on this list is not, then, for personal piety, worship, or individual and communal faith, but to provide the possibility for wider societal reform on a political and cultural level. In that spirit, the idea that reading the Bible might foster a "personal relationship with Jesus or God" is treated as trivial, as it is stated later on in the manifesto.[147] Rather, "European Christendom" is portrayed as "identity, moral, laws and codexes [sic] which has produced the greatest civilisation the world has ever witnessed".[148]

The Bible that is listed as a key textbook, then, is read as part of a library of books that signifies the treasured texts of Western culture. Jean-Yves Camus and Nicolas Lebourg argue that Breivik is rejuvenating a form of "Islamophobic Occidentalism".[149] Rather than a neo-Nazi, or a Norwegian nationalist, he is an Occidentalist.[150] The Bible that appears in the manifesto is part of this Occidentalism, in the production of scripture that is uniquely and originally tied to the West. Önnerfors elucidates the Christian component of this emphasis on Western or Occidental civilisation: "fascism as a modern totalitarian ideology is not in need of religion and itself constitutes a 'political religion' or 'secular faith' but, to counterjihadism, Christianity remains a constitutive feature of European civilization that needs to be strictly defended".[151]

In addition to other key books, a Bible is invoked that is intimately connected with the roots of Europe through particular biblical maxims and values. These maxims and values are deemed to be lost in contemporary society. The Gospel of Luke is cited in the manifesto to make the point that Europe is based on "Judeo-Christian" scriptural foundations: "Our culture, even though we try to forget it, is steeped in a Judeo-Christian morality based on the Golden Rule of reciprocity: 'Do unto others as you would have them do unto you.' (Luke 6:31)". Muslims, on the other hand, are described as "steeped in an Islamic tradition based on Muslim supremacy".[152] Here a

---

[146] Gardell, 'Crusader Dreams', p. 137.
[147] Manifesto, p. 1341. See also, p. 1308.
[148] Ibid., p. 1341.
[149] Camus and Lebourg, *Far-Right Politics in Europe*, p. 112.
[150] Ibid., p. 112.
[151] Önnerfors, 'Between Breivik and PEGIDA', p. 163.
[152] Manifesto, p. 597.

moral supremacy is tied to the Bible, where "the Bible" functions as a general moral compass informing a Judeo-Christian Europe. Anya Topolski has analysed the way the term "Judeo-Christian" has resurfaced in European political debates in the last two decades.[153] As she explains, this signifier functioned in an exclusionary manner in the nineteenth century to designate a contaminated form of Christianity (as opposed to a pure Pauline Christianity).[154] The "signifier Judeo-Christianity is once again being used to create an exclusionary European identity".[155] Though its meaning has shifted, its function remains exclusionary. Whereas it was used to exclude Jews and Catholics from Europe, claims about a Judeo-Christian heritage and values are now used either explicitly or implicitly to exclude Islam.[156] Topolski makes clear the prevalence of this use, from right-wing populists such as Geert Wilders and debates about the European Union, to religious leaders such as Rabbi Jonathan Sacks and Pope Benedict.[157]

The blogger "Vanishing American", cited in the manifesto, laments the contemporary state of Europe. Contemporary society is accused of being biblically "illiterate": unknowledgeable about the Bible and unable or unwilling to read biblical texts.[158] It is proposed that "we today" are generally:

> more ignorant than our ancestors where the Bible and the faith are concerned. If anybody is wrongly handling the word of God, it is likely to be us, not our forefathers. Their brains were at least not addled by nonsense and Political Correctness, and I trust the consensus of our forefathers through the centuries rather than the consensus among today's compromised generation.[159]

If we knew our Bible better, the implication seems to be, we would be better equipped to stand up for European culture. There is a call, then, to read the Bible more—for people in Western Europe to become more biblically

---

[153] Anya Topolski, 'A Genealogy of the 'Judeo-Christian' Signifier: A Tale of Europe's Identity Crisis', in *Is there a Judeo-Christian Tradition? A European Perspective*, edited by Emmanuel Nathan and Anya Topolski (Berlin: De Gruyter, 2016), pp. 267–283.
[154] Ibid., pp. 269–273.
[155] Ibid., p. 275.
[156] Ibid., pp. 278–279.
[157] Ibid., p. 278.
[158] Manifesto, p. 685.
[159] Manifesto, p. 685. The view that biblical literacy is at an all-time low is voiced by various people, as discussed by many of the authors in Katie Edwards, ed., *Rethinking Biblical Literacy* (London: Bloomsbury T&T Clark, 2015).

literate. But here, too, a Bible is produced that represents less a book than a lost past, a part of Europe's cultural core that has become blurred from view, and which needs to be recovered as part of the recovery of a former, more glorious Europe. In this sense we could call this Bible a Civilisation Bible. It is a Bible that is a crucial component in Western Civilisation as a classic text, a provider of maxims and values that are deemed to be central to European culture, and a thing to be recovered in its pre-modern guise. I have already touched on the two first points here—the Bible as classic culture and container of maxims and values—but it is worth examining more closely the third point about a pre-modern Bible. The desire to save "the Bible" from the clutches of the modern world is distinctly tied to an understanding of a biblical-Western civilisation that is under threat from Islam in particular, and modernity more generally. This fear of loss and desire to save the West accounts for the presence of a Civilisation Bible assemblage in the manifesto.

In book three of the manifesto, the idea of a Civilisation Bible is emphasised in the distinction made between a traditional and a modern Bible. A particular Bible is decried as lost, leaving us with a perverted modern Bible. In line with the way contemporary Europe is seen as infiltrated by its supposed "other"—Islam—an idea of the Bible is used to evoke a pure(r) origin point: "we will have to go back to our roots, to the Vulgate, the Versio Vulgata or the original pre-1611 King James Bible".[160] The roots of Europe and the "original" Bible that is sought after, then, is a medieval Europe with its medieval Bible. This "original", more authentic, Bible is affiliated with "a Christendom that propagated self-defence against the infidel Muslims".[161] In contrast, the contemporary Bible is described as "modified", a piece of propaganda with a supremely modern agenda, a "pacifist, gender neutral Bible" that has lost "what God says".[162] What has been obscured according to the manifesto is God's encouragement towards "the ongoing Crusade (self defence)",[163] a message that has been blurred by the "political correctness" of the modern world. Interestingly, the actual Bible versions that are cited in the manifesto do not seem to match this desire for a medieval Bible. Throughout, the biblical references are mostly from the New King James Version, or the King James Version, while some are from the New Revised

---

[160] Ibid., p. 1140.
[161] Ibid.
[162] Ibid.
[163] Ibid.

Standard Version.[164] This mixture points to the way these bits of Bible indicate not one, singular Bible, but a Bible that functions as an assemblage.

The European counterjihad movement sets itself up as the proper interpreter of Western and European civilisation, as Önnerfors notes, positing "a shared European history and culture" "as a counter-force to Islamization".[165] In the same vein as European governments allegedly colluding with Islamic imperialism, the Bible, too, is presented as a corpus that has been ideologically manipulated: "Our modern Bible perversion was written by men using dynamic equivalence. In other words, they are telling you their interpretation and their doctrine, NOT what the manuscripts really say".[166] Interestingly, a new Norwegian translation of the Bible was released in October 2011 (only a few months after Breivik's attacks), from the collaborative work of biblical scholars as well as Norwegian poets and authors, with the aim to offer a more readable and up-to-date Bible, changing for instance the highly debated designation of Mary as a "virgin" to a "young woman". This Bible became a best-seller in Norway in 2012. Again, what this indicates is the way Bibles function as different assemblages. Mapping what I have called the Civilisation Bible assemblage demonstrates the way diffuse notions of Bible are connected to classic culture and Europe's roots, but the new Norwegian Bible produced and published the same year of Breivik's terror attacks is also an assemblage.[167]

For Breivik, though, the Bible becomes a desired foundation tied to a nebulous and nostalgic civilisational past. The Bible is something "we today" have become alienated from. The decay of Western civilisation that is diagnosed today is in this way connected to the perversion of a Bible. The "threats" of a politically correct multiculturalism become an urgent call to reacquaint readers with a perceived "authentic" Bible elusively tied to the perception of a patriarchal past of "our forefathers". The loss of Western civilisation, then, has happened simultaneously with the loss of a traditional Bible. A Civilisation Bible must be reproduced to rebuild Western civilisation today.

---

[164] In the next chapters I unpack where Breivik got his biblical references from, which explains why there is not much consistency between the views about Bible translation that Breivik propagates here and the actual Bible-use. But the point is that there does not seem to be much, if any, awareness of a contradiction here. Indeed, the concern with consistency, coherence, and knowledge of different Bible versions might well be precisely what would be pointed to by people such as Breivik as a peculiarly elitist, liberal, and academic obsession.

[165] Önnerfors, 'Between Breivik and PEGIDA', p. 164.

[166] Manifesto, p. 1140.

[167] I address the question of relativism that arises from the existence of different biblical assemblages in chapter 8 and 9.

The contemporary Church is accused of complicity in the "perverted" Bible with its "pacifist, fanatically egalitarian and gender inclusive language", which, it is argued, "wasn't in the original texts, in the original Bible".[168] The manifesto advocates a salvaging of the Bible from the clutches of the contemporary churches and mainstream society. The Bible is perceived as a victim in need of saving to access its more authentic, original meanings and thus recover the "roots" of Christian Europe.[169] "Lack of guide to scripture" is seen as a source of the problematic understanding of the Bible in contemporary society.[170] The Protestant notion of *sola scriptura* is denounced.[171] In the final parts of the manifesto, a reformed Catholic Church is envisioned as the "necessary guide to the meaning of Scripture".[172] The importance of the Bible as an authentic origin point to Europe that must be authoritatively safeguarded and explicated by "a united, strong and appealing 'Traditional Church'" is found under the heading, "European Political Solutions for the Future".[173] Only through such a return to the "original" pre-modern Bible, aided by the policing of biblical interpretation, can a solution be found for Europe to retrieve "traditional religious values akin to the Bible's injunction to honour thy mother and father".[174]

Breivik himself does not seem to consider his own Bible-use as in need of any guidance from churches, though (as becomes clearer in the ensuing chapters) he does draw on other sources for his Bible-use that are clearly considered authoritative for him. The supposedly dangerous plurality and multivocity of "the Bible" is explicitly raised in the manifesto. In Section 2.83 of the manifesto, attributed to the Norwegian blogger Fjordman, the idea of the Civilisation Bible is embraced, in the statement that "our" Western moral and ethical values are deeply influenced by Judeo-Christian traditions.[175] But it is quickly admitted that once you start reading a Bible, ambiguity sets in. The question is raised as to whether "our openness to outsiders, our democratic system and our Christian compassion, precisely the values that we cherish the most, render the West incapable of withstanding Jihad?"[176]

---

[168] Manifesto, p. 1140.
[169] Ibid.
[170] Ibid., p. 1135.
[171] Ibid.
[172] Ibid.
[173] Ibid., p. 1133. This section comes with the proviso that it is not complete, "due to the complexity of various aspects relating to solutions for Western Europe".
[174] Manifesto, p. 1146.
[175] Ibid., p. 689.
[176] Ibid.

Matthew 5:38–40 and the idea of turning the other cheek and loving one's enemies are mentioned to point to a problematic Bible.[177] This problematic Bible of cheek-turning and enemy-loving is presented as weak. The fact that this Bible is already operating amongst Christians is deemed obvious: "And how can we fight sharia when bishops and church leaders are the first to call for a 'compassionate' immigration policy that allows masses of Muslims to settle here?"[178]

In fact, the reality of multiple Bibles is practically admitted in the manifesto in the distinction between a modern Bible and a so-called authentic Bible. A particular Bible needs to be chosen and safeguarded amongst others. The Bible that contains Matthew 5:38–40 is not one that counterjihadists like Breivik or Fjordman can accept. And yet a Civilisation Bible that will affirm an identity of Europe that can be set up against Islam in the clash of cultures is a useful tool. In that sense, a different Bible to the one embraced by "bishops and church leaders" who campaign for a compassionate immigration policy must be produced and proclaimed. Breivik's manifesto presents this as a return to an original Bible, but of course, "the Vulgate, the Versio Vulgata or the original pre-1611 King James Bible"[179] is not the original Bible. What would constitute an original Bible? What the manifesto calls for is a return to a Bible that is associated with a medieval European Christendom, as a historical prop to support a fantasy of a pure, homogenous Europe in outright conflict with Islam.

The Bible that is invoked in the manifesto is one component of an imagined Europe which acts as foundation, legacy, and prop that aids a different direction in the future. The Christian identity of Europe is affirmed through references to ancient scriptures that have influenced European history and culture. Europe itself is saturated with Christianity. It is a core, an essence to what Europe *is*. And yet, it is also a feeble and precarious part of Europe, now vulnerable to dissipation due to multiculturalism, immigration, and particularly to the presence of Muslims in Europe. As Sørensen writes, Breivik uses constructions of history to create something new;[180] similarly, he uses a construction of a Bible to present the future of European society,

---

[177] Ibid.
[178] Ibid., p. 29.
[179] Ibid., p. 1140.
[180] Sørensen, 'En totalitær mentalitet', p. 107.

a future in which European civilisation is (re)built. Allusions to a "common narrative of the past", to preserve some notion of a pure and in Breivik's case monocultural Europe, is, Wodak argues, a key strategy amongst right-wing populists, and one that Breivik taps into here, too, through the call for a return to an "authentic" Bible.[181] The Civilisation Bible is a prop on which Europe is imagined to be stabilised *as* a territory set apart from Muslim territories. The Bible is also that which fills Europe with "content" in terms of a set of values. A restored Bible from this European past is part of Breivik's vision for a future Europe in which tradition, patriarchy, and purity are "restored", where order will reign and a past will be regained. And yet, it is admitted that there are Bibles that threaten the Civilisation Bible, which is set up in opposition to Islam. There are modern Bibles and Bible-texts about turning the other cheek that destabilise the Bible that Breivik affirms. There are Christians and church leaders who are assembled with those cheek-turning-Bibles that destabilise the Civilisation Bible assemblage, which is part of a machine to produce hate and fear.

Altogether, then, the second biblical assemblage that is at work in the manifesto is the Civilisation Bible. While the War Bible is more confined to the section entitled "The Bible and Self-Defence" in book three of the manifesto, the Civilisation Bible is invoked in different parts of the manifesto. This biblical assemblage is made up of a Bible that is only sparingly opened or read. In other words, it is not invoked by citing lots of biblical verses or stories or through much exegesis of biblical texts. Rather, "the Bible" is referred to as a classic textbook for Europe, a civilisational artefact, and an origin point. Two main non-biblical components are attached to this Civilisation Bible. The first is: other books. The Bible that is invoked here functions as a book that belongs in a canon of "classic" Western literature that is presented as anti-Marxist and conservative. In this sense, it feeds a particular idea and performance of Western culture. The second component that the Bible is connected to as a cultural artefact is the imagined "roots" of Europe. These roots are mourned: Europe is uprooted. Bringing a version of the Bible back is treated as a gesture that will enable a return to the roots of a Europe that can hold its own against Islam in the face of multiculturalism and immigration.

---

[181] Wodak, *The Politics of Fear*, p. 66.

Breivik's Bibles

To sum up this chapter, I have argued that two biblical assemblages form a part of the manifesto: the War Bible and the Civilisation Bible. These biblical assemblages are connected with other non-biblical themes and tenets taken up in the text. The War Bible is an assemblage that is made up of selected biblical verses that take on particular effects when read alongside the Eurabia and counterjihad conspiracies that posit Muslims as an eternal and inherently violent enemy of the Christian West. The biblical verses become confirmation that it is natural for the supposedly European "people of God" to fight an enemy other, and that this fight is righteous. The biblical verses work *with* reconstructions of the crusades and stories of Christian persecution that make up large parts of the manifesto. The War Bible assemblage functions because the biblical verses are strung together with accounts of defensive crusades fought by righteous European knights, defending their land and their people. These bits of a Bible are also situated with repeated stories of Christians being persecuted by Muslims. Altogether, the effect is that of an Islam that is totally threatening, historically and in the present. Along with this narrative of the crusades and the stories of persecution, Christian Europe is in danger, and the Bible offers resources for justifying defensive warfare with God as Lord of war fighting alongside his people.

The Civilisation Bible is a component in the construction of Europe—it forms an assemblage with an imagined Europe. This is a Bible that is connected to the imagined roots of Europe. It is used as an emblem of what Europe has achieved throughout history. It operates as a foundational origin-component to Europe but also as a trajectory that Europe should stay on: regaining "Bibleness" in order to revive European culture. The Civilisation Bible is a prop that helps stabilise notions of Europe as Christian, closed, and superior to other continents. It stands alongside and is inextricably linked to other classic Western literature. It is a Bible that is treated as a victim of political correctness. This political correctness, it is claimed, has tarnished the biblical values that make up European Christendom. Only a return to an "original" Bible can put Europe back on course in the face of the so-called threats of multiculturalism, immigration, and, most particularly, Islam.

The biblical assemblages I have outlined in this chapter are connected to and continuous with other components that make up the manifesto. These connections and continuities are made by their proximity and by their arrangement in the manifesto. Although the manifesto is seemingly contradictory in many ways, the "logic" that is construed in the worldview Breivik presents and propagates works by assembling different elements in order to enhance feelings of victimhood and righteousness, and to stoke hate and fear. Naming the War Bible and the Civilisation Bible aids in identifying particular kinds of Bibles that are produced in the manifesto and which form patterns. No doubt other assemblages could also be identified. But it seems clear that particular ways of thinking about "the Bible" operate in the manifesto and that they are plural. They seem contradictory. How could the idea of a Bible representing the civilisational and benign values of Europe in opposition to a supposedly violent Islamic civilisation work with the idea of a Bible that supports violence? There is no attempt to reconcile these Bibles. These Bibles can make sense in the manifesto if we recognise that in fact two different Bibles are invoked that operate in different ways and with different effects. While the Civilisation Bible works to ground Europe's identity in the clash of civilisations narrative, the War Bible is able to support a violent uprising against those who are deemed the enemy. The fact that a Bible can work as the civilisationally superior (and benign) European cultural content that Breivik is fighting *for* as well as a resource to justify violence and call forth a warrior God, is a testament to the plasticity of the texts associated with "the Bible" and their differing intensities.

In another sense these two Bibles *are* connected: the Civilisation Bible is what needs to be saved to defend Europe; the War Bible is what justifies and calls for a violent defence. Perhaps in the references to David and Goliath there is a reconciliation of the two biblical assemblages, where the story represents both a cultural treasure for the West but also functions to spur on violence from the perspective of an underdog who is fighting for his people. In any case, Breivik did not make up these biblical assemblages. The manifesto is not a closed unit in which these biblical assemblages are arbitrarily embedded. Rather, the manifesto needs to be seen as part of a much wider far-right network. In the next chapter I will map the textual territories from which these biblical assemblages emerge in key sources Breivik drew on.

4
Biblical Connections and Continuities

A few days after the attacks in Norway on 22 July 2011, the Italian Lega Nord politician Mario Borghezio praised Breivik's manifesto, saying that he shared Breivik's opposition to Islam, including his call for a Christian crusade.[1] He added that a significant number of Europeans share Breivik's views.[2] In Britain, a United Kingdom Independence Party candidate, Steve Moxon, openly praised Breivik in a blog post.[3] The Norwegian far-right group Stop the Islamisation of Norway has expressed its admiration for Breivik's actions on several occasions.[4] The perpetrator of the mass shooting in the Al-Noor mosque and Linwood Islamic Centre in New Zealand in March 2019 cited Breivik as an inspiration.[5] Breivik may have acted alone on 22 July 2011, but he was not alone in his worldview.

In the previous chapter I mapped the biblical assemblages that are at work in Breivik's manifesto: the War Bible and the Civilisation Bible. As I emphasised, Breivik's worldview and his Bible-use have to be understood in their connections and continuities with a wider far-right milieu. Paul Jackson has remarked that studies of terrorism are often oriented around analyses of the perpetrators, rather than "the study of the voices that generate the underpinning ideological cultures, the worldviews that help to incubate the rationale for terrorist campaigns".[6] As Jackson points out, the terrorist

---

[1] Berardi, *Heroes*, pp. 96–97.
[2] Ibid., p. 97.
[3] 'Sheffield UKIP Candidate Removed over Blog Post', *BBC News*, 1 May 2012, http://www.bbc.co.uk/news/uk-england-south-yorkshire-17911131 (last accessed 22 June 2022).
[4] Harald Klungtveit and Jonas Skybakmoen, '"Kanskje vi på sikt må slippe ham ut, så vi får ryddet opp": SIAN gjentar Breivik-uttalelser før ny demonstrasjon', *Filter Nyheter*, 12 September 2020, https://filternyheter.no/kanskje-vi-pa-sikt-ma-slippe-ham-ut-sa-vi-far-ryddet-opp-sian-gjentar-breivik-uttalelser-for-ny-demonstrasjon/.
[5] Eleanor Ainge Roy, Harriet Sherwood, and Nazia Parveen, 'Christchurch Attack: Suspect Had White Supremacist Symbols on Weapons', *The Guardian*, 15 March 2019, https://www.theguardian.com/world/2019/mar/15/christchurch-shooting-new-zealand-suspect-white-supremacist-symbols-weapons. The perpetrator of the attack at the Al-Noor Islamic Center in Bærum, Norway, on 10 August 2019, where a gunman opened fire just after the prayers in the mosque had ended, cited Brenton Tarrant as a saint.
[6] Paul Jackson, 'The License to Hate: Peder Jensen's Fascist Rhetoric in Anders Breivik's Manifesto 2083: A European Declaration of Independence', *Democracy and Security* 9 (2013): pp. 247–248.

violence needs to be made desirable before it is carried out.[7] He asks what cultural frameworks give implicit license that foster and fuel hate and violence. Similarly, Lars Erik Berntzen and Sveinung Sandberg have argued that the Breivik case in particular "demonstrates the importance of seeing the terrorism of loners as embedded in, and motivated by, the rhetoric of larger social movements".[8] In his study of the Islamophobia of the contemporary far right in Europe, Mattias Ekman describes the different environments Islamophobic actors emanate from.[9] He mentions those who "produce and distribute 'knowledge' about Muslims and Islam", such as "scholars, writers, journalists and media figures".[10]

In this chapter my focus is on writers on the far right who lament the demise of the Christian West, spread hate, and stoke fear of Muslims, all whilst purportedly propagating "knowledge" about Islam and Christian Europe. Stoking feelings of discontent with the state of the world, these writers are able to garner a far wider appeal than could a perpetrator of violence like Breivik with his sprawling manifesto. Jacob Aasland Ravndal characterises "prominent ideological authorities" as persons "whose writings and statements are widely read and shared" within far-right movements and who have a considerable impact in terms of shaping ideological thinking and, ultimately, though more indirectly, action.[11] Attending to such authorities is a matter of exploring how and where political violence has been "incubated".[12] This chapter focuses on figures who produce "knowledge" about Islam on a more popular level, often posing as intellectuals, but whose main outlet is popular publications, websites, and blogs. I will return to those figures who could be described more straightforwardly as "intellectuals" in the next chapter, but here, too, there is a posturing that takes the shape of intellectual knowledge production, even if they might not be recognised as intellectual authorities outside far-right circles. Counterjihadist groups are able, Andrew Elliott argues, to generate a remarkable amount of popular support "by integrating their rhetoric into a seemingly innocuous form of everyday racism which reconfigures their anti-Muslim sentiments and xenophobia into patriotic defence of the country".[13] In fact, Ravndal has argued that between

[7] Ibid., p. 248.
[8] Berntzen and Sandberg, 'The Collective Nature of Lone Wolf Terrorism', p. 760.
[9] Ekman, 'Online Islamophobia and the Politics of Fear', p. 1990.
[10] Ibid.
[11] Jacob Aasland Ravndal, 'From Bombs to Books, and Back Again? Mapping Strategies of Right-Wing Revolutionary Resistance', *Studies in Conflict and Terrorism* (2021): pp. 13–14.
[12] Jackson, 'The License to Hate', p. 252.
[13] Elliott, *Medievalism, Politics and Mass Media*, p. 157.

2000 and 2010, what he calls a "metapolitical turn" occurred, in which many far-right figures prioritised the spreading and normalising of far-right ideas over violent tactics.[14] In other words, the idea is that "political ideas must be anchored in cultural, intellectual, and public domains, before actual revolutionary change can materialize".[15]

What I aim to do in this chapter, then, is draw out the connections and continuities of the two biblical assemblages I mapped in the previous chapter, by attending to the larger milieu of which Breivik was a part. By identifying the role Bibles play in key figures Breivik cites, I explore to what extent the Civilisation Bible and the War Bible function in contemporary far-right circles. To tease out where the Civilisation Bible and the War Bible in Breivik's manifesto are stabilised and what they are connected to, I focus on five figures who are key to the Islamophobic worldview Breivik propagates: Peder Jensen (known as "Fjordman"),[16] Robert Spencer, Bat Ye'or, Oriana Fallaci, and Bruce Bawer. These names, their worldviews, and their writings, feature centrally in the manifesto as prominent figures in the Eurabia and counterjihad milieu. That is the first reason I have chosen to focus on these figures in this chapter. The second reason is that they all have relatively prominent platforms in digital forums and print culture. They may propagate conspiracy theories and some extreme views, but they are not "extremists" or "terrorists". Collectively, they are the non-violent component of the assemblage that sticks to Breivik and the acts of terror he committed. Without their writings, it is impossible to understand the worldview Breivik embraced in his justification for terrorism.

While all of the five figures I discuss in this chapter are mentioned in the manifesto, it is crucial to point out that I am not confining my analysis to texts and statements by the five that are explicitly cited in the manifesto. Chapter 3 investigated the material that can be found in the manifesto. What I am aiming to do in this chapter and the next two chapters is to move outward, to explore sources that are connected to Breivik's manifesto. So far, to my knowledge, no research has investigated the role Bibles play in the worldview of Breivik and the wider far-right milieu of which he was a part.

This chapter, then, maps the connections and continuities among these five thinkers, the War Bible, and the Civilisation Bible that I argued are at

---

[14] Ravndal, 'From Bombs to Books, and Back Again?', pp. 1–29,
[15] Ibid., p. 10.
[16] I will refer to him as "Fjordman" throughout the chapter.

work in Breivik's manifesto. I begin the chapter by providing a brief overview of these five figures and their shared obsession, namely, the purported decline of Europe. I then turn to the way a Bible is invoked in their writings. Ultimately, I will argue that three modes of Bible-use are at work in the writings of these five figures. I write about "modes" of Bible-use to indicate the different ways biblical assemblages can function, particularly as different assemblages are stabilised through repetition. I use mode to make clear that I am not only seeking to map singular uses of biblical texts or singular constructions of "the Bible". But nor does this use necessarily constitute a trend. Mode indicates the way an assemblage tends towards stabilisation through different kinds of Bible-use. In terms of these three modes, then, first I map the Bible as a machine that produces "biblical values"; second, Jesus as a sword-bearing heroic figure; third, prophetic voice. These three modes of Bible-use are important because they work well to stabilise the War Bible and Civilisation Bible assemblages that I showed were at work in Breivik's manifesto in the previous chapter.

Europe in Decline

Counterjihadism has spread across Europe over the last years, through counterjihadist summits and through websites, books, blog pages, and virtual forums. Rasmus Fleischer suggests that it was during 2007 that a counterjihad milieu began to emerge as a "coordinated movement in North-Western Europe".[17] The UK and Scandinavia counterjihad summit was held in Copenhagen in April 2007, on the initiative of anti-Muslim bloggers. In autumn 2007, another meeting took place inside the European parliament building in Brussels, hosted by Vlaams Beland.[18] Among the invited speakers were the anti-Muslim activists and writers Robert Spencer and Bat Ye'or (her real name is Gisèle Littman).[19] Since 2007, counterjihad summits have featured representatives from European right-wing populist parties such as the Italian Lega Nord and the Swiss Freedom Party.[20] The most obvious ideological authorities for Breivik, as the manifesto demonstrates, are affiliated with counterjihadism.

---

[17] Fleischer, 'Two Fascisms in Contemporary Europe?', p. 62.
[18] Ibid.
[19] Ibid., pp. 62–63.
[20] Ibid., p. 63.

The blogger known as "Fjordman" is, as several scholars have pointed out, Breivik's most important influence.[21] Thirty-seven articles in the manifesto are attributed to Fjordman. A Norwegian by the name of Peder Nøstvold Jensen, he has been an active figure in the Eurabia and counterjihad milieu, and many of the figures in this milieu who feature in the manifesto come through Breivik's citations of articles written by Fjordman. He was a regular contributor to counterjihadist websites such as *Gates of Vienna* and *Brussels Journal*. In his writings he pedals the Eurabia conspiracy that Europe is at war due to an all-powerful Islamic force, and that the people of Europe are being held hostage to Muslim immigrants.[22] Although Fjordman expressed disgust at being cited by Breivik and called it the worst thing that ever happened to him, he remained dedicated to the worldview that he had been propagating prior to the 22 July attacks.[23] In the articles attributed to Fjordman in the manifesto, he writes about different civilisations, separating the "Islamic world" from Christian civilisation.[24] He claims that according to Islamic law, Muslims can accept Christians and Jews only as second-rate citizens, and that Muslims are trying to subjugate the Western world.[25] Complaining about multiculturalism, he writes that the "First Commandment of multiculturalism is: Thou shalt hate Christianity and Judaism".[26] Further, multiculturalists allegedly "also hate nation states, and they even hate the Enlightenment, by insisting that non-Western cultures should be above scrutiny".[27] Fjordman spouts many of the views that are repeated in Breivik's manifesto, about Muslims, multiculturalism, and migration, himself repeating points made by other, more prominent counterjihadist figures, namely Robert Spencer and Bat Ye'or.

Robert Spencer is a prominent figure in the counterjihad scene. An American author and blogger, he founded the blog *Jihad Watch* and co-founded the Stop the Islamization of America organisation. The *Jihad Watch* blog has been active since 2003, and is connected to David Horowitz, who is the director of Freedom Center and the publisher of *FrontPage Magazine*,

---

[21] Gardell, 'Crusader Dreams', pp. 131, 135; Jackson, 'The License to Hate', p. 248.
[22] See Jackson, 'The License to Hate', for more on Fjordman's views.
[23] As Jackson recounts, Fjordman gave an interview to the German right-wing newspaper *Junge Freiheit*. Jackson, 'The License to Hate', p. 269.
[24] Fjordman, 'Western vs. Islamic Science and Religion', cited in Section 1.23 in the manifesto, p. 253.
[25] Fjordman, 'The Church—Part of the Problem or Part of the Solution?', cited in Section 2.83 in the manifesto, p. 686.
[26] Fjordman, 'Thou Shalt Hate Christianity and Judaism', in Section 2.84 of the Manifesto, p. 692.
[27] Ibid.

another key player in the Islamophobic milieu. According to Ekman, *Jihad Watch* has received significant financial contributions to support its activities.[28] The related site, *Gates of Vienna*, is a blog with a more European outlook and has been online since late 2003.[29] Spencer is cited frequently and favourably in Breivik's manifesto. He has published several books, amongst others, *Religion of Peace? Why Christianity Is and Islam Isn't* (2007) and *Not Peace but a Sword: The Great Chasm between Christianity and Islam* (2013). In *Religion of Peace? Why Christianity Is and Islam Isn't*, Spencer bemoans the "lack of cultural self-confidence" marking the West, critiquing the way Christianity—"upon which Western civilization is largely based"—is seen as morally equal to Islam.[30] Spencer believes an Islamic jihad is taking place in Europe, in which Muslims are trying to conquer and subjugate Western non-Muslims. According to him, the choice for people in the West is either to submit to the Islamic social order or stand up for Judeo-Christian values and defend them against the ideological challenge of jihad and sharia.[31]

Egyptian-British writer Bat Ye'or describes herself as a historian of religious minorities under Muslim rule. She has popularised the term "Eurabia", to refer to a state of anti-Americanism and antisemitism in the West in conspiracy with Arabs and radical Islam. Part of Eurabia is her understanding of "dhimmitude", which she describes as a state of Jewish and Christian submission, subordination, and humiliation to Muslims. Liz Fekete discusses the way right-wing and neoconservative think tanks and foundations such as the Henry Jackson Society, the Danish Free Press Society, and the Human Rights Service in Norway have all flirted with the Eurabia theme.[32] *Understanding Dhimmitude: Twenty-One Lectures and Talks on the Position of Non-Muslims in Islamic Societies* is a collection of essays written by Ye'or between 1984 and 2004. Many are based on talks Ye'or delivered at universities in the United States and United Kingdom over these years. Jihad, Ye'or insists, is "a territorial war" "but also a clash of cultures".[33] "One culture, embodied

---

[28] Ekman, 'Online Islamophobia and the Politics of Fear', p. 1991. It allegedly received a financial contribution of $253,250 from the Fairbrook Foundation, and the Freedom Center received $8,380,500 from six different donors.
[29] Ibid., p. 1991.
[30] Robert Spencer, *Religion of Peace? Why Christianity Is and Islam Isn't* (Washington, DC: Regnery Publishing, 2007), p. 1.
[31] Ibid., p. 5.
[32] Liz Fekete, *Europe's Fault Lines: Racism and the Rise of the Right* (London: Verso, 2018), pp. 60–61.
[33] Bat Ye'or, *Understanding Dhimmitude: Twenty-One Lectures and Talks on the Position of Non-Muslims in Islamic Societies* (New York: RVP Press, 2013), p. 70.

BIBLICAL CONNECTIONS AND CONTINUITIES   119

by Arab-Islamic values, convinced of its perfection and its election to rule the world, claims domination in order to extinguish the indigenous local cultures".[34]

Jews and Christians, according to Ye'or, have historically suffered at the hands of Muslims in a struggle that—she states—is a forbidden history and a history that is being reactivated today.[35] As Bangstad notes, the tropes of the Eurabia conspiracy are in circulation in extreme and populist right-wing milieus in Europe and the United States, and have been for some time.[36] Bat Ye'or is, as he points out, no academic, although she is often presented as one.[37] Her husband, David Littman, who shares her views, has represented various NGOs at the UN commission on Human Rights in Geneva.[38] In Bansgtad's words: "It would be an understatement to assert that the work of Gisèle Littman/Bat Ye'or is regarded as failing to meet basic standards of academic research among most qualified historians of Islam and the Middle East".[39] Yet, the appearance of Ye'or's work, full of extensive footnotes and references, is a key part of its claims and its capacities to convince readers.[40] Many of the points she makes are repeated in Breivik's manifesto.[41]

It is important to note here that although the focus for Eurabia and counterjihad movements are on Islam, and Judaism is often referred to also as under threat from Islam, antisemitism is not absent. As Nasar Meer in particular has urged, contemporary antisemitism and Islamophobia should be studied "squarely within the fields of race and racism".[42] While of course antisemitism and Islamophobia have different histories, tenors, and textures, they also share common traits and tendencies, particularly when racialisation is understood as the way people, groups, and minorities become "the sites of racial inscriptions".[43] Meer cites studies that demonstrate the strong relationship between anti-Jewish and anti-Muslim sentiments in the contemporary

---

[34] Ibid., pp. 70–71.
[35] See for instance 'Christians and Jews: The Forbidden History', in Ye'or, *Understanding Dhimmitude*, pp. 46–55.
[36] Bangstad, *Anders Breivik and the Rise of Islamophobia*, p. 145.
[37] Ibid., pp. 145–146.
[38] Ibid., p. 146.
[39] Ibid., pp. 146–147.
[40] Ibid., p. 147. She has been cited approvingly by, for instance, the Harvard historian Niall Ferguson. Ibid., p. 147.
[41] Ibid., p. 150.
[42] Nasar Meer, 'Racialization and Religion: Race, Culture and Difference in the Study of Antisemitism and Islamophobia', in *Racialization and Religion: Race, Culture and Difference in the Study of Antisemitism and Islamophobia*, edited by Nasar Meer (London: Routledge, 2014), p. 2.
[43] Ibid., p. 6.

West, particularly in the United States and Europe.[44] He highlights the "overlapping articulation of both phenomena as something that emerges not in a tiered hierarchy but as a conjoined activity".[45] Meer mentions the widely received conspiracy theory of Eurabia, proposed by Ye'or, and the way the demographic panic it plays into and propels, bears crucial similarities to the antisemitic *Protocols of the Elders of Zion*.[46] While explicit antisemitism might be avoided or played down, it should be kept in mind that more subtle and insidious forms of antisemitism and anti-Judaism are not far off. Jayne Svenungsson has pointed out that although counterjihadist sites, such as *The Gates of Vienna*, include diatribes against Islam next to notes declaring support for Israel, this is less proof of a solidarity with Jews, and more a way of making common cause with radical right-wing groups amongst European Jews.[47] As Omer and Lupo argue, right-wing populist groups "thrive on rearticulated forms of antisemitism" while supporting Israeli policies regarding the occupation of Palestinian lands, embodying the lack of contradiction between Zionism and antisemitism.[48]

Two further figures are worth mentioning when it comes to voices relating to Breivik's manifesto and its ideological authorities, namely Oriana Fallaci and Bruce Bawer, both of whom are cited in the manifesto, albeit not as frequently as Fjordman, Spencer, or Ye'or.[49] They are both closely connected to these figures and the worldview Breivik propagated in the manifesto. Oriana Fallaci (1929–2006) was an Italian journalist who had an illustrious career interviewing high-profile politicians between the 1960s and 1980s. She received several prizes for her journalism. Her writings have been translated into over twenty languages. After the terrorist attacks of 9/11, Fallaci published two books that courted both critique and admiration: *The Rage and the Pride* (2001) and *The Force of Reason* (2004). Both sold in large numbers. In these books, Fallaci decries the state of Europe and the West today. Drawing on Ye'or, she claims that Europe has become "Eurabia". She claims

---

[44] Meer quotes from a Pew Global Attitudes report from 2008 that surveyed 25,000 people across twenty-four countries.

[45] Ibid., p. 8.

[46] Ibid., p. 9. Meer quotes here Matt Carr, 'You Are Now Entering Eurabia', *Race and Class* 48, no. 1 (2006): pp. 1–22.

[47] Jayne Svenungsson, 'Christian Europe: Borders and Boundaries of a Mythological Conception', in *Transcending Europe: Beyond Universalism and Particularism*, edited by S. Lingberg, S. Prozorov, and M. Ojakangas (New York: Palgrave Macmillan, 2014), p. 121.

[48] Omer and Lupo, 'Introduction: The Cultural Logic of White Christian Nationalisms', pp. 9–10.

[49] Bawer is cited directly in the manifesto, at 303–305, 384, 420, 561, 563, 601–603, 629, 738, 804. Fallaci is cited directly at 351, 529, 634.

that a demographic and cultural warfare is taking place whereby Muslims are subtly subjugating Europe. The values and principles of European culture are being lost. Islam is deemed an inferior religious tradition, while European culture is celebrated as superior.

Bruce Bawer is an American journalist, literary critic, and writer who has lived in Norway since the late nineties. In his book *While Europe Slept: How Radical Islam Is Destroying the West from Within* (2006), Bawer complains about the effects of Muslim immigration on Europe. He cites Spencer as an "Islam expert"[50] and praises Ye'or for warning "not only that Europe is on its way to becoming a colony of the Muslim world, but also that this is the result of European design, not neglect".[51] For Bawer, moderate Muslims exist, but they are a minority and they fail to stand up to a more pernicious and prevalent radical Islam. What Muslim immigrants are bringing to Europe according to Bawer is a threat to democracy and liberal values of freedom, tolerance, and equality. Bawer cautions against far-right ideology and calls rather for a "liberal resistance" to radical Islam.[52] What is at stake for him is "modern democratic civilization".[53] The enemy—radical Islam—is clear, clever, and ubiquitous. Multiculturalism and soft laws on immigration are culprits, as he sees it, in enabling radical Islam to gain a foothold in Europe and bring Europe to its knees. Bangstad argues that Bawer's contacts in the transnational Islamophobic network and rhetorical eloquence have made him a key figure in addressing both US and European audiences in a wide range of print and electronic formats. In this sense he has been central in the attempt to mainstream the "Eurabia" literature.[54] As a gay literary critic, he reflects the changes in at least some extreme and populist right-wing environments in Western Europe, which have come to endorse liberal values and LGBTQI rights in their Islamophobic programmes.[55] In the aftermath of the Breivik attacks in July 2011, Bawer's rhetoric has become more strident, suggesting that the "real victims" of the terror attacks in Norway were Bawer and his fellow critics of Islam, as their case would be seriously damaged by Breivik.[56]

---

[50] Bruce Bawer, *While Europe Slept: How Radical Islam Is Destroying the West from Within* (New York: Anchor Books, 2006), p. 218.
[51] Ibid., p. 103.
[52] Ibid., p. 159.
[53] Ibid., p. 157.
[54] Bangstad, *Anders Breivik and the Rise of Islamophobia*, p. 155.
[55] Ibid.
[56] Ibid., p. 162. See Bruce Bawer, *The New Quislings: How the International Left Used the Oslo Massacre to Silence Debate about Islam* (New York: Broadside e-books, 2012).

There is no single or unified voice for figures on the contemporary far right.[57] But as Fekete points out in *Europe's Fault Lines: Racism and the Rise of the Right*, the focus on culture and civilisation has become a shared focus for different figures and movements in Europe.[58] Die-hard neo-Nazis may still speak of racial superiority in Europe, but the new currents of the far right insist instead on Europe's cultural decline and civilisational hierarchies.[59] Ekman discusses the way that reducing complex social and economic issues to "culture" makes it possible for figures on the far right to claim that Europe has a "Muslim problem".[60] The perceived failure of multiculturalism is linked to the accusation that Muslims have failed to integrate in Europe.[61] As Ekman describes it, Muslim immigrants are treated "as an incompatible ontological category predicated on culture".[62] Fjordman, Spencer, Ye'or, Fallaci, and Bawer are all significant contributors to the focus on Islam as an "other" culture that threatens Europe and leads to the decline of Europe and the West.

These figures take different approaches to religion. Fjordman calls himself "not a religious person", although at least in one text by him that Breivik cites, he stresses he is "usually in favor of a revitalisation of Christianity in Europe".[63] He does not cite the Bible much but does argue for the supremacy of Christianity as a progenitor of Western culture and as a religion compatible with reason.[64] Spencer identifies as Catholic, while Ye'or identifies as Jewish. The category of "Judeo-Christian" is central to both Spencer and Ye'or. Biblical texts and invocations of "the Bible" are prominent in Spencer's and Ye'or's writings. Fallaci is an atheist but declares herself a "Christian atheist".[65] Notions of a Bible are not central to her claims, but a particular view of "the Bible" nonetheless props them up in striking ways in her writings. Like Fjordman, Bawer writes obsessively of radical Islam but is less concerned with Christianity or Christian scripture.

As I already alluded, there are three shared modes of Bible-use in the writings of these five figures, although these modes are more intense in some

---

[57] Fekete, *Europe's Fault Lines*, p. 60.
[58] Ibid.
[59] Ibid., p. 62.
[60] Ekman, 'Online Islamophobia and the Politics of Fear', p. 1987.
[61] Ibid.
[62] Ibid.
[63] Fjordman, 'The Church—Part of the Problem or Part of the Solution?', cited in Section 2.83 in the manifesto, p. 686.
[64] Fjordman, 'Thou Shalt Hate Christianity and Judaism', p. 693.
[65] Oriana Fallaci, *The Force of Reason* (New York: Rizzoli International Publications, 2004), p. 185.

and less in others. Bible as a producer of biblical values is key. The invocation of the sword-bearing Jesus is recurrent. Bible-as-prophetic-voice is held up to amplify these five figures' own voices as "prophetic" truth-tellers. In what follows, I will go through these modes, showing how counterjihadist figures construe a particular Bible. These modes are not equally operant in all five figures, and some—such as Bawer—have very little of any of the three modes of Bible-use. But there are nonetheless striking similarities that emerge from their overlapping views of Europe, the West, and Islam. These three modes are significant in the emergence and stabilisation of a War Bible, and even more so for a Civilisation Bible.

Biblical Values

Extolling "biblical values" in opposition to Muslims with their Qur'an is central to Spencer's and Ye'or's writings in particular. These biblical values are treated as fundamental to, and a foundation for, Western civilisation. Spencer claims that "values" and "moral principles" of Western countries are "rooted in Christian premises", values, and principles that are shared with Judaism but "do not carry over into Islam".[66] These principles are "the fount from which modern ethicists have drawn the concept of universal human rights—the foundation of Western secular culture".[67] This is both a celebration of "the foundation of Western secular culture" and a way of grounding Western culture firmly in the "Judeo-Christian".[68] This "truth" must be unapologetically told about Christianity and Judeo-Christian culture.[69] Western bookstores "groan" under an avalanche of anti-Christian books and attacks "on Christian history and doctrine".[70] This is "an integral part of a larger effort to instil a sense of cultural shame in even non-Christian European and American youth—a shame that militates against their thinking the West is even worth defending".[71] Spencer is clear on the current situation and on what is needed:

---

[66] Spencer, *Religion of Peace?*, p. 3.
[67] Ibid.
[68] Ibid.
[69] Ibid.
[70] Ibid., p. 2.
[71] Ibid.

If it is widely recognized, however, that the War on Terror is in fact a struggle against an Islamic jihad that would conquer and subjugate Western non-Muslims, and which is well on its way to doing so in Europe, then Western countries face a choice. They can acquiesce to the demands of their Muslim populations and, little by little, adopt provisions of Islamic sharia law until the Islamic social order is fully implemented. Or they can choose to stand up for Judeo-Christian values and defend them against the ideological challenge of jihad and sharia. Knowledge of the differences between Christianity and Islam is central to this effort.[72]

Judeo-Christian values, therefore, have been forgotten and—worse—repressed, and are key to the effort of standing up for the West and saving it from Islam. Although Fjordman is more ambivalent as to the significance of Christianity, he follows this view, stating that our "Western 'moral and ethical values' are profoundly influenced by Judeo-Christian thinking".[73] In another article he underscores that he "acknowledges and respects the impact of Judeo-Christian thinking on Western culture".[74] Fjordman cites the Catholic historian Christopher Dawson to make the point that religion is what provides a cohesive force in a society and that great religions are the foundations for great civilisations.[75] Further, Fjordman mentions the German philosopher Johann Gottfried von Herder to support the idea that "modern scientific reason was the product of European cultures of reason, the world-historical encounter between Biblical faith and Greek philosophical inquiry".[76]

One of the key arguments of Spencer's *Religion of Peace? Why Christianity Is and Islam Isn't* is that the Bible does not encourage violence, while the Qur'an does. The Bible, in this view, has inspired values of non-violence: this is part of what Spencer sees as the civilisational superiority of the "Judeo-Christian West". The claim is made partly based on interpretations of biblical texts, partly on their impact throughout history, and partly on modes of reading in which Christians and Jews are said to have successfully

---

[72] Ibid., p. 5.
[73] Fjordman, 'The Church—Part of the Problem or Part of the Solution?', p. 689. Fjordman discusses in this article the way Christianity has meant compassion and love of enemies. He considers this form of Christianity to be problematic. See also, 'Thou Shalt Hate Christianity and Judaism', in Section 2.84 of the manifesto.
[74] Fjordman, 'Thou Shalt Hate Christianity and Judaism', p. 691.
[75] Ibid., p. 692.
[76] Ibid., p. 693.

safeguarded their scripture from violent use, whereas Muslims have not. When Spencer mentions Osama bin Laden quoting the Qur'an, he notes that "bin Laden's use of these and other passages in his messages is consistent (as we shall see) with traditional Islamic understandings of the Qur'an".[77] According to Spencer, Islam has "no interpretive tradition of the Qur'an comparable to the traditional Jewish and Christian approaches to the Bible".[78] Christians and Jews have utilised "symbolic, allegorical, historical, or poetic" language and modes of reading, while "Islam is much more literal, even when the text of the Qur'an itself is opaque and confusing—and the jihad passages in the Qur'an are anything but a dead letter".[79] *All* Muslims are said to accept the necessity of jihad, and the aid of jihad is understood as "expansionist, imperialist, totalitarian, and globalist".[80] He concludes that violent passages in the Bible are simply "not equivalent to those in the Qur'an in content, in mainstream interpretation, or in the effect they have had on believers through the ages".[81] It is, according to him, dangerously misleading to act as if Christianity and Islam have similar problems of violence in their scriptural traditions.[82]

Spencer goes on to argue that the Qur'an is much worse than the New Testament also when it comes to slavery,[83] that there are cases of modern slavery in Muslim countries today,[84] and that far from being an occurrence of violent Christianity, the crusades "were a late and small-scale response to Islamic jihad conquests that began 450 years before the First Crusade and overwhelmed what had been up to the time of these conquests over half of Christendom".[85] The "cultural Left" has, according to Spencer, spread notions of the relative equivalence between the Bible and the Qur'an, as well as fostered guilt in the "Western consciousness" about the crusades, to such a detrimental extent that if such attitudes are "not reversed, quickly and decisively, our very survival could be at stake".[86] In this way a Bible of Western values is invoked as a counterpoint to Islam and an ally to the counterjihad cause. The Bible becomes evidence of a civilisational superiority, tied to

---

[77] Spencer, *Religion of Peace?* p. 70.
[78] Ibid.
[79] Ibid.
[80] Ibid., p. 84.
[81] Ibid., pp. 85–86.
[82] Ibid., p. 86.
[83] Ibid., pp. 92–94.
[84] Ibid., p. 97.
[85] Ibid., p. 99.
[86] Ibid., p. 103.

secular governance and non-violent practices. But this Bible is also what is forgotten and undefended in today's world. Recovering pride in the so-called Judeo-Christian values of the Bible is a key part of Spencer's counterjihad agenda.

Similarly, Ye'or undergirds her idea of Eurabia with reference to the shared biblical values of Jews and Christians in opposition to Muslims. In the collected writings, *Understanding Dhimmitude*, Ye'or only intermittently evokes particular biblical texts, but she continuously makes use of the phrase "People of the Book" to signify the joint condition of Jews and Christians as proponents of "Biblical values".[87] She uses the term to cement the "Judeo-Christian" as a strong category with a shared scripture, set apart from Muslims with their scripture. While "biblical values" remains an obscure but omnipresent phrase, these values are taken to be uniquely compatible with and even constitutive of Western civilisation. Western civilisation, in turn, is starkly contrasted with Islam and Muslim countries. Like Spencer, then, Ye'or assumes that a focus on biblical values will erect and hold in place a strong distinction with Islamic or Qur'anic values. Whether or not one is religious is irrelevant; civilisations are seen to be steeped in ancient scriptures that have permeated the history of different territories, cultures, and peoples. Invoking the Bible as a foundation of Western civilisation appears to be a benign way of spouting truisms about the influence of Christianity and its scripture on Europe. But these kinds of truisms can quickly slide into a rhetoric of superiority and essentialised difference. Bible in this setting becomes a machine for producing biblical values. These biblical values are often not specified or outlined; they function more as boundary markers that enclose a "Judeo-Christian" people inside one culture and exclude Muslims from this culture.

Fjordman and Fallaci slide straight into the type of superiority-mongering that is part of this Bible-use. Fjordman compares the Muslim views of God to Jewish and Christian views of God, stating that the former views God as unpredictable while the latter as more predictable.[88] He laments the decline of Western civilisation in relation to what he calls "the most barbaric cultures and regimes on earth".[89] Fjordman claims that Islam has never produced "reasonable and prosperous communities", while "our" "traditional

---

[87] Ye'or, *Understanding Dhimmitude*, pp. 126, 219. Ye'or refers to "People of the Book" throughout the book, because it is the term used of Christians and Jews under Islamic law (also referred to as "dhimmis"). In Islamic law, the status of "People of the Book" signifies the protection rather than the persecution of Christians and Jews.

[88] Fjordman, 'Western vs. Islamic Science and Religion', in Section 1.23 of the manifesto, p. 258.

[89] Ibid., p. 259.

Judeo-Christian religions" have done so.[90] However, as a self-declared "not very religious person", Fjordman is more ambivalent about Christianity and raises the point that Christianity can be "a bridge for Islam to enter the West, rather than a bulwark against it".[91] Citing the blogger Vanishing American, Fjordman acknowledges that "Christianity contains elements of both militancy and pacifism, but it is not one or the other".[92] Ultimately, he believes Christianity has lost some of its medieval elements, which has weakened it,[93] and that church leaders have sold out Christianity.[94]

While Fallaci declares herself an atheist, it is noteworthy that she calls herself a "*Christian* atheist".[95] The "religion in which our culture is steeped" is, she insists, Christianity.[96] In Jesus and in Christianity, Fallaci sees the rejection of death, which she calls the principle that "leads and feeds our civilization".[97] Jesus and Paul are credited with inspiring secularism.[98] Fallaci appeals to the "roots" of Europe to save Western civilisation. She says she is a Christian atheist because she likes the "discourse which stays at the roots of Christianity", not the dogma, liturgies, and priests that have come later.[99] Fallaci is vocal in her criticism of the Catholic Church and of particular Catholic priests. When she laments the effects of "Islamisation" in Italy and more broadly in Europe, it is a loss of Christian culture that she laments. Her polemic about how education in schools is being de-Christianised is telling for how she sees European history, philosophy, art, and music as suffused in Christianity. If Italy continues on its current course, according to her, history lessons could no longer "speak of Jesus nor of his Apostles. Nor of Barabbas and Pontius Pilate. Nor of the Christians and of their Catacombs. Nor of Constantine and of the Holy Roman Empire".[100] She complains:

> Philosophy courses should cancel the world of Saint Augustine and Thomas Aquinas, of Luther and Calvin, of Descartes and Pascal etcetera. History

---

[90] Fjordman, 'Thou Shalt Hate Christianity and Judaism', p. 693.
[91] Fjordman, 'Christianity, Pros and Cons', in Section 2.82 of the manifesto, p. 684.
[92] Ibid., p. 685.
[93] Ibid.
[94] Fjordman, 'The Church—Part of the Problem or Part of the Solution?', cited in Section 2.83 in the manifesto, p. 686.
[95] Fallaci, *The Force of Reason*, pp. 185–186 (my emphasis).
[96] Ibid., p. 111.
[97] Fallaci, *The Force of Reason*, p. 189.
[98] Ibid., p. 188. Fallaci briefly alludes to the story recorded in three of the Gospels known popularly as "Render unto Caesar" (Matthew 22:15–22; Mark 12:13–17; Luke 20:20–26).
[99] Ibid., p. 186.
[100] Ibid., p. 111.

of Art courses should ignore all the Christs and the Madonnas of Giotto and Masaccio, of Beato Angelico and Filippino Lippi, of Verrocchio and Mantegna, of Raffaello and Leonardo da Vinci and Michelangelo. Music should eliminate all the Gregorian chants, all the Requiems starting with Mozart's and Haydn's and Verdi's *Requiem*, and woe betide the teacher who asks to sing Schubert's *Ave Maria*.[101]

Here we have the biblical and the Christian presented as European culture and civilisation. Biblical values are endemic to the Europe she holds up for her readership; Islam, in turn, is presented as an alien force coming from the outside to the inside to destroy the treasures of European civilisation. She talks of safeguarding the "water of our essence, of our civilization. The water of our identity".[102] It is Western civilisation that is at stake here, and the Bible is at the roots of this civilisation.

When it comes to particular views of the Bible, Fallaci complains about "the beautiful monument which stood before the State Judicial Building of Birmingham, Alabama": a marble Bible. On the open pages of the marble Bible the Ten Commandments are listed. Fallaci calls these "the genesis of our moral principles".[103] As she tells the story, this marble Bible was much loved by the people of Birmingham, but "one ugly day the representatives of the tiny Muslim minority began muttering that the Ten Commandments had been written by the Jew Moses, that showing them in public clearly favoured Judaic-Christian culture, and the Politically Correct brigade sided with Allah".[104] The marble Bible itself is a supreme example of the Civilisation Bible, representing "our" "moral principles" or, in Ye'or's term, "biblical values", celebrated as a core fixture of Western identity and culture. The way this Bible is dismantled is symbolic of the much broader sense in which she tells the story of a biblically founded Europe being dismantled due to a sneaking Islamic imperialism. The story Fallaci tells of this Bible in Alabama hints at the role a Bible is supposed to play for Western civilisation: an oversized Bible, monumentalised and memorialised as the marble foundation for Western values.[105] This is not a Bible to be read, but to be revered.

---

[101] Ibid., p. 112.
[102] Ibid., p. 152.
[103] Ibid., p. 250.
[104] Ibid., p. 251.
[105] For a discussion of monumentalising, see Mattias Martinson, 'Towards a "Theology" of Christian Monumentality: Post-Christian Reflections on Grace and Nature', in *Monument and Memory*, edited by Jonna Bornemark, Mattias Martinson, and Jayne Svenungsson (Berlin: Lit Verlag,

Spencer and Ye'or share this idea of the Bible. They invoke a civilisational Bible, denoting the "values" they claim are at the core of Western culture. These foundational core values are in stark opposition to other cultures, primarily, Islamic culture. This is a grand Bible grounded in grandiose claims to civilisational superiority. The Bible is not only a building-block in this construction of Western civilisation, but also its very foundation, preferably fixed in marble, proudly presented on a public square.

The notion of Western values and civilisation for Spencer, Ye'or, Fjordman, and Fallaci, then, is assembled with a Bible that supports the Civilisation Bible assemblage. The Bible I have mapped here is not read but revered and produces "biblical values" that have in turn become Western values. The Jesus that is assembled from biblical texts by Spencer and Fallaci, however, supports the War Bible that we see in Breivik's manifesto.

The Sword-bearing Jesus

As I discussed in the previous chapter, part of the War Bible in Breivik's manifesto is an appeal to the "good soldiers of Christ". Jesus does not come up much otherwise in the manifesto. But the figure of Jesus is more prevalent for Spencer and Fallaci in ways that support Breivik's War Bible: in other words, the idea of defensive violence that is supported by the Bible and by a warmongering Christian God.

While he argues for the peacefulness of Christianity in contrast to Islam, Spencer calls for Christians—and in particular Catholics—to "take up a sword".[106] Citing Jesus's call for a sword (Matthew, 10:34), and Paul's 'sword of the Spirit' (Ephesians 6:17), Spencer encourages a battle against the rise of Islam and the Islamisation of the West. While his argument in many ways hinges on the claim that Christianity and Christian scripture do not encourage violence (in contrast to Islam and the Qur'an), there is a tension in his writings between defence and active violence. Spencer's "sword" is, as he states, "not the sword of conquest and subjugation" but a spiritual sword, namely, Paul's "word of God" (Ephesians 6:17).[107] However, as he does not

2015), pp. 21–42; Mattias Martinson, *Sekularism, populism, xenofobi: En essä om religionsdebatten* (Malmö: Eskaton, 2017).

[106] Robert Spencer, *Not Peace but a Sword: The Great Chasm Between Christianity and Islam* (San Diego, CA: Catholic Answers, 2013), p. 186.
[107] Ibid.

believe in the possibility of interreligious dialogue and affirms repeatedly the "irreconcilability between the calls for Christian-Muslim cooperation and the trend of anti-Christian violence committed by Muslims", what might a solution look like if not a violent uprising, couched in the language of "defence" and heroic (violent) "martyrdom?"[108] Fjordman has a similar style of rhetoric, although he does not cite biblical texts to back up his point. He writes that:

> Christians need to understand that there can be no peace or understanding with the Islamic world. They want to subdue us, pure and simple. Church leaders of all denominations, Protestant, Catholic, Orthodox, must stop stabbing Israel in the back and campaigning for a de facto open borders policy while Muslims are threatening to swamp our lands. Yes, Christianity teaches compassion, but it also teaches identifying evil and standing up to it. At the end of the day, the Church must decide whether, in the defence of civilisation, it wants to be a part of the problem or a part of the solution.[109]

Spencer states that there is not a "new Crusade, but Christians in Muslim lands are being victimized more relentlessly and brutally today than they have been for centuries".[110] The "but" here is significant. The media are, according to him, covering this up and so no action will be taken, except by those such as himself who alert others of the grave dangers of Islam.

In writing repeatedly of "the war against Christians"[111] and "renewed persecution of Christians",[112] Spencer propagates "chilling" stories of Muslims killing their Christian neighbours with their bare hands,[113] blaming "multiculturalist tastes" for the disregard of Islam as a violent force.[114] "Westerners", he writes, must overcome their self-hatred and self-loathing guilt and rise up against the enemy.[115] As Bangstad explains, "central to the popular credibility of the 'Eurabia' genre is the contention that whatever the context, Muslims—regardless of their backgrounds, levels of religious belief and

---

[108] Ibid., p. 17. This book was not published at the time of Breivik's terror on 22 July 2011, but his book *Religion of Peace: Why Christianity Is and Islam Isn't* (Washington, DC: Regnery Publishing, 2007) was published, and Spencer shared many of these views on his blog *Jihad Watch*.
[109] Fjordman, 'The Church—Part of the Problem or Part of the Solution?'.
[110] Spencer, *Not Peace but a Sword*, p. 18.
[111] Ibid., p. 24.
[112] Ibid.
[113] Ibid.
[114] Ibid., p. 28.
[115] Ibid., p. 29.

practice, or political views—are essentially one and the same: instruments of a 1,400-year-old Islamic struggle to establish Islamic control over Europe".[116] Spencer's rhetoric mimics military jargon and calls for bravery in fighting a battle, a trait often used by terrorists in portraying themselves as "(freedom) fighters, if not soldiers".[117] Spencer states that "there is simply no group anywhere in the world today that is committing violent acts and justifying them by quoting the Bible and invoking Christianity. But there are many, many groups committing violent acts and justifying them by quoting the Qur'an and invoking Islam".[118]

Of course—setting aside other examples for the moment—Breivik does precisely this. In his discussion about whether the Bible is as violent as the Qur'an, Spencer emphasises that violent biblical passages are descriptive rather than prescriptive; they "are not commands for all generations to follow, and if they have any applicability, it is only in a spiritualized, parabolic sense".[119] Spencer states that biblical texts do not contain "a call to action for Christians to commit acts of violence".[120] But his insistence on a "defence of the West against today's global jihad" (described as a "wake-up call"),[121] his fearmongering rhetoric, and stories about Muslims killing their Christian neighbours with their bare hands,[122] seem to call precisely for a taking up of arms. The epigraph to *Not Peace but a Sword* is a paean to "Christian martyrs" of Islamic jihad—imagery Breivik adopted in militarised form in his manifesto.

Spencer emphasises the irreconcilability and impossibility of Islamic and Christian cooperation and the insurmountable differences between the two faiths, and he relentlessly sets out the systematic victimisation and victimhood of Christians by Muslims. If the situation is as dire as Spencer paints it, it is not difficult to see how Jesus's and Paul's "spiritual" swords might be swapped for real ones. As I mentioned in the previous chapter, the story of Jesus telling his disciples to buy a sword in Luke 22:36 is cited in Breivik's manifesto: "He [Jesus] said to them, 'But now, the one who has a purse must take it, and likewise a bag. And the one who has no sword must sell his cloak and buy one".[123] As Jackson has shown from analysing writings Breivik cited,

[116] Bangstad, *Anders Breivik and the Rise of Islamophobia*, p. 152.
[117] Hoffman, *Inside Terrorism*, p. 26.
[118] Spencer, *Religion of Peace*, p. 109
[119] Ibid., p. 64.
[120] Ibid., p. 67.
[121] Ibid., p. 4.
[122] Spencer, *Not Peace but a Sword*, p. 24.
[123] Manifesto, p. 1328.

when mainstream politics is presented as untenable then the need for more radical solutions arises, whether such radical solutions are spelled out or not.[124] "Us/them narratives that dehumanize the other make it easier to take life, and metaphors such as 'civil war', 'occupation,' and 'traitors' help justify the use of violence".[125] The potential for violence becomes stronger "when a collective identity is formed around the belief that it is beset by an existential threat, where culture and survival are at stake".[126]

In *The Force of Reason*, Fallaci goes further than Spencer in her celebration of a particular biblical Jesus. She starts by rejecting the idea of a pacifist Jesus. Citing the Gospel of Matthew 10:34–35, she states: "'Think not that I am come to bring peace on earth', he said. 'I came not to bring peace, I came to bring a sword. I came to separate the son from the father, the daughter from the mother, the daughter in law from the mother in law'".[127] In Fallaci's critique of a Catholic priest for being on the side of the Islamic "invaders", she reimagines Jesus's disdain for the Temple's Pharisee merchants turned on the priest. According to Fallaci's assessment of Jesus, he "would have kicked your ass and thrown you out into the square and here he would have smashed so hard your face that today you would not even be able to eat a tomato soup".[128] The Jesus who Fallaci invokes is an ass-kicking brute who seems like a character from a Tarantino film.

Seemingly aware that there is a less antagonistic Jesus in the Bible, she declares that she does not believe in the "masochism of turning the other cheek".[129] Fjordman, too, distances himself from the cheek-turning Jesus by acknowledging that this is part of a Christian Bible that he alleges shows weakness and weakens the battle against "sharia".[130] He warns against what he calls "naive Christian compassion" when it comes to Muslim immigration, and the "disturbing tendency among too many Christian organisations to ally themselves with Muslims".[131] Like Spencer, Fallaci believes in words as weapons, but Fallaci admits that, should words not be enough, she is "ready to make war with something more".[132] Calling the current state of Europe a "war" situation, she states that her war is legitimate, dutiful, and right.[133] Here

---

[124] Jackson, 'The License to Hate'.
[125] Berntzen and Sandberg, 'The Collective Nature of Lone Wolf Terrorism', p. 772.
[126] Ibid.
[127] Fallaci, *The Force of Reason*, p. 19.
[128] Ibid., pp. 179–180.
[129] Ibid., p. 23.
[130] Fjordman, 'The Church—Part of the Problem or Part of the Solution?', p. 689.
[131] Fjordman, 'Thou Shalt Hate Christianity and Judaism', p. 691.
[132] Fallaci, *The Force of Reason*, p. 23.
[133] Ibid., p. 24.

is the War Bible, in which European Christians—atheist or not—are victims of Muslims who are said to "butcher the lambs like Dracula".[134] If Muslims are bloodthirsty and out to make Europe "a province of Islam, a colony of Islam",[135] Fallaci and her sympathisers are merely refusing to turn the other cheek and rather bring not peace but a sword. Muslims, she claims, have always excelled in "invading and conquering and subjugating": their most "coveted prey has always been Europe, the Christian world".[136] Christians in Europe are merely picking up arms, following Jesus, in defensive response to what is portrayed as unambiguous Muslim aggression.

Fallaci appears to suggest that the Jesus of modern Christianity has been "elaborated and distorted",[137] and what she is doing is reactivating a Jesus of the Gospels who can inspire an aggressive response to the status quo as she conveys it. Jesus, she writes, blasts against slavery and "fights" like a man.[138] Again, displaying her knowledge of an alternative Jesus-assemblage, Fallaci calls her readership to forget Jesus's meekness, "his sweetness, his tenderness, his let-the-children-come-to-me".[139] She muses: "I often wonder if Jesus of Nazareth's temperament really was that meek, that sweet, that tender. And each time I answer myself: maybe not, I guess not".[140] Emphasising his manliness, she writes that "he takes his fists to the pharisees and to the rabbis who profit by religion".[141]

To sum up, a sword-bearing Jesus is held up as an icon for both Spencer and Fallaci. With his distaste for the cheek-turning Jesus, it seems likely Fjordman, too, would prefer this hyper-masculine action-man-Jesus. The Jesus they invoke plugs straight into what I called the War Bible, in that they both appeal to "defensive" violence against what they insistently convey as an essentially violent enemy: Islam. Berntzen and Sandberg note that although references to violence and war in anti-Islamic movements are not meant literally, "they serve to highlight the severity of the current situation. In this way, they work as effective motivational framing".[142] "In Breivik's manifesto, the war metaphors of the movement become real".[143] But what does "literally"

---

[134] Ibid., p. 26.
[135] Ibid., p. 34.
[136] Ibid., p. 36.
[137] Ibid., p. 187.
[138] Ibid., p. 189.
[139] Ibid., p. 188.
[140] Ibid.
[141] Ibid.
[142] Berntzen and Sandberg, 'The Collective Nature of Lone Wolf Terrorism', p. 766.
[143] Ibid., p. 771.

mean here? Figures such as Spencer and Fallaci may not endorse Breivik's terrorist violence, but they do call for violence. Bits of Bible are assembled to build a Jesus who does not turn the other cheek—a sword-bearing Jesus who can fight back. While for Spencer, he extols the martyr figure who dies in the fight against Islam, Fallaci celebrates an aggressive macho Jesus figure who does not pull his punches.

The Prophetic Voice

As I already mentioned, Bruce Bawer is the least "biblical" of the five figures I am discussing in this chapter. The only hint at anything biblical in his book *When Europe Slept* comes when Bawer calls the "liberal resistance" to Islamic conquest "prophets and martyrs".[144] The performance of prophetic voice and martyrdom is not isolated, though. As I have just shown, martyrdom as a heroic act against the so-called threats of Islam is called for by Spencer. The self-presentation as prophets is in turn shared with Ye'or and Fallaci. The language of prophecy underlines the way these writers present themselves as unpopular truth-tellers. Further, through their suffering in this truth-telling, they are martyrs for the cause. They are destabilising the status quo, but by invoking the image of themselves or others like them as biblical prophets, they are attempting to situate themselves as righteous, concerned citizens, pointing to the truths most people fail—or refuse—to see.

Bawer uses the language of prophets and martyrs to emphasise the unpopular "truths" being told by brave individuals who sacrifice themselves to the cause of saving Europe from the "threats" of Islam. The Dutch politician and author of *Against the Islamization of Our Culture*, Pim Fortuyn, is one of the prime prophetic voices and martyrs to the cause for Bawer. Fortuyn is held up as Western Europe's "martyred prophet of immigration and integration reform".[145] The Dutch film director Theo Van Gogh is another person who features centrally for Bawer as a "martyr" figure.[146] As someone intent on showing what Bawer thinks is the truth about Islam, Van Gogh's death signals the martyrdom of a truth-teller. While Bawer does not use the language of prophecy about Ayaan Hirsi Ali, she, too, is held up as someone willing to unveil the ugly "truth" about Islam to the world, and who, he laments, is not

---

[144] Bawer, *While Europe Slept*, p. 163.
[145] Ibid., p. 180.
[146] Ibid., pp. 193–200.

sufficiently listened to.[147] Bawer repeatedly complains about the European establishment and the "multicultural elite" supposedly "allied with the Islamic right".[148] This is part of the case made that most people are blinded to this alliance. Only the enlightened and embattled few righteously strive to reveal the truth.[149] Bawer's own book is part of this worldview. The very title—*While Europe Slept*—is a way of positioning him as the prophet who is wide awake while the rest of us are dozing. He states that what is needed are uncomfortable truths regarding Islam and a rejection of "nice" and "naïve" statements about integration and multiculturalism. Bawer's Bible here is slim if at all existent. His language of prophecy is at most a nod to a biblical prophetic tradition. But this admiration for "truth-tellers" who martyr themselves fits nicely into the more explicitly Christian and biblical language of taking up a sword and dying for the cause as a soldier of Christ, which can be found in the counterjihadist writings and in Breivik's manifesto.

Fallaci sees herself as a prophetic type, although she likens herself to a heretic rather than a prophet. For her, organised religion is the historical censor of truth, just as she sees the current-day Catholic Church as taking the side of Muslim immigrants. The trope is similar to the prophetic one, though. Fallaci likens herself to Cassandra, the Trojan priestess in Greek mythology who is cursed to tell the truths that no one believes. The effect of this kind of posturing is that of righteous courage. Fallaci continually speaks of her refusal to give in to criticism, positioning herself as a courageous and heroic prophetic figure, willing to die for her truth. Fallaci does not use the Bible for this posturing, though the anti-establishment, violent Jesus she describes elsewhere connects to her own self-presentation as an angry, courageous truth-teller.

Ye'or similarly presents herself as a truth-teller facing grave danger for the truths she tells. She evokes a Bible to support her prophetic role in a more explicit way. The "truth" Ye'or speaks of is pertinent because, she ceaselessly repeats, it is a history that is being reactivated in the present by Islamic jihad.[150] Islam began as a "conquering faith"[151] and "the knowledge of the

---

[147] Ibid., pp. 190–193. It is interesting that while Ayaan Hirsi Ali was previously considered among the proponents of "New Atheism" she has recently converted to Christianity. See her own account of this conversion: Ayaan Hirsi Ali, 'Why I am Now a Christian: Atheism Can't Equip Us for Civilisational War', *Unherd*, 11 November 2023, https://unherd.com/2023/11/why-i-am-now-a-christian/ (last accessed May 2024).
[148] Bawer, *While Europe Slept*, p. 212.
[149] Ibid.,
[150] Ye'or, *Understanding Dhimmitude*, p. 53.
[151] Ibid., p. 35.

136 THE BIBLES OF THE FAR RIGHT

history of the dhimmi people is essential for a deeper understanding of contemporary events in the Muslim world".[152] The aim of terrorists "is to force us all to live in the shadow of dhimmitude in Europe".[153] This state of affairs engenders fear and cowardice and has, she states, spread from the Muslim world to Europe.[154] These are "acts of war against Europe"; "European leaders are doing nothing".[155] The rising up of a prophetic voice is, then, a lonely one facing the enemy of Islam but also the enemy of indifference. But Ye'or's prophetic voice is also clearly an affirmation of the innocent "lambs" who are being slaughtered by Muslims. In other words, the idea of "righteous victims" is paramount here. Like Spencer, Ye'or argues for the non-violence of the Bible compared to the Qur'an. She admits there are violent elements in biblical texts but qualifies them by suggesting that "the prophetic texts allow different interpretations from the old, legalistic one".[156] Ye'or cites Ezekiel 33:11: "I have no pleasure in the death of the wicked; but that the wicked turn from his way and live".[157] Building on this citation, she explains the need for testimony and responsibility decreed by the Bible. The Bible "testifies to a supra-human and an immanent order of values or, more simply, to a divine presence within the universe and humanity".[158] Genesis 1:27 demonstrates the "partnership between God and man" which is "a dual responsibility freely accepted by man, for keeping or testifying to these supreme ethical norms based on the sanctity of all humans".[159] Ye'or assumes a divine-human partnership in which humans are obliged to stand up for certain norms.

The role of testifier—a role Ye'or clearly casts herself in—is in her view to be assumed by the "People of Israel", due to their history of victimhood.[160] For Ye'or, the Bible "illustrates the constant struggle between the testifier and the destroyer of life or the hater of man".[161] Such a testimony involves "standing up against a tyrant, denouncing injustice, proclaiming the dignity of all humanity", in the hope that the "heart of the tyrant will change".[162] Using the words of the Psalms, she writes: "'I will speak of thy testimonies

[152] Ibid., p. 39.
[153] Ibid., p. 52.
[154] Ibid., p. 53.
[155] Ibid.
[156] Ibid., p. 123.
[157] Ibid., p. 185.
[158] Ibid., pp. 185–186.
[159] Ibid., p. 186.
[160] Ibid.
[161] Ibid.
[162] Ibid.

also before kings, and will not be ashamed' (119:46)".[163] The tyrannical injustice here is clearly intended to be read as Islam. Ye'or speaks of a war against "Europe" and "the West" frequently, and emphatically calls for acknowledgement that jihad is happening not only against Israel but against all non-Muslims. "The will to destroy Israel is linked with the age-old war against Christendom".[164] The Bible, then, is a driver for testimonial "truth-telling", in which Ye'or appears as a pseudo-prophetic figure "on an explosive, dangerous, and lonely path", in a "fight for truth", a message driven home repeatedly in *Understanding Dhimmitude*.[165] The righteous victimhood of Jews and Christians is part of the picture she paints in making Muslims not just other but utterly tyrannical. Ye'or's Bible, then, is one that supports her "prophetic" mission and one that reminds her of the righteous victimhood that is part of the past and, crucially, part of the present.

The focus on prophetic voices and prophets risking martyrdom plays into the War Bible because of its defensive appeal. The counterjihadists are not the aggressors, they are rather the prophets. They are thus cast in the minority, while Muslims and their allies amongst European elites are the majority. The mainstream is presented as people who are naïve to what is going on in the world. Casting their political proclamations about the dangers of Islam as prophetic is a way of claiming truth on their side. It is a way of casting an anti-Islamic message as simply an unveiling of the situation, rather than a hate-filled, toxic racism that fuels xenophobia and stokes violence. Drawing on the biblical prophetic tradition, in which prophets were frequently unpopular and marginalised figures called by God, is a way for counterjihadists to invoke pity and self-present as victims. This sense of pity and righteous defence, favoured by God, is what Breivik's War Bible is fuelled by. The violence of the War Bible is not relished for its violence, but is portrayed as necessary defensive action undertaken by heroic, courageous individuals who are called by God to a task. This task emerges due to the unveiling of the so-called truths that figures like Bawer and Fallaci spout.

Self-presentations of prophets and martyr-like prophets in dangerous situations due to their truth-telling, then, are an important part of the tone and performance of the counterjihadist milieu that Breivik was inspired by. In this milieu, a Bible can function as an archive that demonstrates prophetic

---

[163] Ibid.
[164] Ibid., p. 54.
[165] Ibid., p. 18.

voices of the past, but it can also stand in as a less visible object that supplies vague ideas and memories of prophetic-style voices. Whether they explicitly cite biblical prophetic voices or not, Bawer, Fallaci, and Ye'or function as prophetic mouthpieces and call other anti-Islam activists "prophets" in order to ground their proclamations as truth, as above other viewpoints. As in the case of Bawer, a Bible does not need to be explicit for this Bible-use to function. Bawer's prophetic martyrs can be fully secularised, sanitised of any biblical references. A Bible is not necessarily needed to self-present as a modern-day prophet risking everything to tell the world uncomfortable truths. For others in the counterjihadist milieu, such as Ye'or, the connection between prophetic voice and biblical texts is explicit. In any case, prophetic voice becomes one way to self-present proclamations as unpopular truths and in this way present both the modern-day "prophets" as heroic and the proclamations as matters to die for.

The prophetic voice performance amongst these figures is part of Breivik's War Bible. What is defended is a culture or civilisation rooted in biblical values, which connects the War Bible and the Civilisation Bible. Presenting the counterjihadist movement and its Eurabia followers as "prophetic", even martyred prophets, casts anti-Muslim tirades and conspiracies as a truth that is hidden from most people and that needs to be acted upon. Europe needs to be defended, and only brave individuals who believe the prophets' proclamations will be part of saving Europe. In this way, Breivik's War Bible is stabilised as part of the righteous justification for violence and as part of proper *defensive* action of the "real" victims—namely those prophets who are demonised for telling the truth. Further, the implied divine authority of anyone who casts themselves or others as prophets plays right into Breivik's own War Bible, in which violence is divinely authorised.

Counterjihadist Scripts and Scripture

In this chapter I have turned to the figures on the far right who are central to Breivik's worldview and who are mentioned in the manifesto, though I have examined writings by these figures that are not explicitly cited by Breivik. These thought-leaders have all written books and blogs, given talks and produced web pages that propagate the Eurabia conspiracy and the counterjihadist views that inspired the 22 July terrorist attacks. The material produced by Spencer, Ye'or, Fjordman, Fallaci, and Bawer targets Muslims as the enemy and decries the current state of Europe. In the previous chapter I suggested that the two biblical assemblages at work in Breivik's manifesto were the Civilisation Bible and the War Bible. My aim in this chapter was to analyse the Bible-use in key thought-leaders for Breivik to identify potential connections and continuities. I was not interested in making the case that there is a causal relationship between these texts and Breivik's Bible-use in the manifesto. It is irrelevant whether Breivik did or did not read the texts that I have discussed here. On the contrary, my purpose was to map to what extent the biblical assemblages I identified in Breivik's manifesto are connected to, and continuous with, the kind of Bible-use that is operative in the far-right sources he was most inspired by in his Islamophobic worldview. I outlined three modes of Bible-use that are key for these far-right figures, namely biblical values, the sword-bearing Jesus, and prophetic voice. I pointed to continuities and connections between the Civilisation and War Bibles at work in the manifesto and the kinds of writings produced by Breivik's ideological heroes.

As I discussed in the last chapter, the Civilisation Bible is a Bible that is celebrated and revered in the manifesto, not as a book to be read much, but as a foundation for Western civilisation. The idea of a "Western civilisation" is one that is inextricably associated with the "Judeo-Christian"; it is closed to other civilisations, and it is held up as superior. The clash of cultures that is part of this thinking is grounded in religiously oriented cultures. Spencer, Ye'or, Fjordman, and Fallaci all hold up "biblical values" as core to Western civilisation. They lament a loss of the Bible in mainstream Western culture, which they see in tandem with the decline of the West. Civilisational decay goes hand in hand with biblical decay. A Bible can operate as a machine producing biblical values that will ensure the maintenance of European culture and simultaneously protect this culture from its "outside" elements. Only with a renewed pride in, and recovery of, the scriptural core of Western civilisation can Islam be held at bay.

The War Bible that I argued was at work in Breivik's manifesto consisted of multiple biblical verses strung together to emphasise the idea of a righteous battle, with God on the side of the counterjihadists. This biblical assemblage is not present in quite this form in the counterjihadist writers who inspired Breivik. A version of the War Bible, however, is present. This version highlights Jesus as a sword-bearing heroic figure, willing to fight and die for the cause. The distaste shown by Fjordman and Fallaci towards a cheek-turning Jesus is matched by a desire for a more macho Jesus-figure to "defend" Europe against Muslims. The emphasis on the prophetic voice by Bawer, Fallaci, and Ye'or plays into notions of a righteous truth-teller who is telling uncomfortable and unpopular truths for the sake of the good, but is not heard, and is even in danger of being martyred for the cause. The figures in the counterjihadist milieu who propagate the Eurabia conspiracy, then, operate with particular invocations of a Bible that support their anti-Islam cause.

But there are other connections and continuities that are important to tease out when it comes to the War Bible and the Civilisation Bible—connections and continuities that are less directly tied to the counterjihadist milieu I have examined in this chapter. More oblique references that do not point towards the central figures in the far-right worldview that Breivik bought into are also at work. There is more to these assemblages, both inside and outside Breivik's own citational network in the manifesto, when it comes to mapping the emergence and stabilisation of these biblical assemblages. I will continue to ask, then, about the emergence of the War Bible and Civilisation Bible in far-right circles, about how these biblical assemblages work, and what past and present Bible-use play a part in making these assemblages function effectively. In the next chapter I will examine more closely the War Bible and its relations to contemporary US discourses and practices relating to Bibles and politics, as well as to War Bibles of the past.

5
The War Bible

For the far-right Rassemblement National in France, Joan of Arc is an iconic religious-nationalist figure whose annual celebration day has been a trademark for the party since 1978.[1] The founder of the party, Jean-Marie Le Pen, connected the legendary figure of Joan of Arc with Jesus, when he stated, quoting the Gospel of Matthew (10:34), that she did not come to bring peace but a sword.[2] The far-right British National Party produced an election poster in 2009 that featured a picture of Jesus and his words as recorded in the Gospel of John (15:20): "If they have persecuted me, they will also persecute you".[3] Paul Golding of Britain First stated in 2021 on social media that his favourite biblical verse is 2 Timothy 2:3: "You therefore must endure hardship, as a good solider of Christ".[4] Violence, persecution, and militant imagery is part and parcel of the contemporary European far right, whether this rhetoric and imagery is practiced or threatened, graphic or more discreet. Bits of Bible have appeared in demonstrations, proclamations, and social media posts over the years, as these examples demonstrate. None of the Bibles that I have mapped so far operate in isolation. Mapping the way Bibles feature and the way biblical texts function in the worldview that Breivik reproduced in his manifesto is only a starting point. These biblical assemblages are, as I have argued, using Sara Ahmed's term, sticky. The biblical assemblages I have mapped are themselves part of larger assemblages. Non-biblical components stick to the biblical assemblages and ensure that they work.

In this and the next chapter, I analyse more closely the War Bible and the Civilization Bible that I identified in chapter 3. This involves digging further into the citational network of Breivik's manifesto. It also involves addressing geographical spread and historical distance. This and the next chapter

---

[1] Roy, 'The French National Front: From Christian Identity to Laïcité', p. 86.
[2] Ibid.
[3] Timothy Peace, 'Religion and Populism in Britain: An Infertile Breeding Ground?', in *Saving the People: How Populists Hijack Religion*, edited by Nadia Marzouki, Duncan McDonnell, and Olivier Roy (London: Hurst & Co, 2016), p. 107.
[4] Britain First official Telegram account, post, 16 April 2021 (last accessed February 2022).

follow a similar structure. First, I tease out further connections in Bible-use through the citational network that Breivik created with his manifesto, then I ask how the War Bible and Civilization Bible activate past Bibles that share tendencies in Bible-use, and third, I gesture towards key non-biblical elements that make these Bibles work. I begin in this chapter with the War Bible, proposing three interrelated arguments. First, I argue that Breivik's War Bible assemblage is connected to two American sources mentioned in the manifesto that are less obviously part of the counterjihadist milieu I covered in the previous chapter. Second, I argue that Breivik's War Bible assemblage cannot be understood as an actualisation only of these two American sources, but of past Bibles used in warfare. Third, and finally, I argue that two non-biblical elements in particular stick to Breivik's War Bible assemblage, namely, the Middle Ages and masculinity.

Continuing my exploration of the figures that appear in Breivik's orbit through the references in his manifesto, I begin this chapter by examining further sources that are highly pertinent for understanding the emergence and stabilisation of the War Bible assemblage I identified in chapter 3. In the previous chapter I began to unpack the way invocations of a sword-bearing Jesus and performances of prophetic voice function in the counterjihadist writings that furnish Breivik's far-right worldview. This Bible-use supports the War Bible found in Breivik's manifesto. But there are also sources alluded to in the manifesto that more directly provide material for the War Bible, at least in terms of the biblical material. I turn, then, first of all to the figures that Mattias Gardell cites as key for Breivik's references to Christianity in his study of Breivik's sources. As I already alluded to in chapter 3, Gardell mentions the fact that Breivik turned to American right-wing Christians for his references to the Bible.[5] As Gardell writes, "Breivik looked across the Atlantic to American right-wing preachers Michael Bradley, founder of the evangelical Bible-Knowledge Ministries, and Joseph Francis Farah, author of the Tea Party manifesto, and editor-in-chief of the conspiracy peddling World Daily Net that Breivik frequented, both of whom are popular among Militia members, the Patriot movement, and Tea Party activists".[6]

In the second part of the chapter, I explore connections with past Bible-use. Histories of Bible-use stick to the War Bible assemblage I have mapped. I aim, then, to begin to map broader historical connections and shared

---

[5] Gardell, 'Crusader Dreams', pp. 145–146.
[6] Ibid., p. 145.

tendencies in Bible-use. I draw out connections with past War Bibles, particularly crusader uses of biblical texts in the Middle Ages and Bible-use during the First World War. My intention is not to exhaustively map all possible connections between the War Bible as I have described it in this study and all Bible-use in warfare—clearly an impossible task. Rather, I have chosen examples of past Bible-use in warfare that shed light on particular tendencies and affects in Bible-use. As I show, part of the "value" of a Bible in warfare can be precisely that it transforms violence into something other than unpalatable violence, such as heroic sacrifice, dutiful defence, even purification.

But there are also non-biblical elements that stick to a Bible to make it work at a particular time. Returning to the present-day far-right uses of a War Bible, then, the final part of the chapter analyses non-biblical components that stick to this biblical assemblage to make it work in the worldview that is propagated. I focus particularly on the Middle Ages and masculinity. These components stick to the War Bible assemblage I have analysed in ways that are relevant far beyond the Breivik case, to far-right ideology and practice more generally, where obsessions with the crusades and fantasies of masculinity are prevalent.

Biblical Battles at Bible-Knwoledge.com

In chapter 3, I mentioned that the main biblical material that makes up Breivik's War Bible assemblage is gathered in one part of the manifesto, namely in the third book. The case I made was that the citations of biblical verses relating to warfare and violence do not operate alone, but work *with* the Eurabia conspiracy and counterjihadist ideology that is so central to the manifesto. These bits of Bible work *with* constructions of the medieval crusades and *alongside* stories about Muslim persecutions of Christians. Together, these components make up a War Bible, where bits of biblical text provide divine authority and protection in the battle, but key motivations and affects that drive this Bible-use lie in the image of the knightly and righteous hero taking up a battle reaching back to the crusades and defending innocent Christians from an eternally threatening Muslim enemy. I demonstrated in chapter 4 that Breivik's War Bible resonates with key far-right thought-leaders, although they do not embrace the acts of violence Breivik actually committed. But the War Bible has further connections than the Eurabia conspiracy-peddlers and the counterjihadist milieu. There are both more direct sources from which Breivik derived his War Bible, and more diffuse networks in which this Bible plays a part. One of these sources is a web page called Bible-Knowledge.com.

Breivik cites this web page as a source for his Bible battle verse selection in the third book of the manifesto. The page is set up and managed by two American brothers, Michael and Chris Bradley. According to the "About us" section on Bible-Knoweldge.com, their "online ministry" started in 2004 and the page went live at the start of 2005.[7] The page is designed, Chris Bradley writes, to "help people grow in their walk with the Lord".[8] He describes how it began with his brother Michael responding to people's problems via email. As a result, they felt "led by the Lord to take these teachings to the world".[9] Michael Bradley died in 2012, but Chris Bradley continues to update the web page, and comments that they have gone from seventy articles on the Bible to four hundred. Chris Bradley describes the development of what he calls "The Power Verse System":

> I have put about 1500 of the most powerful verses in all of the Bible on individual index cards. Each of these Bible verses are grouped into appropriate categories covering different aspects of our walk with the Lord. This is why we have decided to name our website Bible Knowledge. We will be covering a wide range of topics and issues giving you all of the appropriate verses from Scripture to back up what is being taught per subject matter.

The web page has multiple links to articles written on different themes, such as "How the Holy Spirit Communicates to Us" and "Healing Verses of the Bible".[10] The part of the Bradley brothers' web page that is relevant to the War Bible assemblage, and that Breivik cites in a footnote, is their "Battle Verses of the Bible" page. It is attributed to Michael Bradley, but was last updated 23 February 2021.[11] It is not, then, the same as when Breivik consulted it. As I will show, though, there are startling similarities between the biblical verses on the web page and those Breivik cites. In fact, in many cases it seems as if

---

[7] Bible Knowledge Ministries—Bible Teaching Website, https://www.bible-knowledge.com/about-us/ (last accessed June 2024).
[8] Ibid.
[9] Ibid.
[10] At the time of writing, three additional author names have been added to the web page. All three are American women and all are described as Christian authors.
[11] As the article is still attributed to Michael Bradley, I will continue to refer to him as the author even if changes were made to the article after his death.

Breivik has lifted verses directly out of the web page and into his manifesto. The Bible version the Bradley brothers cite is the New King James Version, which is mostly the English-Bible version that Breivik uses in the manifesto.

The "Battle Verses of the Bible" page starts by Bradley positing that he will give the reader "100 of the best battle verses from the Bible", adding that he "cannot stress enough the power that is on these particular verses".[12] Bradley then states that those who have read the Old Testament will know that God does not hesitate to go into battle for his chosen people, the Jews. Bradley emphasises an "absolutely ferocious God" in his defence of his people, and a "strong righteous wrath" in "self-defence".[13] Bradley comments that just as God was defensive of the Jewish people, he is just as defensive of his children today. He is keen to urge Christians to arm themselves for a "spiritual warfare" as "many of God's children are getting beat to a pulp in the playing field of life".[14] He refers to "horror after horror" in the news. Robberies, abductions, and murders are mentioned. The index card method is recommended here, too.[15] It is suggested that the battle verses listed on this page should be written on index cards: "If you are willing to take this kind of extra step with the Lord, then you will have right at your fingertips all of the main battle verses of the Bible".[16] Bradley notes that these battle verses should be incorporated into "your own personal battle prayers when engaging with whatever enemy may have come your way".[17]

As I detailed in chapter 3, the idea of a God who is on the side of his people, the idea of defensive battle, and a God of war are all tenets that make up Breivik's War Bible assemblage. Bradley writes: "Once you have the knowledge on how to get God to move on your behalf in a battle situation—defeating whatever enemy has come your way can then become quite easy, since God is all-powerful and there is nothing that He cannot do—which would include handling any type of storm cloud that may have just come your way".[18] These lines closely resemble the line in Breivik's manifesto: "God can anoint you with His supernatural power to defeat any enemy that may come your way".[19] It is, as Bradley states, a matter of putting these verses to use

---

[12] Bible Knowledge Ministries—Bible Teaching Website (last accessed November 2022).
[13] Ibid.
[14] Ibid.
[15] Ibid.
[16] Ibid.
[17] Ibid.
[18] Ibid.
[19] Manifesto, p. 1331.

against "whatever enemy may have come your way".[20] In a highlighted section in bold, Bradley writes about "God the Father" as a "Man of War", and that "He can be stirred up to go into battle for you. And the way that you stir up God the Father to go into battle for you is to form out the appropriate battle prayers that will fit the specific battle situation you may be facing".[21] Before listing the verses, Bradley writes again that they are:

> all showing you the "war side" to God the Father's personality and how ferociously He can go into battle for you to defeat any enemy that may try and come against you in this life. These are whopper power verses, and I mean whopper power verses!

This is Breivik's War Bible assemblage, highlighting the "war side" of God and picking out biblical verses to motivate for battle. Bradley concludes the main page for Battle Verses of the Bible: "All of the above Scripture verses will give you more than enough live ammunition should you ever need them to face any enemy or storm cloud head on".[22] Breivik similarly wrote: "All of the above Scripture verses are definitely telling you that God can anoint you with His power whenever that power is going to be needed to take on any kind of enemy or challenge".[23]

There are multiple sub-pages to the Battle Verses page, all of which furnish further biblical verses. Many of the verses cited on these pages can be found also in Breivik's manifesto, specifically in what I called the War Bible assemblage. For instance, on the sub-page "Going on the Offensive Against Your Enemies",[24] Bradley writes that if "there is one major secret I feel the Lord has given to me in the area of spiritual warfare—it has to be the strategy of going on the offensive against whatever enemy is coming against you—just like David did with Goliath".[25] As I discussed in chapter 3, David and Goliath come up several times in Breivik's manifesto.[26] Leviticus 26:3 is cited on the sub-page "Walk in All of God's Ways—Keep All of God's Commandments",

---

[20] Bible Knowledge Ministries—Bible Teaching Website (last accessed November 2022).
[21] Ibid.
[22] Ibid.
[23] Manifesto, p. 1331.
[24] Bible Knowledge Ministries—Bible Teaching Website, also attributed to Michael Bradley and last updated 14 November 2018 (last accessed November 2021).
[25] Bible Knowledge Ministries—Bible Teaching Website (last accessed November 2022).
[26] Manifesto, pp. 33, 1158, 1329.

which Breivik also cites.[27] In "God Will Run Protection for You",[28] Bradley writes that sometimes "God will want you to go into the battle, and then He will fight the battle through you to defeat your enemy".[29] Similarly, Breivik writes that in addition to sometimes running "a protective shield around you where nothing can get through to attack you", God is depicted as stepping in himself: "This is where God will literally take your enemy head on and do battle with it".[30] Isaiah 42:13, where God is likened to a mighty man and a man of war, is listed in the article "God Will Fight Your Battles", as well as by Breivik.[31] In "Battle Angels", Bradley writes that sometimes "God will take up the battle for you and take your enemy head on all by Himself", a line that Breivik directly repeats: "This is where God will literally take your enemy head on and do battle with it".[32]

It is not exactly clear what kind of battle is imagined by the Bradley brothers. They make multiple mentions of "any enemy" you may be facing. They make reference to "spiritual warfare" rather than physical war, but nowhere do they say this could not also be physical violence. Prayers to battle cancer are mentioned.[33] On the sub-page "God Will Anoint You for Battle",[34] further examples are listed detailing what sort of trials readers may be undergoing to need God's help. The list refers to divorce, being sued, being cheated on, being abused, or your children having drug problems.[35] In the "Testimonies" page (as it is available at the time of writing), the stories are mostly about finding a new job, robberies, lawsuits, suicide, and divorce.[36] As far as I could find, there are no references to Muslims or immigrants as enemies, or anything that would be associated with the Eurabia conspiracy and counterjihad milieu. The "battles" that are imagined on this web page,

---

[27] Bible Knowledge Ministries—Bible Teaching Website (last accessed November 2022); manifesto, p. 1330.
[28] Bible Knowledge Ministries—Bible Teaching Website, also attributed to Michael Bradley and last updated 23 February 2021 (last accessed November 2021.)
[29] Bible Knowledge Ministries—Bible Teaching Website (last accessed November 2022).
[30] Manifesto, p. 1332. This sentiment is repeated in the sub-page, 'God Will Fight your Battles', https://www.bible-knowledge.com/god-will-fight-your-battles/, attributed to Michael Bradley and last updated 14 January 2020 (last accessed 5 November 2021.)
[31] Bible Knowledge Ministries—Bible Teaching Website last accessed November 2022; manifesto, p. 1332. Other biblical verses that Breivik repeats include Daniel 11:32, 1 Corinthians 1:20, Isaiah 54:17, and Psalm 144:1.
[32] Bible Knowledge Ministries—Bible Teaching Website, https://www.bible-knowledge.com/battle-angels/, last accessed November 2022; Manifesto, p. 1332.
[33] Bible Knowledge Ministries—Bible Teaching Website (last accessed November 2022).
[34] Bible Knowledge Ministries—Bible Teaching Website, also attributed to Michael Bradley and last updated 18 December 2020 (last accessed November 2021.)
[35] Bible Knowledge Ministries—Bible Teaching Website (last accessed November 2022).
[36] Bible Knowledge Ministries—Bible Teaching Website.

then, are not exactly the "battle" in which Breivik imagined himself a warrior. Nor is this exactly the conflict that counterjihadist figures such as Robert Spencer, Bat Ye'or, and Oriana Fallaci have insisted is taking place between Christian Europe and Islam.

There are also some important differences between Breivik's War Bible assemblage and Bradley's Bible-use. One difference is that Bradley includes a section at the bottom of the main Bible battle verses page where he says that God wants us to remain "humble with all of this, along with making sure that we treat all of our enemies with love, respect, and kindness".[37] His own War Bible assemblage includes two verses that complicate at least to some extent the Bible where God is a Man of War. Proverbs 24:17 is cited: "Do not rejoice when your enemy falls, and do not let your heart be glad when he stumbles; lest the Lord see it, and it displeases Him, and He turn away His wrath from him".[38] Proverbs 25:21 is also cited: "If your enemy is hungry, give him bread to eat; and if he is thirsty, give him water to drink; for so you will heap coals of fire on his head, and the Lord will reward you".[39] Clearly, the Bradley brothers are imagining a different kind of battle and a different form of warfare than Breivik. It is nonetheless clear that Breivik's War Bible in many ways can be said to come fairly straightforwardly from the Bradley brothers' Bible-Knowledge web page. Most of the biblical texts cited in the third book of the manifesto can be found also in the series of articles under the general headline "Battle Verses". There is no trace of the Eurabia conspiracy and counterjihad ideology that was stuck to Breivik's War Bible, as far as I can find.

The War Bible that operates in the Bradley brothers' Battle verses page, then, is taken up by Breivik in terms of the bits of Bible, but it is also about picking up a mode of Bible-use, where individual texts function as intensive sources of power. This is part of Breivik's Bible-use, where individual texts are listed without much or any comment, as if they give power merely by being listed and invoked. Content does matter. The verses are, after all, tailored to be about battles, God's support for you, enemies, and warfare—spiritual or otherwise. But the verses themselves are near-talismanic. If carried on index cards—or inscribed in a manifesto—they can furnish power. The biblical battle verses are continuously described by the Bradley brothers as "powerful", as "God-torpedoes" that can be used "to shoot at whatever enemy may

[37] Bible Knowledge Ministries—Bible Teaching Website (last accessed November 2022).
[38] Ibid.
[39] Ibid.

come your way—whether it be human, demonic, or any kind of illness or disease".[40]

Right-Wing Evangelical Battles

Gardell calls the Bradley brothers right-wing Evangelical preachers.[41] Zooming out from the Bradley brothers specifically, there may be connections between Breivik's use of a War Bible to fuel hatred and violence, and recent US political movements in which a Bible plays a part, even if this is not exactly a War Bible. Rhys Williams discusses the way immigration has become an important theme for white Evangelical Protestants.[42] Particularly in the second decade of the twenty-first century, anti-immigrant and nativist tendencies amongst white Evangelicals are clear.[43] Anti-immigration and nativist sentiments have been on the rise and have gained traction in the Republican Party, particularly during Donald Trump's presidency. Williams demonstrates the way biblical citations have played a key part in white Evangelical Protestant campaigns to rail against immigration and promote Christian nationalism.[44] The story of Nehemiah is a particularly recurring biblical text that is used to support the building of walls.[45] As Williams shows, the "importance of walls for protection of the 'innocent' is an interesting motif" that recurs amongst white Evangelical Protestants, and bits of Bible play a key part in the cases made for why walls are not only necessary but "biblical". Nehemiah 4:17–18 is also mentioned in Breivik's manifesto, where the building of a wall is described.[46] Of course, much of the rhetoric that Williams describes comes after Breivik's manifesto was compiled. The point is not that Breivik copied it. The point is that Breivik's manifesto should be seen as part of a much more far-ranging network of Bible-use that connects

---

[40] Ibid.
[41] Gardell, 'Crusader Dreams', p. 145.
[42] Rhys H. Williams, 'Mobilizing Religion in Twenty-First-Century Nativism in the United States', in *Religion in Rebellions, Revolutions, and Social Movements*, edited by Warren S. Goldstein and Jean-Pierre Reed (London: Routledge, 2022), pp. 199–218.
[43] Ibid., p. 200. See also Rhys Williams, 'Civil Religion and the Cultural Politics of Immigration in Obama's America', *Journal for the Scientific Study of Religion* 52, no. 2 (2013): pp. 239–257.
[44] Williams, 'Mobilizing Religion in Twenty-First-Century Nativism in the United States', p. 210. Nehemiah 4:17–18 is mentioned in Breivik's manifesto at p. 1329.
[45] Williams, 'Mobilizing Religion in Twenty-First-Century Nativism in the United States', p. 210. Nehemiah 4:17–18 is mentioned in Breivik's manifesto at p. 1329.
[46] Manifesto, p. 1329.

across geographical borders and overlaps with ideological proclivities and proclamations that have only picked up speed since the terror attacks in 2011.

But there is another key source for Breivik's War Bible that I will now turn to, which links the War Bible further to US Evangelical movements. The Bible connections are less direct than the shared stock of biblical verses found in the manifesto and drawn from the Bradley brothers' web page, but the continuities with the War Bible assemblage are nonetheless striking.

The Bible as a Radical Document

In addition to the Bradley brothers, the other relevant source that Gardell mentions in regard to Breivik's Bible-use is Joseph Farah and his *The Tea Party Manifesto: A Vision for an American Rebirth*, published in 2010.[47] The Tea Party manifesto is not directly cited in Breivik's manifesto. But Farah is cited as editor-in-chief of the conspiracy peddling World Net Daily website that Breivik frequented. I am here going to focus on Farah's Tea Party manifesto, because although this does not feature directly in the manifesto, Breivik is influenced by Farah, and Farah produces a version of a War Bible in his Tea Party manifesto that resonates with Breivik's War Bible. Again, then, I am not interested in questions of causation but in the ways the War Bible I identified in Breivik's manifesto reveals connections and continuities that operate through interlinking, but not altogether overlapping, ideologies that spread across borders. Resonating with the counterjihadists' War Bible assemblage I mapped in chapters 3 and 4, Farah's Bible-use inspires sacrifice—even martyrdom—and legitimises resistance to the governing authorities, even violent resistance. It involves mining biblical texts for courageous heroes who fight back, thriving on alarmist statements about the urgency of current problems, and glorifying a Bible as a radical document, alongside other documents such as the US Constitution. I begin, though, by providing some background to the Tea Party movement, as Farah's Bible operates within Tea Party activism.

The Tea Party is an American movement which emerged in 2009, with close ties to the Republican Party. Although not numerically large, the movement has received considerable media coverage for its protests and

---

[47] Joseph Farah, *The Tea Party Manifesto: A Vision for an American Rebirth* (Washington, DC: WND books, 2010).

proclamations.[48] Studies have shown that Tea Party activists have had considerable influence on electoral success and policy changes.[49] Although the movement is decentralised and far from homogenous, scholars have argued that members largely characterise themselves as "strongly conservative".[50] Tea Party activists to a large extent share views on economic and social issues with conservative Republican politicians.[51] As Kevin Arceneaux and Stephen P. Nicholson make clear, supporters of the Tea Party are predominantly white, male, Republican, and conservative.[52] Government spending and lowering taxes are key issues. Tighter restriction on immigration has also been a rallying point.[53] There is considerable overlap between the Tea Party and the Christian right in the United States, with Tea Party activists critiquing government as amoral and socialist and holding firm views about the founding of America as a testament to American exceptionalism.[54] Like the Christian right, the Tea Party movement emerged and grew by mobilising large numbers of white conservative Christians through grassroots organisations, working to gain political influence. Many Tea Party–backed candidates who came into office in 2010 were evangelical Christians.[55]

Although the religious makeup of the Tea Party movement is by no means straightforward, a majority of its members—including members not identifying as religious—profess that America is a Christian nation.[56] As Ruth Braunstein and Malaena Taylor indicate, this point demonstrates the way the rhetoric of America as a Christian nation, even for non-Christians, can operate as a "form of boundary-work that marks certain groups as political 'others'".[57]

---

[48] Amber M. Gaffney, David E. Rast III, Justin D. Hackett, and Michael A. Hogg, 'Further to the Right: Uncertainty, Political Polarization and the American "Tea Party" movement', *Social Influence* 9, no. 4 (2014): p. 272.
[49] Michael A. Bailey, Jonathan Mummolo, and Hans Noel, 'Tea Party Influence: A Story of Activists and Elites', *American Politics Research* 40, no. 5 (2012): p. 793. Braunstein and Taylor note that although some Tea Party movement groups are not nearly as active as they were in 2009 and 2010, large numbers of Americans continue to express support for the movement's core aims and ideas. Ruth Braunstein and Malaena Taylor, 'Is the Tea Party a "Religious" Movement? Religiosity in the Tea Party versus the Religious Right', *Sociology of Religion: A Quarterly Review* 78, no.1 (2017): p. 34.
[50] Gaffney, et al., 'Further to the Right', p. 273.
[51] Bailey, et al., 'Tea Party Influence', p. 771.
[52] Kevin Arceneaux and Stephen P. Nicholson, 'Who Wants to Have a Tea Party? The Who, What, and Why of the Tea Party Movement', *Political Science and Politics* 45, no. 4 (2012): p. 701.
[53] Bailey, et al., 'Tea Party Influence', p. 771.
[54] Angelia R. Wilson and Cynthia Burack, '"Where Liberty Reigns and God Is Supreme": The Christian Right and the Tea Party Movement', *New Political Science* 34, no. 2 (2012): p. 174.
[55] Braunstein and Taylor, 'Is the Tea Party a "Religious" Movement?', p. 36.
[56] Ibid., p. 35.
[57] Ibid.

With Sarah Palin, Joseph Farah was a keynote speaker at the first Tea Party Convention in Nashville, Tennessee, in 2010. He is the author of several books, including *Taking America Back: A Radical Plan to Revive Freedom, Morality and Justice* and *None of the Above: Why 2008 Is the Year to Cast the Ultimate Protest Vote*. Farah is the editor-in-chief of the far-right news website World Net Daily, which is cited several times in Breivik's manifesto.[58] In the 1990s, he co-wrote a book with the right-wing radio presenter Rush Limbaugh, *See, I Told You So*.[59] Farah identifies as a "tea partier" and a political activist, aiming to "wake up" America from "its political sleepwalk".[60] The Tea Party manifesto is his effort to provide a simple and coherent "visionary mission statement"[61] for Americans who are no longer content with the status quo. The Tea Party manifesto conforms to classic populist traits and is not explicitly preoccupied with Muslims or migrants. It is concerned with the "elite" powers and "cultural institutions" which Farah argues are "threatening America's very existence as a sovereign, free, vibrant, cohesive, self-governing nation-state".[62] It is about taking power away from "Washington" and focusing on "the will of the people".[63] He desires "a government of the people, by the people, and for the people".[64] The Tea Partiers desire to, as Farah puts it, "take America back from the precipice", to restore the founding fathers' vision of America, and to set in motion a "moral renewal".[65]

For Farah, the vision of a renewed America is decidedly spiritual. He describes the American dream as under spiritual attack and the necessary action as a spiritual battle.[66] One point that Farah makes repeatedly is that Tea Party activism should not only be about economic issues and materialism. A "spiritual core" is needed.[67] This concern reflects a tension that has arisen in the Christian right's relationship to the Republican Party, where economic issues have sometimes been seen to eclipse moral issues to do with sexuality and reproduction, for instance.[68] Unlike the Christian right in the United States, Tea Partiers did not have a habit of collectively engaging in religious

---

[58] The pages Breivik cites are no longer available.
[59] Joseph Farah and Rush Limbaugh, *See, I Told You So* (New York: Pocket Books, 1994).
[60] Farah, *The Tea Party Manifesto*, p. 15.
[61] Ibid., p. 17.
[62] Ibid., p. 21.
[63] Ibid., pp. 27, 66–67, 116. "Washington" is constantly used as metonymy for the US political elites; see Farah, *The Tea Party Manifesto*, pp. 63, 66–67, 71, 115.
[64] Ibid., p. 73.
[65] Ibid., p. 23.
[66] Ibid., p. 24.
[67] Ibid., p. 55.
[68] Wilson and Burack, '"Where Liberty Reigns and God Is Supreme"', p. 178.

practices like prayer or Bible study.[69] Instead, scholars have commented on the "civil religious" practices of reciting the Pledge of Allegiance and group studies of the Constitution amongst Tea Party groups.[70] With his manifesto, Farah is clearly hoping to steer Tea Party members towards a Christian understanding of the movement's political agenda. References to God in Farah's manifesto are frequent, particularly to the God who "grants inalienable rights to life, liberty, and the pursuit of happiness", and a God who people are accountable to.[71] The founding fathers of the United States are frequently referenced as understanding that "only a moral people with knowledge and reverence for God's role in our lives can ever be capable of self-government".[72]

As Farah sees it, one is accountable either to God or to government. He calls this a "biblical principle".[73] America is supposedly in trouble because it has forgotten God.[74] Taking back "America's soul" needs to be done "in a way that will please God".[75] Success in fact depends on God.[76] The Tea Party movement, he proclaims, is a movement of prayerful people who love God, a people who go to "church and synagogue".[77] This is the only place in the manifesto where Farah implies Christians and Jews are part of the movement. No other religious group is included. Muslims are not mentioned. The point about Jews and Christians, however, is emphasised further by Farah making reference to "Judeo-Christian values".[78] This reference to Judeo-Christian values resonates with the counterjihadist writers whom Breivik cited and that I discussed in chapter 4.

The Constitution of the United States and the American Declaration of Independence are two near-sacred sources for Farah, but a Bible plays a role, too, as I have already indicated. When Farah mentions how certain groups are demonised in the contemporary United States, "Bible-believing Christians" are one of his examples.[79] Farah cites 2 Corinthians 7:14: "If my people, which are called by my name, shall humble themselves, and pray, and seek my face, and turn from their wicked ways; then will I hear from

[69] Braunstein and Taylor, 'Is the Tea Party a "Religious" Movement?', p. 37.
[70] Ibid.
[71] Farah, *The Tea Party Manifesto*, pp. 24, 28, 30, 44, 51.
[72] Ibid., p. 58.
[73] Ibid., p. 30.
[74] Ibid., p. 42.
[75] Ibid., p. 125.
[76] Ibid., pp. 125, 130.
[77] Ibid., p. 45.
[78] Ibid., p. 96.
[79] Ibid., pp. 39–40. Somewhat comically, smokers are the other example! These two groups are compared to "Native Americans and homosexuals".

heaven, and will forgive their sin, and will heal their land".[80] In other words, if people repent and change the status quo in contemporary America, then there is a chance of redemption from what he sees as the demise of the United States. These biblical references are fairly fleeting. Arguably the most significant way a Bible is invoked in the manifesto is as a radical document that inspires sacrifice—even martyrdom—and legitimises resistance towards the governing authorities, even violent resistance.

The founders, as Farah writes, were inspired by a "radical document—the Bible".[81] Farah laments that many pastors, church leaders, and theologians now have a "timid" view of "biblical faith in the public square".[82] He writes that some even think the Bible condemns resistance to tyranny.[83] Elaborating on this point, he cites Paul's letter to the Romans (13:1–7), where Paul urges his readers to submit to the governing authorities.[84] But in response to this, Farah suggests that it is problematic to read too much into these verses, to the exclusion of the rest of Christian scripture.[85] He argues that Paul is exhorting us not to overthrow the government as an institution, but that this does not hold for resisting unjust laws or rulers.[86] He goes on to state that "the Bible is also teeming with acts of civil disobedience and deliverance from tyranny".[87] He mentions Pharaoh's daughter, Moses's mother and Moses in Exodus, and Daniel praying in defiance of the king in Daniel 6.[88] Farah then gives what he calls a striking example of the "way the Bible actually celebrates heroes of the faith who take extraordinary, even violent actions to liberate themselves from ungodly rulers".[89] He recounts the story in the book of Judges, chapter 3, where Ehud assassinates the ruler of the Moabites, who had conquered the Israelites.[90] Farah makes the connection to "our own leaders when they break trust with the Constitution and God's law", warning them in the words of Psalm 149:5–9:

---

[80] Ibid., p. 58.
[81] Ibid., p. 74.
[82] Ibid.
[83] Ibid.
[84] Ibid., pp. 74–75.
[85] Ibid., p. 76.
[86] Ibid., p. 77. He comes back to Romans 13. Ibid., p. 80.
[87] Ibid., p. 77.
[88] Ibid., pp. 77–78.
[89] Ibid., p. 78.
[90] Ibid., p. 79.

Let the saints be joyful in glory: let them sing aloud upon their beds. Let the high praises of God be in their mouth, and a two-edged sword in their hand; To execute vengeance upon the heathen, and punishment upon the people; To bind their kings with chains, and their nobles with fetters of iron; To execute upon them the judgement written: this honour have all his saints. Praise ye the LORD.[91]

There is no qualifying statement from Farah to not use these texts to justify actual violence. In fact, he complains about Barack Obama for treating the Constitution and the Bible as documents that contain great ideas, rather than to be taken seriously and read literally.[92]

What is significant about Farah's radical Bible is the way it is assembled with repetitive alarmist statements, appealing to the urgency of the situation as he describes it: "the very future of our nation is at stake",[93] there is a need to "fight to regain what we have lost".[94] Farah states that the enemy is in control and must be combatted.[95] There are frequent references to the founders, who "risked and sacrificed everything",[96] to betrayal,[97] and to the elites in Washington being the "lawless ones", the ones "who are perverting justice and morality and order".[98] Farah argues that "we need to become resistance fighters".[99] "We need to be willing to sacrifice our comfort—maybe even our lives, our fortunes, and our sacred honour".[100] The founders are described as "prophets of old who were willing to challenge the establishment even if it meant their deaths".[101] He writes that "it's time for freedom-loving Americans to go on the offense",[102] the time for debate is over.[103] Moreover, he urges readers not to wait for a leader to guide them, but that: "YOU are the leader".[104] Armies are mentioned when Farah states that he would "rather have a smaller army with God on my side than the largest army in the world

---

[91] Ibid., pp. 80–81.
[92] Ibid., p. 106.
[93] Ibid., p. 59.
[94] Ibid., p. 122.
[95] Ibid., p. 130.
[96] Ibid., p. 70.
[97] Ibid.
[98] Ibid., p. 83.
[99] Ibid.
[100] Ibid.
[101] Ibid., p. 95.
[102] Ibid., p. 97.
[103] Ibid., p. 98.
[104] Ibid., p. 99.

devoid of God".[105] The radical Bible that Farah invokes is full of biblical figures who resist tyranny. It is assembled with both the founding fathers, who sacrificed everything, and the contemporary resistance fighters in the Tea Party movement.

Similar to Breivik's War Bible, there is a focus on sacrifice, heroism, and the necessity to fight defensively to save, in Farah's case, the United States, and in Breivik's case, Europe. For both Farah and Breivik there is an emphasis on saving *Christianity* in the United States/Europe. Breivik uses different examples to Farah, but the mention of manly characters in Christian scripture who fight with God on their side against the enemies of "the people" are similar. Breivik's self-conception as a leader figure, a knight or soldier of Christ, is as if a direct response to Farah's appeal to not wait for a political leader to solve societal problems but to take a stand and fight the battle yourself. Although Farah does not frame the battle as one against migration and Islam in the Tea Party manifesto, as Breivik does, there is a similar focus on the evil of the status quo, the urgent need to take action, a return to a golden age, a conservative vision of the family, and a rejection of secularism.

Although Farah himself does not mention immigration, Islam, or nativist ideas directly in the manifesto, it is important to note that the Tea Party movement is well known for dealing in racial resentment and complaints about immigration, even if this does not apply to all Tea Party supporters.[106] Although resentment about taxes and immigration is not directed primarily or explicitly at Muslims, the narrative of racial minorities "freeloading" off the hard-earned money of "hard-working" people and the anxiety and anger directed at societal change linked to immigration is not far from Breivik's own antagonism towards immigrants and the supposed effects of immigration in Norway and Europe more broadly.[107] Further, the fact that the Tea Party movement appeals to both religious and non-religious supporters is noteworthy. As Braunstein and Taylor have shown, the Tea Party movement appeals to a broader audience than does the Christian right in the United

---

[105] Ibid., p. 126.
[106] Arceneaux and Nicholson, 'Who Wants to Have a Tea Party?', p. 701. In their study of data surveyed from the US 2010 midterm elections, Arceneaux and Nicholson complicate the conventional characterisation of the Tea Party when it comes to key issues of race and government spending by pointing to more heterogeneity in the movement than is sometimes allowed. One result of their findings is that although they confirm the sense that the Tea Party movement is fundamentally white, male, and conservative, they did not find much evidence of the idea that the movement consists of working poor whites. Rather, the Tea Party supporters tend to be wealthier than the general population. Arceneaux and Nicholson, 'Who Wants to Have a Tea Party?', p. 708.
[107] Ibid., p. 701.

States. This broader appeal may be significant for "followers" such as Breivik who may draw on parts of the Tea Party discourse or from Tea Party activists without fitting the movement or being an outright supporter.[108] Braunstein and Taylor discuss the fact that the Tea Party movement has attracted a relatively high proportion of secular members, with at least 17% of members who identified as atheist, agnostic, or nothing in particular, and yet, as they also found, a majority of their members shared a belief that America is a Christian nation. As a form of "boundary-work", they suggest, the claim about a Christian America "defines non-Christians as outsiders, interlopers or even enemies".[109] This could reflect the construction of a religious *outgroup*, and Tea Partiers' shared concern about rising immigration, particularly Muslim immigrants.[110]

The focus on Christian America, for both Christians and non-Christians, then, becomes a "subtle means of marginalizing members of religious traditions, like Islam, that they viewed as threats to the American way of life".[111] This is important in understanding how ideas about a Christian nation or continent such as America or Europe "can operate as a form of symbolic boundary work", how it can be used to construct out-groups, "even in the absence of a shared in-group religious identity".[112]

There is much on the Bradley brothers' Bible-Knowledge web page about biblical battle verses and in Farah's Tea Party manifesto on a Bible that promotes heroic violence against political rulers, that connects explicitly or more implicitly to Breivik's War Bible assemblage. In these sources, a War Bible gains speed, and this can instill confidence to face your enemy with God on your side and provide justification for a violent uprising against perceived unjust conditions and purportedly tyrannical rulers. What is missing from the War Bible assemblage in these sources is the counterjihadist and Eurabia conspiracies that stick so squarely to Breivik's War Bible. Versions of the War Bible assemblage I identified in Breivik's manifesto operate, then, in different arenas, some of which are connected to, and continuous with, Breivik's Bible-use either ideologically or in practice. It is not the case that the Bible-use I have discussed operates in the same way in all these contexts. Quite clearly it does not. A Bible that is inspiring for battle can operate in overlapping and

---

[108] Braunstein and Taylor, 'Is the Tea Party a "Religious" Movement?', p. 54.
[109] Ibid., p. 55.
[110] Ibid.
[111] Ibid.
[112] Ibid.

interconnecting ways, provoking powerful affects of righteous anger, heroism, and courage, as well as comfort and confidence that God is on your side. There are also disconnections and discontinuities. But I have tried to show that the War Bible that operates in Breivik's manifesto is connected to networks of Bible-use that cross geographical boundaries. They demonstrate political and religious entanglements and function in explicitly and implicitly anti-immigrant and xenophobic ways.

The use of the War Bible is not unique to these contemporary settings, however. Nor do the battle verses and uses of heroic-insurgent biblical stories spell out anything particularly innovative in the history of Bible-use. In actual warfare, Bibles have been used on multiple occasions throughout history. To broaden the discussion and tease out what shared tendencies might be at work to make the War Bible effective, I want to gesture briefly towards examples of past Bible-use. Some recurring features are noteworthy in Bible-use that justifies violence and warfare. In the examples I have looked at so far, selectivity is key. Particular bits of Bible are cited. Other bits of Bible are left out. Further, constructions of an enemy are important. Breivik's War Bible is not the first time Bible-use has functioned to other Muslims. Affects of righteousness, desires for comfort, and framing the violence as necessary but defensive action, are also crucial.

War Bibles

It would be impossible to summarise or extensively cover here the ways in which Bibles have been used in warfare. As far as Bibles *have* frequently been used in warfare, though, it would be possible to speak of multiple War Bible assemblages. In order to convey more broadly the reasons why the War Bible I have been analysing might be useful and the way selectivity can function effectively, I want to gesture towards examples that, I suggest, are relevant for the case I am analysing in this book, starting with Bible-use during the crusades, before turning to Bibles during the First World War. I focus on these examples due to the tendencies they illuminate in Bibles used in warfare, namely to shore up animosity towards a (Muslim) enemy and posit this animosity as righteous, and to confirm that God is on one's side and provide comfort that violence is justified.

During the crusades, biblical texts were cited and interpreted to justify violence and shore up animosity towards the enemy. Katherine Allen Smith discusses the way biblical texts were used to endow important events during the crusades with meaning. She highlights two biblical stories in particular, namely the "cleansing of the Temple" and the "legend of the innocents". In June 1099, after a siege of five weeks, a fraction of the original First Crusade armies reached Jerusalem and conquered the Holy City and massacred the majority of its inhabitants.[113] One biblical story that became connected to the 1099 conquest was the "cleansing of the Temple" story, when Christ drove the merchants and moneychangers from the Temple in Jerusalem—a story that can be found in Matthew 21:12-14; Mark 11:15-18; Luke 19:45-47; and John 2:13-16. Allen Smith calls the story "a typological drama", in which crusaders "collectively played the role of Christ and Muslims stood in for the merchants and moneychangers of the Gospel accounts".[114] Particularly the account in John 2:13-16 became popular, she argues, in which Christ yields a whip of knotted cords.[115] This rare moment of violence on Jesus's part in the Gospels is seized upon. Jerusalem becomes the Temple. The crusaders all get to play Christ, showing anger at the merchants and moneychangers— who during the 1099 attack become Muslims. Crusaders become an angry Christ.

"By the time of the First Crusade, the Temple had come to symbolise not only Christ's body but the entire body of believers, the corpus Christianorum who collectively participated in the mystery of the Eucharist and bore responsibility for safeguarding the Temple's purity".[116] The Temple is not only Jerusalem as Holy Land, then, but a living body of Christ—to be defended. After the crusading army breached Jerusalem's walls on July 15, 1099, the Christians carried out one of the most infamous massacres of medieval warfare. Some of the bloodiest scenes took place on the Temple Mount, where thousands of Muslims were killed inside the al-Aqsa Mosque, which Latin Christians referred to as the Temple of Solomon, and outside the Dome of the Rock, which Latin Christians referred to as the Temple of the Lord. As Allen Smith explains it, the Christian chroniclers presented these massacres as a cleansing process, often describing the crusaders' actions with the verb *mundare*, which conveys the sense not only of a physical purification but a

---

[113] Katherine Allen Smith, 'The Crusader Conquest of Jerusalem and Christ's Cleansing of the Temple', in *The Uses of the Bible in Crusader Sources*, edited by Elizabeth Lapina and Nicholas Morton (Leiden: Brill, 2017), p. 19.
[114] Ibid., p. 20.
[115] Ibid., p. 21.
[116] Ibid., p. 24.

purging of sin.[117] The Muslims killed were linked to other hated groups, seen as enemies of the Church—simoniacs, heretics, usurers, and Jews. In this way, extreme acts of violence like the massacre of July 1099 could be read as "acts of purification".[118] A sense of righteous anger could be channelled into acts of violence.[119] The Bible that is invoked here, then, is part of a process of producing feelings of righteous anger. In this use of a Bible, the violence becomes purification, cleansing. The crusaders are not brutal soldiers but become Christs.

Part of the righteousness of the War Bible seems to involve situating the owners of this Bible as innocent, defending themselves against cruelty and tyranny. The "legend of the innocents" is key in this regard and was another biblical story which became familiar during the Middle Ages, particularly through medieval literature, art, and plays.[120] In Matthew 2:16–18, Herod is furious that the Magi have not delivered over Jesus to him. In his anger, he orders that all the boys in Bethlehem who are two years old or younger should be killed. Allen Smith notes how Herod's massacre became a symbol of ultimate cruelty in medieval literature and art. The baby boys become known as the "innocents"—the innocent victims of cruel brutality. Crusader sources share these ideas, presenting the "innocents" as examples for "the whole crusading community in their capacity to be the first *athletae Christi* to sacrifice themselves in military conflict to serve Christ".[121] Crusader sources from the twelfth and thirteenth centuries emphasise the spiritual characteristics of children—innocence, purity, humility.[122] Bernard of Clairvaux, the most famous preacher of the crusades, called people to give their heart to a child Jesus in order to themselves become innocent and pure as children.[123] In crusader sources, the Muslim enemy—the Saracen—is the source of cruelty towards children and is depicted as carrying the original sword Herod used for the massacre of innocents.[124] In this instance, the Muslim enemy has become not merchants and moneychangers but the evil child-killing Herod. The crusaders here are no longer Christs but innocent young

---

[117] Ibid., p. 31.
[118] Ibid., p. 34.
[119] Ibid., p. 37.
[120] Sini Kangas, 'The Slaughter of the Innocents and the Depiction of Children in Twelfth- and Thirteenth-Century Sources of the Crusades', in *The Uses of the Bible in Crusader Sources*, edited by Lapina and Morton, p. 78.
[121] Ibid., p. 79.
[122] Ibid., p. 86.
[123] Ibid., p. 79.
[124] Ibid., p. 92.

children, purely good in their encounter with the cruelty of the Muslims/ Herod. A Bible can support the becoming-innocent of violent crusaders and the becoming-Herod of Muslims.

The Bible-use briefly sketched here, then, is one that holds up the righteous anger and violence of Jesus and the greed and brutality of the Muslim enemy. This Bible-use ensures that the Christian crusaders are the pure and good—as either Christs or children—and that the enemy are unworthy and cruel—moneychangers, merchants, and Herods. By using particular biblical texts to frame key events of the crusades, the violence of the crusaders is made righteous. They are Jesus. They are the "innocents". The enemy is a desecrator of sacred sites. The enemy is a baby-killer. Breivik's War Bible similarly plays on feelings of righteousness, conjuring up hatred of the designated enemy, through anecdotes about Muslims being brutal and bloodthirsty. It is hardly insignificant that Breivik dressed himself up as a crusader and insisted he was part of a Knights Templar network.[125] Similarly, as I have shown, the sword-bearing Jesus in the Eurabia and counterjihadist circles I discussed in chapter 4 plug into this desired violence of the Christ-figure standing up to Muslims. The Bradley brothers' battle verses and Farah's Bible-as-radical-document posit resistance as righteous and defensive-heroic action with God on one's side as legitimate.

"The Bible" as a source of comfort in the face of an enemy has been another key feature of War Bibles. This feature is marked in Breivik's manifesto and the Bradley brothers' battle verses, as select verses are used as sources for power when confronting problems. During the First World War, Bibles were used in this way. Preachers and theologians were not unaware of a Bible that could challenge the militarism and violence of warfare. But nor were they blind to the bits of Bible that could play a part in the war effort. A Bible was assembled that could join the forces of war, where some biblical components were put to work while others were unworkable and therefore could either be overwritten or downplayed. Amongst British soldiers, Bibles proliferated in the First World War, as scripture became a source of comfort.[126] A Bible which provides a divine agent on the side of the vulnerable soldier is understandably a welcome component in the trenches. Michael Snape highlights Exodus 14:14, which was read by two English soldiers before an attack in

---

[125] He later retracted this.
[126] Michael Snape, *God and the British Soldier: Religion and the British Army in the First and Second World Wars* (London: Routledge, 2005), pp. 233–236.

November 1917, 'The Lord will fight for you'.[127] But Bibles could also be used as a motivating "force for morale" and to incite "righteous enthusiasm" for the cause.[128] This was not straightforward, though, as a Bible fit for war had to be properly assembled to avoid confusion or contradiction to the war cause. A. J. Hoover discusses how preachers during the First World War grappled with biblical principles and passages.[129] He argues that, generally, both German and British preachers, for instance, posited 'love of enemy' as an ethical principle that should be evaluated before applying it absolutely.[130] Defence of "family, nation, truth, Christ, or God" could trump this principle.[131]

It is acknowledged, then, that different bits of Bible can produce different sentiments, principles, and actions. Different bits can be emphasised and highlighted. Other bits are downplayed or relativised. Biblical passages that seem to endorse militant self-defence or celebrate the status of the soldier are welcomed to justify war, while passages that do not become less important or inapplicable.[132] Building on Anglican and Lutheran statements about the lawfulness of Christian soldiers,[133] clergy argued that the Bible is "free of any antimilitarianism", and identified New Testament passages that seemed to endorse, or at least not critique, soldiers.[134] In fact, praise of the soldier by British and German preachers was enhanced with reference to Christ, Paul, and biblical precepts that encouraged sacrifice and duty. John 15:13 is an obvious example: "No one has greater love than this, to lay down one's life for one's friends".[135] Violence during war is justified by the public nature of the cause (rather than private violence). The sword that is wielded is "the sword of community justice, not a private sword".[136] A Bible that condoned some forms of militarism and violence needed to fit what was conceived as the "essence of Christianity", as Hoover puts it, "heroism, love, sacrifice, devotion to duty".[137]

---

[127] Ibid., p. 245.
[128] Ibid.
[129] A. J. Hoover, *God, Germany, and Britain in the Great War* (London: Praeger, 1989), p. 106.
[130] Ibid.
[131] Ibid., p. 106.
[132] Hoover mentions for instance the reference in Matthew 27:54, where a Roman soldier recognises the greatness of Christ and is called a "true son of God". He further explains how lines in the Sermon on the Mount about peacemakers came to be seen as inapplicable to war between nations. Ibid., pp. 104–107.
[133] Such as Article 37 of the Anglican Articles of Religion, the Lutheran Augsburg Confession (1550), the Presbyterian Westminster Confession of Faith (1647), and the Congregationalist Savoy Declaration of Faith and Order (1658). Ibid., p. 106.
[134] Ibid., pp. 106–107.
[135] Ibid., p. 108.
[136] Ibid., p. 107.
[137] Ibid., p. 108.

The War Bible that emerges here, then, is not a brutal and blunt part of the war effort. Rather, it beautifies and biblicises the violence of the war as heroic sacrifice and duty. In this way, echoes of the Christ who willingly went to his death are in the background, too. To lay down one's life for one's friends (John 15:13) becomes tied to thousands and thousands of deaths on the battlefield as heroic, Christ-like self-sacrifices. The Bible of war in this case is one of comfort to soldiers and one that justifies violence as duty and death as sacrifice. The tendencies in the War Bibles I have discussed in relation to crusaders and the First World War are in many ways shared by the War Bible assemblage of the far right that I have been mapping. Of course, there are disconnections and discontinuities in these forms of Bible-use, particularly if we begin to look in more detail. But I have offered a short account here to tease out particular shared tendencies in order to highlight why a War Bible might be effective and why it might be activated and reactivated in different forms over time. Producing affects of righteous anger, courage, and comfort; framing violence as defensive and sacrificial; providing heroic figures and ideals to imitate; encouraging resistance to an enemy who is construed as evil, where one is on the side of God—these are all features that characterise the War Bibles I have analysed. All of these features make violence less unpalatable and more justifiable, excusing or even glamourising the perpetrator.

But War Bibles are made up not only of bits of Bible. I want to now highlight two components that are crucial to make Breivik's War Bible work, that I already began to outline in chapter 3, namely, connections to the Middle Ages and masculinity. I touched on the way particularly the medieval crusades feature in the manifesto in chapter 3, but I now expand this to demonstrate the way the Crusades are used more broadly by far-right movements. It is important to highlight these other components that stick to the far-right War Bible I have been mapping, as they are crucial elements in making it work. While the analysis in chapter 3 focused inwards on the manifesto, the following discussion moves outwards to demonstrate the way these non-biblical components that stick to a far-right War Bible are relevant far beyond the Breivik case.

Crusader Scripts

Medieval scholars have drawn attention to the way the Middle Ages is used by figures on the far right, from medieval motifs and crosses to the Latin phrase "Deus vult". I already began to discuss in chapter 3 how a "Middle Ages" is assembled that plugs into the War Bible in Breivik's manifesto. But this non-biblical component in Breivik's worldview resonates across contemporary far-right ideology and practice. In this way, the crusader use of a Bible I discussed earlier is quite clearly being reactivated, sometimes explicitly with a Bible and sometimes with other crusader symbols, texts, and artefacts.

The Middle Ages is used in a fantasy for a "homogenously white, universally Christian" Europe.[138] The group of neo-Nazis who marched through Charlottesville, Virginia, in 2017, for instance, wielded clubs and shields with medieval insignia.[139] As William Diebold notes, the motif on the Charlottesville shield was also depicted on the cover of the manifesto written by the perpetrator of the attack on two mosques in Christchurch, New Zealand, in 2019, which killed fifty-one people. The perpetrator cited Breivik as an inspiration. As Diebold shows, the way the contemporary far right uses the Middle Ages is connected to the Nazi self-conception and its obsession with that period in history.[140]

The Celtic cross is another symbol that has been taken up in far-right circles. Maggie Williams discusses the way the Celtic cross has become part of nationalist and racist discourse, such as that on the website Stormfront: "Because we can't use the swastika is why we use the Celtic Cross. It symbolises Christendom and Christianity and also the white, pre-Christian tribes in Europe".[141] White supremacists mobilise the Celtic cross against Black and Jewish people.[142] The image of the cross in the Stormfront post consists of a white, equal-armed cross, outlined in black and set within a black circle. Stormfront's version of the cross includes the slogan "White Pride World Wide" around the ring. In the ancient world, such designs appeared in Scandinavia, central Europe, Ireland, and elsewhere, but they are pre-Christian in date and therefore did not originally symbolise "Christendom and Christianity", as the Stormfront post would have it.[143] As Williams

---

[138] David Perry, 'Introduction', in *Whose Middle Ages? Teachable Moments for an Ill-Used Past*, edited by Andrew Albin, Mary C. Erler, Thomas O'Donnell, Nicholas L. Paul, and Nina Rowe (New York: Fordham University Press, 2019), p. 6.
[139] Ibid.
[140] William Diebold, 'The Nazi Middle Ages', in *Whose Middle Ages?*, edited by Albin, Erler, O'Donnell, Paul, and Rowe, pp. 104–105.
[141] Maggie Williams, '"Celtic" Crosses and the Myth of Whiteness', in *Whose Middle Ages*, edited by Albin, Erler, O'Donnell, Paul, and Rowe, p. 220.
[142] Ibid., p. 221.
[143] Ibid.

points out, discourse on the far right fantasises about a "pre-national Europe, where they envision a blended culture of pale-skinned people—Celts, Vikings, Anglo-Saxons—whom they can classify as 'white'".[144] But this is a fantasy. Each of these groups was already more diverse than they imagine.[145] "Conflating a pre-Christian deity with the Christian notion of a cross in this way serves to construct an indefinite sense of 'white' Christian culture that fuses very different contexts into a single, convenient narrative and symbol of dominance".[146]

The Latin phrase "Deus vult" ("God wills") has come to the centre of recent discourse of hatred and violence towards Muslims.[147] Adam Bishop discusses the way #deusvult is associated with far-right politics and particularly anti-Islamic messages on social media platforms.[148] In the United States, mosques in Arkansas were vandalised with the phrase in October 2016; in Scotland in December 2016, the phrase also appeared on a mosque. Deus vult was a battle cry in the First Crusade and in later crusades in the twelfth and thirteenth centuries. Pope Urban II's speech in November 1095 called upon Christians of Western Europe to send military assistance to the Byzantine Empire, which was under attack from the Muslim Seljuk Turks.[149] Clearly, then, this reference to take up arms against a Muslim enemy is what is reactivated in the reuse of the phrase today. Bishop emphasises the way white supremacists who use the phrase Deus vult would like to re-create a Christian utopia they imagine existed in the past. He argues that in this sense they are not misusing the phrase; in fact, their usage is completely in line with its original intent. "The crusaders really believed that God wanted them to kill Muslims and restore and preserve Christian rule".[150]

These revitalisations and reconstructions of the crusades can be understood as the "revived pasts" that Kristin Skottki describes as the "memories, imaginations and re-enactments of historical events that still (or again) surround us today".[151] The idea of a "revived past" highlights "the performative

---

[144] Ibid.
[145] Ibid.
[146] Ibid., p. 222.
[147] Adam M. Bishop, '#DeusVult', in *Whose Middle Ages?*, edited by Albin, Erler, O'Donnell, Paul, and Rowe, p. 256.
[148] Ibid.
[149] Ibid., p. 257.
[150] Ibid., p. 260.
[151] Kristin Skottki, 'The Dead, the Revived and the Recreated Pasts: "Structural Amnesia" in Representations of Crusade History', in *Perceptions of the Crusades from the Nineteenth to the Twenty-First Century, Engaging the Crusades vol. 1*, edited by Mike Horswell and Jonathan Phillips (London: Routledge, 2018), p. 110.

and constructed character of 'historical culture' (*Geschichtskultur*) and draws attention to non-academic representations of, and engagements with, the past".[152] The function of the revived past of the crusades in Breivik's manifesto is to foreground the "righteous violence" of Christian Europe against Islam, in a battle raging from the Middle Ages until today. This sort of assembling of bits of history and fantasies of a past are modes that enable "later communities to constitute and sustain themselves".[153] It is not a unique feature of Breivik's manifesto or of his War Bible assemblage. Rather, it is both a result of, and part of propagating, a worldview in which violence is necessary to protect an imagined white Europe, dedicated to Christendom.

Skottki provides important background as to *why* and *how* the crusades have come to the fore in recent public debate, particularly since George W. Bush's infamous description in 2001 of the war on terror as a crusade.[154] After 9/11 some voices in the public sphere characterised the acts of terror as a to some extent understandable response to Western atrocities against Muslim societies, harking back to the crusades. In response to these views, some intellectuals "used the concept of the 'Clash of Civilizations' to turn this argument around, portraying religious violence as deeply rooted in Islamic culture and religion itself. In this version, the crusades were presented as an early, necessary attempt to stop the violent sprawl of Islam".[155] Perhaps the most prominent intellectual participating in this debate is Thomas Madden, an American historian, former chair of the History Department at Saint Louis University in St. Louis, Missouri, and director of Saint Louis University's Center for Medieval and Renaissance Studies. As mentioned earlier, Madden is cited by Breivik. Madden claims that during the crusades the "violence was all on the Muslim side. At some point what was left of the Christian world would have to defend itself or simply succumb to Islamic conquest. [. . .] In other words, the Crusades were from the beginning a defensive war".[156] As Skottki puts it, Islamist violence is in these accounts "'fetishized' as the essence of Islam, reifying the image of the everlasting medieval-ness

---

[152] Ibid.
[153] Elizabeth A. Castelli, *Martyrdom and Memory: Early Christian Culture Making* (New York: Columbia University Press, 2004), p. 5.
[154] Of course, Osama bin Laden also accused the United States and Israel of being crusaders. For a discussion of this in relation to discourses about religion after 9/11, see Ulrich Schmiedel, *Terror und Theologie: Der religionstheoretische Diskurs der 9/11-Dekade* (Tübingen: Mohr Siebeck, 2021), particularly chapter 1, pp. 1–38.
[155] Skottki, 'The Dead, the Revived and the Recreated Pasts', p. 121.
[156] Thomas F. Madden, 'Crusade Myths', *Catholic Dossier* 1 (2002); Madden, *The Crusades Controversy: Setting the Record Straight* (North Palm Beach, FL: Wellspring, 2017).

of Muslims".[157] Dressed up as knights, white supremacists chant "Deus vult" and carry crusader flags and banners, imagining they are Templars fighting against Muslims to defend a white Christian Europe and North America.[158] This is of course precisely what Breivik did. The construction of the Middle Ages at work in this discourse feeds into a War Bible in which manly soldiers of Christ are invoked, taking up the sword Christ ordered his followers to buy, bringing not peace but a sword. The God of Breivik's War Bible is a God of "Deus vult" who wills violence against the enemy of "his people".

As I mentioned in chapter 1, Andrew Elliott writes about the reuse and remediation of the Middle Ages across media platforms. Elliott calls the medievalism at work in much of this reuse and remediation "banal medievalism". In his analysis of the banal medievalism that appears in Breivik's manifesto, he points to the way Breivik's medievalism "offered him a way to explain current world events": "The banal medievalism of Crusades, Templars and jihad thus offered Breivik a parallel fantasy world of shared heritage, a myth of racial purity and a false sense of national identity".[159] In Breivik's self-understanding, his attacks were a part of a broader crusade.[160] Elliott describes the rise of far-right online platforms and the proliferation of social media networks in which the "interconnected medieval language used by the counterjihad bloggers" assumes new significance in Breivik's self-styled image as a Templar knight.[161] The recirculation of banal medievalisms in these circles occurs with memes, jokes, and snippets of quotations.[162] As Elliott puts it:

> It is this closed loop, and the freedom of the internet and unpoliced social media, which allow for the warm embrace of extremist positions to circulate in isolation, far from the prying eyes of alternative or moderate opinions and without the necessity for fact-checking or historical scrutiny, or the demands of peer-review. It is in this closed loop that Breivik's own medievalist ideology was thus formed and perpetuated.[163]

---

[157] Skottki, 'The Dead, the Revived and the Recreated Pasts', p. 122.
[158] Bishop, '#DeusVult', p. 264.
[159] Elliott, *Medievalism, Politics and Mass Media*, p. 141.
[160] Ibid., p. 142.
[161] Ibid., p. 141.
[162] Ibid., p. 153.
[163] Ibid., p. 154.

Elliott draws attention to the wider networks of banal medievalism in far-right circles. He describes the "counterjihad filter bubble" to designate the closed circuit of networks that provide confirmation and reinforcement of paranoid fantasies about a clash of civilisations taking place.[164] This sort of counterjihad filter bubble can lead to an "immersive radicalization", a "self-contained and immersive loop of extremist propaganda".[165] He discusses the "spreadability" of banal medievalism,[166] particularly in portraying Islam as inherently medieval and thus "other". He describes online networks of "closed, and highly influential, counterjihadist websites trading memes, photos, cartoons and medievalist references to a clash of civilizations".[167]

As Elliott points out, one of the ways counterjihadist ideology works is by positing violence as self-defence.[168] A narrative is obsessively repeated of Islam as a medieval and barbaric religion incapable of adaptation to modernity.[169] Couched in the language of defence, "the counterjihadists sidestep accusations of exclusionary racism by celebrating a common (though wholly invented) medieval past among white Europeans; and second, by insisting that Islam is itself medieval, ideological objections are rooted in an antagonistic, dichotomous, and ultimately zero-sum language of the broader counterjihad movement, according to which there is 'no room' for tolerance in the face of temporally incompatible cultures".[170] What Elliott terms "participatory patriotism" is a means of rewriting the past used by far-right groups to "sidestep accusations of racism by adopting a celebratory mode of medievalism".[171] "According to this selective medievalism, the Middle Ages find themselves rewritten to offer an imagined heritage in the form of Templars (a model for united European efforts to 'combat' Islamisation), St George (a model of specifically English national identity), or the Crusades (a model for European Christian co-operation against a common enemy) as indices of national identity to nurture ideas of autochthonous belonging and entitlement".[172]

---

[164] Ibid., p. 173.
[165] Ibid., p. 174.
[166] Elliott uses this term, p. 8. But it comes from Henry Jenkins, Sam Ford, and Joshua Green, *Spreadable Media: Creating Value and Meaning in a Networked Culture* (New York: New York University Press, 2013).
[167] Ibid., p. 176.
[168] Ibid.
[169] Ibid., p. 177.
[170] Ibid., p. 178.
[171] Ibid.
[172] Ibid., p. 179.

In examining the War Bible assemblage, then, as it operates in Breivik's counterjihadist milieu, it is not enough to explain only the bits of Bible and the mode of Bible-use that operates in the assemblage. Non-biblical components are crucial, too. The Middle Ages is one part of the War Bible assemblage as I analysed it in chapter 3. In this section I have elaborated on this connection, to demonstrate the way the Middle Ages, particularly the crusades, are a crucial feature to examine in contemporary far-right ideology and practice. Using the Middle Ages may or may not connect to Bible-use. In Breivik's case, however, it does. A reliance on a particular narrative of the crusades is in part what makes Breivik's War Bible legible, with his bits of Bible fuelling war and violence alongside his self-presentation as a knight. But the Middle Ages functions more broadly in far-right circles in ways that might continue to produce versions of a War Bible. As I showed in my brief discussion of crusader Bible-use, there are highly relevant parallels to the depiction of Muslims that could continue to resonate with contemporary far-right groups, keen to seek legitimation and justification by turning to a Bible the way Breivik did. But another non-biblical—although it can also be biblical—component of Breivik's War Bible is masculinity. To understand how this War Bible works, it is necessary to turn to the way desires for masculinity stick to a particular kind of violent Bible, not just for the Breivik case.

Masculinity

From what I have discussed so far, it will be clear to most that gender issues are highly pertinent in the Breivik case and in the politics of contemporary far-right movements more generally. A crucial way in which the War Bible works is as a component that combines well with the calls for a re-invigorated patriarchy in Breivik's far-right milieu and his own fantasies about masculine heroism. In a telling comment in the manifesto, Breivik brings together his antagonism towards feminism and modern approaches to the Bible when he bemoans the way "traditional courses on 'dead white males' (such as Shakespeare, Milton and Chaucer)" are being replaced "with courses on women's studies or 'The Bible as Literature' (a course designed to denigrate the Bible as cleverly crafted fiction instead of God's truth)".[173] Here, the denigration of white men that he assumes is taking place in Western societies goes

[173] Manifesto, p. 35.

hand in hand with the denigration of the "word of God". He complains about how so-called Cultural Marxists designate "Muslims, Feminist women, homosexuals and some additional minority groups as virtuous and they view ethnic Christian European men as evil".[174]

Jorunn Økland points out that when Breivik surrendered to the police, he named multiculturalism, cultural Marxism, and feminism as the reasons for his attack.[175] Some weeks later, feminism was quietly dropped from public discussions.[176] Økland discusses the significance of one of Breivik's main targets in the terror attacks being Norway's first female prime minister, Gro Harlem Brundtland. Brundtland was on the island of Utøya earlier in the day on 22 July 2011; she was seen by Breivik as a dangerous feminist responsible for the decline of Norwegian society.[177] Økland proposes that feminism was not a major discussion point after the terror attacks because—even in Norwegian society, where gender equality is one of the social issues held in highest regard—it had increasingly become a culturally uncomfortable position to hold. Breivik, then, was tapping into antifeminist discourses that were already in place.[178] I have suggested that "masculinity" is a component of the War Bible that is non-biblical. But, of course, in many ways this component could be seen as eminently biblical, as Økland also points out. The Bible has primarily been cast as a protector of the patriarchy. Økland compares the misogyny in the Book of Revelation to Breivik's own hateful views of women as expressed in the manifesto. But Økland also points in another direction that is extra-biblical, and that is Michael Kimmel's notions of aggrieved entitlement, for understanding the importance of masculinity in Breivik's manifesto, and as I am suggesting, more broadly in right-wing movements.[179]

As Økland so clearly shows, patriarchal visions of society and desires for a hegemonic masculinity form a part of Breivik's worldview. In a rant about political correctness early on in the manifesto, Breivik writes that those who defy political correctness "must behave according to the old rules of our culture, not the new rules the cultural Marxists lay down".[180] The "old rules of our culture" are highly gendered: "Ladies should be wives and homemakers, not cops or soldiers, and men should still hold doors open for ladies. Children

---

[174] Ibid., p. 20.
[175] Økland, 'Manifestos, Gender, Self-Canonization, and Violence', p. 19.
[176] Ibid., p. 20.
[177] Ibid., pp. 18–19.
[178] Ibid., p. 21.
[179] Ibid., p. 22.
[180] Manifesto, p. 21.

should not be born out of wedlock. Glorification of homosexuality should be shunned. Jurors should not accept Islam as an excuse for murder".[181] Again, the suspicion towards Muslims as murderers is connected to the idea that women are no longer first and foremost "wives and homemakers". These patriarchal and misogynistic positions are connected to Breivik's War Bible and make it work. The War Bible is made up of references to David fighting Goliath; it is made in conjunction with Breivik's dress-up as a policeman on Utøya, with his game-playing of World of Warcraft, with his crusader costume, his paganly named weapons, and his car named after Thor's wagon. Connecting the Breivik case to Kimmel's discussion of aggrieved entitlement points towards broader tendencies relating to violence and masculinity, particularly as they function in right-wing ideology and practice.

In *Angry White Men: American Masculinity at the End of an Era*, the sociologist Michael Kimmel travelled around the United States "to take the pulse of angry American white men".[182] He discusses the way downward mobility, economic instability, and the shifts in gender politics and employment structures have led many men to experience a sense of loss in their lives. Rights to a secure job, stable family life, respect and status in society, are perceived by these men as their entitlement. Sexual insecurity and humiliation are part of this narrative of loss. What links the different groups Kimmel discusses is what he calls "aggrieved entitlement".[183]

Aggrieved entitlement, he argues, has led to "sporadic outbursts, clandestine terrorist conspiracies, and paranoid political thinking".[184] The sense of entitlement Kimmel diagnoses belongs to middle- and upper-class white men. They operate with a nostalgic longing for a past world where they no longer feel like victims of the contemporary social order.[185] As Kimmel puts it: "Angry White Men look to the past for their imagined and desired future".[186]

Arguably, aggrieved entitlement is an important component in Breivik's worldview, too, where there is a clear nostalgia expressed for a "golden age" in which men were men and women were women. A desire for a re-invigorated masculinity is part of the call for a white Europe free of foreign influence.

---

[181] Ibid.
[182] Michael Kimmel, *Angry White Men: American Masculinity at the End of an Era* (New York: Nation Books, 2013), p. 9.
[183] Ibid., p. 18.
[184] Ibid., p. 276.
[185] Ibid., p. 17.
[186] Ibid., p. 21.

Aggrieved entitlement leads to a misdirected anger, Kimmel explains, frequently towards those further down on the social-economic ladder. This leads to a scapegoating, particularly of Jews, minorities, immigrants, and women.[187] The anger is fuelled towards "a generalized ethnic and racial 'other'—who is seen as threatening to transform America from a Christian (read: white) nation into a multicultural polyglot with no center of racial gravity".[188] This is not a problem peculiar to the United States. In Breivik's brand of the far right there is arguably also an anger fuelled and intensified against Muslim immigrants who are racialised as "other". Kimmel writes, if "your despair can be massaged into this Manichaean struggle between Us and Them, you, too, can be mobilized into the army of Angry White Men".[189] When threatened, the sense of entitlement "can be manipulated into an enraged protectionism, a sense that the threat to 'us' is internal, those undeserving others who want to take for themselves what we have rightfully earned".[190] This is a virtual social movement, organised virtually in chatrooms, on websites, and in cyberspace. It focuses on the promise of empowering men. White supremacist organisations that stoke and exploit the anger of aggrieved entitlement produce websites "saturated with images of warrior-like men, donning weaponry, shields, and armor".[191]

A form of aggrieved entitlement works with Breivik's War Bible. Anger is expressed at what has been lost in Europe and towards the enemy who is perceived as the cause of this loss. The ranting against multiculturalism and the demonisation of Muslims stems from feelings of aggrieved entitlement. Multiculturalism and Muslim immigrants are blamed for everything from the loss of European Christian values and the decline of European culture to women's liberation and divorce rates. The War Bible works with aggrieved entitlement because it can furnish a set of examples of heroic masculinity, modelled in a God of War—akin to the ultimate masculine general and his uber-masculine soldiers. It puts God firmly on the side of the soldiers rallying against "Eurabia", shoring up righteous anger and an innocent violence masked as defence against an evil enemy.

"Toxic masculinity" is one term that could be used about Breivik and his brand of patriarchal misogyny. Toxic masculinity might in fact be a crucial

---

[187] Ibid., p. 24.
[188] Ibid., p. 28.
[189] Ibid., p. 32.
[190] Ibid., p. 35.
[191] Ibid., p. 264.

component in Breivik's War Bible: a vision of crusaders and good soldiers of Christ, of dying for your friends and taking up Jesus's sword, and fighting in God's name, is arguably a toxic combination of fantasies of re-invigorated masculinity associated with strength, militancy, and aggression, and particular Bible texts as well as snippets of Christian history. In her study of English Defence League activists, Elizabeth Pearson cautions against using the label "toxic masculinity" for men on the far right, though. Notions of masculinity, and even hyper-masculinity, are certainly operant in far-right circles, as Pearson also demonstrates. Particular ideas about size, the potential for violence, and desires not to be victimised, or perceived as victimised, are part of the far-right milieu she examines. Aggressive "masculine behaviours, rituals and practices that appear threatening to—or indeed threaten—others feel *positive*".[192] Through her interviews with English Defence League activists between 2016 and 2018, she seeks, however, to problematise notions of "toxicity". Pearson argues that what is clear is that EDL protesters activate notions of masculinity that are already there in society.[193] There is "continuity between EDL masculine identities and wider—patriarchal—norms dating from well before the emergence of the counter-jihad scene. The EDL is a microcosm of sections of wider British society".[194] Her point is not to dismiss the role masculinity plays, but to suggest that labelling it as "toxic" occludes its continuities with wider patriarchal norms.[195] When individual men are regarded as the problem, she writes, "the issue becomes not one of patriarchy, or society, but of agency in specific groups, and the responsibility for 'fixing' patriarchy is pushed onto them".[196] Particular men, then, are designated as uniquely toxic, and therefore problematic notions of masculinity are not explored in broader ways. It is a way of distinguishing between good and bad men.[197] This could also be seen as a problem with the Breivik case, where he becomes an exceptional figure who is dismissed as irrelevant for broader trends and tendencies. Økland raises an important question when she asks why it seemed to be so hard to talk about, and push back against, Breivik's antifeminism, in the aftermath of the terror attacks.[198] Was Breivik's own antifeminism connected to broader, albeit weaker, backlashes against

---

[192] Pearson, 'Extremism and Toxic Masculinity: The Man Question Re-posed', p. 1268.
[193] Ibid.
[194] Ibid.
[195] Ibid.
[196] Ibid., p. 1269.
[197] Ibid.
[198] Økland, 'Manifestos, Gender, Self-Canonization, and Violence', p. 20.

feminism, as Økland suggests? In any case, it is dangerous to assume that a figure such as Breivik can be isolated as the problematic exception, while the rest of the society of which he himself is a part is untouched by antifeminist tendencies.

No Bible-use in warfare or for violent purposes functions only with biblical elements. The War Bible assemblage needs also non-biblical components to work effectively. There may be some circles in which mostly biblical components can furnish a worldview, inform agendas, and spur on action. But Breivik's far-right milieu is more diverse than that, occupying territories that are not biblical or Christian or religious. The Middle Ages and masculinity are two elements that stick to Breivik's War Bible. I highlighted these because I contend that they are important for broader far-right trends. The use of the Middle Ages in far-right circles, such as Breivk's own use, play upon the idea of a loss of a golden age. This non-biblical component of the War Bible provides an image of a past of white European Christendom when men were brave and valiant crusaders and women knew their place. Aggrieved entitlement is a key component of the War Bible because it stokes a sense—particularly among middle-class men—of loss and nostalgia for a past when everything was better. Anger arises from this loss and is directed against particular groups who are blamed for the loss, however misdirected this anger is. In Breivik's worldview the anger is directed at Muslims and particularly Muslim immigrants. The War Bible is fuelled by aggrieved entitlement. It plays into a loss of masculinity and pride which is intensified and played upon to re-inforce particular views of masculinity as valour, strength, and honour.

Activating a War Bible

In this chapter I have connected the War Bible at work in Breivik's manifesto to two sources mentioned in the manifesto, the "battle verses" from the Bible-Knowledge webpage, and Joseph Farah's Tea Party manifesto. The biblical texts concerning violence that Breivik cites come from the Bradley brothers' web page and resonate with Farah's Bible as radical document to fight the so-called governing elites. The War Bible that I argue is at work in Breivik's manifesto could be connected to Bibles throughout history that have been taken up as part of warfare. In particular, two tendencies at work are the encouragement of righteous animosity against a Muslim enemy and the providing of comfort and confidence in alleging that violence is justified and even divinely ordained. The contemporary far-right War Bible that Breivik takes up is particularly effective because it is stuck also to non-biblical components, such as the Middle Ages and masculinity. When the War Bible is at work it can produce important effects and affects: to situate the group who lays claim to a Bible as innocent victims against an evil enemy, to sanctify violence-as-sacrifice, and to situate oneself as the righteous victim with God on one's side. A Bible is territorialised in Breivik's manifesto, which reactivates potencies in Bible-use that have previously been activated in very different settings by very different actors. The affects the War Bible play on and produce are nostalgia for an imagined past that is lost. Righteous anger is part of this Bible towards an enemy who is conceived of as brutal and "other". A sense of honour is tied to the War Bible as images of masculine valour and courage are invoked. The War Bible is effective and affective in its ability to provide a clear-cut enemy and inspire fantasies of masculinity tied to valour and glorified violence. But as I have already made clear, the War Bible assemblage is not the only way Bible-use operates in far-right milieus. The Civilisation Bible operates with another set of interlocutors, milieus, histories, affects, and materials. It is to this less violent—though not non-violent—assemblage that I now turn.

6
The Civilisation Bible

On 19 December 2020, the leader of British far-right organisation Britain First, Paul Golding, quoted Proverbs 3:3 on the group's social media profile on Telegram: "Don't let kindness and truth forsake you. Bring them around your neck. Write them on the tablet of your heart". The quote was accompanied by the message: "The Bible includes 66 separate books written over thousands of years by dozens of authors. But these disparate writings all tell a single story and narrative, a remarkable feat! Nothing else like it exists. It is a truly remarkable document and Western civilisation is based upon it . . .".[1] Paul Golding's Bible in this Telegram post is not an isolated Bible. It activates the Civilisation Bible assemblage that I mapped in Breivik's manifesto and in the wider far-right milieu of which he is a part. The post is in many ways simply repeating a claim that many, across the political spectrum and regardless of faith, would make about the importance and influence of the Christian Bible.[2] But crucially, Golding's post is specifically connecting to an anti-Islam campaign which is assembled also with biblical texts and with Bibles.

In this chapter I focus on the Civilisation Bible. In the first part of the chapter, I continue exploring figures who are cited in Breivik's manifesto, turning to two figures who are mentioned in the manifesto but who do not self-identify with the Eurabia and counterjihad network: Rémi Brague and Roger Scruton. Neither would be obviously connected to Breivik's far-right milieu; they are minor voices as they are cited in the manifesto, in contrast to the more major voices I discussed in chapter 4. Brague and Scruton are both well-known philosophers. Both have published on European culture and Western civilisation, topics that have been taken up by the European far-right in recent years. I examine the books by Scruton and Brague that are

---

[1] For a discussion of Britain First's Bible-use, see Hannah Strømmen, 'Crusades, Christ and Christmas: Islamophobia and the Bible in the European Far-Right after 9/11', *Zeitschrift für Religion, Gesellschaft und Politik* (2023): https://doi.org/10.1007/s41682-023-00148-1.

[2] Sometimes, as I have shown, it is "Judeo-Christian" scripture that is presented as the source of Western values, but often the "Jewish" elements of Bible are not included.

mentioned in the manifesto, scrutinising what Bible appears in their writings and how their own constructions of a Bible might be drawn into Breivik's counterjihad milieu, particularly to accelerate the Civilisation Bible assemblage. My intention is not to taint Scruton and Brague by association with Breivik. As Mattias Ekman argues, it is important to make a distinction between the intellectuals who participate actively in counterjihadist networks and those who are used as "validators" in the discourse.[3] Brague and Scruton are used as validators: thinkers whose writings are used to validate an Islamophobic position and programme. Even if the Bible that appears in their writings is not explicitly taken up in Breivik's manifesto, I identify connections and disconnections in the milieu that are created through Breivik's manifesto and its multiple statements and citations. Scruton's and Brague's arguments and articulations take different directions to those I discussed in chapter 4 by Fjordman, Spencer, Ye'or, Fallaci, and Bawer. Their own mode of Bible-use differs also from that of the Bradley brothers and Joseph Farah that I discussed in the previous chapter.

As in the last chapter, this one, too, has three interrelated arguments. First, I argue that Breivik's Civilisation Bible assemblage needs to be understood in connection with forms of Bible-use that emphasise the biblical form and content of European culture and Western civilisation. Second, the Civilisation Bible assemblage I have analysed activates past Bibles, particularly claims to "the Bible" as cultural heritage and as civilisational-colonial tool in early modern European developments. Third, elements that particularly stick to the Civilisation Bible to make it work are the clash of civilisations thesis and the dominant constructions of "culture" and "religion" that are part and parcel of the clash thesis.

The Biblical Form of Europe

Rémi Brague is a French historian of philosophy, born in 1947. Educated at the École Normale Supérieure, he studied ancient Greek thought, Hebrew, and Arabic. He is professor emeritus of Arabic and religious philosophy at the Sorbonne and holds the Romano Guardini chair of philosophy at the Ludwig-Maximilians-Universität of Munich. Brague is the author of multiple books and articles in French and in English. He is perhaps most well known

---

[3] Ekman, 'Online Islamophobia and the Politics of Fear', p. 1991.

in the English-speaking world for his book *Eccentric Culture: A Theory of Western Civilization*, from 1992. It is this book that is mentioned in Breivik's manifesto, in an article written by Fjordman and cited by Breivik.[4] The part of this book that is cited in the manifesto is not about a Bible. Nonetheless, it is the parts about Christian scripture that I will focus on, after explaining briefly the case Brague makes in *Eccentric Culture*. I am not trying to make the argument that Breivik, or Fjordman, in some sense copied or were inspired directly by Brague's writings on "the Bible". Rather, I am teasing out what notions of Bible circulate in the sources that are cited by Breivik, in order to identify what biblical assemblages operate in the wider discourse of which Breivik was a part—even if Breivik or Fjordman never paid any conscious or explicit attention to Brague's Bible.

In *Eccentric Culture*, Brague reflects on what the essence of Europe is. Ultimately, Brague concludes that "Romanity" is at the heart of Europe. Romanity for Brague is the Roman tendency to borrow from other cultures: "To be Roman is to experience the ancient as new and as something renewed by its transplantation in new soil, a transplantation that makes the old a principle of new developments. The experience of the commencement as a (re)commencement is what it is to be Roman".[5] To be Roman is to answer a call to renew the ancient.[6] Brague therefore valorises what he calls "secondarity". In many ways Brague's central argument counters the far-right ideological tendencies I have described as linked to the Eurabia and counterjihad milieu. He has no patience for desires for cultural purity or nativist notions of belonging. Brague insists that "culture" is always acquired, never innate. Every culture is "a land of immigration".[7] Even "Romanity" does not signify a pure essence for Europe to celebrate as its own achievement. Romanity is not a "return to what is proper to the culture and which would have existed in all its purity at the time of the founding origins".[8] "On the contrary, it tends toward a source located *outside* of European culture—in this case, in Greco-Latin antiquity".[9] Brague is aware of the xenophobic pitfalls that open up when searching for the essence of a culture. As Brague reflects, discussions of "what is proper to a culture" often lead to the exclusion of what

---

[4] Fjordman, 'Western vs. Islamic science and religion'.
[5] Rémi Brague, *Eccentric Culture: A Theory of Western Civilization* (South Bend, IN: St. Augustine's Press, 2002 [1992]), p. 34.
[6] Ibid., p. 35.
[7] Ibid., p. 122.
[8] Ibid., pp. 122–123.
[9] Ibid., p. 123.

is considered improper.[10] He wants to avoid this tendency of othering. His own "model of relation to oneself and to the other", he reflects, makes this othering tricky.[11] "Culture cannot be, for the European, something that he possesses and that constitutes his identity".[12] If the model to imitate is outside, then the greatness to recall must be that of the other.[13] Brague therefore avoids any simplistic definition or definitive characterisation of Western civilisation and Europe. He explicitly avoids the superiority-mongering of figures such as Fallaci, Fjordman, and Spencer. Brague does not hold on to any closed or clear-cut notion of a Western civilisation cut off from Islam. Interactions between Europe and the Islamic world throughout history have been important.

In *Eccentric Culture*, Brague is not simply interested in mapping the *content* of European culture as if that would proffer the answer as to what Europe *is*. He is more interested in the *form* Europe takes, particularly the form Europe takes in relation to its culture. Here, the sacred scripture of Christians comes to play an important role. But a particular Bible comes up as the content of Europe, too. I will sketch this Bible first, before turning to the biblical form of Europe, as Brague sees it. Uncontroversially, Christianity forms part of the content of European culture for Brague, alongside other elements such as the Greco-Roman and Jewish heritages.[14] When it comes to Bibles, he argues that the Christian Bible—Old and New Testament—constitutes an important part of the European cultural content. The list of the "Old Testament's cultural influences on Europe" could be "quickly drawn up", but it would also be an enormous undertaking.[15] Brague nonetheless lists some examples, such as the idea of the supremacy of man over the rest of creation. The idea of a temporality that is radically non-cyclical, given an absolute beginning (the Creation), and maybe an end, is, he writes "obviously Biblical in origin".[16] The idea that man's relation to God is realised especially through moral practices came to Europe from the prophets of the Old Covenant.[17] The anthropology of Western civilisation, sense of time, and morality, are in this way indebted to a Christian Bible. Although these references could all

---

[10] Ibid., p. 135.
[11] Ibid.
[12] Ibid.
[13] Ibid., p. 138.
[14] Ibid., p. 176.
[15] Ibid., p. 53.
[16] Ibid.
[17] Ibid.

refer to the Jewish scriptures, Brague clearly posits that the Bible's influence in Europe is refracted through a Christian lens.

The other way that a Bible informs the content of European culture is through a Christianity which "distinguishes the temporal and the spiritual, the religious and the political".[18] Here he draws a contrast between Christianity and the Islamic world.[19] Several biblical verses are cited to demonstrate this separation, which essentially conjures up Europe's secular proclivities. Samuel's choice of Saul in 1 Samuel, he writes, "set in place a lasting antagonism between politics and religion".[20] The preaching of Jesus is also key. The distinction between the religious and the political "was formulated in the words of Christ on the necessity of rendering to Caesar what belongs to Caesar, and to God what belongs to God (Matthew 22:17 and parallels)".[21] Further, citing John 6:15, Brague notes that Jesus refused to be king.[22] The incarnation is key for secularity, too. According to Brague, *"the emergence of a profane domain, and its consequences in European history, including the possibility of 'secular' societies—and even of radical atheism—is made possible by the idea of incarnation"*.[23] In Brague's invocation of a Bible that tends towards separating the religious from the political, we get an origin point for the later secular inflections of European culture.

This is a form of the Civilisation Bible, wherein the origins of Western Civilisation are rooted in a Bible that brings a particular view of humanity, morality, temporality, and secularity. It is not controversial to make the case that Bibles have had a huge influence on Europe and the West more broadly. Most would agree that this is the case. But the trajectories this influence has taken are more nebulous and complex than Brague explains. Perhaps more importantly, though, pointing directly back to a Bible as a founding influence, rather than the making of Bibles—its uses and understandings—is a way of eliding the processes in which Bibles have been made in the image of the user/interpreter as much as the other way around.

More importantly, for Brague, however, a Bible shapes the very form of Europe. The Bible that Brague invokes is in fact precisely the model of Romanity that he celebrates as Europe's essence. Like the Romans, Christians borrowed from others. "Christianity superimposed itself on what

---

[18] Ibid., p. 157.
[19] Ibid.
[20] Ibid., p. 158.
[21] Ibid.
[22] Ibid.
[23] Ibid., p. 165. Emphasis in original.

already existed. It grafted itself on a civilisation that was already organized according to its own laws".[24] Christianity "constitutes the very *form* of the European relationship to its cultural heritage".[25] Brague sees Christianity's relationship to its past, to the "Old Covenant", that is, to Judaism, as the very structure of secondarity that he values in the Romans.[26] In other words, the structure of the New Testament following an Old Testament without the former rejecting or replacing the latter is a religious version of Romanity. "The Christians are essentially 'Romans' in that they have their 'Greeks' to which they are tied by an indivisible bond. *Our Greeks are the Jews.* To say it a little less quickly: Christianity is to the Old Covenant what the Romans were to the Greeks".[27] Brague cites Paul (Romans 11:24) to signify the way the Christians are grafted onto the Jewish people.[28] In the relationship Brague sees Christianity having with Judaism, he draws a contrast with Islam.

> While Islam rejects the authenticity of the documents on which Judaism and Christianity are founded, Christianity, in the worst case, recognizes at least that the Jews are the faithful guardians of a text that it considers as sacred as the text which is properly its own. In this way, the relationship of secondarity toward a preceeding religion is found between Christianity and Judaism and between these two alone.[29]

Marcionism comes up several times in *Eccentric Culture* as a tendency to be critiqued. The cutting off of the past that Marcionism represents in Brague's understanding is what impedes the Romanity he values. In Islam's relationship to the scripture of the Jews and Christians, Muslims fail for Brague as a religious people in this Romanity.

Ultimately, for Brague, Europe is not only the validation of other cultures and religions as part of the European self that is unique to Europe. It is the very universal nature that such a validation signifies that marks Europe. Brague writes, therefore, that "the content of Europe, it is just to be a container, to be open to the universal".[30] The understanding of Europe and of Christianity as particularly tied to notions of the universal is of course not unique to Brague.

[24] Ibid.
[25] Ibid., p. 176.
[26] Ibid.
[27] Ibid., p. 54.
[28] Ibid.
[29] Ibid., p. 64.
[30] Ibid., p. 146.

It is a much-discussed idea that has garnered critique, particularly in recent years. By implication, non-Europeans, and Jews and Muslims, become the particular and the exclusive. In Fjordman's article, which Breivik cites in the manifesto, the point is made that Brague claims Muslims traditionally lack the instinct for self-criticism and appreciation of "the other".[31] Brague is taken up, then, to draw distinctions between (Christian) Europe and Islam, in which the latter are in some important and definitive sense lacking. Extrapolating on Brague, it is clear that he is contributing to a long tradition of celebrating Christianity as the universal and indicting Judaism as the particularistic. Islam, too, for Brague, is cast as deficient. These tendencies have been extensively critiqued as hugely problematic in its understanding of these religious traditions as well as in the effects this kind of view has had on non-Christians.

Jayne Svenungsson has traced back notions of Christian Europe to the influential eighteenth-century German Romanticist thinker known as Novalis.[32] As she shows, Novalis yearned for a revitalisation of a cosmopolitan spirit he sees in the Middle Ages. When read in his own historical context, he cannot easily be cast as a proponent of exclusivist notions of Christian Europe.[33] Nonetheless, his writings have inspired modes of conceptualising Europe that are problematic and that are apparent in Brague's Christian Europe.[34] One such problem is precisely the issue of universalism. Svenungsson situates Novalis in a universalist tradition that runs deep in Christianity, and that Brague arguably also taps into. While universalism, as Svenungsson argues, has no doubt in many ways been a positive resource throughout history, it is also problematic, particularly in relation to other traditions, Judaism especially.[35] Throughout the history of Christianity, the Jewish tradition has consistently been cast as exclusive and discriminatory in contrast to Christianity's message of universal salvation. Further, the idea that Christianity has superseded Judaism as a progressive and superior form of religion has frequently been tied to these perceptions of Christianity as universal and Judaism as exclusive.[36] While celebrations of Christian Europe

---

[31] Fjordman, 'Western vs. Islamic Science and Religion', cited in Section 1.23 in the manifesto, p. 255.
[32] Svenungsson, 'Christian Europe: Borders and Boundaries of a Mythological Conception', pp. 120–134.
[33] Ibid., pp. 123–124.
[34] Ibid., p. 125.
[35] Ibid., p. 128.
[36] Ibid. Svenungsson mentions key thinkers for Europe and Christianity such as Joachim of Fiore, Friedrich Schleiermacher, and Immanuel Kant. See also Jayne Svenungsson, *Divining*

as a proponent of universalism might seem benign, Svenungsson warns against ignoring the stereotyping of Judaism and Jews that underlies this universalism as its other. As she argues, these age-old anti-Jewish tropes are resurfacing on a structural level in contemporary anti-Islamic movements.[37]

While Brague's description of Europe differs in important ways from the articulations of counterjihadist writers such as Spencer and Fjordman, there are connections between Brague's Bible and the Bible that appears in Breivik's manifesto—particularly the Bible I call the Civilisation Bible. It is perhaps unsurprising that Breivik himself and the counterjihadist milieu he predominantly cites lack the detail and historical awareness of a philosopher such as Brague. But they do repeat certain tenets that Brague emphasises, relating specifically to the Christian Bible as a key legacy for Europe, particularly when it comes to the cultural legacy of Christian scripture and to distinctions between the sacred and secular in Europe. This is a version of a Civilisation Bible, in which a Bible furnishes Europe with civilisational shape and cultural content. Brague, too, draws a line between (Christian) European culture and Islam. If the very form and content of Europe is indebted to a Bible in a profound way for Brague, then this is one elemental feature that distinguishes Europe from Islam, in which the Qur'an is not seen to inspire or instill the notions of "Romanity" that Brague's Christian Bible does. Brague himself does not draw this line in a xenophobic manner in the way figures such as Breivik obviously did. But the Civilisation Bible that he invokes is in many ways reactivated in Breivik's manifesto, through the voices, citations, and references that fill that massive text.

The point is not that Brague's Bible is exactly what is repeated in Breivik's manifesto, or whether Fjordman, for instance, took any interest in Brague's comments about Christian scripture. The point is that versions of the Civilisation Bible assemblage circulate in particular times and places, and a version of this assemblage operates in the network that is made through Breivik's manifesto. Another reason I highlight this version of the Civilisation Bible, though, is that whereas Breivik's manifesto lies on the extreme end of the far-right spectrum and will most likely be read by like-minded people

---

History: Prophetism, Messianism and the Development of the Spirit, translated by Stephen Donovan (New York: Berghahn, 2016) and Jayne Svenungsson, 'Religion and Secularity as Supersessionist Categories', *Zeitschrift für Religion, Gesellschaft und Politik* (2023): https://doi.org/10.1007/s41682-023-00156-1.

[37] Svenungsson, 'Christian Europe', p. 131.

and scholars who are studying it, the versions the Civilisation Bible take in a thinker like Brague's writings enjoy a much wider reach and obviously enjoy far greater respectability. I am not suggesting that Brague's Civilisation Bible in any simple or straightforward way *leads to* Breivik's violence or to a counterjihadist worldview. But it does contribute to the intensification of a particular kind of Bible-use that positions a Bible alongside Europe's roots, and as a distinctive assemblage set apart from Islamic culture and its scripture.

Scruton and the High Culture of the Bible

Roger Scruton (1944–2020) was a British philosopher and conservative thinker who held academic positions at several universities in the United Kingdom and the United States, amongst other places at Birkbeck College London and the University of Oxford. He edited the conservative political journal *The Salisbury Review* between 1982 and 2001 and was a senior fellow of the conservative American think tank Ethics and Public Policy Centre. He accepted a British knighthood in 2016 and the Order of Merit of Hungary from the Hungarian prime minister, Viktor Orbán, in 2019. By conservative scholars who share his views, Scruton has been called "the greatest living conservative thinker".[38] In response to Scruton's death in 2020, the British Conservative prime minister at the time, Boris Johnson, tweeted that the world had lost its greatest conservative thinker.[39] Like Brague, Scruton is the author of numerous books and articles, also for a more popular audience. Scruton's books *Modern Culture* (1998) and *The West and the Rest: Globalization and the Terrorist Threat* (2002) are mentioned in Breivik's manifesto.[40] I focus on these specific books, investigating to what extent a Bible is constructed in these sources and whether it connects or disconnects to Breivik's biblical assemblages. Again, as with Brague, it is not Scruton's references to a Bible that are directly quoted or mentioned in Breivik's manifesto. Nonetheless, after recounting briefly Scruton's focus in these books,

---

[38] Peter Augustine Lawler, 'Roger Scruton's Conservatism: Between Xenophobia and Oikophobia', *Perspectives on Political Science* 45, no. 4 (2016): p. 251.
[39] 'Roger Scruton: Conservative Thinker Dies at 75', *BBC News*, 13 January 2020, https://www.bbc.co.uk/news/uk-51084248.
[40] Manifesto, pp. 63, 333, 540–541.

I turn to his biblical references to demonstrate the way these references play into a Civilisation Bible assemblage.

In *Modern Culture*, Roger Scruton is much less detailed on the role that Christianity and Christian scripture have played in Western culture than Brague is in *Eccentric Culture*. All the same, religion and a Bible do turn out to play important roles in the book. Scruton is interested specifically in modern culture, in what he calls common culture and in what he calls high culture. As Scruton diagnoses the modern condition, people "no longer know what to do or what to feel; the meaninglessness of our world is a projection of our numbness towards it".[41] Culture supplies what is missing. We may have lost community in modern life, but culture can, through the imagination, recuperate "the old experience of home".[42] Modern life for Scruton spells out the loss of common culture. Due to the decline of a common culture that dignifies people and moralises their actions,[43] we need culture—specifically high culture—to sustain the ethical life.[44] If common culture "dignifies people, by setting their desires and projects within an enduring context", and provides "the words, gestures, rituals and beliefs which moralise our actions", then high culture is what keeps "these things alive".[45] High culture does so "by giving imaginative reality to the long-term view of things, and by setting us in the context of an imagined redemption".[46]

According to Scruton, the core of common culture is religion.[47] With the decline of religion, again, it is high culture that can take the place of religion.

> It seems to me that the art of our high culture—and not only of ours—has drawn upon and amplified the experiences which are given in less conscious form by religion: experiences of the sacred and the profane, of redemption from sin and the immersion in it, of guilt, sorrow and their overcoming through forgiveness and the one-ness of a community restored. Art has grown from the sacred view of life.[48]

---

[41] Roger Scruton, *Modern Culture* (London: Bloomsbury, 2018 [1998]), p. 155.
[42] Ibid.
[43] Ibid., p. 67.
[44] Ibid., p. 46.
[45] Ibid., p. 67.
[46] Ibid.
[47] Ibid., p. 5.
[48] Ibid., p. 40.

Scruton accepts the fact that religion has largely disappeared from modern culture. He argues that "culture is rooted in religion, and that the true effort of a high culture is to perpetuate the common culture from which it grew—to perpetuate it not as religion but as art, with the ethical life transfixed within the aesthetic gaze".[49] The relationship between culture and religion is, then, a tightly intertwined one, even if religion is only a ghostly presence in the culture we can embrace and be elevated by in modern society.

Throughout *Modern Culture* Scruton indicts kitsch and pop culture. He calls for a validation of high culture to ameliorate the feelings of meaninglessness and alienation that mark the loss of common culture in modern life. In this sense, the culture he values is very much marked by religion, particularly Christian scripture. In fact, through Scruton's encomium for high culture, he invokes a form of the Civilisation Bible. Scruton's Bible comes not through reference to biblical texts but through Western cultural artefacts. Scruton calls T. S. Eliot's *The Waste Land* "a founding document of modern English literature". The modern city Eliot invokes "calls for the refreshing rain of Christ's passion": "And the alienated observer is both Christ and the pilgrim seeking him—the soul for whom suffering is also a mystical redemption".[50] The story of Moses and Aaron is invoked through Arnold Schoenberg and his unfinished opera, *Moses and Aaron*.[51] Scruton points out that we "should not be surprised to find that so many modernists have been religious traditionalists", mentioning Igor Stravinsky, Olivier Messiaen, Benjamin Britten, Henri Matisse, and Henry Moore.[52]

In his argument for why imagination is a superior source of culture than fantasy, he invokes idolatry as the corollary to fantasy. Discussing idolatry, he turns to Exodus and the story of Moses, Aaron, and the golden calf. But Scruton's Bible is made from art rather than text. He discusses a painting, Nicolas Poussin's *Golden Calf,* in the National Gallery in London. The foreground is dominated by the calf, raised on its pedestal. The idol is a glowing surrogate, lifelike but dead, with the emphatic deadness of metal. Aaron gestures with priestly pride to his creation, while the people, drunk, helpless, and in the grip of collective delusion, dance like brainless animals around this thing less sacred than themselves. In focusing on the calf, their emotions are also out of focus—bewildered, diseased, gyrating in a void. In

---

[49] Ibid., p. 149.
[50] Ibid., p. 79.
[51] Ibid., p. 82.
[52] Ibid., p. 82.

the distance, barely visible, is the figure of Moses, descending from Mount Sinai with the tables of the law: the abstract decrees of an abstract God who can be understood through no earthly image but only through law.[53] Moses throws the stone tablets to the ground, breaking not the law but its earthly record. "The contrast here is between the active work of imagination, which points to a God beyond the sensory world, and the passive force of fantasy, which creates its own god out of sensory desires".[54] Proper worship over idolatry—which is here aligned with imagination over fantasy—is something a Bible has taught us. This is not a biblical text, however, but a Bible-as-art. A civilisational-cultural Bible can teach us the lessons that are already part of our cultural repository.

Like Brague, Scruton's Christian Bible is associated with universality. Scruton suggests that it is religions whose deities reside in texts that are "universal". The textual nature of Christianity is in this way highlighted as key for the development of high culture.[55] As he points out, the God of Israel showed no great inclination for "graven images".[56] As he sees it, part of the close connection between religion and culture comes from the sacred scripture of religions. Western civilisation, he writes, "is founded upon the written record".[57] The "core religions" of the West—Judaism and Christianity—are religions of the book, "in which Latin, Greek and Ancient Hebrew have achieved the sacred status of the voice of God, precisely through being written down".[58] "Our worldview descends from a common culture *founded* on a sacred text".[59] For Scruton, this is a status that is shared with Islam as another religion of the book.

Like Brague, Scruton seems to be aware of the fact that cultures as he conceives them might be perceived as exclusive or even xenophobic in the emphasis on what is common to those "within" the culture.[60] Scruton does not draw on Brague's argument about secondarity and Romanity. Nor does he develop a similar argument. However, he does hint at something similar. He notes that "our own common culture, which grew within the cosmopolitan order of the Roman Empire, under the inspired leadership of St Paul—an

---

[53] Ibid., p. 60.
[54] Ibid., p. 60.
[55] Ibid., p. 19.
[56] Ibid.
[57] Ibid., p.139.
[58] Ibid.
[59] Ibid., p. 140.
[60] Ibid., p. 127.

uprooted Jew who was also a Roman citizen—is expressly outward-going, a culture of merchants, adventurers and tradesmen, of seafarers and city-builders, for whom life among strangers is the norm".[61] Through his understanding of Paul, Scruton paves a way for Christianity to be the source of an open and outgoing culture. As Scruton explains it, Paul borrows the concept of corporate personality for the Christian idea of membership from Roman law: we are "members in Christ". From the outset, the church is "universal". "In brief, Christianity offers a membership that is available to all, which promises a new life, and which is not bound by the laws of the ancestors".[62] Here, the focus on the universality of Christianity and its connection to notions of community in Europe are similar to Brague's. Nonetheless, as if fearing this tendency might undo Scruton's emphasis on the common culture of a people, Scruton argues that despite "its universal claims, the Christian religion distinguishes the member from the outsider, and defines the rites of passage which safeguard social reproduction".[63] Anyone can be a member, then, but not everyone is a member. There are outsiders.

Like for Brague, Scruton sees Christianity's uniqueness coming into visibility through reference to secularity. Islam is not mentioned by Scruton in this context, but Christianity is heralded as different to most religions when it comes to secularity.[64] "The Christian religion permits and encourages a legal organisation which is purely secular, and which lays claim to no divine authority".[65] Scruton does not speculate at length on the historical causes of this, but he tellingly mentions "Christ's parable of the Tribute money, or St Paul's astute use of the Roman Law to claim protection for his new religion" as possibilities. For Scruton, the "respect for secular law has made Christianity more hospitable than other faiths to the idea of secular government".[66] In fact, he goes so far as to say that the Enlightenment view of politics "is already implicit in the faith which Enlightenment put in question".[67]

In *The West and the Rest*, the other book by Scruton that is cited in Breivik's manifesto, Scruton continues many of the themes laid out in *Modern Culture*. Here, however, Islam comes to the fore more visibly as a threat. Scruton rails against trends of globalisation that he sees as having resulted in a "culture of

---

[61] Ibid.
[62] Ibid.
[63] Ibid.
[64] Ibid., pp. 127–128.
[65] Ibid., p. 128.
[66] Ibid.
[67] Ibid.

repudiation".[68] Since its publication, a year after 9/11, Scruton's complaints have become familiar; complaints about "losing control" of borders, the culture of the West "bent on a path of self-destruction".[69] Political correctness is rallied against for denigrating what is "felt to be most especially *ours*".[70] Radical feminists have apparently "set out to deconstruct the family entirely".[71] Multiculturalism is described as "a form of apartheid".[72] Elites are spoken of as drivers of the change that Scruton sees as so detrimental to tradition, territory, national feeling, and the family.[73] Territorial jurisdiction and national loyalty are what Scruton lauds as peculiarly Western, as well as what is under threat in a globalised world. Religion plays a key role for Scruton in *The West and the Rest*. In fact, interestingly, Scruton starts the book with the word "religion". Christianity and Islam are key focal points that Scruton returns to repeatedly to make his case about what constitutes "the West" and what constitutes "the rest". As is clear from the title of the book, Scruton is keen to make stark distinctions between the West and its others. Early in the book, Scruton writes that "the difference between the West and the rest is that Western societies are governed by politics; the rest are ruled by power".[74] As this line makes clear, the book contains more starkly phrased claims than it does careful arguments, empirical evidence, or theoretical reflection. Although Scruton frequently discusses historical issues and incidents throughout the book, he announces that his theme is not historical but conceptual.[75]

One of the key "others" for Scruton is Islam. He writes that "there seems to be no room in Islamic thinking for the idea—vital to the history of Western constitutional government—of an office that works for the benefit of the community, regardless of the virtues and vices of the one who fills it".[76] Whereas Western politics involves a process of negotiation, compromise, and the work of offices and committees, Islamic societies deal with "immovable and eternal decrees" laid down by a holy book or by a religious authority.[77]

---

[68] Roger Scruton, *The West and the Rest: Globalization and the Terrorist Threat* (London: Continuum, 2002), p. x..
[69] Ibid., p. 149.
[70] Ibid., pp. 72–73.
[71] Ibid., p. 71.
[72] Ibid., p. 63.
[73] Ibid., p. 71,
[74] Ibid., p. 7.
[75] Ibid., p. xi.
[76] Ibid., p. 94.
[77] Ibid., p. 91.

One of the key distinctions for Scruton is the relationship between the public and the private. According to Scruton, the Qur'an makes no distinction between private and public spheres.[78] As he puts it, "everything is owed to God, with the consequence that nothing is owed to Caesar".[79] The West, Scruton pontificates, "enjoys a *single* political culture, with the nation state as the object of a common loyalty, and a secular conception of law, which makes religion a concern of family and society, but not of the state".[80]

Islam is in many ways a major problem for Scruton, though not the only one. The EU, immigration, and globalisation also feature highly as problems. Scruton refers to "Islam" as if it were a monolithic entity and does at times speak of a "single aim and purpose" for Muslims in a context where this singularity is decidedly threatening. But Scruton is not like figures such as Spencer and Ye'or, either, in that occasional statements indicate the awareness that not all Muslims are the same. Scruton writes that the "terrorism of the al-Qaeda kind is an abnormality, repudiated by the majority of Muslims".[81] He qualifies this, however, by continuing to argue that Islamism is not an "accidental product" of the contemporary world but is part of a crisis in Islam and must be understood in relation to "the fundamental tenets of the faith".[82] He also writes, in the preface to the book, that putting the blame on Islam for the problems of Western civilisation is a "superficial response".[83] It is true that Islam is not the only problem for Scruton. Globalisation is also at fault. He writes that he does not think there are only two camps—the West and the rest—but he does nonetheless want to insist on "a great difference" between Western and non-Western culture. He focuses on Islam because he says it "offers such a clear alternative" to the political project that has marked the West.[84]

But there is a clear underlying—or not so underlying—agenda in Scruton's book. Although Islam is merely referred to as one example of the "rest" that threatens "the West", this example is repeatedly invoked to shore up the problems Western society supposedly faces today. It is noteworthy that already in the preface to the book Scruton invokes Huntington's clash of civilisations thesis, positing that it is more credible now than it was on its

[78] Ibid., pp. 91–92.
[79] Ibid., p. 92.
[80] Ibid., p. 63.
[81] Ibid., p. 109.
[82] Ibid., p. 110.
[83] Ibid., p. x.
[84] Ibid., p. xi.

initial publication in the early 1990s.[85] Scruton lauds the "open discussion, trial and error, and the ubiquitousness of doubt" that he posits as endemic to Western society.[86] Meanwhile, echoing Bernard Lewis's "The Roots of Muslim Rage", Muslim migrants are mentioned in the next breath in relation to the "hatred" "many of these Muslim refugees begin to conceive" in and for the West.[87] Scruton highlights the need for revenge this hatred sows, a revenge that he diagnoses as a desire for "final destruction".[88] The Qur'an is mentioned frequently, with respect to what Scruton calls its "continual refrain" of conquest, victory, and triumph.[89] At one point, Scruton calls it "a great and dignified text" and seems to admire the tendency of some Muslims to commit the Qur'an to memory. This admiration is linked to the Civilisation Bible, as Scruton's complaint is that "most modern people" lack a "repertoire of quotations, maxims, and well-crafted sayings upon which to draw in one's daily life and relationships".[90] It is not so much the content of the sacred text that is important, then, but its capacity to provide classic sayings that contribute to culture.

As he did in *Modern Culture*, Scruton laments the "religious deficit in modern societies", although he is referring specifically to the way rituals and traditions induct young people into national cultures and instill loyalty in people to their national territories.[91] In contrast to Islam, Scruton writes favourably about the Christian legacy of "the West".[92] He claims that two "great institutions intervene between the modern world and its premonition in ancient Greece", namely Roman law, which he says represents "a universal jurisdiction", and Christianity, which he says represents "a universal church".[93] Scruton again invokes the figure of Paul as a Roman citizen, who, he writes, conceived of the universal citizen.[94] Again, he makes the point that this corresponds to Christ's vision in the story Jesus tells about giving to God what is God's and to Caesar what is Caesar's.[95] Scruton draws a strong distinction between the biblical text and the Qur'an, writing that this story

---

[85] Ibid., p. vii.
[86] Ibid., p. ix.
[87] Ibid., p. ix. Lewis, 'The Roots of Muslim Rage'.
[88] Ibid., p. ix.
[89] Ibid., p. 120.
[90] Ibid., p. 106.
[91] Ibid., pp. 81–82.
[92] Ibid., p. 35.
[93] Ibid., p. 3.
[94] Ibid.
[95] Ibid., pp. 3–4.

"contrasts radically with the vision set before us in the Koran, according to which sovereignty rests with God and his Prophet, and legal order is founded in divine command".[96] Whereas Christianity and the secular are compatible for Scruton, then, nothing like this exists in Islamic sacred texts or tradition.[97] For Scruton, Jesus's statements are about encouraging personal ideas, not political projects.[98] The Civilisation Bible that I analysed in the previous chapter is here on bright display, with a Christian Bible presented as a progenitor and prop for Western civilisation.

Although the Civilisation Bible is clearly dominant in Scruton's books, the War Bible can arguably also be glimpsed in *The West and the Rest*. It is noteworthy that in his defence of national territories, Scruton discusses sacrificing your life and the idea of the "patriot who dies in defence of territory".[99] Scruton claims that this possibility is diminishing due to the weakening ties of individuals to their nation. He laments that we have become a "community of strangers".[100] But when a crisis takes place, it is "*we who now must fight, must put our backs to the wheel*".[101] Interestingly, Scruton mentions the apostle Paul in this context as giving voice to the idea that strangers must be united in a common membership by saying "we are members one of another".[102] As if Paul is here admonishing people to sacrifice themselves for their country, Scruton states that "people have an instinct to defend their territory" and that this can be a source of sacrifice, talking of such sacrifice as heroism.[103] Without the possibility of renouncing our lives for the common good, there is no way a society under threat can survive.[104] Further, Scruton suggests that Jesus's injunction to turn the other cheek does not result in pacifism but is perfectly "compatible with defensive warfare" (though apparently incompatible with terrorism).[105] Breivik's War Bible assemblage was precisely one of ostensibly defensive warfare. Although Scruton repudiates terrorism, he is careful to insist that Jesus would not be a pacifist and that notions of heroic sacrifice are part of the Bible he invokes.

[96] Ibid., p. 4.
[97] Ibid., p. 5.
[98] Ibid., p. 38.
[99] Ibid., p. 59.
[100] Ibid., p. 57.
[101] Ibid.
[102] Ibid., p. 56. Although Scruton makes clear that Paul envisaged this membership as potentially global, Scruton thinks such global membership is problematic and holds that it is necessary to think instead in terms of a particular temporal community.
[103] Ibid., p. 55.
[104] Ibid.
[105] Ibid., pp. 38–39.

While a Civilisation Bible is predominant in Scruton's *Modern Culture* and *The West and the Rest*, then, there is a glimpse of a possible War Bible in the latter text.

A Bible is prominent for both Brague and Scruton as a progenitor and a prop. For both, this Bible supports some form of secularism. Their Bibles are immensely influential beyond the strictly "religious" spheres, to prop up notions of culture and civilisational properties. In fact, taken together, their Bibles are key to the development of Western ideas of humanity, morality, temporality, community, and culture. Brague is not interested in cheap notions of cultural purity, populist distinctions between a good people and an evil people, nor in bullish attacks on Islam. Scruton is far more simplistic in his characterisation of Islam, repeating clichés that also appear in far-right circles. Both emphasise the uniqueness of Christianity and tie this uniqueness to the Bible. For both of them, this uniqueness is particularly tied to secularism. And for both, the distinctions between Christianity's heritage and Islam are crucial. In this sense, both philosophers contribute to the construction of a Civilisation Bible that connects not only European culture and Western civilisation to a Christian Bible, but also to a Bible antithetical to Islam.

It is noteworthy that Breivik's Civilisation Bible is echoed in Brague's and Scruton's notions of a Bible, although there are also crucial differences. In this sense, their Bibles take other forms and with other elements. But as an assemblage, the Civilisation Bible that operates in Breivik's manifesto is connected to these broader philosophical reflections on Western culture and the heritage of Christian scripture.

However, neither Brague nor Scruton are the progenitors of the Civilisation Bible assemblage. What I would like to do next, then, is turn to the histories of Christian scripture that stick to the contemporary Civilisation Bible I have discussed in terms of far-right ideas and practices. Past practices of Bible-use and biblical interpretations are not visible in the same way as the references to thinkers and writings that I have been mapping from Breivik's manifesto. But by tugging at the historical ties that arguably stick to the current-day Civilisation Bible, it is possible to elucidate what past versions of Bibles continue to operate in contemporary political terrains. I argue that in particular, early modern Europe and the colonial period furnish versions of a Bible that are repeated in, and resonate with, current-day Bibles, particularly the Civilisation Bible assemblage.

Cultural Heritage

In many ways the idea of Christian scripture as influential and formative for European culture is neither strange nor surprising. It seems natural to posit that part of the specificity of European societies when it comes to their shape and content is due to an indebtedness to interpretations and uses of a Bible. But the notion of a Bible as a foundation for Western culture and formative for European civilisation has intensified in particular periods and become dominant as a result of particular processes.

Jonathan Sheehan has persuasively shown that the Enlightenment period produced a dominant conception of the Bible as an icon of cultural heritage rather than, first and foremost, a theological authority.[106] In *The Enlightenment Bible: Translation, Scholarship, Culture*, Sheehan describes and explains the complex processes particularly in England and Germany after the Reformation, which put the Bible centre-stage in sixteenth-century Europe, and which set the stage for shifting struggles over the bodies of Bibles. For the sixteenth-century reformers, theology depended on Christian scripture. "The Bible" was a theological authority, and the authority of the Bible was guaranteed by theology. Sheehan explains that a different conception of the Bible emerged during the Enlightenment period in Europe, when the essential link between theology and Christian scripture was broken. From the movement of radical Pietists to the activities of biblical scholars in Germany, a separation between "the Bible and divine speech" grew.[107] In the late seventeenth century, a crisis in religion could be felt across Europe. "Whether from isolated philosophers, clandestine networks of freethinkers, or organized cabals of atheists, Christianity at the turn of the eighteenth century was, for many, a religion in danger".[108] Spinoza's *Theologico-Political Treatise* from 1670 became notorious for its blistering criticism of the Bible. A tension arose between admitting the human elements of the Bible and losing any authority the Bible could still claim. It was in this tension that different approaches to the identity of "the Bible" began to accelerate.[109]

By the middle of the eighteenth century, Germany had become the leading force for research on the Bible, in which the Bible was ceaselessly questioned

---

[106] Jonathan Sheehan, *The Enlightenment Bible: Translation, Scholarship, Culture* (Princeton, NJ: Princeton University Press, 2013).
[107] Ibid., p. 90.
[108] Ibid., p. 32.
[109] Ibid., p. 47.

and debated. "If the old answer to the old question 'What is the ultimate source of biblical authority?' was 'theological truth,' the new answers were distributed across a variety of humanistic and historical disciplines".[110] The Bible that emerged during the Enlightenment was plural in character, belonging not primarily to the domain of theological truth as unified Scripture.

> Just as political discussion in the period was distributed across a variety of new outlets—newspapers, coffee houses, or what have you—so too was the Bible distributed across a variety of genres, scholarly practices, and disciplines. It was not an accident that the Enlightenment Bible had no single center, that it was not an object as much as a project.[111]

In Christian Europe, the Bible had previously functioned essentially as a unified text upon which theological truth could be built. The post-theological Enlightenment Bible had no one centre for its authority, but rather coalesced particularly around four domains: philology, pedagogy, poetry, and history. Each of these domains offered an answer to the question of biblical authority, and each enabled the Bible to survive in the modern climate suspicious of theological truth claims based on a sacred unquestionable and authoritative text.[112] Michael Legaspi has called this historical development the "death of Scripture" and the birth of a different kind of Bible.[113] For many, scripture could no longer function meaningfully "as an authoritative anthology of unified, authoritative writings belonging to the Church".[114] The Reformation and the concurrent splitting of Christianity and the Bible into different camps and canons turned scripture into contested territory. As a contested text, the Bible could no longer successfully function as a self-authorising, unifying authority in European culture.[115] Rather, the Bible was claimed as a "common cultural inheritance".[116]

Sheehan explains how, over time, the decentring of biblical authority laid the foundation for "the production of a fully cultural Bible, a Bible whose

---

[110] Ibid., p. 91.
[111] Ibid.
[112] Ibid.
[113] Michael Legaspi, *The Death of Scripture and the Rise of Biblical Studies* (Oxford: Oxford University Press, 2010).
[114] Ibid., p. 3.
[115] Ibid., p. 5.
[116] Ibid.

legitimacy and authority was embedded no longer in theology, but in that complex of literature, teaching, scholarship, and history that came to be called culture".[117] This was aided by the translation of Bibles into literary artefacts, denoting different national or linguistic cultures.[118] Philologists, pedagogues, poets, and historians "invented a distributed, ramified, diverse Bible, but one independent of theology, one that could survive embedded within the matrix of 'culture' ".[119]

This cultural Bible took shape also in England, albeit with different contextual nuances. As in Germany, however, it was built on key developments during the eighteenth century, from the conviction that a post-theological Bible would be authenticated through the practices of poetry, scholarship, history, and pedagogy. "And it was built, above all, upon the German practices and ideals of biblical scholarship that developed in the early nineteenth century as the flow of scholarly innovation reversed and Germany became the model for English scholars eager to reinvent a Bible strong enough to survive the climate of modernity".[120] In England and Germany, Sheehan argues, a cultural Bible was related to "the effort to create a religion and a culture free from alien influences".[121] This was the transformation of the Bible from a theological text to a cultural icon. Through culture a Bible could emerge that moved beyond what could be seen as a "talismanic fetishism for the Scriptures" that was seen to characterise Jews and Muslims; through culture a Bible could emerge as "the condensed heritage of the West".[122]

In the face of uncertainties about the theological authority of the Bible as a result of critical debate and scholarship in the sixteenth to eighteenth centuries, then, a Bible became re-invested with *cultural* authority as a marker of "our" Western heritage. Because it is first and foremost as a *cultural icon* that Christian scripture survived in the modern age, Sheehan labels this dominant attitude to the Bible the "Cultural Bible". James Crossley points to the way the phenomenon of the Cultural Bible that Sheehan describes is crucially related to the way biblical readers and interpreters were interacting with developing ideas of secularisation.[123] "Only the cultural Bible, in short,

[117] Sheehan, *The Enlightenment Bible*, p. 92.
[118] Ibid.
[119] Ibid., p. 220.
[120] Ibid., p. 247.
[121] Ibid., p. 255.
[122] Ibid., p. 257.
[123] James G. Crossley, *Harnessing Chaos: The Bible in English Political Discourse since 1968*, revised edition (London: Bloomsbury T&T Clark, 2016 [2014]), p. 11.

could preserve the essential core of Christianity and inject it into the veins of modern society".[124] In a modern age that was suspicious of theological claims and claims of a theological Bible, German and English scholars and literati could behold a new Bible "reconstructed for a posttheological age": "Beyond inspiration, beyond the Word of God, this Bible would stand on its own as a modern classic".[125] The idea of a normative culture, grounded on the Bible, could celebrate "the virtues of Western culture".[126] Sheehan suggests that the near-universal admittance of the cultural relevance of the Bible today—from academics to jurists, from the devout to doubters—is a sign of the prevalence of this Enlightenment legacy.[127] This kind of Bible can then also be made compatible with secularising developments in society, which is then fully worked out in the Bibles of thinkers such as Brage and Scruton, in which Christian scripture is not only compatible with secularity but also endemic to secular ideals.

This Cultural Bible is very much a forerunner of Breivik's Civilisation Bible. Less about theological authority or dogma, the Cultural Bible that feeds the Civilisation Bible shores up a confidence in Western culture and its civilisational treasures, of which a Bible plays a major part. It is a version of Sheehan's Cultural Bible that is activated by figures such as Brague and Scruton who continue to present a Bible that is not a set of books to be read for their sacred status or theological truth, but as a foundation for Western culture and civilisation. I have called Breivik's biblical assemblage a Civilisation Bible rather than a Cultural Bible, in order to indicate a biblical assemblage as a foundation for the West, in the sense of Huntington's Christian Western Civilisation as an imagined political actor. Sheehan's Cultural Bible emerged during the Enlightenment period as a source for pedagogy, ancient history, poetry, and philology in a way that does not necessarily imply this sort of civilisational unity. As Sheehan notes, though (and as I, too, have tried to show), there is no way to separate the Cultural Bible from the Civilisation Bible in any clear-cut way. I do so here only to shed light on different processes and emphases. Sheehan himself makes the connection between the Cultural Bible he analyses and recent concerns invoked in the "clash of civilizations" thesis: "The Bible is seen, in this normative language, as the fountain of the literary, artistic, spiritual, jurisprudential, and moral

---

[124] Sheehan, *The Enlightenment Bible*, p. 258.
[125] Ibid.
[126] Ibid., p. 259.
[127] Ibid.

virtues that infuse what we call Western civilization".[128] The celebration of Western civilisation as founded on "biblical values" and in opposition to Islam, then, is a version of Sheehan's Cultural Bible.

A Bible with cultural authority can be revered as an identity marker of the West for those with and those without a Christian *faith*—such as Breivik, who insisted he was a cultural Christian. Due to the uncontroversial nature of these claims about the Bible—some notion of the Cultural Bible is generally accepted—it can be easy to miss the problematic way it can come to work for a far-right cause and the problematic affects it plays on and produces. Again, the point is not that a version of the Civilisation Bible assemblage *necessarily* becomes far-right or is necessarily problematic. The point is that it has been activated in an anti-Islam manner by figures on the far right and could continue to function in this problematic way.[129]

Colonial Tools

Claims of superiority are not necessarily part of Sheehan's Cultural Bible. But as Crossley points out, the developments that Sheehan discusses were taking place at a time of emerging and intensifying nationalism and Orientalism in nineteenth-century Europe.[130] One Bible that can be identified as explicitly tied to culture and claims of superiority from a similar time frame, then, is the Bible of the European colonial era. It might seem misleading to dub this Colonial Bible as separate from the Cultural Bible that Sheehan discusses. I am separating them from each other in order to highlight particular features of Bible-use that operate in different ways, even if there is also overlap. This separation is not absolute or intended to signal biblical assemblages that are easily separated. I nonetheless speak of both the Cultural Bible and the Colonial Bible because this naming allows me to shed light on different processes, tendencies, and trajectories. Most important for this discussion, the Cultural Bible functions well within Europe to shore up notions of cultural heritage and deal with emerging secular ideas in European societies.

---

[128] Ibid.
[129] James Crossley discusses the way the idea of the Cultural Bible has been taken up in the United Kingdom in the political arena, mostly for conservative ends, and particularly centred on the King James Version of the Bible as a bastion for English culture and language. See James G. Crossley, 'What the Bible Really Means: Biblical Literacy in English Political Discourse', in *Rethinking Biblical Literacy*, edited by Katie Edwards (London: Bloomsbury T&T Clark, 2015), pp. 29–33.
[130] Crossley, *Harnessing Chaos*, p. 11.

The Colonial Bible may share many properties with the Cultural Bible, but it is key to note the way it functions beyond Europe to act as a tool and a weapon in the European colonial projects around the globe. It is used *on* non-Europeans as well as altered *by* non-Europeans who came into contact with the Colonial Bible assemblage.

Although there is of course far from "one" Bible during the complex and varied set of practices of different European colonial powers from the sixteenth through the nineteenth and early twentieth centuries, I want to highlight how a Bible was used to consolidate claims to a superior culture. These claims legitimated imperial territorial violence as well as the "civilizing" aims of empire. The idea of possessing a superior Bible denoting civilisational prowess is repeated in the far-right discourse I have discussed, and this idea can be connected to the Colonial Bible. These old Bibles stick to the current-day biblical assemblage that operates in the contemporary Islamophobic far right in Europe. They are part of what makes the current-day biblical assemblages work, perhaps because invocations of these current-day assemblages feel familiar.

During the sixteenth century, Spanish adventurers were conquering the "new world" of Latin America and the "Indians" who lived in these lands. The evangelisation of the Indians became a justification for the conquest. As Michael Prior explains, the "Catholic kings were authorized to engage in a holy war which would implant the true faith in the regions of the infidel".[131] Christopher Columbus saw in his discoveries the fulfilment of scripture: "For I am about to create new heaves and a new earth" (Isaiah 65:17; also Revelation 21:1).[132] In general for Christian theologians during this period, the unbelief of Indians justified the occupation of their lands. "Many Indians accepted Christianity enthusiastically. Soon the Church became a powerful and wealthy institution which permeated the new colonial order and became a bastion of European culture and civilization throughout the colonial era".[133] Yvonne Sherwood argues, however, that the Bible of the Spanish Empire was an unwieldy and heterogeneous corpus, "a book that was not yet organised by quasi-colonial management structures", as it would come to be for instance in the late British Empire.[134] Michael Prior

---

[131] Michael Prior, *The Bible and Colonialism: A Moral Critique* (Sheffield: Sheffield Academic Press, 1997), p. 53.
[132] Ibid. "Justification for violence was based on the conquest of Canaan by the Israelites." See Deuteronomy 9:5; 18:9–14; Leviticus 18:24–25. Ibid., p. 59.
[133] Ibid., p. 57.
[134] Yvonne Sherwood, 'Comparing the "Telegraph Bible" of the Late British Empire to the Chaotic Bible of the Sixteenth Century Spanish Empire: Beyond the Canaan Mandate into Anxious Parables

demonstrates this, too, when he points to the tug-and-pull of passages of the Bible for the pro- and anti-colonial cause. Those who espoused theocratic imperialism and supported imperialism with the language of holy war avoided much of the Hebrew prophetic tradition, a tradition which was taken up by those laypeople, priests, and bishops who opposed imperialism.[135]

Other parts of the Bible were also emphasised by critics of colonialism. "The voices dissenting from theological support for European colonization compared the situation of the Indians with that of the suffering Israelites in exile, whether in Egypt or Babylon, or of the early Church in its persecution by the Roman Empire".[136] Identifying themselves as John the Baptist crying in the wilderness, these dissenting voices prepared "to pay the ultimate sacrifice for their prophetic protest (Mark 6.17--20)".[137] The Bible, during this time, is openly conflicted.[138] Although there are, of course, counter-Bibles to later Colonial Bibles, Sherwood's point is that during these early days of empire, there is far more open and public flux around the meanings of "the Bible", its role, and identity. Eventually, a more fixed Colonial Bible emerges, however. Counter-Bibles or alternative biblical assemblages never disappeared, but they became arguably minor assemblages in the face of more major assemblages.

If we turn to the nineteenth-century British Empire, it is clear, as Brian Stanley argues, that British Christians understood their duty to propagate a Christian message alongside "the imagined benefits of Western civilization".[139] Although some missionaries allowed their personal experiences of other cultures to alter their perception of notions of civilisation, there was a widespread anticipation that a transformation of colonised "pagan" societies would take place through "the civilizing agency of the gospel".[140] Missionary society secretaries, for instance, who testified to the parliamentary select committee on aborigines in 1836–37, proclaimed unambiguously their confidence in "'the tendency and efficacy of Christianity to

---

of the Land', in *In the Name of God: The Bible in the Colonial Discourse of Empire*, edited by C. L. Crouch and Jonathan Stökl (Leiden: Brill, 2014), p. 20.

[135] Prior, *The Bible and Colonialism*, p. 59.
[136] Ibid., p. 62.
[137] Ibid.
[138] Sherwood, 'Comparing the "Telegraph Bible" of the Late British Empire to the Chaotic Bible of the Sixteenth Century Spanish Empire: Beyond the Canaan Mandate into Anxious Parables of the Land', p. 22.
[139] Brian Stanley, *The Bible and the Flag: Protestant Missions and British Imperialism in the Nineteenth and Twentieth Centuries* (Leicester: Apollos, 1990), p. 157.
[140] Ibid., p. 160.

civilize mankind'".[141] Stanley argues that the close association in missionary thinking between Christianity and civilisation rested on at least four prior assumptions. The first was that the cultures to which missionaries were going were "heathen" societies that needed to be saved from perdition.[142] The second was "the supposition that nineteenth-century Britain constituted a model of Christian culture and society".[143] Stanley recounts the way missionary magazines contained graphic descriptions of a pre-Christian Britain as primitive, barbarous, and idolatrous. "The Bible had made Britain great. She was the archetype of the Christian nation, and God's design was to create more Christian nations on the same pattern".[144] The culture of Victorian Britain was shaped by the Bible and evangelical Protestantism in a way that meant the importance and salvific values of the Bible were assumed. Third, there was an "implicit faith in human progress which was one of the legacies of the Enlightenment to Christian thought".[145] Fourth, the idea of civilising the "heathen" was attractive and effective because it was thought to have worked.[146]

The Gospel in itself was held to be "the civilizing agent".[147] "Part of the package of civilization which Christianity was thought to bring in its train was freedom and justice".[148] As Stanley explains, this belief in Britain as a model of Christian society became more and more vulnerable towards the end of the nineteenth century.[149] Before this, however, the notion of a "Protestant West" bringing civilisation and culture was deeply ingrained in many missionary and colonial envoys.[150] The Colonial Bible we might speak of during this time, then, is related to Sheehan's Cultural Bible: a Bible that denotes the treasures of Western civilisation and that feeds the confidence of the West. Of course, part of the colonial project regarding the Bible was to bring it as a "civilizing agent", as Stanley puts it. That could be also part of current-day far-right agendas in some forms, but it is not necessarily a driving force. The Bible invoked in the far-right milieu I have examined does not seem to be a missionising Bible. It is not a mobile Bible to be brought to faraway lands. It is

---

[141] Ibid. Quoted by Stanley.
[142] Ibid., p. 161.
[143] Ibid.
[144] Ibid.
[145] Ibid.
[146] Ibid., p. 162.
[147] Ibid., p. 171.
[148] Ibid., p. 172.
[149] Ibid., p. 165.
[150] Ibid.

a deeply internal and immobile Bible—a Bible that is the roots of Europe, to be kept deep in the soil of Europe. Or, as Fallaci desired it, the Bible takes the shape of a marble slab in a public square. But the strong focus on the superiority of the Bible, as we saw for instance in Spencer's and Fallaci's writings, is arguably a reactivation of elements of the Colonial Bible. Elements of the Cultural Bible and the Colonial Bible could all be said to come together in the far-right Civilisation Bible that I have been mapping. This Civilisation Bible assemblage is assembled with the institutions and artefacts of high art found across Europe's galleries and museums, with literary canons and musical giants such as Shakespeare and Bach; it is assembled with the notions of secularity that are seen as shaping European societies; it is assembled with the colonial missions that celebrated Western superiority with an unparalleled confidence. Most of these associations or components are not and do not need to be spelled out when the Civilisation Bible is invoked. Therefore, claims such as Paul Golding's, about the Bible being a foundation for Western civilisation, sound familiar, even commonsense.

The histories of the Civilisation Bible stick to contemporary Bible-use. The Civilisation Bible assemblage in Breivik's worldview, then, works because it is reterritorialising Bibles that were operative in the past, in the making of modern Europe, particularly in theological developments during the Enlightenment and Europe's colonial era. But there are also non-biblical elements that are crucial to make the Civilisation Bible effective. In the final part of this chapter, I gesture towards one such non-biblical element, namely the clash of civilisations thesis, which operates as a narrative about history and a construction of the present that crucially makes the Civilisation Bible work as an effective part of a far-right worldview in which the othering of Islam is central.

The Workings of the Civilisation Bible

The Civilisation Bible is arguably an effective component in far-right discourse also because it plugs into non-biblical components. In this final part of the chapter, I will examine a particularly important non-biblical component, namely Samuel Huntington's clash of civilisations thesis. As I go on to explain, the clash thesis works effectively *with* a Civilisation Bible because it connects to what Seyla Benhabib has called a "reductionist sociology of culture",[151] as well as dominant understandings of religion, as elaborated by Elizabeth Shakman Hurd in *Beyond Religious Freedom: The New Global Politics of Religion*. This non-biblical component is not the only element that sticks to the Civilisation Bible as I have described it, but in the context of Breivik's worldview it is, I suggest, crucial for making the Civilisation Bible operant and effective. In other words, this might go some way to show why this kind of Bible seemed to be of use to a figure such as Breivik. Without understanding this part of the Civilisation Bible, it is difficult to see how assumptions around, and constructions of, a Civilisation Bible could emerge, take shape, and work effectively. In other words, the Civilisation Bible would not be part of far-right discourse if it did not serve some purpose and produce particular effects and affects.

As I have already touched on, Huntington captured the narrative of a conflict between cultures in his concept of the clash of civilisations in the 1990s.[152] In Huntington's construct of the clash of civilisations, there is a marked attention to the West. It is noteworthy that he does not juxtapose the West with the East. Instead, the West is in conflict with Islam, and Islam is in conflict with the West. What is "the West"? The concept allows for the characterisation and classification of societies into different categories, such as Western and non-Western. For Huntington, this classification is important. What runs through it is the idea that the West, while built on Christian foundations, is secular. Christianity is seen to have learnt *not* to meddle in politics: churches are separated from the state. Islam, however, has not learned this lesson. As a consequence, Huntington suggests that the "centuries-old military interaction between the West and Islam is unlikely to decline".[153] Quite the contrary, it could become "more virulent".[154]

It is clear to see how the clash of civilisations thesis is adopted by Breivik and those he admired. The conflict between the West and Islam is at the very centre of the Eurabia and counterjihad milieu. The idea of a clash is never questioned, but insistently stated and restated in the writings of Spencer, Ye'or, Fallaci, and Bawer. As Hans-Georg Betz points out, it is not fair to call Huntington a right-wing extremist, but the arguments he has advanced are taken up by far-right figures in Western Europe to aid their anti-immigration

---

[151] Seyla Benhabib, *The Claims of Culture: Equality and Diversity in the Global Era* (Princeton, NJ: Princeton University Press, 2002), p. 4.
[152] See Huntington, *The Clash of Civilizations and the Remaking of World Order*.
[153] Huntington, 'The Clash of Civilizations', p. 31.
[154] Ibid.

campaign, particularly against Muslims.[155] While it would be unfair, then, to place historians such as Huntington and Lewis alongside Spencer, Ye'or, Fallaci, and Bawer, it is almost impossible to imagine the writings of the latter four appearing without the (in)famous clash of civilisations thesis. Huntington is not responsible for all the ways his thesis has been taken up. In any case, his thesis alone would not be enough in and of itself to set in motion a far-right discourse that is virulently anti-Islam. The idea of starkly opposed cultures based on different religions relies on a number of assumptions about the nature of "culture" and "religion". Seyla Benhabib and Elizabeth Shakman Hurd have examined the ways in which particular conceptions of culture and religion have been taken up in public discourse and become dominant. Their arguments shed important light on the way these conceptions are operant also in far-right discourse.

In *The Claims of Culture: Equality and Diversity in the Global Era*, Benhabib traces the way in which *culture* "has become a ubiquitous synonym for *identity*, an identity marker and differentiator".[156] While in the Romantic period, culture and civilisation were seen as contrasts, Benhabib observes that in contemporary uses of the two terms, such distinctions are gone.[157] This is certainly the case in the far-right texts I have examined, where civilisation and culture are frequently treated as interchangeable terms. For the Romantic writer Johann Gottfried Herder, *Kultur* meant the unique, shared values, meanings, linguistic signs, and symbols of a people. *Civilisation*, on the other hand, referred to the material values and practices that are shared with other peoples and that do not reflect the individuality of a people.

Benhabib argues that the dominant idea of culture today lies in an egalitarian understanding of culture propagated by social anthropologists who were critical of Eurocentric cultural presumptions.[158] Culture here is the "totality of social systems and practices of signification, representation, and symbolism that have an autonomous logic of their own, a logic separated from and not reducible to the intentions of those through whose actions and doings it emerges and is reproduced".[159] Nonetheless, Herder's

---

[155] Hans-Georg Betz, 'Against the "Green Totalitarianism": Anti-Islamic Nativism in Contemporary Radical Right-Wing Populism in Western Europe', in *Europe for the Europeans: The Foreign and Security Policy of the Populist Radical Right*, edited by Christina Schori Liang (Aldershot: Ashgate, 2007), p. 37.
[156] Benhabib, *The Claims of Culture* p. 1.
[157] Ibid., p. 2.
[158] Ibid., p. 3.
[159] Ibid.

"identification of a people's genius with expressions of its cultural identity persists".[160] Benhabib is describing what she sees as a wide-ranging problem in the way cultures are talked about and dealt with legally, in the media, and in the political domain. Benhabib diagnoses the dominant tendency in understanding cultures as a "reductionist sociology of culture". Cultures are treated as easily distinguishable units; they are seen as matching particular population groups; a straightforward account of the culture of a population is assumed to be possible and unproblematic.[161] As she puts it, it is often taken for granted by politicians and policy-makers, in courts and in the media, that every human group "has" some kind of "culture" and that the borders distinguishing these groups and the "contours of their cultures" are not only identifiable but fairly straightforward to specify.[162]

The reductionist account of culture has many risks that are evident in the far-right milieus I have been discussing. Culture risks being essentialised as the property of an ethnicity or race. Cultures are reified as distinct entities through overemphasis of boundaries and difference. The internal homogeneity of cultures is overemphasised. Cultures become fetishised badges of group identity that are placed beyond critical analysis.[163] The emphasis on homogeneity and tendency to fetishisation is at work in the Civilisation Bible, in which a Bible of sprawlingly different and diverse texts from the Middle East full of complexity, ambiguity, and difference, is set aside in favour of a Bible of Western culture that is monolithic and monumentalised.[164] The risks that Benhabib sketched are all issues we see in Breivik's far-right milieu but that are not exclusive to the far right. Quite the contrary, according to Benhabib these notions of culture have become mainstream. Religion has come to play a role in relation to culture that is key for understanding how these ideas of culture are mobilised, including in particularly problematic ways by proponents of the far right.

Arguably, religion has become a category that is attractive to "fill in" the content of "cultures", as Benhabib describes them. In *Beyond Religious Freedom: The New Global Politics of Religion*, Hurd is critical of the way religious-rights discourse has become a dominant mode of defining identity and of gaining recognition in the public sphere, particularly for legal

---

[160] Ibid.
[161] Ibid., p. 4.
[162] Ibid.
[163] Ibid.
[164] See Martinson, 'Towards a "Theology" of Christian Monumentality: Post-Christian Reflections on Grace and Nature', pp. 21–42.

rights.[165] She argues that "privileging religion as an official marker of difference engenders an 'ecology of affiliation' that presupposes and produces hard and fast religious identities that trump other modes of belonging".[166] Divisions in society become defined in religious terms (rather than, say, generational, linguistic, class, gender, citizenship, or other), where "bounded religious communities and identities are taken for granted".[167] For far-right groups, then, it makes sense to draw on religious identity claims in a social arena in which assumptions operate about the boundedness of religious groups as discrete—and therefore potentially opposing—identities.

Hurd draws attention to the "two faces of religion" paradigm which has grown increasingly prevalent in political debate in the last decades, where religion is seen as split between a potential for irenic, peace-building, tolerant effects and sectarian, conflict-inducing, intolerant effects.[168] In this paradigm, the category of religion is split into the *problem* of so-called bad religion, which is sectarian and intolerant, and therefore requires discipline and surveillance, and *the solution* of so-called good religion, which is irenic, peace-building, and respectful of rights, freedom, and tolerance.[169] Hurd argues that this "global dynamics of good religion–bad religion"[170] was accelerated by Huntington's clash of civilisations thesis in the 1990s and gained momentum after 9/11.[171] As a category, religion became a way of identifying a particular problem. For example, naming something "*Islamic* terrorism" is a way of diagnosing the religiosity of the terrorism as a distinct social ill (and of course such an invocation is entangled in the "politics of the example").[172] But religion also functions as a category that designates a solution in the form of "good" religion. As a solution (rather than a problem), religion is that which is harnessed by organisations, experts, and aid agencies to prevent radicalisation and encourage tolerance between religious groups. "Irenic religion, in this narrative, enhances international public order by providing moral sustenance and support for international human rights, facilitating

---

[165] Elizabeth Shakman Hurd, *Beyond Religious Freedom: The New Global Politics of Religion* (Princeton, NJ: Princeton University Press, 2015).
[166] Ibid., p. 42.
[167] Ibid., p. 111.
[168] Ibid., p. 24.
[169] Ibid., pp. 22–24.
[170] Ibid., p. 22.
[171] Ibid., p. 23.
[172] Michael Naas, 'Introduction: For Example', in *The Other Heading: Reflections on Today's Europe*, translated by Pascale-Anne Brault and Michael B. Naas (Bloomington: Indiana University Press, 1992), p. xviii.

the spread of freedom, and promoting human flourishing through advocacy for religious tolerance and interfaith understanding".[173]

Huntington's clash of civilisations thesis sticks to the Civilisation Bible assemblage in crucial ways by providing a framing of global politics in which Christianity clashes with Islam. The popular acceptance of this vision means it plugs effortlessly into a Bible that forms and informs "Christian" Western civilisation in a clash against Islam. Part of this clash thesis is notions of culture and religion that also work with the Civilisation Bible. Assumptions that cultures are closed and essentialised and that religion belongs to separate groups ensure that a Civilisation Bible works and picks up speed in the perceived conflict with Islam. Hurd's good religion–bad religion paradigm can be seen in Breivik's worldview, in which Islam is solidified as a "bad" religion. As I discussed in chapter 3, the protection of the religious rights of Christians in the Middle East from persecution is a key issue for much far-right propaganda. Christianity—sometimes Judeo-Christianity—becomes slotted into the discursive apparatus as the "good" and "saving" religion as well as the victim of bad religion. Breivik's far-right milieu is plugging into discourses about religion already accepted in the more mainstream arenas of public debate and legal rights.

Activating a Civilisation Bible

In this chapter I have examined two more marginal figures who are connected to Breivik's worldview through citations and references in his manifesto. Examining Rémi Brague's and Roger Scruton's arguments about Western civilisation and European culture, a Bible emerged that connects to Breivik's Civilisation Bible and arguably accelerates the Civilization Bible by providing philosophical and (semi-)historical grounds for this Bible. Neither the counterjihad milieu nor the philosophical traditions of which Brague and Scruton are a part operates in a vacuum when it comes to constructing Bibles. As Alastair Hunter has put it, "history has a habit of leaking into the present".[174] Trajectories of Bibles in the past elucidate how particular

---

[173] Hurd, *Beyond Religious Freedom*, p. 24.
[174] Alastair G. Hunter, '(De)Nominating Amalek: Racist Stereotyping in the Bible and the Justification of Discrimination', in *Sanctified Aggression: Legacies of Biblical and Post-Biblical Vocabularies of Violence*, edited by Yvonne Sherwood and Jonneke Bekkenkamp (London: T&T Clark, 2003), p. 97.

Bibles are assembled and made effective in the present. Particularly for the Civilisation Bible, I argued that the Bible-use emerging in early modern Europe, where scripture becomes a repository for Western culture and a crucial colonial tool, is activated in the contemporary Civilisation Bible assemblage. The Civilisation Bible assemblage works effectively and affectively in the present because it plugs into the clash of civilisations thesis, which cuts the world up into clearly delineated civilisations operating with starkly separate religiously defined cultures. One way in which the glories of European culture, its civilisational triumphs, superiority, and specialness, then, are held up and held together is with the help of the Civilisation Bible. The Civilisation Bible can also stoke affects of fear at a lost religious culture that should be treasured and defended, hence connecting to the War Bible assemblage I discussed in the previous chapter. Now that I have discussed key aspects of the War Bible and Civilisation Bible assemblage, I turn in the next chapter to the way biblical scholars have responded to violence in Bible-use.

7
The Problem of Biblical Violence

The Bible has been called "the most dangerous of books", "endowed with the power to kill".[1] Mieke Bal, who made these statements, is not alone in her assessment (although some might quip that Bibles do not kill people, people/guns kill people). In his discussion about the problematic nature of the Bible, aptly named *Wolf in the Sheepfold: The Bible as Problematic for Theology*, Robert Carroll warns that the Bible can "make a good servant" but a "bad master".[2] In this chapter, I want to move beyond the details of the War Bible and the Civilisation Bible in the networks I have been mapping. Having asked *which* biblical assemblages operate in far-right contexts, I now turn to possible responses to these assemblages. As I have already discussed, the biblical assemblages I have analysed are not always violent. They are not only the possession of the far-right terrorism which is the starting point of this book. The War Bible and the Civilisation Bible assemblages that I have identified are not static objects that operate according to set trajectories. They are contingent and contextual assemblages that function according to a particular logic in the networks I have mapped. Part of this logic is the way they work with constructions of Europe as mono-racial, anti-immigration, and anti-Islam. In this chapter, I articulate and assess four responses that are based on trends and tendencies in biblical scholarship on violence. As a shorthand, I have called these four responses historicising biblical texts, battling selectivity, challenging biblical authority, and resistant reading. I focus on these four, not because they are exhaustive, but because they represent responses from a wide range of perspectives in biblical scholarship, from the more explicitly confessional to the more avowedly secular and atheist, as well as from historical-critical to feminist-womanist perspectives.

My aim is to determine to what extent these responses are helpful for the case discussed in this book. I begin by explaining what I mean by the

---

[1] Mieke Bal, *Anti-Covenant: Counter-Reading Women's Lives in the Hebrew Bible* (Sheffield: Almond, 1989), p. 14.
[2] Carroll, *Wolf in the Sheepfold*, p. 5.

phrase "biblical violence". I go on to discuss the discipline of biblical studies and what is often considered its remit, and then turn to the four responses. Ultimately, I argue that what is crucial in responding to biblical violence is attention to the affective investments that inform how biblical texts are read and how Bibles are invoked, by examining the fluid and flexible modes of Bible-use on the ground that go beyond reading and interpretation of texts. In the next chapter, I build on this discussion to put forward my own proposal for responding to the varied and varying workings of biblical assemblages.

Biblical Violence

Biblical texts featuring violence are not scarce. There is Cain's killing of his brother Abel in Genesis 4; God's destruction of the world in Genesis 7; the unnamed woman in Judges 19 who is gang-raped and cut into twelve pieces; the Lord's injunction to brutally conquer and kill the Canaanites in Deuteronomy and Joshua; the rape of Tamar in 2 Samuel 13; Paul's call for those who disagree with him to castrate themselves in Galatians 15:12; and the rider of the white horse in Revelation 19 from whose mouth comes a sharp sword to strike down the nations. And this is just a selection drawn from the canonical texts of Jews and Christians. Then there is the use of biblical texts for violent ends. As Eryl Davies writes, Bibles have "proved to be a useful weapon in the armoury of those who have sought to discriminate against race, colour, gender, class, religion or sexual orientation, and divine authority has been claimed for all kinds of abominable practices which have resulted in the marginalization and persecution of oppressed minorities".[3]

It is clear, then, that biblical violence operates on different levels. Eric Seibert articulates these different levels as description (of, for instance, rape, murder, warfare), prescription (violence that is sanctioned, even prescribed), the pronouncement of violence against others (desiring or calling for the Lord's vengeance on one's enemies in the form of judgement and divine retribution, for instance), and violent ideologies that do harm either explicitly or implicitly (for example, patriarchy, ethnocentrism).[4] Clearly, each of these levels of biblical violence could be unpacked further, differentiated, and

---

[3] Eryl W. Davies, *The Immoral Bible: Approaches to Biblical Ethics* (London: Bloomsbury, 2010), p. 1.
[4] Eric A. Seibert, *The Violence of Scripture: Overcoming the Old Testament's Troubling Legacy* (Minneapolis, MN: Fortress Press, 2012), p. 10.

explicated with more precision. But in basic terms, to talk about "biblical violence" is to say something about both the content of biblical texts and the way biblical texts and Bibles can be read and used in ways that endorse or encourage violence.[5]

When I use the phrase "biblical violence" in this chapter, I use it as a deliberately capacious term to include these different levels. Trying to constrain exactly what "biblical violence" is would imply that the kinds of violence described in biblical texts, or justified through use of a Bible, can be clearly marked off as a distinct zone of dangerous Bible-ness. This would close down discussion about potentially unexpected Bible-use. It would also artificially demarcate in advance what dangers scholars will see.[6] Rather than close down discussion about the effects and affects of Bibles, a more capacious and heuristic use of the term "biblical violence" can prompt further reflection on the kinds of violence that are described in biblical texts and the kinds of violence that have come from the use of Bibles. Violence can involve physical harm to bodies, or it can take the form of psychological damage; it can include oppression and aggression; be collective or individual; and be severe or subtle. What constitutes "violence" and "harm" needs, in my view, to be discussed concretely in relation to each case in which a Bible or biblical text is used. As Yvonne Sherwood and Jonneke Bekkenkamp warn against, it might be tempting to think we can "identify key minefields and troublespots in the biblical and postbiblical landscape and then ... attempt to diffuse them, put barbed wire around them, or hold peace summits around them", as if it is straightforward to disentangle the "good" texts from the "bad".[7] What is crucial is to identify how Bibles are "recycled, appealed to, exploited, banalized, as they circulate as part of ongoing vocabularies", and how this Bible-use plays out on the ground.[8]

---

[5] Ibid., p. 10.
[6] For an excellent and expansive discussion of the ways we might understand violence in the Christian canon of scripture, see Helen Paynter, *Blessed are the Peacemakers: A Biblical Theology of Human Violence* (Grand Rapids, MI: Zondervan, 2023).
[7] Yvonne Sherwood and Jonneke Bekkenkamp, 'Introduction: The Thin Blade of Difference between Real Swords and Words about "Sharp-Edged Things"—Reflections on How People Use the Word', in *Sanctified Aggression: Legacies of Biblical and Post-Biblical Vocabularies of Violence*, edited by Yvonne Sherwood and Jonneke Bekkenkamp (London: T&T Clark, 2003), p. 3.
[8] Ibid.

The Business of Biblical Studies

What are biblical scholars supposed to do with the violence in the texts that are their bread and butter? What are they, or we, supposed to do with the violent interpretations and practices that have accompanied biblical texts throughout history? As I argued in chapter 2, mainstream biblical scholarship has been mostly concerned with historical questions. At major biblical studies conferences, there are sessions dedicated to ethical questions, to the theme of violence, as well as to the reception of biblical texts. But these are in the minority when it comes to confronting biblical violence as problematic. Feminist, womanist, postcolonial, African American, and contextual biblical scholars in particular have long been doing biblical scholarship in which ethical questions and issues of power and violence are paramount. No feminist, as Sherwood writes, has been prepared "bleakly to catalogue women's oppression" in, and as an effect of, biblical texts, rather than actively combat this oppression.[9] But the approaches taken by these scholars are often treated as alternative approaches to biblical texts—"aberrations", as Wongi Park puts it.[10] Chapters and books introducing feminist biblical scholarship frequently lament that however far feminism seems to have come, it remains in the margins of the discipline as an optional concern.[11] The approaches named earlier, then, have dedicated research and teaching to issues of biblical violence, but this has not necessarily changed the dominant currents of biblical scholarship.

Other biblical scholars who have grappled with responses to biblical violence take a more theological approach or explicitly address a faith-based readership. L. Daniel Hawk, for instance, begins his book *The Violence of the Biblical God: Canonical Narrative and Christian Faith* with "the question of divine violence and how it should inform Christian faith and practice".[12] These scholars are keen to address the issue of violence in the Bible

---

[9] Yvonne Sherwood, 'Feminist Scholarship', in *The Oxford Illustrated History of the Bible*, edited by John Rogerson (Oxford: Oxford University Press, 2001), p. 311.
[10] Wongi Park, 'Multiracial Biblical Studies', *Journal of Biblical Literature* 140, no. 3 (2021): p. 446.
[11] See for instance Sherwood, 'Feminist Scholarship', p. 299; Susanne Scholz, 'Introduction: The Past, the Present, and the Future of Feminist Hebrew Bible Interpretation', in *Feminist Interpretation of the Hebrew Bible in Retrospect, Volume I: Biblical Books*, edited by Susanne Scholz (Sheffield: Sheffield Phoenix Press, 2017 [2013]), p. 9. Scholz is quoting Esther Fuchs when she makes this comment, who bemoaned this fact in 2008, but Scholz argues it still holds true.
[12] L. Daniel Hawk, *The Violence of the Biblical God: Canonical Narrative and Christian Faith* (Grand Rapids, MI: William B. Eerdmans, 2019), p. xiv. A good example of this kind of scholarly discussion from explicitly Christian perspectives can be found in Helen Paynter and Trevor Laurence's volume, *Violent Biblical Texts: New Approaches* (Sheffield: Sheffield Phoenix Press, 2022).

"without jettisoning belief in the Bible as the word of God".[13] Some, such as Eric Seibert, set out to "overcome" the "Old Testament's troubling legacy" as a scholar, teacher, *and* a "committed Christian who actively participates in the life of the church and affirms the essential role of Scripture for Christian faith and practice".[14] Seibert also makes clear that the New Testament is "extremely problematic" in terms of its content and legacy, for justifying slavery, antisemitism, and violence against women and children. He makes the case that he focuses on the Old Testament due to issues of scope as well as his specialism being in Old Testament studies.[15] Here, the motivation to deal with biblical violence arises from a relationship with a particular faith community for whom biblical texts are of existential importance. These texts may be loved, revered, respected, authoritative, difficult, obscure, and challenging. The fact that scholars such as Seibert state emphatically that biblical texts "should never be used to inspire, promote, or justify acts of violence", or to "oppress or otherwise harm people",[16] and seek to find ways of dealing with biblical violence, makes perfect sense, perhaps especially when one is part of a faith community where Bible-use is central.

However, not all biblical scholars think biblical violence is a problem. For instance, the contributions to *Encountering Violence in the Bible*, edited by Markus Zehnder and Hallvard Hagelia, mostly defend biblical violence. In their introduction, Zehnder and Hagelia critique biblical scholars who claim violence is always wrong. They oppose the idea that violence in the Bible must always be critiqued.[17] Their argument is that this position leaves no room "for studying each biblical text on its own terms and trying to listen to it in order to find out how it could be brought into a fruitful dialogue with the challenges of the present-day world".[18] Zehnder and Hagelia note that the "theme of the beneficiary character of God's 'violence' to contain and overcome evil forms of human violence" is "perhaps the single most important motif and element of common agreement running through a good number of the articles presented in this volume".[19]

---

[13] M. Daniel Carroll R. and J. Blair Wilgus, eds., *Wrestling with the Violence of God: Soundings in the Old Testament* (Winona Lake, IN: Eisenbrauns, 2015), p. viii.
[14] Seibert, *The Violence of Scripture*, pp. 3, 5.
[15] Ibid., p. 5.
[16] Ibid., p. 2.
[17] Hallvard Hagelia and Markus Zehnder, 'Introduction', in *Encountering Violence in the Bible*, edited by Markus Zehnder and Hallvard Hagelia (Sheffield: Sheffield Phoenix Press, 2013), pp. 1–12.
[18] Ibid., p. 5.
[19] Ibid., p. 9. The most representative chapter for this position is perhaps Dana M. Harris, 'Understanding Images of Violence in the Book of Revelation', in *Encountering Violence in the Bible*, edited by Zehnder and Hagelia, pp. 148–164.

Many biblical scholars might argue, though, that it is not the job of biblical scholars to "solve" the problem of biblical violence or to diagnose it as a problem. That kind of task is better left to clergy or theologians. Confronting this perception, Ed Noort asks about "what the 'real work' of our discipline is or should be".[20] Without minimising the exegetical craft and painstaking work of biblical scholarship, he argues that as biblical texts have been conceived as authoritative and used as texts of terror, "the exegete has an extended task":

> He or she should not only offer a descriptive explanation, but he or she also may be charged with posing a normative judgement. Of course it depends on the audience and the questions posed, but in the wide range in which these texts still have meaning for parts of the public, stepping back onto the safe side of a historical or philological explanation only signifies extraditing the texts to arbitrariness in the present public domain.[21]

Noort asks how equipped biblical scholars actually are for such work.[22] "As long as we act as philologically schooled historians trying to interpret texts in their own contexts and their 'original' meaning we have done our usual job in academia".[23] He asks: "can we ignore the reception history of these texts, which continues up until today?"[24] These questions touch on what the "real work" of biblical scholars is.[25] Noort suggests that the task of the exegete must be expanded with reception history, including normative judgements, in addition to exegetical work and analysis.[26]

As I have already begun to outline, however, some biblical scholars *have* been concerned with biblical violence. Further, those who have not been overly concerned with biblical violence as a problem might still put forward a response to biblical violence that draws on the historical interest at the heart of mainstream biblical studies.

---

[20] Ed Noort, 'Biblical Violence and the Task of the Exegete', in *The Present State of Old Testament Studies in the Low Countries*, edited by Klaas Spronk (Leiden: Brill, 2016), p. 190.
[21] Ibid., p. 190.
[22] Ibid.
[23] Ibid.
[24] Ibid., p. 182.
[25] Ibid., p. 190.
[26] Ibid.

Historicising Biblical Texts

The first point that could be raised as a response to the kind of Bible-use I have outlined in this book is that it is the result of an ahistorical and anachronistic use of biblical texts. Given what I already noted about the field of biblical studies, this is probably the most obvious scholarly approach to the violence of biblical texts. It is also a response that has frequently been put to me when I talk about my work on far-right Bible-use. Put simply, the idea is that as biblical texts are of ancient origin, written by ancient authors, and for ancient audiences, they have little relevance to a modern audience when it comes to how to one should live one's life. People who cite specific biblical texts, or hold up a Bible more generally, to justify violence in the contemporary world are misusing or abusing these ancient texts. They have not understood what "the Bible" is.

Bibles are, in this view, ancient archives. The ancient texts that make up Bibles belong in their ancient contexts. Forms of Bible-use that ignore this are ahistorical and anachronistic. Why should we expect Bibles to be relevant to modern societies, to modern-day ethical or political questions, and to human-rights charters? In this vein, Hallvard Hagelia cautions: "seen from a modern perspective, the God of Israel is 'violent'", but "we should be careful not to read the Bible too much from a modern perspective; it should be read on its own terms".[27] These texts might be used to speak to contemporary situations, but that is the result of confusion, ignorance, and error.

The language around "misuse" and "abuse" of the Bible is popular and understandably appealing. Talking about misuse and abuse of the Bible can function as a shorthand for condemnation of any situation where a biblical text or a Bible is used to do harm. There may be an important role for this language in particular contexts, such as on placards in marches and protests or in snappy social media posts. But in an academic context, what this language implies is that something improper is done to biblical texts when they are interpreted in ways that might go against the intentions of the ancient authors of the texts—of their *Sitz im Leben*, their original setting.

John Dominic Crossan's influential work exemplifies the argument that biblical violence can be dealt with through historical understanding. Crossan makes the case for why a historical knowledge of biblical texts is not just the

---

[27] Hallvard Hagelia, 'Violence, Judgment and Ethics in the Book of Amos', in *Encountering Violence in the Bible*, edited by Zehnder and Hagelia, p. 146.

province of academic biblical scholars but should also be how faith-based communities grapple with biblical violence. In *How to Read the Bible and Still Be a Christian*, Crossan urges his readers to attend "to the original matrix of a story and respect for the story's purpose within its world" in order to "allow ancient voices to speak fully and clearly".[28] He argues that it is necessary to reflect on the climax of the Neolithic Revolution, on Mesopotamia and the Epic of Gilgamesh for "correctly understanding" Genesis 2–3.[29] To understand the story of Cain and Abel, it is necessary to put it in the context of the Sumerian dispute between the divine brothers Shepherd God and Farmer God.[30] To make sense of Deuteronomy, which is full of violent curses and a violent God, it is necessary to understand the ascendancy of the (Neo) Assyrian Empire.[31] Using imperial terror as a military strategy and foreign policy, the Assyrian Empire influenced the Israelite understanding of God's covenant.[32] Crossan argues that with a figure such as Paul, it is important to understand the way Paul's message about love and justice were co-opted even within the texts that have made it into Christian Bibles. Understanding the history of these texts, the way not all texts ascribed to "Paul" in the New Testament reflect Paul's views, helps readers of biblical texts to sift through these texts to get to "original" ideas, deep in the folds of history, that can be—in Crossan's view—mined for a non-violent message today.

What is valuable about the approach of historicising biblical texts is that it brings in the different temporal and geographical dimensions of the texts that make up Christian Bibles. They are not just attached to their current-day forms and locations. They are not stand-alone texts that can easily travel

---

[28] John Dominic Crossan, *How to Read the Bible and Still Be a Christian* (New York: Harper Collins, 2015), p. 37.
[29] Ibid., pp. 43, 46.
[30] Ibid., p. 60.
[31] Ibid., p. 91.
[32] Ibid. Crossan's point is not to turn the Bible into a historical archive, though, or to turn all Bible readers into historical-critical scholars. He is addressing a Christian audience which continues to use Bibles in worship and faith life. Crossan's approach is to identify an "original" Bible by turning to history. Violence, according to Crossan, came in reaction to the radical nature of Jesus's message. The original Bible containing Jesus's radical message which Crossan seeks is not just a Bible prior to the interpretations that have come *after* it was canonised. Rather, the Christian Bible itself already contains interpretations that are contrary to the original message. In other words, it is necessary to locate a Bible in a Bible by historical means. Essentially, what Crossan argues, through different examples in the Christian biblical canon, is that the biblical corpus plays out—again and again—a struggle between what he calls the radicality of God and what he calls "the normalcy of civilization". Crossan writes about "a rhythm of assertion-and-subversion" throughout the Bible in which a "vision of the radicality of God is put forth, and then later, we see that vision domesticated and integrated into the normalcy of civilization so that the established order of life is maintained". When it comes to Jesus, Crossan spells out that it "is not that Jesus the Christ changed his mind", but that "Christianity changed its Jesus".

between different historical times as if their meanings are obvious and can simply be translated directly into other times and places. These texts are not solely owned or simply possessed by people who are alive today. Ancient authors, listeners, geographies, vocabularies, ideologies, and materials are stuck to Bibles in multi-dimensional ways. Biblical texts are also marked by their formation and usage in a past that is far removed from, even radically different to, our own modern world. In *The Realness of Things Past*, the historian Greg Anderson argues for an ontological turn when it comes to the past, in which we recognise the claims to truth and the realness of the life-worlds of ancient people despite the potentially radical alterity of the past to our present.[33] Understanding ancient times, places, and peoples on their own ontological terms, as he puts it,[34] does not mean we can access things "as they really were", but it does entail an attempt to recover "whatever past peoples could say about their present".[35] We would have to ask about the "elemental metaphysical commitments" of past peoples, of the commitments that "made possible the world as they knew and experienced it" rather than assuming a direct line of development or continuity between a past and our present.[36]

Assuming continuity between the texts of a Bible and a present-day context bulldozes over the concrete realities and experiences of the people who first wrote, listened to, and passed on these texts. Trying to understand them on terms that are different from our own, in a past that has its own unique and distinct conditions, is about paying respect to this past as well as opening one's self up for curiosity about different—sometimes radically different— modes of thinking, embodying, feeling, and living. This confrontation with the ontological otherness of a past of which texts are a part can be both enthralling and unsettling. We lose something if we flatten these texts into messages that speak directly only to our own contexts, commitments, and culture.

But sticking to the "origins" of biblical texts and their "original" meanings is also a form of flattening. As I already pointed out, it is also not how a lot of Bible-use actually works. Lots of people and communities use Bibles as texts to be guided by rather than as ancient archives. Most obviously, Jews and Christians relate to Bibles in ways that denote these texts are more than

---

[33] Greg Anderson, *The Realness of Things Past: Ancient Greece and Ontological History* (Oxford: Oxford University Press, 2018), p. 123
[34] Ibid., p. 117.
[35] Ibid., p. 119.
[36] Ibid.

just remnants from the past. The approach of historicising biblical texts assumes that more *knowledge* is what it takes to change Bible-use that incites or involves violence. There is nothing wrong with aiming for more knowledge about biblical texts. That is a key part of what biblical scholarship does. As Clare Foster puts it, "corrective expertise" has an important role, particularly in the digital present.[37] But simply correcting or attempting to police particular kinds of Bible-use is not necessarily effective, and moreover, it mistakes how much Bible-use works. It is also potentially arrogant—as if biblical scholars always know best how texts can and should be used.

Vested interests in particular understandings and uses of Bibles that operate on a more emotional, or affective, level are crucial, and are often forgotten when the focus lies squarely in educating people to have more knowledge about biblical texts. I will go on to discuss different understandings of affect, but one way of understanding affect is as emotion. As Sara Ahmed puts it, emotions "shape the very surfaces of bodies, which take shape through the repetition of actions over time, as well as through orientations towards and away from others".[38] She asks not what emotions are, but what they do.[39] Emotions are not just something I have; they are relational; "they involve (re)actions or relations of 'towardness' or 'awayness' in relation" to different objects.[40] Ahmed moves away from the idea of emotions as interior states to more sociological and anthropological models that see emotions as social and cultural practices.[41] "Rather than emotions being understood as coming from within and moving outwards, emotions are assumed to *come from without and move inward*".[42]

The main point here is that emotions are not just something personal, private, and internal, but are also embedded in social practices, habits, and interactions. To take account of affect is to probe what Karen Bray and Stephen Moore call the "often unremarkable yet frequently momentous feelings for which we have many names: love, hatred, anger, rage, madness,

---

[37] Clare L. E. Foster, 'Familiarity and Recognition: Towards a New Vocabulary for Classical Reception Studies', in *Framing Classical Reception Studies,* edited by Maarten De Pourcq, Nathalie De Haan, and David Rijser (Leiden: Brill, 2020), p. 62. Foster, too, argues that such corrective expertise is not enough: "A shift of interest towards how we know, rather than what we know, is long overdue". Foster, 'Familiarity and Recognition: Towards a New Vocabulary for Classical Reception Studies', p. 62.
[38] Ahmed, *The Cultural Politics of Emotion* p. 4.
[39] Ibid.
[40] Ibid., p. 8.
[41] Ibid., p. 9.
[42] Ibid.

loneliness, paranoia, depression, despair, envy, anxiety, shame, boredom, joy, happiness, ecstasy, contentment, optimism, pessimism".[43] Of course humans do not only operate rationally, intellectually, or cerebrally, but are feeling creatures who respond emotionally to objects and others. Fiona Black and Jennifer Koosed suggest that affect, in the sense of emotion, "is not just about individual and interior states but always also about how emotion is a socially produced sensation; affects circulate body to body, produced by and producing certain political and cultural phenomena".[44] How do feelings "get coded within cultures" and how do "they come to stick to certain kinds of bodies, objects, and choices"?[45] "Affect theory confronts us with the ontological, epistemological, and religious significance of the nonlinguistic and the nonrational".[46]

This needs to be part of our way of thinking about Bible-use, too. Responding to Bible-use cannot only be about a classroom lesson in ancient history. Justine Esta Ellis has made a similar argument in relation to calls for improvements in religious literacy. Taking for granted notions of rationality, neutrality, autonomy, and interiority, such calls tend to forget and sideline "the embodied experiences and emotional attachments involved in formalizing knowledge".[47] To be clear, my critique is not that figures on the far right might not be changed by more historical knowledge and therefore the response falls flat. That is not the bar I set for any response to biblical violence. Rather, it is a question more generally of how changes can occur in how people read and relate to biblical texts and how they lay claim to Bibles. For the affective investments people have in Bibles, biblical texts, or particular interpretations, a response based on more knowledge of the past may not hit home in any meaningful way. When the theologian and civil-rights leader Howard Thurman recounts the way he would read biblical stories to his grandmother, who had been a slave, he remembers the way she would not allow him to read Paul's letters.[48] When he asked her why, she told him that the white preacher on the plantation used to preach from Paul's letters,

---

[43] Bray and Moore, 'Introduction: Mappings and Crossings', p. 3.
[44] Black and Koosed, 'Introduction: Some Ways to Read with Feeling', p. 9.
[45] Bray and Moore, 'Introduction: Mappings and Crossings', p. 3.
[46] Ibid., p. 6.
[47] Justine Esta Ellis, *The Politics of Religious Literacy: Education and Emotion in a Secular Age* (Leiden: Brill, 2022), p. 4.
[48] As recounted and discussed by Grey Gundaker, in Grey Gundaker, 'The Bible *as* and *at* a Threshold: Reading, Performance, and Blessed Space', in *African Americans and the Bible: Sacred Texts and Social Textures*, edited by Vincent Wimbush (Eugene, OR: Wipf & Stock, 2000), p. 757. An occasional exception was 1 Corinthians 13.

particularly the parts admonishing slaves to obey their masters. She vowed to herself that if she was ever free and learned to read, she would never read those parts of Christian scripture.[49] This does not seem an irrational response to the trauma of slavery and the Bible-use that was involved. This use and understanding of Paul's letters offers a particularly strong example of the way more historical knowledge about Paul's writings, or insisting on situating them in their ancient context, will most likely neither change the way Thurman's grandmother relates to these texts nor adequately address the problems the text presents.

Ahmed discusses the way texts generate effects.[50] Texts, particularly classics and canonical texts, are stuck to histories of association. The way these associations orbit a text and make it thick with what Ahmed calls "affective value" is often concealed.[51] She talks about the effects of repetition, but also of the concealment of the work of this repetition.[52] Partly, the things that stick, stick because there is a vested interest in propagating particular structures and their effects. The Slavery Bible in the United States is a good example of a Bible that accumulated affective value amongst white people who wanted to legitimate white supremacy and the enslavement of Black people. But the "European-Americanization of the Bible"[53] more generally, as Vincent Wimbush has put it, has had more subtle effects, too, as I tried to show in relation to the Civilisation Bible. There are multiple other examples of Bibles that have accumulated affective value. A Bible that is used to propagate patriarchal structures in society, for instance, will be perpetuated according to patriarchal interests, perspectives, and practices. As Ahmed puts it, emotions accumulate over time as "a form of affective value".[54] Ahmed's attention to emotions and stickiness in relation to politics is about asking why some societal structures are so persistent, even when they have been met with resistance. Why is change so hard? Her answer is that the accumulated affective value of a practice or position may override thoughtful and evidence-based rebuttals of these practices and positions. Emotional investments in particular ways of life structure the way the world is encountered and experienced. Undoing emotional entanglements is not a matter of saying "stop

---

[49] Gundaker, 'The Bible *as* and *at* a Threshold', p. 757.
[50] Ahmed, *The Cultural Politics of Emotion*, p. 13.
[51] Ibid., pp. 11, 13.
[52] Ibid., p. 12.
[53] Wimbush, 'Introduction: Reading Darkness, Reading Scriptures', p. 757.
[54] Ahmed, *The Cultural Politics of Emotion*, p. 11.

feeling like that". Emotional investments and interests may be resistant to arguments that operate on a rational or intellectual level.

It is important to point out here that I am not suggesting that "ordinary" Bible-users are beholden to these affective investments, while biblical scholars look upon biblical texts with a cool, trained eye from above the fray of emotions. As Rita Felski has discussed in relation to art and literary critics,[55] there is not enough scholarly reflection on why scholars themselves have affective investments in texts. Some Bibles make us feel good. Others will make us shudder or cringe. What affects are produced by what Bible will depend on our affective investments, on our beliefs, commitments, contexts, and experiences. The way people *become* invested in particular Bibles, and help form and transmit biblical assemblages, is key for thinking about responses to biblical violence. Biblical scholars have as many affective investments as the next person, and probably more affective investments in particular Bibles, than most.

Altogether, then, the historicising biblical texts approach, as I have called it, responds to biblical violence by insisting on biblical texts being understood in their ancient context. Responding to biblical violence with a demand to historicise the Bible, as a canon and collection of texts, has a value in that it defamiliarises these texts as the straightforward possessions of "us" today, whichever "us" is laying claim to a Bible. Paying attention to the historical dimensions of Bibles is about acknowledging and exploring the temporal and geographical textures of these texts. These texts do not belong only to whoever has most recently laid their hands on a Bible. They do not speak straightforwardly or easily into a present. Ancient authors, listeners, geographies, vocabularies, ideologies, and materials are stuck to Bibles in multi-dimensional ways. This is a point that effectively reveals the multi-dimensionality of Bibles as assemblages that operate across different temporal and geographical dimensions, that cut across cultures and are stuck to ontological commitments that might seem alien to present-day reality. Taking this multi-dimensionality seriously is about revelling in, and paying respect to, the historical otherness of biblical texts. However, there are limitations to this response. Confidence in historical knowledge of biblical texts stopping "bad" use of Bibles is, as I have argued, misplaced. It forgets that the majority of Bible-users relate to Bibles in diverse, complex, and ambiguous ways that are not set apart entirely from academic concerns, but do not

---

[55] Felski, *Hooked*.

wholly overlap with academic concerns, either. Affective ties to Bibles and biblical texts are crucial for understanding the way Bible-use functions (also when it comes to the affective ties of biblical scholars).

Battling Selectivity

The second point that can be raised about the political Bible-use I have discussed is that it is the result of selectivity. The mere act of selectivity could be critiqued as illegitimate Bible-use. Individual biblical verses are lifted out of their larger textual surroundings and serve a purpose that they could never have served had they been left in their larger context. This larger context might refer to the longer text in which a verse or chapter is found, or it might mean the context of "the Bible" itself as a canon of texts, depending on which canon one is committed to. Selectivity is often bemoaned when it comes to political Bible-use. It is an understandable concern. Most people would be frustrated if a line from an email they sent was cited and used to mean something that it could not have meant if the line was read in the context of the entire email or the chain of emails in which it is a part. Arguing for the problem with lifting bits of text out of the chapter or book they are in is so obvious to biblical scholars that it barely needs to be made in critiquing selective forms of Bible-use.

In the case I have been analysing in this book, it is easy to see how the selectivity of bits of Bible in Breivik's manifesto could be described as opportunistic and cynical. The bits of biblical text are cut out of longer texts and made to fit a different kind of text—a far-right manifesto shared online as a PDF, full of different quotes and different kinds of texts pasted together. Many biblical passages are ignored altogether, hence my case for mapping the particular biblical assemblage that is constructed based on specific biblical texts as well as the other elements that are stuck to these bits of Bible. As Mieke Bal notes, because of the unique status of Christian scripture in Western culture, bits of Bible lend themselves to a "politics of allusion".[56] "Even the tiniest allusion is enough to invoke an entire story" or a "legacy of interpretation".[57]

---

[56] Mieke Bal, 'Seduction, the Biblical Imagination, and Activating Art', in *The Bible and Feminism: Remapping the Field*, edited by Yvonne Sherwood with the assistance of Anna Fisk (Oxford: Oxford University Press, 2017), p. 590.

[57] Ibid.

But deeming it problematic to take bits of biblical text out of their chapter and book relies on a particular understanding of practices of reading and of texts themselves. Simply assuming that all texts should be read from start to finish, in which every sentence or smaller narrative unit is read within its whole, does not correspond to actual reading practices in many cases. This is particularly the case when it comes to histories of reading biblical texts, in which often texts have functioned not *as* texts with clear beginnings and ends but as pieces of music or as images in the form of paintings or stained-glass windows. In church liturgies, parts of biblical texts are read or sung. Priests and ministers often reflect on one or two verses in their sermons.

With the rise of social media, the way biblical texts are engaged with has changed further. Peter Phillips has argued that if scholars want to understand biblical literacy in contemporary culture, "we need to make a shift away from thinking that biblical literacy is exclusively about people reading the Bible".[58] Phillips has made the case that digital Bible engagement shows a trend from the sharing of propositional statements such as John 3:16 to the sharing of more therapeutic-style verses, such as Jeremiah 29:11.[59] The purpose of the bit of Bible shared is not to see it as part of a narrative or primarily as a text to be read but as words that feel good or as an inspirational slogan that resonates with people. Bits of Bible have become caught up in social media trends, then, where short text-snippets are key. Jennifer de Paola and Eemeli Hakoköngäs have discussed the exponential growth of "bite-size" content on social media, much of it centred on "positive thinking".[60] As they point out, this might be "inspirational memes, quotes, aphorisms, proverbs and other types of motivational text that social media users have digitally superimposed on an image".[61] These posts are meant to add meaningfulness and inspiration to the social media content. It is about creating "a graphically and aesthetically appealing quote".[62] De Paola and Hakoköngäs discuss the celebrity/authority endorsement technique as one function in the visual aspects of a meme, where a celebrity is cited as the author of the quote or a quote is introduced by "science says . . ." or "psychology says . . ."[63]. With

---

[58] Peter Phillips, 'The Pixelated Text: Reading the Bible within Digital Culture', *Theology* 121, no. 6 (2018): p. 403.
[59] Peter Phillips, *The Bible, Social Media, and Digital Culture* (London: Routledge, 2019), p. 21.
[60] Jennifer De Paola and Eemeli Hakoköngäs, 'This Must Surely Be the Way to Happiness! Divergent "Bite-Size" Wisdoms" about Happpiness in Inspirational Internet Memes', *Culture Unbound: Journal of Current Cultural Research* 12, no. 3 (2020): p. 591. Ibid.,
[61] Ibid., pp. 591–592.
[62] Ibid., p. 592.
[63] Ibid., p. 604.

a quote from a Bible, it is the "Bibleness" that provides authority—and for some, celebrity—to the verse that is shared. This is not about *reading* biblical texts so much as it is about seeing or enjoying a biblical verse. It is about how a bit of text *feels*. Selectivity, then, is key.

Tom de Bruin's research on Bible verses shared online points to the way selectivity is paramount for appealing to audiences. In these acts of selection, biblical canons and biblical passages are transformed and even, in a sense, rewritten.[64] De Bruin focuses on the way biblical verses are shared as images, superimposed on picture backgrounds, and so the rewriting of the text is part of understanding the effects of this text-image. For the case of Breivik and his biblical assemblages, the biblical texts are shared in a massive PDF document rather than as tweets or Facebook posts. But other contemporary far-right groups with similar viewpoints to Breivik's have made use of Bible verses in their social media feeds.[65] The point is that selectivity is only a problem if we assume that texts *should* or *must* be read in particular ways, such as from start to finish, and where quotations have to always be placed in their larger contexts. Much contemporary Bible engagement does not look like this, though, nor has it historically.

The appeal to a larger biblical context in which individual biblical texts should be used and understood often comes from scholars who are addressing a faith-based readership. This makes sense due to faith commitments to particular canons. Reading Bible-as-canon can address tendencies to select bits of Bible in ways that go against other biblical texts. Focusing on canonicity is a way of challenging the nit-picking of individual biblical texts or snippets of text by pointing out that for Christians, for instance, there is an accepted canon which indicates a whole set of texts that are deemed "biblical" and which therefore should all have weight when it comes to Christian faith and practice. It is a matter of seeing "the Bible", again in Crossan's words, "as a completed volume, as an organized unity, and as an integrated totality".[66] This approach requires confessional commitments, as it depends on your allegiance to the outcome of historical processes whereby a Bible became *the Bible* for a particular group of people.

---

[64] Tom de Bruin, 'Seeing Is Believing: The Digital Bible and Bible Verses Online', *Spec Christiana* 31, no. 1 (2020): p. 145.

[65] See Strømmen, 'Crusades, Christ and Christmas: Islamophobia and the Bible in the European Far-Right after 9/11'.

[66] Crossan, *How to Read the Bible and Still Be a Christian*, p. 20.

Eryl Davies explains the way a canonical approach to a Bible allows violent passages to "resonate with their wider canonical context" and can in this way be seen in a different light.[67] Davies outlines how the attempt to view the Bible as a whole has significant implications for how individual texts are read and understood. Violent biblical texts are potentially only problematic if read in isolation. The individual parts of the Bible should be understood through the order and shape of the canon as a whole.[68] When the whole biblical canon is taken into account, respecting "its overarching perspective and overall intention, the ethically objectionable passages would not prove to be quite such a stumbling-block as is often supposed".[69] Weighing up violent biblical texts by insisting on their connection with other biblical texts that make up a biblical canon could have a "moderating effect" and take "the edge off" the more extreme and explicit violence in light of non-violent texts.[70]

Another point about reading "the Bible" as a set of chosen texts that are brought together for the purposes of a faith community is that a theological lens is used to weigh up different texts and their meaning. For Christians, a "Christological hermeneutic", as Jerome Creach argues, is one way of making sense of biblical texts. In *Violence in Scripture: Resources for the Use of Scripture in the Church*, Creach states that it is "probably necessary to read the Bible with some organizing center as a guide to understanding the whole".[71] He suggests that reading the Bible with Christ as a centre "may aid in understanding passages that seem to promote violence".[72] Ultimately this allows him to conclude that the Bible is anti-violence, by arguing that the violence that occurs is either human violence (and therefore sinful), or a "divine response to and correction of the violence of humans".[73] God's violence is therefore corrective and redemptive, whereas human violence is wrong. In this way the Bible becomes "a grand testimony against violence".[74]

---

[67] Davies, *The Immoral Bible*, p. 80.
[68] Jerome F. D. Creach, *Violence in Scripture: Resources for the Use of Scripture in the Church* (Louisville, KY: Westminster John Knox Press, 2013), p. 5..
[69] Davies, *The Immoral Bible*, p. 80.
[70] Ibid., p. 81.
[71] Creach, *Violence in Scripture*, p. 3.
[72] Ibid.
[73] Ibid., p. 5.
[74] Ibid. Crossan argues similarly in *How to Read the Bible and Still Be a Christian*. Crossan asserts that the historical Jesus "is the norm and criterion of the Christian Bible. In other words, the meaning of that Bible's story is in its *middle*, in the story of Jesus in the Gospels and the early writings of Paul; the climax of its narrative is in the *center*; and the sense of its nonviolent center judges the (non) sense of its violent ending". Erik A. Seibert, *Disturbing Divine Behaviour: Troubling Old Testament Images of God* (Minneapolis, MN: Fortress Press, 2009), Kenton Sparks's *Sacred Word, Broken Word: Biblical Authority and the Dark Side of Scripture* (Grand Rapids, MI: Eerdmans, 2012), and

The strength of the canonical approach lies in the fact that it points to the diversity of biblical texts gathered together into one book. It becomes difficult to see a Bible as anything but pluriform, despite the texts being bound together in one book or as a fixed canon. As Hawk reflects, there can be no "imposition of an absolutizing template"; the complexity and diversity of the Bible fosters different interpretive positions and can therefore prompt "dialogue among faithful readers who read and think differently about God's violence and what Christians should make of it".[75] The Christological hermeneutic demonstrates the way theological interpretations will to a large extent determine Bible-use. It shows that for most Christians in principle, and probably all Christians in practice, biblical texts are not all read the same way or without a more overarching theological lens. There are some problems with this approach, though. How are the diversity and difference of texts contained in a canon actually dealt with? The Christological hermeneutic addresses the issue of the diversity of the canon. But does that approach lead to "functional Marcionites",[76] where particular New Testament passages about Jesus trump so-called Old Testament texts? Reading the Christian Bible with a Christological hermeneutic has been a way for Christians to do violence to Jews, by reading Jesus into Jewish texts and denigrating and demonising Jews for not accepting these readings. Although Christians will undoubtedly continue to see Jesus as an—or the—key figure for interpreting Christian scripture, a Christological hermeneutic that does not confront this violent history risks doing further violence.

It goes without saying that a canonical approach, or a Christological hermeneutic, are not approaches that work if you are not already committed to the canonical shape of a Bible or the idea of Jesus as the centre for your reading and use of a Bible. As I discussed in chapter 2, it is important to recognise the way Bible-use operates also outside faith communities. Breivik and other figures on the far right lay claim to religious communities without "belonging" to them in any obvious or traditional sense. There may be no sense of commitment to canonical readings or theological hermeneutics, even if references to Christian tradition and culture feature. As I discussed in chapter 1, Breivik does not look like a Christian in a way many would

---

Crossan's *How to Read the Bible and Still Be a Christian*, for instance, all utilise a Christological hermeneutic in responding to biblical violence.

[75] Hawk, *The Violence of the Biblical God*, pp. 200–201.
[76] For a discussion of this point, see Carroll R. and Wilgus, *Wrestling with the Violence of God*, p. 6.

recognise as "Christian". At the same time, he lays claim to a form of cultural Christianity that he deems real and significant. As I have shown, he is not alone in this understanding of Christianity. Bibles do not belong only to faith communities, even if some people might wish they did. In practice, secular, political, and cultural uses of Bibles characterise Western societies. Any response to biblical violence needs to take into account that this response cannot be addressed to recognised faith communities alone. But also, as with the previous approach, it could be argued that it should not, and cannot, be a matter of theologians and faith leaders telling communities of faith how to read and relate to scripture. Further, affect is an issue in this case, too, where complex feelings, emotions, and relations to biblical texts inform the use of these texts.

Altogether, then, it makes sense to bemoan selectivity when it comes to biblical violence. Picking out a lone verse to serve violent ends or cutting out part of a story to exemplify the violence of the Bible is irritating when you know that the larger context in which these verses and stories are nestled might complicate or completely change the picture. These larger contexts might diffuse the violence. They might diminish or destroy the interpretive confidence that violence can be justified as a result of the bit of text. Just as Bibles cannot be seen as isolated entities when it comes to understanding their content, capacities, and features, but must be seen as assembled with multiple different elements, so it must be recognised that small bits of biblical text sometimes do carry weight as components alongside other factors. Even if scholars think this is bad practice or hermeneutically problematic, it is important to keep in mind that texts do not function in only one way, as literary wholes to be read from start to finish. Texts function in all sorts of ways. And they are not always read or interpreted. A commitment to particular theological ways of reading or to canonicity are ways of critiquing selectivity. But there are limitations to the critique of selectivity as the problem. Canonical approaches are tricky: how do you measure the multiple different biblical texts against each other all at once to avoid creating hierarchies? Further, biblical texts do not belong only to faith leaders, committees, or religious communities, where particular theological perspectives and appeals to canonicity might hold sway.

Biblical Authority

The third point that could be raised in response to biblical violence is that the problem lies not so much in individual biblical texts as it does in the authority invested in that thing we call "the Bible". The Civilisation Bible operates effectively due to its currency as a cultural-theological authority. The famous image of then-president Donald Trump holding a Bible in Washington, DC, in June 2020 is an example of the authority invested in the physical book. Appealing to a Bible is an appeal to a certain kind of authority. For the ideas and practices of Breivik, this authority is attached to the presumed status of Christian scripture.

Critiquing the authority of Bibles is most frequently tied up in critiquing theological claims that see the Bible as a source of *divine* authority. In his 2002 presidential address to the Society of Biblical Literature, John J. Collins blamed the violence executed in the name of the Bible on "its presumed divine authority, which gives an aura of certitude to any position it can be shown to support".[77] The Bible has been seen as conferring certitude—a certitude that transcends human discussion and argumentation. Because of this, it has contributed to violence in the world.[78] In other words, as Regina Schwartz discusses, the authority of Bibles has been invoked both to justify slavery and to abolish it, to support missionary imperialism and revolutionary response, in the rhetoric of Zionism and the liberation theologies of Latin America and South Africa.[79] As the variety of these examples demonstrates, the problem is less with biblical texts themselves, which could be interpreted to justify all sorts of positions and programmes, and more the authority of a Bible that can be used to legitimate dogmatic certainties and non-negotiable positions. Schwartz writes that the "ancient agonistic values" of biblical texts "are far too dangerous to continue authorizing".[80]

Collins suggests that biblical scholars can lessen "the contribution of the Bible to violence in the world" by showing that "certitude is an illusion".[81] He writes:

---

[77] Collins, *Does the Bible Justify Violence?*, p. 32.
[78] Ibid., pp. 32–33.
[79] Regina Schwartz, *The Curse of Cain: The Violent Legacy of Monotheism* (Chicago: University of Chicago Press, 1997), p. 8.
[80] Ibid., p. 176.
[81] Collins, *Does the Bible Justify Violence?*, p. 33.

The biblical portrayal of human reality becomes pernicious only when it is vested with authority and assumed to reflect, without qualification or differentiation, the wisdom of God or the will of God. The Bible does not demystify or demythologise itself. But neither does it claim that the stories it tells are paradigms for human action in all times and places.[82]

Biblical scholars can point to the contradictory and diverse texts of the Bible to undermine any clear-cut certitude in one position over another.[83] This involves a demystifying and demythologising approach to Bibles in which any aura of authority is questioned and challenged. The demystifying and demythologising of biblical texts is arguably exactly what many, if not most, biblical scholars do in their scholarly activities by talking about textual composition, complexities around authorship, the ambiguities of words and their meanings, and difficulties in verifying the veracity of biblical accounts of events.

However, some biblical scholars argue that the discipline has not done enough when it comes to challenging the authority Bibles enjoy in society. This failure has potentially allowed for the authority of Bibles to remain intact in modern societies despite the secularised characteristics marking biblical studies.[84] Most prominently, Hector Avalos has claimed that biblical scholars have more often than not "maintained the value of religious texts that promote or endorse violence".[85] He critiques hermeneutical strategies that, as he puts it, "sanitize violence".[86] In *Fighting Words: The Origin of Religious Violence*, Avalos accuses scholars of religion and biblical scholars of being complicit with "creating and propagating the value of violent texts".[87] These actions by scholars may be done for apologetic reasons in defending religious traditions, in seeking to remain neutral in describing and explaining religious traditions, or in maintaining the aesthetic value of biblical texts. He makes similar critiques of sanitising biblical texts and engaging in apologetics for biblical texts in *Slavery, Abolitionism and the Ethics of Biblical Scholarship* and *The Bad Jesus: The Ethics of New Testament Ethics*.[88] Most

---

[82] Ibid., p. 31.
[83] Ibid., p. 30.
[84] Legaspi discusses the secularisation of the field in *The Death of Scripture and the Rise of Biblical Studies*.
[85] Hector Avalos, *Fighting Words: The Origins of Religious Violence* (New York: Prometheus Books, 2005), p. 23.
[86] Ibid., p. 23.
[87] Ibid., p. 381.
[88] Hector Avalos, *Slavery, Abolitionism, and the Ethics of Biblical Scholarship* (Sheffield: Sheffield Phoenix Press, 2013); Hector Avalos, *The Bad Jesus: The Ethics of New Testament Ethics*

biblical scholarship, in his view, is "part of an imperialist enterprise bent on preserving the authority" of a set of texts that Avalos sees as fundamentally problematic.[89]

In *Fighting Words*, Avalos's own response to biblical violence is "to undermine the value of any scripture that endorses violence".[90] He subscribes to what he calls a "zero-tolerance" approach to the Bible, indeed to any religious text that contains and endorses violence.[91] He argues that there is no other solution to violence done in the name of the Bible. He talks therefore of the "folly" of reappropriating ancient religious texts for a modern context, calling it a "morally sordid game", "morally reprehensible", and "vacuous".[92] For Avalos there is no way to "save" the Bible from violence, both in terms of its content and in terms of Bible-use. Scholars like Collins and, to an even greater extent, Avalos, want to challenge the authority of "the Bible" so that this set of texts is not elevated beyond question, debate, and critique. Avalos in particular pushes his argument towards the rejection of particular biblical texts altogether, resulting in their decanonisation. Further, Avalos argues that Jesus is considered a paradigm of ethics in New Testament scholarship. As he sees it, "biblical scholarship is still largely operating as part of the detritus of Christian empires, which often used the Bible as their textual authority".[93] Therefore, it is this textual authority that has to be not only challenged but rejected.[94] For Avalos, ancient biblical texts should play no role in determining modern ethics.[95] Ethics "should not be based on textual authority", only on scientifically verifiable phenomena and empathy as a biological constituent of humanity.[96] As he concludes in *Slavery, Abolitionism, and the Ethics of Biblical Scholarship*, "the modern world must completely unshackle itself from using the Bible as any sort of ethical or social authority".[97]

Schwartz, too, is interested in the way the authority tied to biblical canons have "fixed" particular memories and narratives, both proliferating

---

(Sheffield: Sheffield Phoenix Press, 2015). Cavan Concannon has made a similar case in relation to Paul's writings, that scholars have been part of a sanitising of Paul that is deeply problematic. Cavan W. Concannon, *Profaning Paul* (Chicago: University of Chicago Press, 2021).

[89] Avalos, *The Bad Jesus*, p. 28.
[90] Avalos, *Fighting Words*, p. 382.
[91] Ibid., p. 360.
[92] Ibid., p. 362.
[93] Avalos, *The Bad Jesus*, p. 377.
[94] Ibid., p. 377.
[95] Ibid., p. 378.
[96] Ibid.
[97] Avalos, *Slavery, Abolitionism, and the Ethics of Biblical Scholarship*, p. 288.

memories and limiting memories.[98] Commenting on the way biblical stories of conquest have far-reaching political afterlives, Schwartz suggests that whatever clever nuances biblical scholars might provide on the historicity of these biblical stories, they may simply be too subtle to change the political effects of the biblical texts, particularly because these texts enjoy an authoritative status.[99] It might be more effective, she suggests, instead of seeking to rewrite the historical narrative in which a biblical story is embedded, to rewrite the biblical narrative.[100] Ultimately, Schwartz calls for an opening of "the biblical canon": "and by that I do not mean some partial commentary of sanctified unalterable authoritative texts, but a genuine rewriting of traditions: new creation stories, new exoduses, new losses, and new recoveries of what is lost".[101] Due to the authority biblical stories hold in faith communities and their role also in secular cultural registers, people in the modern West are probably not able to "completely escape biblical myths as our cultural inheritance, and so the best we can do is rewrite them in a new key".[102] Her revisioning of "the Bible" takes the form of an "alternative Bible that subverts the dominant vision of violence and scarcity with an ideal of plenitude and its corollary ethical imperative of generosity"; it is a Bible "embracing multiplicity instead of monotheism".[103]

The value of the approach of challenging biblical authority lies in its focus on the status Bibles have as more than just any book or collection of texts. It recognises the power of the sticky histories of Bible-use in terms of the feelings of reverence and respect that endow Bibles with theological and cultural capital. As James Bielo posits, individuals and groups "appropriate the Bible as a resource—often because of its intense cultural capital—to support and persuade, impose and resist".[104] The approach of challenging biblical authority moves us beyond the details and content of a biblical text and its interpretation to the attitudes and assumptions that underlie Bible-use in the past and the present. Tackling biblical violence, then, has to include attention to the authority of "the Bible" as sacred scripture, literary classic, and cultural canon.

---

[98] Schwartz, *The Curse of Cain*, p. 144.
[99] Ibid., p. 158.
[100] Ibid.
[101] Ibid., p. 175.
[102] Ibid., p. 176.
[103] Ibid.
[104] James S. Bielo, 'Introduction: Encountering Biblicism', in *The Social Life of Scriptures: Cross-Cultural Perspectives on Biblicism*, edited by James S. Bielo (New Brunswick, NJ: Rutgers University Press, 2009), p. 6.

However, there are also problems with this approach. While Collins suggests that the destabilisation of biblical authority can be done by demonstrating the diversity of biblical texts and the way these texts contradict one another, he does not discuss to what extent this would actually be effective. It is hardly news that Bibles are collections of texts. Every single introduction to every introductory book on "the Bible" talks about it as a library, *ta biblia*. Even if it is the case that the diversity of biblical texts in Bibles should be emphasised more, an important question would be to ask how this can be done in a way that is effective and not just pedantic or patronising. How authority works can be complex, as Dawn Llewellyn demonstrates in her study of the way post-Christian women can be highly critical of the authoritative status sticking to biblical literature while not rejecting biblical texts.[105] Llewellyn calls this a process of "filtering".[106] The women Llewellyn studies reject straightforward claims to the authority of "the Bible". At the same time, this does not entail an outright rejection of biblical texts altogether. In fact, many of them incorporate biblical material into their lives in creative and critical ways.[107]

It is not spelled out by either Avalos or Schwartz how a decanonising or rewriting process of biblical books would or could take place. Is it imagined this should be done by the faith communities for whom Bibles are important? Or amongst anyone, of faith or none? Should it be a bottom-up process or a top-down agenda? The authority of Bibles is clearly a crucial issue for legitimating violent acts and ideologies. But thinking through how to tackle this authority is not straightforward, given the long history of revering Bibles as sacred scripture, as canonical literature, and as a cultural classic. Again, questions of affect would need to be addressed to tease out *how* authority is invested in a particular book or mode of reading, how some figures and interpretive perspectives become endowed with authority, and how perceptions of canonicity itself might continue to structure what possibilities exist for change.

The approach of challenging biblical authority, then, takes seriously the problematic elements in Bibles and in Bible-use, allowing for serious critique and even rejection and rewriting of some biblical texts. Claiming

---

[105] Dawn Llewellyn, '"But I still read the Bible!" Post-Christian Women's Biblicalism', in *The Bible and Feminism*, edited by Sherwood with the assistance of Fisk, p. 582.

[106] Ibid., pp. 582–583. She also refers to Lynn Resnick Dufour's term "sifting". Lynn Resnick Dufour, '"Sifting through Tradition": The Creation of Jewish Feminist Identities', *Journal for the Scientific Study of Religion* 39, no.1 (2000): pp. 90–106.

[107] Llewellyn, '"But I still read the Bible!"', p. 582.

certainty about the meanings of biblical texts and using this certainty to hurt others is explicitly challenged. The aura of authority attached to a Bible can, and should in this view, be dispelled. Biblical texts are drawn down from so-called divine heights to be seen as: the products of humans, the result of editorial machinations, and faulty and flawed texts that are frequently contradictory and often outright problematic. Rather than challenge biblical violence by providing historical contextualisation of biblical texts, though, the challenging biblical authority approach directs its attention to the theological and cultural capital of Bibles. It is the aura of authority Bibles enjoy that has to be problematised, rather than simply reinterpreting individual biblical texts or adding historical nuance and detail to violent texts. Demonstrating the internal inconsistencies of biblical canons and their diversity can lessen the confidence of claims as to what "'the Bible' says". But it is no secret that Bibles are collections of disparate texts with different meanings and messages. It is not clear how insisting on this point will make any difference. Decanonising and rewriting biblical texts are two more radical suggestions for how to challenge the authority of Bibles and biblical canons. The problem with this response, though, is that there is not much reflection on the multifaceted way the authority that is associated with Bibles actually works. This comes back to affective ties and investments as well as long histories of Bibles accumulating cultural and theological capital. It is not clear how proposals to decanonise or rewrite biblical texts would work in practice, who would decide, and for whom this would actually change anything when it comes to Bible-use.

Resistant Reading

The fourth point that could be made about the Bible-use I have discussed is that the problem of biblical texts lies in their intractable patriarchal biases and misogynistic tendencies. To combat this problem, it is necessary to foster strategies of resistance to the worldviews, attitudes, and behaviours biblical texts put forward as normal and normative. A resistant reading approach is not primarily about critiquing the authority of the Bible, though it could do that, too, but about engaging in critical resistance to biblical narratives that contain or condone violence, producing interpretations that challenge biblical material, and actively questioning the assumptions that inform biblical stories of violence. This approach could also be characterised as reading with a hermeneutics of suspicion,[108] though, as I will go on to discuss, resistance does not have to take the form of suspicion. What a resistant mode of engagement with biblical texts entails is a critical stance that refuses to accept the terms the texts set, the narrative point of view, and the presented worldview.

Responses to biblical violence of the resistant reading kind have often come from feminist and womanist biblical scholarship. These biblical scholars have been tireless in exposing the violence of biblical texts. The violence described in biblical texts is frequently perpetuated against named or unnamed women. The effects of Bible-use on women have impacted their lives in violent ways through misogynistic attitudes and patriarchal practices, from everyday harassment and discrimination to domestic violence, sexual violence, and murder. There is of course no one response to biblical violence from feminist and womanist biblical scholars. But reading with resistance to biblical violence is one way of naming an important set of approaches taken to the patriarchal assumptions in, and misogyny of, biblical texts. Phyllis Trible's seminal *Texts of Terror* has been hugely influential in responding to biblical violence from a position of resistance. She makes clear that for women in the Bible, as well as women reading the Bible, the texts of the Bible are full of the horrors of violence in ancient Israel: "Hagar, the slave used, abused, and rejected; Tamar, the princess raped and discarded; an unnamed woman, the concubine raped, murdered, and dismembered; and the daughter of Jephthah, a virgin slain and sacrificed".[109] Trible's response is grounded in her vision of feminism as "a prophetic movement, examining the status quo, pronouncing judgement, and calling for repentance".[110]

According to Trible, feminist scholars can resist biblical violence by highlighting this violence and by evaluating "neglected data that show the inferiority, subordination, and abuse of the female in ancient Israel and the early church".[111] Further, they can uphold forgotten texts and reinterpret "familiar ones to shape a remnant theology that challenges the sexism of scripture".[112] Most of all, for Trible, scholars can resist the acceptability and prevalence

---

[108] Elisabeth Schüssler Fiorenza's work has been paramount here, see for instance *In Memory of Her: A Feminist Theological Reconstruction of Christian Origins* (Chicago: Independent Publishers Group, 1994 [1983]); *Bread Not Stone: The Challenge of Feminist Biblical Interpretation* (Boston: Beacon Press, 1985); *But She Said: Feminist Practices of Biblical Interpretation* (Boston: Beacon Press, 1993 [1992]).
[109] Phyllis Trible, *Texts of Terror: Literary-Feminist Readings of Biblical Narratives* (Philadelphia: Fortress Press, 1984), p. 1.
[110] Ibid., p. 3.
[111] Ibid.
[112] Ibid.

of biblical violence against women by recounting "tales of terror in memoriam to offer sympathetic readings of abused women".[113] Trible is invested in recovering neglected stories and histories in an act of remembering a past that remains relevant for the present, and to work towards the cessation of these terrors in the future.[114]

Additionally, part of Trible's resistance to biblical violence lies in constructing a "positive counter-canon".[115] This can be done by drawing attention to other parts of the Bible and offering unfamiliar applications of them in conjunction with the texts of terror she reflects on, such as the suffering servant songs of Second Isaiah or the passion narratives of the Gospels. Beverly Stratton points out that though narratives of terror as found for instance in Judges 19–20 are "irredeemable", Trible urges attention to biblical texts following Judges that emphasise hospitality and sympathetic attention to women: Hannah in 1 Samuel and Ruth and Naomi in the book of Ruth.[116] What Trible offers as an approach, then, is a resistance to biblical violence by refusing to forget or side-step it and unearthing positive resources in the biblical corpus to counteract or dialogue with the violent passages. Bringing quite different biblical texts together demonstrates the way she situates herself as a resistant reader in an active interpretive and responsive role, not tied to a historical-critical engagement with sources, origins, and intentions that seeks neutrality. There are some clear parallels here to both the battling selectivity approach and the challenging biblical authority approach.

Resistant reading can also take the form of resisting the dominant perspective and protagonists of biblical stories, thereby actively challenging the narrative point of view. J. Cheryl Exum refuses passivity for herself or for female characters when encountering biblical violence, articulating the way scholars can "give the victims of literary murder their own voice, a voice that identifies and protests the crimes against them and that thereby claims for them a measure of that autonomy denied them by their literary executioners".[117] In her reflection on feminist scholarship on the Books of Joshua and Judges, Stratton similarly comments on the way feminist biblical

---

[113] Ibid.
[114] Ibid.
[115] Sherwood, 'Feminist Scholarship', p. 313.
[116] Beverly J. Stratton, 'Consider, Take Counsel, and Speak: Re(Membering) Women in the Book of Joshua and Judges', in *Feminist Interpretation of the Hebrew Bible in Retrospect: Volume 1: Biblical Books*, edited by Scholz, p. 100.
[117] J. Cheryl Exum, 'Murder They Wrote', in *Fragmented Women: Feminist (Sub)versions of Biblical Narrative* (Valley Forge, PA: Trinity Press International, 1993), p. 41.

scholars have taken up a resistant position in interpreting against the narrator, plot, and biblical tradition by showing compassion and attention to the victims of violence—a compassion and attention mostly denied them within the world of the texts themselves.[118] In his overview and evaluation of the efficacy of different strategies for coming to terms "with the ethically problematic passages of Scripture", Eryl Davies commends this kind of approach, because it challenges the way "readers have been conditioned to remain slavishly respectful to the text's claims and to respond to its demands with uncritical obeisance".[119]

Resistant reading strategies can go further than resisting the realities described in the world of biblical texts where women are frequently portrayed as expendable objects. A resistant reading approach can also involve resisting the misogyny and patriarchal attitudes justified by biblical texts in contemporary communities. Womanist scholars such as Renita Weems and Valerie Cooper bring the biblical texts they analyse into conversation with Black women's realities to speak up against contemporary domestic violence.[120] As activists, not just scholars, they see the discipline as a vantage point from which to shape and influence public discourse and engage with the lives of real women.[121] In the practice of reading biblical texts with communities of "ordinary readers", the commitment to change is explicit.[122] In this sense, the resistant reading approach has strategies for dealing concretely with the authority of Bibles and biblical interpretations that do harm by perpetuating and legitimating patriarchal attitudes. Faith communities can examine their own material realities in conjunction with the biblical text, judge what God—through scripture—calls them to do, and then act on this call to work against violence in their own local communities.[123] It is a matter of ensuring that "women and men in *our* world who live amid war, under the legacy of past colonisation or the cloud of newer empires, and whose lives are disrupted through patriarchal oppression and violence" are not "'raped by the pen' of the Bible's enduring cultural legacy".[124] Here again the focus on potential or

---

[118] Stratton, 'Consider, Take Counsel, and Speak', p. 101.
[119] Davies, *The Immoral Bible*, pp. 1, 122.
[120] Stratton, 'Consider, Take Counsel, and Speak', p. 96.
[121] Ibid., p.108.
[122] Ibid.
[123] Ibid.
[124] Ibid., p. 109.

THE PROBLEM OF BIBLICAL VIOLENCE   237

actual victims of Bibles is at the forefront, through the work of examining the effects and affects of Bibles in different communities.[125]

Although I have foregrounded the above approaches as promoting forms of resistant reading, Rhiannon Graybill has critiqued the way some feminist biblical scholarship on violent biblical texts results less in modes of resistance and more in "telling sad stories". In *Texts after Terror: Rape, Sexual Violence, and the Hebrew Bible*, Graybill reflects on how it is tempting "to take scissors to the Bible and remove its most troubling stories", its "texts of terror",[126] or to "relish the terror, to draw out every ounce of horror as a performance of voyeurism and catharsis".[127] Graybill argues that to effectively resist the violence in biblical texts from a feminist viewpoint is "to stay with the fuzzy, messy, and icky, even or especially when such readings seem difficult".[128] Graybill contends that "ethical practice requires telling and retelling stories" not only to revel in their sadness, but to uncover their complexities, tensions, and ambiguities.[129] She elaborates on the importance of these complexities, tensions, and ambiguities with the everyday language of fuzzy, messy, icky. Graybill's resistance to biblical violence—though she does not use the word "resistance"—pushes biblical scholars to think again about what it means to grapple with the violence in biblical texts.

Graybill, then, can be seen as another proponent of a resistant reading approach. Her version lies in uncovering new ways of telling these old stories, ways that do not only repeat these stories as if they are already-known.[130] Graybill articulates a set of tactics for reading that takes us beyond "telling sad stories". She summarises them as: "refusing to claim a position of innocence, resisting paranoia and paranoid reading, following the traces of sticky affect, and reading with and through literature".[131] These tactics are about rejecting the idea that violent stories must include innocent victims or that we ever encounter these stories from an innocent position. This entails refusing easy solutions and fitting challenging biblical texts into frameworks with which

---

[125] Contextual biblical scholarship could similarly be said to provide a resistant approach to biblical violence, and in many ways emerges out of feminist biblical criticism. I will come back to this approach in the next chapter.
[126] Rhiannon Graybill, *Texts after Terror: Rape, Sexual Violence, and the Hebrew Bible* (Oxford: Oxford University Press, 2021), p. 175.
[127] Ibid., p. 176.
[128] Ibid.
[129] Ibid., p. 110.
[130] Graybill draws on Barbara Johnson for this concept of the "already-known" text. Melissa Feuerstein, Bill Johnson Gonzáles, Lili Porten, and Keja L. Valens, eds., *The Barbara Johnson Reader: The Surprise of Otherness* (Durham, NC: Duke University Press, 2014).
[131] Ibid., p. 173.

we are already familiar in order to not have to think too hard about the problematic nature of these texts and their violence. The point about paranoid reading is related to this in that it is about not trying to fit the text into the perspective in which we already know who is bad and who is good, as if such static frames fit the text or our own reality. "Paranoid readings offer strong theories: *Everything in this text can be explained by misogyny*".[132] If we already know the Bible is full of violence, we look for this violence everywhere and see its tendencies to do violence everywhere—a paranoid position.

Graybill's point about resistant modes of reading is also meant to critique faith in exposure: we already know there are violent stories in biblical texts, so it is not enough to simply expose this violence. No single theory can explain all the features of a violent story. Sticky affect is about recognising the way biblical stories of violence touch us and each other, sticking to us and each other, in ways that are frequently uncomfortable and unsettling. It is crucial to "attend to sensations, to feelings, to emotions, to what lurks at the edges of our responses to texts and other things in the world".[133] Reading violent stories with and through literary texts—Graybill mostly reads biblical texts with contemporary fiction, but also, for instance, with memoirs and films—expands and opens up the ways we think about the violence in these texts in creative and provocative ways.

The resistant reading approach is valuable in that it pushes readers of biblical texts to confront the patriarchal assumptions and misogynistic attitudes that inform these texts. It refuses to let these texts off the hook. In explicitly taking a normative position that arises from the fact that women are frequently the victims of violence in biblical texts and in light of the interpretive legacies of biblical texts, biblical violence is challenged. Resisting biblical violence can take different forms, but revealing and critiquing the patriarchal perspectives that are part and parcel of the world biblical texts describe and prescribe is a key part. Resisting a position of innocence is important, though, because it opens up questions beyond binaries of perpetrator and victim, to more complex questions about complicity.

The limitation of the resistant reading approach as I have described it, though, is that it is arguably too focused on *interpretation* and the *content* of biblical texts. The focus lies primarily in the power of stories and the way these stories are read. As my analysis in earlier chapters has shown, however,

---

[132] Ibid., p. 22. Emphasis in original.
[133] Ibid., p. 23.

THE PROBLEM OF BIBLICAL VIOLENCE   239

sometimes—even often—it is not about stories and interpretations of biblical stories, but about snippets of text, about the status of "the Bible", about frameworks imposed on particular Bibles, histories of Bible-use, and Bibles as material and symbolic objects. As Bielo emphasises, Bibles are not only a "textual object of discourse" but "also a material object of use and signification".[134] Phillips asks: "Do we need to explore more embedded, material, creative ways to engage in both Bible research and Bible study? Not just with material Bibles but with mediated Bibles? Is there not something more holistic in embracing a Bible explored through all our senses, a mediated Bible rather than simply printed or digitally rendered Bibles?"[135] Inner-textual details and questions of interpretation are privileged over Bible-use more broadly construed. The way Bibles function as assemblages alongside a number of non-biblical components, then, can be overlooked or downplayed. The complex ways that biblical interpretation, and Bible-use, function is of course not unknown to feminist biblical scholars.[136] My point is not that scholars are not aware of the way Bibles function also beyond a textual register as things to be interpreted, but rather to characterise a particular approach in responding to biblical violence that focuses on resistance as re-interpretation and retelling.

What I have wanted to capture with the resistant reading approach is the call to actively question, challenge, and resist the violence that abounds in biblical texts, the patriarchal assumptions and misogynistic attitudes that produce this violence, as well as its effects. Resistant reading is a response to biblical violence that is about active commitment to challenge biblical violence in all the forms it takes, grounded in normative judgements of biblical texts, and committed to addressing the real-life repercussions of biblical violence. This is not just about being sad about biblical violence against women, hoping that the exposure of biblical violence will bring change, but also about interrogating the messiness of these texts, as Graybill urges. The limitation of the resistant readings approach, though, is that it is focused on fostering alternative interpretations of biblical texts, of performing close readings that prompt sympathy for victims and survivors of violence, and

[134] Bielo, 'Introduction: Encountering Biblicism', p. 6.
[135] Phillips, 'The Pixelated Text', p. 406.
[136] Appraisals of feminist biblical scholarship, such as Yvonne Sherwood's edited volume *The Bible and Feminism: Remapping the Field*, tackle precisely the way "the Bible" "functions as ideal image, icon, myth or putative foundation". Sherwood, 'Introduction: The Bible and Feminism: Remapping the Field', in *The Bible and Feminism: Remapping the Field*, edited by Sherwood with the assistance of Fisk, p. 10.

therefore focused mostly on Bible-as-content and Bible-as-text. The focus lies on reading otherwise, or telling biblical stories differently, rather than on Bibles as material and symbolic objects, or on Bibles as components that are used alongside and with other objects to produce particular effects and affects.

Beyond Biblical Violence

In conclusion, I began this chapter with the different kinds of violence in biblical texts and legitimated through the use of Bibles. I asked how biblical scholars should respond to the kind of Bible-use I have been discussing in this book. To a large extent, modern biblical scholars do not see it as their job to respond to the ethical questions raised by violent Bible-use, despite the fact that violence is common in biblical texts and in the history of interpretation and use of these texts. There are, however, notable responses that have emerged from the discipline of biblical studies when it comes to biblical violence. I outlined and assessed four responses to violent Bible-use that could all be raised in relation to the case discussed in this book, pointing to the value and limitations of these responses: historicising texts, battling selectivity, challenging authority, and resistant reading. All approaches shed light on valuable possibilities for grappling with biblical violence, such as better understanding of the otherness of biblical texts as part of another time and place, disrupting simple notions of biblical authority, and resistance to the patriarchy that permeates this collection of texts.

Building on these approaches, though, and thinking with them, I have argued that there are points that would benefit from being emphasised more, particularly the complex affective investments people have in biblical texts and Bibles, and the way these texts function beyond the textual. My push would be towards refocusing attention on Bible-use on the ground, rather than on dominant norms for biblical scholars. It could be objected that just because something is a particular way does not mean that biblical scholars should accept this state of affairs rather than problematise, for instance, anachronistic interpretations, selectivity, or a passionate belief in the unquestionable authority of "the Bible" as sacred scripture. Such objections would miss my point. I have argued that scholarship needs to take seriously the weight of trends and tendencies in Bible-use. I want to put attention on actual Bible-use, which in many ways is not very well known. It is about accounting for the "social life" of scripture, as James Bielo has put it. In other words, "posing questions about how actual people, in actual social encounters, amid actual institutional conditions interact with their sacred texts".[137] What are the "identifiable principles and processes—social, cognitive, linguistic, or otherwise—that structure the interactions that occur between the Bible and its many and varied interlocuters?"[138] The scope for research here is wide, from "dominant and marginalized Christians, widespread and narrowly represented communities, historical and emerging expressions".[139]

Bielo is focused on Christian communities, but I have argued that it is also crucial to map Bible-use beyond communities and people who are recognisably "Christian". As I already briefly mentioned, Llewellyn has provided an interesting example of such attention by exploring the way women who have left Christianity—whom she calls post-Christian women—still engage with Bibles. As she points out, as a group who "might be considered unlikely to engage with the Christian texts on account of their deliberate departure from this tradition", their biblical engagement has "largely gone unnoticed".[140] Bible-use should also be investigated beyond groups who do identify or used to identify with Christianity, however, to take account of people for whom Bibles are important for cultural or political reasons or who have been influenced in some way—perhaps indirectly and vaguely—by biblical interpretations.[141] After all, "biblical stories continue to haunt the cultural imagination",[142] through everything from art to advertising.[143]

While many trends—perhaps particularly social media trends—change rapidly, I emphasise how Bible-use already functions on the ground rather than in the ivory towers of the academy. While this distinction and its implications are problematic—as if non-academics are largely ignorant and somehow more earthy, and as if academics are not embedded in life pursuits and social milieus much like anyone else—it is perhaps good to keep in mind

---

[137] Bielo, 'Introduction: Encountering Biblicism', p. 5.
[138] Ibid., p. 2.
[139] Ibid.
[140] Llewellyn, '"But I still read the Bible!" Post-Christian Women's Biblicalism', p. 571.
[141] One example of research into a non-religious group and its biblical engagement is David G. Ford, *Reading the Bible Outside the Church: A Case-Study* (London: Pickwick, 2018).
[142] Bal, 'Seduction, the Biblical Imagination, and Activating Art', p. 589.
[143] See for instance Natasha O'Hear and Anthony O'Hear, *Picturing the Apocalypse: The Book of Revelation in the Arts over Two Millennia* (Oxford: Oxford University Press, 2015) and Katie B. Edwards, *Admen and Eve: The Bible in Contemporary Advertising* (Sheffield: Sheffield Phoenix Press, 2012).

that biblical scholarship is not the standard of all Bible engagement. Drawing on Felski, however, I would contend that it is ultimately just as important to study the way biblical scholars are affectively invested in particular methods and Bibles as it is to study Bible-use outside the academy. Biblical scholars are not set apart from trends in Bible-use, but form a heterogenous group of Bible-users.

Now that I have surveyed four approaches—historicising texts, battling selectivity, challenging authority, resistant reading—to biblical violence that could form responses to the far-right Bible-use I analysed in earlier chapters, I build on this discussion in the next chapter to put forward a proposal for how to respond to biblical violence.

8
Deterritorialising Biblical Assemblages

Identifying the composition of biblical assemblages is crucial for understanding how Bibles work in the world. In earlier chapters, I identified two biblical assemblages in contemporary far-right networks and discussed how they work: the Civilisation Bible and the War Bible. Following Deleuze and Guattari, I talked about this as mapping biblical assemblages. Identifying biblical assemblages and analysing how they work is, as I put forward in chapter 2, what constitutes mapping. Mapping, as I have envisioned it, does not reveal a particular landscape that was simply there, waiting to be discovered. Rather, mapping is the result of analysis that helps scholars to see connections, developments, stabilisations, and destabilisations in the forms Bibles take and in the use of biblical texts. There is another aspect of mapping that I have not touched on explicitly yet, though, namely, the deterritorialisation of biblical assemblages. All assemblages undergo territorialisation, deterritorialisation, and reterritorialisation. In this chapter, I address the issue of major versus minor assemblages and make a case for how biblical scholars can play a part in deterritorialising major assemblages.

In the previous chapter I discussed responses to biblical violence. Biblical texts do not only belong to and in the present, but are stuck to other times, places, and peoples. Bibles can be creatively, critically, and constructively engaged with in ways that challenge their authority and the perspectives assumed in and by biblical texts. Attention to the larger contexts in which bits of biblical text are found can destabilise particular assumptions and arguments about what bits of Bible mean. This is also the case for acts of reading biblical stories resistantly. More knowledge of the historical contexts of biblical texts, though, or a call to decanonise biblical texts may fall flat. Reading resistantly will convince some who are already on board with feminist critiques of patriarchy, but not others who may be affectively invested in perpetuating particular perspectives and positions. People do not only have intellectual or rational responses to Bibles and biblical texts. Affective investments—understood as emotions or feelings—are important for understanding the power and traction of particular biblical assemblages. More knowledge about biblical texts will not necessarily change Bible-use. The way the authority of Bibles works needs to be interrogated. How can particular biblical assemblages—such as the biblical canon of a particular faith community—be challenged in such a way that this challenge makes a difference? Putting forward new interpretations of biblical texts is valuable but could risk neglecting the multi-faceted ways biblical texts function alongside other components, are stuck to histories of Bible-use, and are caught up in complex relations to other texts, traditions, people, and things. I argue that attention to how the deterritorialisation of assemblages works furnishes a possibility for challenging biblical violence that builds on the responses I discussed but also goes further in addressing complex questions of change.

I begin by returning to the notion of "mapping" that I discussed at the outset, drawing out its connection to Deleuze and Guattari's concept of deterritorialisation. I then turn to the idea of minority Bibles. Building particularly on postcolonial and minority biblical scholarship, I explore how minority Bibles can challenge majority Bibles. This leads me to the question of change. To think through how change works, I discuss affect and attachment. Here, I address a way of understanding "affect" that is less tied to emotion and feeling and more to potential and change. For thinking about how change comes about, affect is a productive concept to explore how things could be otherwise. Taking seriously modes of attachment to Bibles demonstrates the relational and multi-dimensional ways that biblical assemblages operate. I ask: How are Bibles deterritorialised, and what role can scholars play in relation to the territorialisation and deterritorialisation of Bibles? Finally, drawing on Erin Manning's SenseLab project, I propose "BibleLab" as a mode of experimentation with biblical assemblages.

Mapping and Normativity

How can a biblical assemblage be challenged? How might it change? How can other biblical assemblages become? Separating a descriptive from a normative task in biblical studies is not possible if the aim is to map biblical assemblages. It is also not a luxury scholars can afford, in light of the actual and potential capacities Bibles have to do harm. It is arguably highly problematic to leave the normative aspect to those who have been most harmed by Bible-use, pawning it off to feminist, womanist, queer, Asian, Latinx, and African American biblical criticism, as if everyone else—white scholars—can continue to operate on a descriptive "scholarly" plane. As Vincent Wimbush notes, neutrality can only be believed "by the dominants".[1]

For those who buy into strong distinctions between theology and religious studies, where biblical studies is placed in the latter camp, there might be discomfort with my proposal for mapping as a mode of biblical reception. Simply put, the idea of the descriptive versus the normative lies in the distinction between what is and what ought to be. Thomas A. Lewis has recounted the tensions in debates about normative claims versus a neutral stance that has haunted theology and the study of religion seemingly more than any other discipline.[2] I draw here on Lewis's broad conception of normativity as a wide range of judgements of value, whether implicitly or explicitly expressed, that are inevitable to any enterprise, regardless of discipline.[3] As he articulates, in addition "to presupposing or defending norms for the practice of academic work itself, scholars also inevitably make normative judgements regarding the materials and people they are studying".[4] That no biblical scholarship is undertaken from a value-neutral position or a disinterested stance is of course hardly news. Pushing back against claims of disinterestedness and neutrality in biblical studies has been particularly championed by feminist, womanist, postcolonial, and poststructuralist scholars. In the words of Randall Bailey, Tat-siong Benny Liew, and Fernando F. Segovia, the "academic rhetoric of objectivity, or the pretence that difference makes no difference, is itself premised on a particular set of differences in terms of race, gender, class, and sexuality".[5]

Admittedly, just because it is accepted that there can be no neutral standpoint from which a scholar works, it does not follow that a normative task is part of a scholar's work. A commitment to critique might be accepted, as well as a commitment to self-reflection on one's own positionality. Venturing into the *normative*, though, might strike some as going too far into the terrain of the preachy, or of succumbing to a dangerous hubris in setting out to solve world problems with misplaced normative prescriptions. Potential

---

[1] Wimbush, 'Introduction: Reading Darkness, Reading Scriptures', p. 9.
[2] Thomas A. Lewis, 'On the Role of Normativity in Religious Studies', in *The Cambridge Companion to Religious Study*, edited by Robert Orsi (Cambridge: Cambridge University Press, 2011), pp. 168–185.
[3] Ibid., pp. 171–172.
[4] Ibid., p. 172.
[5] Randall C. Bailey, Tat-siong Benny Liew, and Fernando F. Segovia, 'Toward Minority Criticism: Framework, Contours, Dynamics', in *They Were All Together in One Place? Toward Minority Biblical Criticism*, edited by Randall C. Bailey, Tat-siong Benny Liew, and Fernando F. Segovia (Atlanta: SBL Press, 2009), p. 7.

pitfalls with normative judgements in scholarship on religion are raised well by Robert Orsi at the end of *Between Heaven and Earth*. He warns against tendencies to judge when studying different forms of religion. Orsi calls for a disciplined suspension of the impulse to locate the other "securely in relation to one's own cosmos" and a willingness to "make one's own self-conceptions vulnerable to the radically destabilising possibilities of a genuine encounter with an unfamiliar way of life".[6] Yet, Orsi, too, has a normative vision of scholarship in this mode as "transformative".[7] Indeed, he calls the study of religion "a moral discipline in its cultivation of a disciplined attentiveness to the many different ways men, women, and children have lived with the gods and to the things, terrible and good, violent and peaceful, they have done with the gods to themselves and to others".[8] I agree with Orsi about the risk of falling too quickly into judgements that confirm dominant views of religiosity or of the world. But in developing my response to biblical violence, and far-right Bibles in particular, I contend that it is not possible or desirable to keep the descriptive and the normative apart, particularly in the sense of biblical reception as mapping, following Deleuze and Guattari.

For Deleuze and Guattari, mapping is not a descriptive exercise. Mapping is understood in contrast to tracing. Eugene Holland explains that for Deleuze and Guattari, the aim of mapping is not to represent the world as it is "but to survey and map its tendencies or becomings, for better and for worse".[9] While tracing reproduces the object, fixed in a representation, mapping indicates an object's tendency and potential for change.[10] In naming the Civilisation Bible assemblage and War Bible assemblage in earlier chapters, and analysing the way these assemblages work, I have attempted to demonstrate particular tendencies in how Bibles are constructed and used—tendencies relating both to past Bibles and to the potential for future biblical reception. Indicating a thing's tendency to stabilise and its potential for change is already a normative task, as it opens up for change. Tracing stabilises.[11] "Mapping, by contrast, follows various lines of a multiplicity, evaluates and experiments with their escape-velocities, evaluates their potential for transformation, and highlights or intensifies the lines of flight".[12] In

---

[6] Robert A. Orsi, *Between Heaven and Earth: The Religious Worlds People Make and the Scholars Who Study Them* (Princeton, NJ: Princeton University Press, 2005), p. 198.
[7] Ibid., p. 199.
[8] Ibid., p. 203.
[9] Holland, *Deleuze and Guattari's A Thousand Plateaus*, p. 37.
[10] Ibid., p. 40.
[11] Ibid.
[12] Ibid.

other words, mapping can demonstrate where and in what ways a concrete assemblage has been territorialised and it points to the places where stability is open to change—what Deleuze and Guattari call a deterritorialisation, or a line of flight.

Deterritorialisation

To understand how deterritorialisation occurs, Deleuze and Guattari's illustration of an assemblage as a musical refrain is helpful. They call a refrain *"any aggregate of matters of expression that draws a territory and develops into territorial motifs and landscapes"*.[13] The "bird sings to mark its territory".[14] But the refrain can be changed. If the bird wants to attract a mate, the refrain might be altered accordingly. In other words, the assemblage changes depending on different dynamics and desires, different conditions and circumstances. What might have been a bird-territory-refrain-assemblage is changed by an encounter with something outside its assemblage, to become a new bird-family-nest-assemblage. Deleuze and Guattari call changes like these deterritorialisations. Deterritorialisation names the way assemblages continually transform themselves.[15] Each *"multiplicity is already composed of heterogeneous terms in symbiosis"*; each *"multiplicity is continually transforming itself into a string of other multiplicities, according to its thresholds and doors"*.[16] Change is a matter of "passages, bridges and tunnels".[17]

All assemblages are subject to territorialisation, deterritorialisation, and reterritorialisation. Nothing is fixed. All things undergo change, sometimes slow change and sometimes speedy change. Some assemblages stagnate, others are given to rapid change. We constantly move between deterritorialisation—freeing ourselves from the restrictions and boundaries of controlled spaces—and reterritorialisation—repositioning ourselves within new regimes of delineated spaces.[18] Deterritorialisation is a

---

[13] Deleuze and Guattari, *A Thousand Plateaus*, p. 376. Emphasis in the original.
[14] Ibid., p. 363.
[15] Nail, 'What Is an Assemblage?', p. 34.
[16] Deleuze and Guattari, *A Thousand Plateaus*, p. 291. Emphasis in the original.
[17] Ibid., p. 375.
[18] Jessica Ringrose, 'Beyond Discourse? Using Deleuze and Guattari's Schizoanalysis to Explore Affective Assemblages, Heterosexually Striated Space, and Lines of Flight Online and at School', *Educational Philosophy and Theory* 43, no. 6 (2011): pp. 602–603.

positive power that has thresholds and degrees. It is always relative and has "reterritorialization as its flipside or complement".[19] Assemblages are never homogenous or static: "All assemblages are always undergoing some kind of adaptation or change. The question is, 'What kind of process of transformation are they undergoing?'"[20]

To indicate where change occurs, Deleuze and Guattari speak of the cutting edges of deterritorialisation.[21] The deterritorialising edge can be found wherever an assemblage comes into contact with its outside.[22] As the example of the bird's refrain indicates, the outside of an assemblage does not need to be thought in spatial terms. Deleuze and Guattari define an assemblage in terms of "external relations (its ways of affecting and being affected)".[23] What is meant by outside is an assemblage's combination with something that was not previously part of it. "Any boundary established by an assemblage is always temporary and porous, whether it be a boundary between slowly shifting tectonic plates or within a rapidly developing conversation at a party that continually shifts as people join or leave the group".[24] "This constant negotiation of shifting intensities, whether on a short or a long temporal scale, is the site where the new is created".[25]

Languages give a good sense of how deterritorialisation occurs. Languages could be described as different language-assemblages, made up of words and grammatic rules, but also of schools, parents, national language committees, cultural institutions, mouths and tongues, socio-economic conditions, neighbourhoods, geo-political interventions, and sticky histories. Every language is characterised by territorialisation and deterritorialisation.[26] "When language users subvert standard pronunciations, syntactic structures or meanings, they 'deterritorialize' the language".[27] "Conversely, when users reinforce linguistic norms, they 'territorialize' and 'reterritorialize' the language".[28] Deterritorialisation and reterritorialisation in language goes on all the time.[29] Deleuze and Guattari write about major and minor languages to

---

[19] Deleuze and Guattari, *A Thousand Plateaus*, p. 62.
[20] Nail, 'What Is an Assemblage?', p. 35.
[21] Deleuze and Guattari, *A Thousand Plateaus*, p. 65.
[22] Adkins, *Deleuze and Guattari's* A Thousand Plateaus, p. 247.
[23] Ibid.
[24] Ibid.
[25] Ibid.
[26] Ronald Bogue, 'The Minor', in *Giles Deleuze: Key Concepts*, edited by Charles J. Stivale (Montreal: McGill-Queen's University Press, 2005), p. 112.
[27] Ibid., p. 111.
[28] Ibid., p. 112.
[29] Ibid.

explain the way there are different language assemblages within the "same" language, with different intensities, economies, laws, and powers. A major language is the official language of a state, or the language taught in schools, the official, written language that has grammatical rules, conventions, and a history as the dominant language. Minor languages are the more unofficial dialects and language styles that crop up in minority circles. People who do not have English as their mother tongue do not oppose their way of speaking to official English, they transform English.

Minor languages do not exist in themselves: "they exist only in relation to a major language and are also investments of that language for the purpose of making it minor".[30] Major languages are homogenising and stabilising, working to reinforce their majoritarianness.[31] Major languages territorialise. The minoritarian, however, signals "potential, creative and created, becoming".[32] Minority languages, then, deterritorialise. Major languages often reterritorialise minor languages, through schooling or bureaucratic requirements, legal procedures and grammar rules, but minor languages can constantly challenge the major language through forms of deterritorialisation that escape these rules, regiments, and regulations.

Deleuze and Guattari speak of the changes deterritorialisations bring about as lines of flight. Lines of flight, they explain, do not "consist in running away from the world but rather in causing runoffs, as when you drill a hole in a pipe; there is no social system that does not leak from all directions, even if it makes its segments increasingly rigid in order to seal the lines of flight".[33] Because Deleuze and Guattari highlight change (in order to challenge the idea that things have a static, universal, eternal essence), it might seem as if they privilege change over stability. Adkins points out that the "danger of an unrestricted tendency toward change is just as great as that of an unrestricted tendency toward stability".[34] But if a Bible emerges and becomes stabilised in a particular milieu, where it seems to, or actually does, tend towards xenophobia and violence, then it is crucial to show where its tendencies to change might lie. In emphasising the desirability of the minority and the minor over major assemblages given to stabilisation, I do not want to imply that this desirability lies only or mainly in the creativity of becoming that comes from

[30] Deleuze and Guattari, *A Thousand Plateaus*, p. 122.
[31] Ibid., p. 123.
[32] Ibid.
[33] Ibid., p. 239.
[34] Adkins, *Deleuze and Guattari's* A Thousand Plateaus, p. 14.

the minor as opposed to the major. Rather, it is about power differentials, about voice, and about systems of oppression that reside in dominant centres of power. To come back to questions of normativity, then, when I emphasise the need to analyse tendencies towards stabilising and change in biblical assemblages—what I call biblical reception as mapping—it is, put simply, with a view to liberation for those who are at the periphery, often without a voice that is heard and who are denied agency.

Mapping, then, is about exploring tendencies or becomings in the world. It surveys the way assemblages are subject to both stasis and change. Mapping demonstrates where, and in what ways, a particular assemblage has been territorialised; it points to the places where the assemblage is vulnerable to change. This change is what Deleuze and Guattari call a deterritorialisation, or a line of flight. Languages are examples of assemblages that can become dominant and stable. An official national language in a country is one such assemblage. This assemblage territorialises through regimes that enforce its status as a major language. But it is given to change through the becoming of minor languages. Minor languages are assemblages made up of other components than the major language. Dialects, street corners, text messages, poetry, might all form a language assemblage that is minor and far more given to change than a majority language with its grammatical rules, institutions, and bureaucracy. These minority-language assemblages are deterritorialising. But how should these different kinds of assemblages be evaluated? And how do they relate to biblical assemblages?

Minor and Major Bibles

As I already mentioned, one of the key questions for the territorialisation, deterritorialisation, and reterritorialisation of assemblages is: What kind of change is occurring? It is no secret that Deleuze and Guattari value change—or deterritorialisation—to stasis—territorialisation. But that does not mean they value all and any change. Does the change that is occurring tend towards stabilising or towards becoming? For Deleuze and Guattari, it is the minority that signals becoming. Majority assemblages are always stabilising—or territorialising. Stabilisation is dominating, fixing, and tied to a status quo that seeks to limit creativity and change. "Becoming", for Deleuze and Guattari, denotes the creativity of potency, of change. Although deterritorialisation is not always or straightforwardly desirable in their view, forms of becoming are desirable because they eschew the dominating tendencies that result in stasis and oppression. Stabilisation is dangerous because it can lead to tyranny and despotism.

Deleuze and Guattari state: "All becoming is minoritarian".[35] Coming back to the example of language-assemblages, the notion of minor languages is helpful for clarifying the oppressive potential of major assemblages and the possibilities for liberation that minor assemblages can set in motion. As they explain it, minor languages are:

> potential agents of the major language's entering into a becoming-minoritarian of all of its dimensions and elements. We should distinguish between minor languages, the major language, and the becoming-minor of the major language. Minorities, of course, are objectively definable states, states of language, ethnicity or sex with their own ghetto territorialities, but they must also be thought of as seeds, crystals of becoming whole value is to trigger uncontrollable movements and deterritorializations of the mean or majority.[36]

Similar to minor and major languages, we could talk about minor and major Bibles. A minor Bible can challenge and change the status of a major Bible. The minority or majority status of a Bible is a matter of power, stabilisation, and intensity. Major Bibles are not necessarily bad, just as the majority language of a place is not inherently bad. But tendencies toward stabilisation of languages *can* lead (and often have led) to tyranny over minorities and castigation of difference amongst peoples who use a language. It is easy to see how the institutional backing of a major Bible translation will ensure the status of a particular Bible version. When it comes to the way Bibles are made from interpretive trends and other non-biblical elements, power is also operative, such as economic, institutional, and theological power. What "outside" elements can act as the cutting edges of deterritorialisation for a particular biblical assemblage? What are minor Bibles and major Bibles? And how can minor Bibles become seeds or crystals of becoming that can trigger deterritorialisations of major Bibles?

---

[35] Deleuze and Guattari, *A Thousand Plateaus*, p. 123.
[36] Ibid.

Colonial and postcolonial approaches to Bibles are instructive for understanding the way Bibles are territorialised and deterritorialised.[37] Colonial Bibles have played important and devastating parts in the "civilizing" operations of European imperialism. It is well known how Bibles were brought, for instance, to African territories and used to "educate" people in European religion and culture. These Bibles were territorialised in and through colonising practices in which the Bibles were seen as both symbolic of European civilisation and quite literally as material to be imbibed by the "natives" to become more like Europeans. In connection to colonialism, the Civilisation Bible I discussed could be seen as a prime example of a major biblical assemblage. As I discussed in chapter 6, it is a dominant biblical assemblage that has stabilised a Bible as European cultural heritage, as part of the art and literature of Western societies, with civilisational pride, but also, particularly through colonialism, with practices of domination, oppression, and violence against those deemed uncivilised. It is an assemblage that is territorialised in and through the sticky histories that make it seem obvious that a Bible is a symbol of cultural identity and civilisational pride. It is territorialised through the biblical art covering gallery walls in the West. It is territorialised through its impact, or the perception of its impact, on national languages and cultures. Bibles used for colonisation were majority Bibles that were taken for granted as the norm and normative when it came to how to be socialised into a European culture that was assumed to be not only dominant but the rightful dominant power.[38]

But Bibles have also been deterritorialised in colonial encounters. Musa Dube and R. S. Wafula's *Postcoloniality, Translation and the Bible in Africa* contains multiple examples of deterritorialised Bibles. While contributors to this book do not operate with the language of territorialisation and deterritorialisation of Bibles, their attention to the way Bibles are made and unmade provides key insights into how minor Bibles can challenge major Bibles. Johnson Kiriaku Kinyua, for instance, explains the way colonisers were keen to translate their English Bible into vernacular African languages

---

[37] There are many examples that could be used, though, to explore minor Bibles. Queer biblical interpretation would be another crucial approach to the territorialisation and deterritorialisation of Bibles.

[38] Another way of talking about major and minor Bibles is foregrounded by Yvonne Sherwood in *A Biblical Text and its Afterlives: The Survival of Jonah in Western Culture* (Cambridge: Cambridge University Press, 2001), where Sherwood begins with "Mainstream" readings of Jonah and then turns to what she calls "Backwater" readings to highlight more alternative and minority perspectives on Jonah.

to make it more accessible to the colonised peoples. Unsurprisingly, "Bible translation remained entrenched in the consciousness and will of the colonial discourse that assumed its own dominance and superiority".[39] "The study of the translation of the Gĩkũyũ New Testament reveals a hierarchal process in which the missionary-translators ascribed to themselves the power to investigate, describe, name, define, and translate the source biblical texts to the Gĩkũyũ version of the New Testament".[40] The colonisers, then, wanting to be in charge, put measures in place to limit the power of Africans themselves to impact the translation process. The United Kikuyu Language Committee, for instance, ruled that any translation of the Bible for general publication had to be submitted to it for approval.[41]

Similarly, there was an attempt to standardise languages across African countries to ensure greater stability and uniformity in language use. This involved reducing the Gĩkũyũ language "into a suave uniformity that the translators could control".[42] Translation functioned in this case as a "hegemonic process that facilitated the domestication as well as homogenization of the idiom through the predetermined process of cooption and expansion of the linguistic tools".[43] However, as Kiriaku Kinyua points out, Bibles have the "potential of becoming both a solution and a problem, both an oppressor and a liberator".[44] He argues that the "untranslatability of African religious terminologies opened an interstice that transformed the colonized from the passive victims of translation to active translators" who recognised that they had forms of power to affect the Bible imposed on them.[45] "Translation became a performative act of decolonization".[46] There was room for hybridity, and creative modes of engaging this Bible opened up spaces for the negotiation of native words, terms, and concepts. Ambivalences and contractions, uses of words and their impossible translations, meant a counter-Bible could emerge.[47]

---

[39] Johnson Kiriaku Kinyua, 'A Postcolonial Analysis of Bible Translation and its Effectiveness in Shaping and Enhancing the Discourse of Colonialism and the Discourse of Resistance: The Gĩkũyũ New Testament—A Case Study', in *Postcoloniality, Translation and the Bible in Africa*, edited by Musa Dube and R. S. Wafula (Eugene, OR: Pickwick, 2017), p. 69.
[40] Ibid.
[41] Ibid., pp. 72–73.
[42] Ibid., p. 79.
[43] Ibid., p. 81.
[44] Ibid., p. 59.
[45] Ibid., p. 83.
[46] Ibid.
[47] Ibid., p. 90.

In her introduction to the volume, Musa Dube reflects on these subversive Bibles through the use of African languages. She argues that "the use of African languages and concepts are inevitably rewriting the biblical text and giving it a new meaning".[48] What she calls "savage readings" are creative and courageous challenges to, and re-creations of, colonial Bibles. These re-creations "highlight the multiple border-crossing of African cultural beliefs into the translated biblical text and underline how African cultures have and continue to translate the meaning/use/impact of the biblical text in the process".[49] The oral cultures that African readings bring to the missionary-colonial biblical assemblage can be seen as a form of deterritorialisation.[50] It is not just a matter of the internal "reading" of the texts, though. These are minority Bibles deterritorialising the majority colonial-missionary Bible assemblage. What the concepts of assemblage, territorialising, and deterritorialising help biblical scholars to see is that it would be mistaken to assume that "the Bible"—proper and pristine—was brought to Africa and then "Africanized". The Bibles that came to different places on the African continent were themselves already assemblages that relied on a number of factors—material and conceptual—to function.

Wimbush, too, has proffered examples of the way minor Bibles have emerged in response to encounters with colonial powers and uses of a Bible to enslave Africans. In his study of *The Interesting Narrative of the Life of Olaudah Equiano or Gustavus Vassa, the African. Written by Himself* from 1789, Wimbush writes about Olaudah Equiano's experiences as a Black slave and his time in Britain. As Wimbush highlights, Equiano structures his own story as a biblical story. But crucially, Wimbush argues, "Equiano does not merely quote the Bible; he is not an unthinking mimic of British evangelicalism; he makes his story about the phenomenon of the Bible as part of the construction of the world of the dominants, with the focus on the British".[51] To understand how Equiano's story works, "the reader has to come to understand that he came to understand the Bible as the fetishized center-object around which British society was structured".[52] That set of texts referred to as "scripture" or "the Bible" is significant "insofar as Equiano understands

---

[48] Musa Dube, 'Introduction: Silenced Nights, Bible Translation and the African Contact Zones', in *Postcoloniality, Translation and the Bible in Africa*, edited by Dube and Wafula, p. xxiv.
[49] Ibid., p. xxiv
[50] Ibid.
[51] Vincent L. Wimbush, *White Men's Magic: Scripturalization as Slavery* (Oxford: Oxford University Press, 2012), pp. 17–18.
[52] Ibid.

that the dominant social and political structures in place are built around the Bible, drawing justification and power therefrom".[53] In other words, this is a territorialised Bible used to justify the colonisers' notions of themselves and others. It is a major Bible. Equiano constructs the events of his life in relation to biblical texts in a way that deterritorialises the British colonial Bible. It is not a matter of submitting to the powers of a colonial Bible, then, a major assemblage, but of deterritorialising this assemblage through his own biblically inflected story. This could be seen as a *retelling* of biblical stories, but it is far more than that, since Equiano is the colonised, enslaved subject who imagines a more radically inclusive social order with his story and thereby prompts a minor Bible to emerge as a challenge to the territorialising colonial Bible that was used to subjugate Black people under British colonial rule. Equiano's story, then, displays an emerging minor Bible that deterritorialises the coloniser's majority British-colonial Bible.

The way a major Slavery Bible has been deterritorialised by a minor anti-racist and anti-slavery Bible gaining steam is similarly significant for understanding changes to Bibles. These Bibles could also be called a major White Bible and a minor Black Bible. On the experience of African Americans, Wimbush writes about how almost from the very beginning of their engagement with biblical texts, African Americans "interpreted the Bible differently from those who introduced them to it".[54] Cheryl Sanders writes that slaves were critical of white preachers in particular, who were used by plantation owners to sanction slavery. "The Southern white evangelical defence of slavery on biblical grounds was widely regarded as a joke", though it did cause some to reject not only the Bible that was being used to oppress them but the status and significance that Christian scripture could have at all.[55] The story of God freeing the Israelites from bondage in Egypt loomed large, as well as beliefs in a just God and the slaves' affirmation of their own God-given humanity.[56]

Sterling Stuckey writes about Frederick Douglass, who escaped from slavery in the United States and became an influential abolitionist leader. Douglass learned to read through exposure to biblical texts, despite the fact that his master forbade him from accessing a Bible—something Douglass

---

[53] Ibid.
[54] Wimbush, 'Introduction: Reading Darkness, Reading Scriptures', p. 17.
[55] Cheryl J. Sanders, 'African Americans, the Bible, and Spiritual Formation', in *African Americans and the Bible: Sacred Texts and Social Textures,* edited by Vincent L. Wimbush (Eugene, OR: Wipf & Stock, 2000), p. 591.
[56] Ibid.

ignored. He even taught many slaves to read with the help of biblical texts. Stuckey details the way Douglass gathered pages of a Bible from the gutter, "a telling indication of the inaccessibility of the Bible to slaves".[57] The biblical assemblage that emerged in Douglass's Bible-use was one that rejected the uses Christianity was put to in justifying slavery[58] and was made up not only of biblical texts but also of the books that had informed Douglass in his hatred and rejection of slavery.[59] He understood the power of a Bible in the "slave masters' admission of the potential explosiveness of slaves' exposure to the Bible" and their "clever yet sorry efforts to focus mainly on slaves obeying their masters".[60] Chanta Haywood explains the way a particular use of a Bible framed Blacks in nineteenth-century United States as inferior in order to keep them in social and physical bondage.[61] Particular stories such as the "Curse of Ham" from Genesis 9:25–27 and Paul's injunctions for slaves to obey their masters made up a Slavery Bible. As Grey Gundaker notes, for "African Americans who endured the dual evils of slavery and racism to make the Bible fully a part of their religious faith, the book and its associations had to be reconsecrated into a positive frame of reference".[62]

Haywood describes the way nineteenth-century African American women, as a minority in terms of race and gender, courageously engaged a Bible that rejected the Slavery Bible.[63] Some deliberately excised Paul's letters—or at least the parts about slaves obeying their masters—from the minor Bible emerging amongst Black people in America.[64] Psalm 68:31 was a much-loved text.[65] The minor Bible assemblage that gained force amongst African Americans is neither singular nor homogenous. Abolitionists and activists, male and female preachers, but also artists, were working on a Bible that challenged the Slavery Bible. Leslie King-Hammond writes about this challenge as a revisioning of the Bible that was construed to support slavery and oppress Black people.[66] "The African and African American artist

---

[57] Sterling Stuckey, '"My Burden Lightened": Frederick Douglass, the Bible, and Slave Culture', in *African Americans and the Bible: Sacred Texts and Social Textures*, edited by Wimbush, p. 253.
[58] Ibid., p. 258.
[59] Ibid., p. 261.
[60] Ibid., p. 263.
[61] Chanta M. Haywood, 'Prophesying Daughters: Nineteenth-Century Black Religious Women, the Bible, and Black Literary History', in *African Americans and the Bible: Sacred Texts and Social Textures*, edited by Wimbush, p. 359.
[62] Gundaker, 'The Bible *as* and *at* a Threshold', p. 754.
[63] Haywood, 'Prophesying Daughters', p. 360.
[64] Ibid., p. 361.
[65] Ibid., p. 363.
[66] Leslie King-Hammond, 'The Bible and the Aesthetics of Sacred Space in Twentieth-Century African American Experience', in *African Americans and the Bible: Sacred Texts and Social Textures*,

saw the Bible as a fascinating vehicle for the interpretation of the African American experience" and thus took the Bible that was denied to them by their slave masters and re-visioned it also with "African-centered belief systems and sensibilities".[67]

In the post–Second World War context, an anti-racism Bible gathered speed in the hands and mouths of figures such as Martin Luther King Jr. and Fannie Lou Hamer.[68] Harding writes that Hamer, who often sang bits of Bible, "encouraged others to claim the texts so that they could transform the sacred stanzas", "creating new realities, responding to the transformative power of the movement with audacious transformations of the text".[69] Gundaker proffers further examples of the creative and critical challenges to the Slavery Bible that came from African Americans through performance and material culture. Biblical phrases and images circulated among "media, genres, and contexts in culture", invigorating traditions and innovating with Bibles.[70] Gundaker emphasises the way bits of Bible were materially represented on, for instance, signs in front of peoples' houses, and the way Western and Central African practices, rites, and references complemented this Bible-use.[71] What he calls a "transatlantic expressive network"[72] is what I have been calling an assemblage.

Another challenge to major Bibles has been spearheaded by biblical scholars who articulate what they do as "minority biblical criticism". Publications such as *They Were All Together in One Place? Toward Minority Biblical Criticism* from 2009, edited by Randall C. Bailey, Tat-siong Benny Liew, and Fernando Segovia, and its sequel, *Reading Biblical Texts Together: Pursuing Minoritized Criticism* from 2022, edited by Tat-siong Benny Liew and Fernando Segovia, have argued for the transformation of biblical studies through alliances and coalitions of minority scholars. They do so in response to the power differentials, racially and ethnically, that affect scholarship, as they do all areas of life, but also due to the way claims about

---

edited by Wimbush, pp. 437–438. See also Abraham Smith, 'Aaron Douglas, the Harlem Renaissance, and Biblical Art: Toward a Radical Politics of Identity', in *African Americans and the Bible: Sacred Texts and Social Textures*, edited by Wimbush.

[67] Ibid., pp. 438, 446.
[68] Vincent Harding, 'The Annointed Ones: Hamer, King, and the Bible in the Southern Freedom Movement', in *African Americans and the Bible: Sacred Texts and Social Textures*, edited by Wimbush.
[69] Ibid., p. 544.
[70] Gundaker, 'The Bible *as* and *at* a Threshold', p. 755.
[71] Ibid., p. 756.
[72] Ibid.

"the Bible" more specifically as the word of God have functioned to oppress minorities in the past and the present. Minority criticism relativises "dominant criticism" by contextualising claims to objectivity and universality in scholarship.[73] Having a viewpoint, being marked by values and perspectives, is not only a thing of the periphery but also of the centre.[74]

Minority biblical scholarship could be described as a form of deterritorialisation. It is directed at the Bible that emerges as an object of study in dominant biblical studies criticism—a Bible that is produced and reproduced through teaching and academic endeavours such as conferences, committees, and conversations. As Bailey, Liew, and Segovia explain, minority is less about numbers and more about power.[75] This type of minority criticism is a reckoning with what I have talked about as major biblical assemblages that have stabilised over time, to set in motion possibilities for something new and other—what Deleuze and Guattari call becoming. Minority persons, as Bailey, Liew, and Segovia write, "can turn the undeniable power differential that they suffer into springboards for new interpretations and critical interventions".[76] Atalia Omer and Joshua Lupo call for attention to the "religious and political agency of feminist and nonmilitant interpreters of religious traditions" to counter the louder voices of masculine, militant claims. Such attention allows for "new avenues of interpretation" to emerge.[77]

There is of course no simple or straightforward way for such new avenues or becomings. It requires alliances or coalitions. Navigating such alliances and coalitions is fraught with complexity, while being potentially hugely productive and promising, as these volumes demonstrate. Bailey, Segovia, and Liew argue, though (and feminists have similarly argued about patriarchy), that the way racialisation works requires the forging of coalitions, intellectually and politically, to create change.[78] Both *They Were All Together in One Place?* and *Reading Biblical Texts Together* focus on readings of biblical texts and what happens when biblical texts are read from the perspectives of minority biblical scholars. While both could be said to deal with the reception of biblical texts in the sense of how biblical texts are read and interpreted, they are less focused on the kind of biblical reception as mapping that I have been foregrounding. More dedicated to the interpretation of individual

---

[73] Bailey, Liew, and Segovia, 'Toward Minority Criticism: Framework, Contours, Dynamics', p. 27.
[74] Ibid.
[75] Ibid., p. 6.
[76] Ibid., p. 7.
[77] Omer and Joshua Lupo, 'Introduction: The Cultural Logic of White Christian Nationalisms', p. 6.
[78] Bailey, Liew, and Segovia, 'Toward Minority Criticism: Framework, Contours, Dynamics', p. 13.

biblical texts, their focus does not lie on Bibles as constructed objects stuck to other elements, or to the trends in stabilisation and destabilisation that characterise biblical assemblages on a more overarching level. In *Reading Biblical Texts Together: Pursuing Minoritized Criticism*, though, Segovia mentions one of the pathways forward that is foregrounded already in the earlier volume by Evelyn L. Parker, to expand their focus "beyond text and interpretations", to the differing elements that frame biblical texts and to the political ends that are tied in with uses of biblical texts.[79] While commending this pathway forward, Segovia explains why the volume remains focused on precisely the act of reading biblical texts together. Reception as mapping and deterritorialising major biblical assemblages picks up on the attempts to articulate and intervene into the power dynamics that structure biblical texts and Bible-use that goes beyond reading and interpretation.

So far, I have mentioned that mapping is not (only) a descriptive exercise. It is a matter of following lines of connection and pointing to the tendencies towards stasis and the potential for change in any given assemblage. Like refrains or language-use, biblical assemblages might be classics and canons that remain relatively fixed and stable for long periods of time, or they may be more given to flux and flexibility. I highlighted examples of major Bibles being deterritorialised in their encounter with an "outside". I have suggested that colonial and postcolonial Bible-use and Bible-use to sanction and to fight slavery demonstrate the way Bibles are territorialised and deterritorialised. It is important to point out that I am not contending that these are linear developments or signs of straightforward progress. As I have discussed, there are versions of the Colonial Bible still being activated, as are versions of a White Bible assemblage. I have also hinted that biblical scholars are not only perching from above and watching territorialisations and deterritorialisations taking place. In mapping assemblages, they can be part of deterritorialising Bibles. Deterritorialisation as I have articulated it takes up the call from feminist biblical scholars to resist the stabilisations of major assemblages that are easy to take for granted as natural rather than contingent. It takes up the creativity called for in radically destabilising texts that have become classics and part of canons. By pointing to the tendency to change in a biblical assemblage, or to its resistance to change, biblical

---

[79] Fernando F. Segovia, 'Minority Biblical Criticism: Reading Texts Together as Critical Project', in *Reading Biblical Texts Together: Pursuing Minoritized Biblical Criticism*, edited by Liew and Segovia, p. 9.

scholars are contributing to the possibilities for destabilising major Bibles that have become oppressive. But there are further possibilities for biblical scholarship to curate possibilities for change. To outline how I think this curation can take place, I will first discuss notions of affect and attachment, before turning to a more practical consideration of how deterritorialisation of Bibles can take place.

Affect and Attachment

In the previous chapter I pointed to problems in scholarly responses to biblical violence, particularly problems relating to a predominantly knowledge-focused approach, the lack of reflection around how authority works, and the focus on *interpretations* (or reinterpretations) of biblical texts. Biblical assemblages can be resilient and stubborn, accumulating theological and cultural capital over time, and stabilised in peoples' assumptions about what "the Bible" is. Drawing on Brian Massumi's understanding of affect is, I suggest, helpful for thinking about how biblical assemblages might change and what part biblical scholars can play in experimenting with old and new Bibles. For Deleuze and Guattari the question is: "What *might* we become?"[80] It is a matter of beginning with the situation as it is—*in medias res*—and experimenting with the possibilities for becoming that are there. As Adkins points out, this is not a matter of destroying all structures of stability, but of a careful experimentation.[81] "Creating the new requires first of all an understanding of the conditions of possibility for the new".[82] Understanding comes from having mapped an assemblage's tendency to stasis and change.

I have touched on the importance of affect understood as emotion or feeling. Here, however, I want to turn to another understanding of affect— an understanding closely associated with Deleuze. As Stephen Moore and Karen Bray explain, "Deleuzian affect is purely processual: it is logically prior to structured sensory perception, conscious cognition, and linguistic representation. It is even prior to feelings".[83] Affect in this sense should not be equated to feeling or emotion. Massumi builds on Deleuze, presenting affect, in Baruch Spinoza's sense, as a body's ability to affect or be affected.[84]

---

[80] Adkins, *Deleuze and Guattari's* A Thousand Plateaus, p. 247.
[81] Ibid.
[82] Ibid.
[83] Bray and Moore, 'Introduction: Mappings and Crossings', p. 2.
[84] Massumi, *Politics of Affect*, p. 4.

Affect is about potentiality—the capacities of a body to come to be or come to do.[85] It is a matter of capacities for change, for modes of activity that result in some change. It is "directly relational, because it places affect in the space of relation: between an affecting and a being affected".[86] In Robert Paul Seesengood's words, attending to affect "is attending to how Things affect us, the automatic, involuntary, and pre/pan-cognitive ways we regard or respond and how those responses are a form, themselves of meaning".[87] Affect is in-betweenness and becomingness.[88] Affect is the connection between humans, non-humans, plants, systems, things.[89]

As Massumi explains, thinking of affect as the potential for change—for something to affect and be affected—is a matter of focusing on the next experimental step rather than a big utopian picture.[90] Thinking about affect is a matter of what Massumi calls a "pragmatic politics of the in-between".[91] "When you start in-between, what you're in the middle of is a region of relation".[92] But relations are anything but stable. Being in-between is always also to be in-movement, even if this is slow movement. He asks whether it makes sense to think of society as a structure. Is it not more useful to think of it as a *process*? "A process is dynamic and open-ended, composed of ongoing variations on itself. It fundamentally lacks the groundedness of a structure. Any stabilising structuring is *emergent*, and self-improvised".[93] How are particular ideas, institutions, relations "enabled to *re-emerge,* across the variations, in always new forms?"[94] Affect, then, is about the attunement between different bodies "in a joint activity of becoming".[95]

How are bodies affected, and how do bodies affect? Massumi suggests that bodies "can be inducted into, or attuned to, certain regions of tendency, futurity and potential, they can be induced into inhabiting the same affective environment, even if there is no assurance they will act alike in that environment".[96] There is "a complexity and diversity in the field that you can't

---

[85] Ibid., pp. 5–7.
[86] Massumi, *Politics of Affect*, p. 91.
[87] Seesengood, 'Bespoke Words: The Bible, Fashion, and the Mechanism(s) of Things', p. 50.
[88] Ibid.
[89] Ibid.
[90] Massumi, *Politics of Affect*, p. 3.
[91] Ibid., p. 18
[92] Ibid., p. 50.
[93] Ibid., p. 87.
[94] Ibid.
[95] Ibid., pp. 94–95.
[96] Ibid., pp. 56–57.

possibly comprehend completely, and you're changing with it. Because of this, the approach has to be heuristic and experimental".[97]

An example might be Deleuze and Guattari's discussion of the musical refrain and about improvisations with tunes to discover new possibilities in an otherwise well-known melody. Musicians might come together to play a familiar melody, but may, in their relational encounter, begin to alter that melody through improvisation. Who knows what the melody will become? Who knows what the musicians can become in their encounter with each other, the particular environment, location, their instruments, and audience? Or, with languages, it could be a matter of thinking about how major languages are deterritorialised not by inventing a totally new language, but through experimentation with the tendencies in a major language, where slippages in grammar tend to occur, where pronunciations alter familiar words and become familiar for a minority, where misspellings accumulate and become part of a different language assemblage. This is not planned or systematised, but—as Massumi argues—heuristic and experimental, in which the people who are deterritorialising the major language assemblage are also part of the minor language assemblage, and changing with it. Affect, Moore suggests, is also an "action word", naming "the perpetual becoming, the incessant movement—at times glacially slow, at other times lightning fast" that marks all bodies.[98] The becoming of a minor language is an ongoing process, and it is necessarily relational, happening between and amongst people who use a language.

A crucial reason for taking seriously how change can occur is because *attachments* to particular biblical assemblages matter. I have talked about affective investment, about cultural currency, and theological capital, all economic terms for the value a biblical assemblage is endowed with. But another term that captures the relationality that is integral to any biblical assemblage and the traction it has is "attachment". More knowledge about the historical context of Paul's letters may change how I feel about these texts—but it may not. I may be attached to Paul's letters in a way that is linked to my upbringing, to habits of reading, to people for whom Paul is an authority, to institutions I am embedded in, to groups I identify with, to histories of interpretation I am not aware of, but that have structured the way I relate to Paul's writings. Taking seriously different forms of attachment to Bibles is

---

[97] Ibid., p. 124.
[98] Moore, *The Bible after Deleuze*, p. 38.

key for thinking about the authority of Bibles and how this authority works. Or, as I have described it, it is key to think about how territorialised Bibles are stabilised as well as the possibility of a Bible being deterritorialised.

Rita Felski urges attention to attachment in her *Hooked: Art and Attachment*. She is writing about art, but her argument is, I suggest, highly relevant for thinking about Bibles. As Felski points out, attachments "involve thought as well as feeling, values and judgements as well as gut response".[99] Attachment can mean "warm and fuzzy feelings (irony, as we'll see, can be a powerful tie); it allows for, but does not stipulate, relations to a social group or collective (one can feel as closely connected to a film, a painting, or a song as to another person)".[100] Further, attachments "are made and unmade over time, intensify or fade away, are oriented to the future as well as the past, can assume new forms and point in surprising directions".[101] Attachment, then, is not only about emotion, but about *relation*.[102] Attachments "are the result not of a single all-powerful cause steering things behind the scenes but of different things coming together in ways that are often hard to pin down".[103] "Attachments are, by their very nature, selective: we cannot care for everything equally".[104] Our attachments to art or to Bibles are charged by "affective intensities, spectacular effects, moments of transport or enchantment, different registers of perception and feeling".[105] It is not about attachments mattering because they are inner, subjective states which indicate strong feelings for something. Attachments can be deeply political, ethical, and intellectual.[106] "Instead of prescribing what kinds of responses people should have, we might start by getting a better handle on attachments they *do* have".[107]

Getting a handle on what attachments people have is arguably a version of what I have been trying to do in identifying what biblical assemblages are operative in a loosely connected milieu. It is also what I have been calling for in making a case for the importance of biblical reception. But I also suggest that attachment is important because it can help biblical scholars to reflect on how attachments form, how they are made and unmade. Many biblical

---

[99] Felski, *Hooked*, p. ix.
[100] Ibid., p. ix.
[101] Ibid., p. ix.
[102] Ibid., p. 5.
[103] Ibid., p. 9.
[104] Ibid., p. 35.
[105] Ibid.
[106] Ibid.
[107] Ibid.

scholars have experienced the way attachments to Bibles and particular biblical texts or authors are destabilised and changed when students study these texts with them. Historical knowledge of the origins of biblical texts can radically alter attachments to biblical texts as either culturally or theologically authoritative. This can happen in a classroom, lecture, or field trip encounter among texts, peers, and lecturers. This is why the response to biblical violence that I discussed in the previous chapter that calls for more historical contextualisations of Bibles can be powerful. But it does not do enough to address the different kinds of attachment to Bibles that exist in the world and that act as scaffolding for major biblical assemblages. More historical knowledge about biblical texts used in the anti-abortion campaign, for instance, will probably not address the strong affective investments in a Bible that is perceived to be supremely and essentially anti-abortion.

Affect and attachment are two ways of thinking about change and relationality. Affect, as Massumi understands it, is about potency and the capacity of bodies to do things. Attachment is about the relationship we have to artworks, books, people, and institutions. Taking seriously affect as a way of thinking about what change is possible, and paying attention to the attachments that make this change more or less possible, is crucial for thinking about Bibles as assemblages that are territorialised and deterritorialised. What can we do with this, though, more concretely? I have tried to show in previous chapters what mapping biblical assemblages can look like in terms of academic analysis. I would now like to turn to questions of praxis and pedagogy. Drawing on Erin Manning and Brian Massumi's work on SenseLab, I suggest that "BibleLab" can name a strategy for addressing territorialisations of Bibles and for experimenting with possibilities of deterritorialisation.

SenseLab

Manning and Massumi have experimented with how change occurs concretely and creatively in the SenseLab project, which Manning founded in 2004. Erin Manning holds a University Research Chair in Relational Art and Philosophy in the Faculty of Fine Arts at Concordia University in Montreal. As well as being the director of SenseLab, she is a philosopher, cultural theorist, and practising artist. In her book, co-written with Brian Massumi, *Thought in the Act: Passages in the Ecology of Experience*, they explain how

SenseLab arose as a response to the pressures artists and academics are facing in gaining funding and institutional support.[108] SenseLab is not an organisation or an institution, nor is it a collective identity. Ultimately, it can be summarised as: concept-work, collective concern, and creative practice. It is not the first or the only group of academics, artists, and activists to experiment with the production of knowledge, with pedagogy, presentation, and group work. Due to the way its tactics can be drawn on to respond to the problems I articulated in the previous chapter, though, I focus on SenseLab in some detail. This will help me in turn to put forward the politics and pedagogy side to mapping biblical assemblages.

On her web page, Manning calls SenseLab "a laboratory that explores the intersections between art practice and philosophy".[109] SenseLab generates events. It is concerned with experimental forms of research creation that enable activities and relations "that ripple into distant pools of potential".[110] "It was conceived as a flexible meeting ground whose organizational form would arise as a function of its projects, and change as the projects evolved".[111] SenseLab's mode of existence is entirely project-based.[112] Membership is based on collective affinities. Anyone who considers themself a member can be one. Projects have brought together "a shifting mix of students and professors, theorists and practitioners" from different disciplines and practices.[113] In *Thought in the Act*, Manning and Massumi outline SenseLab projects that display their variety and adaptations over time. SenseLab projects are driven by the collective concern participants bring to the given project. These projects set out to trigger events consisting of collective experimentation and creative expression.[114] A particular project is given a name according to a chosen theme, brings together participants over a period of time, and usually involves a set of shared readings and activities. How long a time period, who and in what way participants meet, and how the event unfolds vary from project to project.

For instance, the first project was called *Dancing the Virtual* and took place in 2005. It brought together philosophers, dancers, and choreographers to

---

[108] Erin Manning and Brian Massumi, *Thought in the Act: Passages in the Ecology of Experiences* (Minneapolis: University of Minnesota Press, 2014), pp. 84–89.
[109] Erin Manning, http://erinmovement.com (last accessed June 2024).
[110] Manning and Massumi, *Thought in the Act*, p. 151.
[111] Ibid., p. 90.
[112] Ibid., p. 145.
[113] Ibid., p. 90.
[114] Ibid., p. 151.

work through what "thought in movement" means. The goal was not to reach agreement among participants on philosophical issues relating to movement, the virtual, and embodiment. The goal instead was to stage those issues, live, in on-site interaction, to see if work with concepts and embodied encounters would "bring something new to participants' practices".[115] Philosophers were invited to think with their bodies, and dancers engaged with theoretical material relating to movement. Crucially, participants with very different backgrounds and skills did this exploration together. Manning and Massumi discuss how the design of the event was crucial to get philosophers to move and dancers untrained in philosophy to grapple with theory.[116] At the same time, participants were invited to actively collude in how the event transpired in order to make it their own.[117] Manning wanted to open forms of doing research that would change how participants thought by focusing not on thought alone, but on affect and bodies. "The aim is to coordinate a heterogeneity of energies, transforming them, in the back-and-forth between small-group interaction and whole-group interaction, into creative synergies".[118] Process is emphasised over products or "deliverables".[119]

For SenseLab not to become just like another academic seminar or symposium, Manning and Massumi share a number of strategies. For instance, in order to "enter the event together", they write about how they aim to avoid traditional self-introductions that tend to bring people together based on pre-established identities such as professor, student, artist, theorist, "with histories of past accomplishments shoring up that identity".[120] These identities hierarchise and divide, however humbly they are proffered. People cannot of course simply leave these identities behind. But SenseLab is about asking what other ways there are of coming together "that do not cement us to our preformatted ideas of what we have to bring and who we will be for the event".[121] In one project, each participant was asked to bring a wrapped gift, which would be given anonymously to another participant, but not *for* that participant. Rather, the gift was for the event. The giving of these gifts functioned in place of normal introductions. "Its role was to energize the opening of the event".[122]

[115] Ibid., p. 91.
[116] Ibid., p. 91.
[117] Ibid., p. 92.
[118] Ibid., p. 138.
[119] Ibid., p. 90.
[120] Ibid., p. 141.
[121] Ibid.
[122] Ibid.

The physical space and layout where a SenseLab event takes place is important. Manning has experimented with placing different kinds of fabrics around a room, asking participants to choose the fabric they are most attracted to in order to divide the group into smaller groups in ways in which what they share is related to touch and texture, and in which unpredictable groupings might arise.[123] Groupings are thus not based on rank or expertise or where participants might turn based on background and prior experience. Participants should be released from their "habitual presuppositions", "those tendencies engrained in all of us by the conventional genres of interaction in the art and academic worlds".[124] It is a matter of opening "the field of participation to unforeseeable interactions without destabilising participants, rendering them reticent or defensive".[125] Manning comments on the importance of signalling to participants that what was coming is different to the norm, but in an inviting and even comforting way.[126] She calls this "hospitable estrangement".[127] Playfulness is key. "A degree of play creates the potential for the emergence of the new, not in frontal assault against structure but at the edges and in its pores".[128] The identities of participants are not denied. It is not about pretending differences do not matter or as if it would be possible to step outside of everyday structures. The purpose is to prime people's capacity for creative play, enable new connections to emerge, and open up for unexpected interactions.[129]

Creating care for the event[130] and a hospitable environment that opens up for possibilities of something new emerging is crucial. Concern for the event is important to develop.[131] An atmosphere must be "generated that sustains that concern".[132] SenseLab participants "are invited to bring their care, their concerns, their affinities, their passions, and most especially the techniques in which these are performatively invested".[133] The events assume no ethos of consensus. It assumes no community in the sense of a defining identity[134] that precedes a collectivity's coming together with set boundaries.[135] In any

[123] Ibid., pp. 98–99.
[124] Ibid., p. 98.
[125] Ibid.
[126] Ibid.
[127] Ibid.
[128] Ibid., p. 99.
[129] Ibid., p. 100.
[130] Ibid., p. 108.
[131] Ibid., p. 147.
[132] Ibid.
[133] Ibid., p. 141.
[134] Ibid., p. 108.
[135] Ibid., p. 110.

SenseLab project, the particular constellation of people who participate commit to certain practices, habits, and rites such as the sharing of meals and group work. It is about generating a shared ethos and a sustained collective concern relating to the chosen topic. Collaborations and attachments develop as a result of events that take on a life of their own.[136] The projects usually include concept work assemblies involving close collective readings of a selection of philosophical texts.[137] This might be undertaken by small groups and then shared with the larger group. One way of cultivating a group dynamic, as Manning and Massumi explain, is to draw on the idea of affinity groups. An affinity group is, as they describe it, "an autonomous decision-making unit, usually composed of five to fifteen people, networked horizontally".[138] The aim of these groups is to form a non-hierarchical group. Manning and Massumi address the importance of avoiding too-fixed affinity groups, as "cross-solidarities" are key to develop across groups to "facilitate concept and technique contagion", and preventing "the organizational structure from ossifying into rigid segmentations".[139]

Enabling constraints are used to trigger different collaborations and processes. It is not about letting things flow.[140] Unconstrained interaction typically leads to lack of rigor, intensity, and interest for those not directly involved.[141] These kinds of free-flow interactions are low on follow-up effects.[142] Rather, it is about commitment to a topic and intensive exchange.[143] An example of an enabling constraint is that everyone reads the same texts in advance of the event or as part of concept-work during an event.[144] This makes possible the activation of ideas on-site. "To prevent one group or individual from being silenced or disqualified, each would be encouraged to 'activate' what they knew or could do in a way that was anchored in a shared and always available print-based resource".[145] This also addresses the difficulty of different backgrounds and specialisms, in an attempt to avoid elitism, exclusion, and intimidation.

---

[136] Ibid., p. 76.
[137] Ibid., p. 143.
[138] Ibid., p. 138.
[139] Ibid., p. 140.
[140] Ibid., p. 93.
[141] Ibid.
[142] Ibid., p. 94.
[143] Ibid.
[144] Ibid., p. 95.
[145] Ibid., p. 96.

When smaller groups undertake concept-work, then, this is ultimately shared with the larger group. But this feeding back of concept-work should not take the form of description or explanation, but be activated collaboratively on-site, "entering the relational fray as one creative factor among others".[146] The commonly used technique of summary reporting to explain what happened in a small group to a larger group tends to break the movement and dampen the mood, making people feel listless, bored, and distracted.[147] A concept-working group instead should activate what they had done for the larger group, such as re-performing a discussion of a philosophical problem in a movement exercise.[148] It is about creating modalities of transition that capture not the content of the last exercise (whether it is artistic or philosophical) but its affective intensity, its generative force.[149]

Conceptual speed-dating is another method that is used. Half of the group is classified as "posts". Their job is to sit or stand in a circular formation at the edges of the room. The other half is "flows". Flows move from one post to another, clockwise, at timed intervals. A concept is chosen that should be part of the theme and related to a text that is central to the project but that is not obviously central or popularly known. "This is where the real work comes in: the concept has to be understated enough that it has not yet entered common understanding and undergone the generalization that comes with that, but it must be active enough that the whole conceptual field of the work feeds through it".[150] For the *Dancing the Virtual* project, they used the term "terminus", found in William James's work. For the conceptual speed-dating, the group is given the term as well as a passage or page number to start from. In five-minute intervals, the flows move from one post to another, trying to sort out the concept. The concept is worked through in pairs, but the interactions change and are begun and ended repeatedly, building on previous conversations in stop-and-start ways. This instigates a collective thinking process that can be built on further. Individual ideas are disseminated and mutate through continually displaced pairings. This gave *Dancing the Virtual* a pivot concept around which to unfold.[151]

---

[146] Ibid., p. 90.
[147] Ibid., p. 97.
[148] Ibid., p. 98.
[149] Ibid.
[150] Ibid., pp. 96–97.
[151] Ibid., p. 97.

Forms of creative expression are, as already mentioned, used.[152] This could be in the form of collective activities, some kind of collective creative practice, or the construction of a work or several works by groups. Activities are generated from smaller groups that might change and rotate.[153] To think about relationality, bodies, and thought in the creation of concepts and change, meal-sharing and preparation have also become a staple of SenseLab projects. Groups might be responsible for taking turns in preparing meals, and meals themselves can become informal assemblies. Manning and Massumi write about the importance of involving participants in "a logistics of mutual care".[154] Attending to the body is important for concept-work and research creation as well as creative practice, so they discuss the way they make sure that food is plentiful and that there are rituals of conviviality. Times for naps and quiet refuges for participants might also be provided.[155] The event's undertakings are tentative and germinal. The product is the process.[156] "Our hope was to touch on how creative practices, and how art and politics, can co-compose in research-creation".[157] "The measure of success would be the intensity of the next event this one seeded, as well as the creative partnerships formed through SenseLab participants spinning off into extra-SenseLab collaborations".[158]

Massumi and Manning are guided by Deleuze and Guattari's understanding of philosophy as "the creation of concepts whose mission is to augment capacities to act, feel and perceive, in addition to think. So we approach philosophy as a creative practice".[159] It is about forging techniques of relation.[160] But their understanding of creative expression and philosophy is not set apart from some notion of the political. They think in terms of the micropolitical:

> By micropolitical we mean returning to the generative moment of experience, at the dawning of an event, to produce a modulatory commotion internal to the constitution of the event. It's a question of reconnecting

[152] Ibid., p. 143.
[153] Ibid.
[154] Ibid., p. 139.
[155] Ibid., p. 100.
[156] Ibid., p. 146.
[157] Ibid.
[158] Ibid., pp. 146–147.
[159] Massumi and Manning, *Politics of Affect*, p. 77.
[160] Ibid., p. 78.

processually with what's germinal in your living, with the conditions of emergence of the situations you live through.[161]

The idea and practice of SenseLab, then, is to produce an environment of potential and "to live in that moveable environment of potential".[162] It is a project-based way of working that is about experimenting with concepts through embodied practices and creative expression. It is sustained by collective concern and care for the chosen topic. SenseLab attempts to work through collaborative engagement that elides standard hierarchies and rigid disciplinary (or other) identities. It is about setting in motion new pathways for thinking conceptually, other ways of embodying these concepts, the creation of hospitable environments, and new and surprising attachments that spawn future projects. Doing this kind of work, Manning and Massumi argue, sustains a "pragmatics of potential" that avoids the paralysis of hopelessness.[163] Micropolitics is not programmatic; it is not about generating policy proposals or proposing global solutions. But it is not divorced from the more macropolitical activity.[164] "Macropolitical intervention targets minimal conditions of survival. Micropolitics complements that by fostering an excess of conditions of emergence. That inventiveness is where new solutions start to crystallize".[165]

BibleLab

Drawing on SenseLab and the concrete practices Manning and Massumi discuss in *Thought in the Act*, I propose BibleLab as a laboratory for experimentation with biblical assemblages. BibleLab names a project-based way of experimenting with Bibles—the way Bibles are invoked, constructed, perpetuated, and constituted by and through affects and attachments. The spaces for any BibleLab project could be those that are traditionally linked to learning, such as classrooms (at schools or universities). They could also be spaces where Bibles are likely to be found and already in frequent use, such as Jewish and Christian communities. In this sense, BibleLab could

[161] Ibid., p. 79.
[162] Ibid., p. 80.
[163] Ibid., p. 80.
[164] Ibid., p. 81.
[165] Ibid.

simply look like Bible study groups or university seminar sessions on biblical interpretation, where familiar patterns and practices continue to play out along well-established lines. But it is crucial to think through the ways in which these patterns and practices might be rejigged and reoriented through concept-work, collective concern, and creative practice. Less familiar spaces for working with Bibles are therefore also important—spaces where biblical assemblages might be deterritorialised, beyond classrooms and communities for whom a Bible is important.

Ultimately, the point is to think concretely about affect and attachment in relation to biblical assemblages. How might bodies affect and be affected in encounters that are curated in a project that engages with a major biblical assemblage? What relations can be explored between participants' assumptions about, and attitudes to, "the Bible", and each other? What processes can be set in motion through projects that take as a theme a particular Bible? Instead of thinking in terms of large-scale change—the big picture—how can such projects constitute the next small experimental step that nonetheless relates to the politics of Bible-use on a larger scale? To develop in some more detail how BibleLab might work, I begin with the more obvious spaces of the classroom and Bible study amongst faith communities. I do so by way of Felski's reflection on attachments in the classroom, and by way of the Ujamaa Centre's Contextual Bible Study approach for faith communities. I then turn to further possibilities for spaces that are less obviously connected to Bibles.

Felski asks how ties to artworks are sustained, suppressed, and reconfigured in spaces like the classroom.[166] Rather than focus on interpretations of paintings or novels, Felski enquires about attachments. Flipping network on its head, she speaks of work-nets: the way people become bound together by a work.[167] One place this sort of binding together takes place is the classroom. A class is, as she puts it, "a fragile collective with its own habits, quirks, and rhythms that will dissolve at semester's end"; interactions are mediated by poems, paintings, films, or whatever work is discussed collectively.[168] The classroom is "a heterogeneous and messy space".[169] Every part of it, including every single student, is a network: "what looks like stable units turn out to be fragile composites made up of many parts. The point holds

---

[166] Felski, *Hooked*, p. viii.
[167] Ibid., p. 156.
[168] Ibid., p. 156.
[169] Ibid., p. 157.

for persons as well as institutions; internally differentiated as well as externally connected, human beings are unstable compounds with permeable borders".[170] Why do particular identifications occur? What gets connected to what?[171] By examining work-nets, it is possible to get a better understanding of how connections are made; how identifications arise; and how those involved are affected by, and affect, the work—the novel, the poem, the film, the painting—that is the reason these people have come together.

Any cultural artefact is constituted by acts of reception. "Can we encourage students to become more attached—or differently attached—to literature and art?"[172] Felski writes about the "reorienting force of narratives, forms, ideas, values, and meanings".[173] For "a work to (partially) remake who we are, we must also co-make it".[174] Taking part in the classroom means in many ways to allow oneself to be reoriented by others.[175] Felski sees potential here to care more and care better.[176] Teaching cannot be a matter of trying to manufacture more generous people, but it can, she suggests, be a space for enabling "more generous forms of interpretation".[177] It is a case of being "exposed to unfamiliar works or being exposed differently to familiar ones; learning new languages of analysis and habits of attention; becoming attuned to the formal composition and intricate subtleties of a previously unnoted poem or painting—such practices of engagement and interpretation can alter the vectors of our attachments".[178] Felski's attention to the dynamics of a classroom and the attachments teachers and students bring to a classroom setting is useful for reflecting on the fact that very few people, particularly in Europe or North America, come to a class on biblical texts without some prior attachments to a Bible. Even a student who has never read a single biblical text is caught up in the history of Bible-use that informs European and North American history, culture, and society. But paying attention to what can happen to these attachments in a class demonstrates the potential for transformation that is present in the relational ties that are forged among students, teachers, texts, and cultural artefacts, and that alter and develop over time spent together.

[170] Ibid., p. 159.
[171] Ibid.
[172] Ibid., p. 129.
[173] Ibid., p. 147.
[174] Ibid.
[175] Ibid., p. 149.
[176] Ibid., p. 150.
[177] Ibid., p. 130.
[178] Ibid., p. 155.

In a classroom, any BibleLab project would need to break down ordinary pre-ordained roles such as student and lecturer, through the avoidance of typical introductions, as Manning and Massumi propose. Teaching in this mode would need to be project-based. A project would arise from the concerns participants bring to the class. It could not be top-down, decided by a pre-ordained curriculum, a lecturer, or a leadership committee. A group of students with a lecturer could start a project by introducing themselves in ways that challenge the hierarchy of those identities: students and lecturer—to become co-participants in a project. The point is not to pretend that such differences can be erased or eradicated. That is not the aim, either. The lecturer can have an important role as facilitator. Their expertise and experience can play an important part in the project. But so can the students' expertise and experience. What is crucial is that all participants experience the project as their own, with a responsibility to keep it going, and accountability for how it works.

For example, the theme that students are concerned with could be racism, perhaps wishing to explore more specifically "race and religion". A number of readings could be used, on colonial Bible-use, for example, reading for instance academic texts on the history of European colonial missions; and on the transatlantic slave trade and the role religion and a particular Bible played. Other readings could be biblical texts on slavery, including those that have been used to justify racism, such as the so-called Curse of Ham text in Genesis 9; texts by postcolonial biblical scholars; texts on the concept of race; and intersectional perspectives on gender, class, and race; as well as photographs, diaries, and records of people subject to slavery. Texts could be suggested by the lecturer and students, and ultimately which texts to focus on should be decided on as a group.[179] Finding resources to read together would be part of the project, in thinking about what questions and concerns participants bring to the project. These readings function as enabling constraints, allowing participants common material to work with and discuss, and providing the scope to focus the project.

The aim in this early phase is to identify what actual or potential roles a Bible plays in relation to the theme. The territorialisation of a particular Bible should be identified. The Civilisation Bible assemblage might be named as a major Bible that has played a role in constructions of race through its

---

[179] As my mention of photographs indicates, this process does not have to be so text-heavy; it could include documentaries, films, art, materials, music, or anything the group thinks might be useful.

connections to civilisational pride, cultural identity, and European heritage. Or a Colonial Bible might be named as a more specific set of texts, people, histories, materials, and symbols that were used in colonial encounters. Discussing examples in which a particular major biblical assemblage has been stabilised is a key aim at this stage, identifying different elements in the assemblage, not exhaustively but exploratively. An important part of this early phase of the project would also be to include activities that probe participants' own experiences and attachments to structures in the world that enable and perpetuate racism, for instance. Exactly what materials are relevant would need to arise from the discussion at the start of the project when the theme is chosen.

There could then be work done collectively over a given period of time, such as on different forms of creative expression. The group splits into smaller groups, and each group decides on a form of creative expression to work on together. The aim in this part is to reflect on the territorialised Bible discussed earlier and its tendencies for change. Where is it open to change? What might happen to it in the encounter with something outside the biblical assemblage that has been identified? How might this deterritorialisation happen? Ample time should be given to this planning phase, where the activity is planned, the purpose reflected on and related to the readings, tasks delineated, and steps outlined. After a set amount of time, participants could benefit from changing groups in different rotating constellations, thereby ensuring that what is created is the result of the whole larger group. Actual physical Bibles might be used to quite literally experiment with, cutting up bits of text or gluing in bits of text and image, working with the materials a Bible is made from, with the order of texts, or the shape and scale of texts. Biblical canons might be altered. Rewritings might take place. Non-biblical texts might be added to particular biblical texts. Or particular biblical texts might be staged by visual or oral means, or through the bodies of the participants themselves.

Of course, what is done with a Bible would need to be discussed in the group sensitively, taking seriously what attachments participants might have to a Bible and what participants feel comfortable with. Such comforts might need to be challenged, but an important point in this kind of work would be to address the attachments people have to Bibles and their feelings about what can and should be done with a Bible. Some participants might self-identify as Jewish or Christian and may feel deeply uncomfortable with cutting up a Bible, for instance. Others might think of a Bible as just another book. Reflecting on different kinds of Bible-use and different notions of what a Bible is, is precisely the point of BibleLab.

The purpose, though, is not what is created at the end. Rather, it is the work done to re-imagine creatively and critically what a particular biblical assemblage is, how it works, and with which non-biblical elements. The upshot would be to enable participants to engage with the affects and attachments to different biblical assemblages in ways that are not focused on a policy or programme or an aesthetically valuable product. The result is not, however, devoid of political relevance or aesthetic interest. But the aim is the process itself, the relations that occur as participants work together, with one another and with biblical texts and particular biblical assemblages. There is no "event" planned except whatever happens when participants do the project together. At the end, participants in the project might come together to debrief, to reflect on how they felt during the process, on what happened while working together, on what questions they might now have, and on what relations have emerged as a result of the project.

A second space for BibleLab would be projects done with faith communities. Bible studies are common amongst many faith communities. BibleLab could function like a kind of Bible study, but more along the lines of the Contextual Bible Study approach (CBS). In many ways, CBS is already doing the kind of work I am proposing BibleLab can do. I outline this kind of work in some detail here, particularly the work done at the Ujamaa Centre, before elaborating on the way its work with Bibles might relate to BibleLab and my discussion of affect, attachment, and biblical assemblages.

The Ujamaa Centre describes itself as a centre for community development and research, oriented particularly around praxis.[180] It was established in the 1980s, and is based at the University of KwaZulu-Natal in South Africa. The Centre operates between academic biblical studies and "ordinary" or non-academic African users of biblical texts in faith communities. The Centre facilitates workshops that grapple with biblical texts. The Ujamaa Centre's Manual from 2014 lists five steps for a Contextual Bible Study.[181] The first is to identify a theme, which should be guided "by the issues or themes that a particular local community is dealing with".[182] The second is

---

[180] Ujamaa Centre web page, http://ujamaa.ukzn.ac.za/WHATisUJAMAA.aspx (last accessed June 2024).
[181] The Ujamaa Centre for Community Development & Research, *Doing Contextual Bible Study: A Resource Manual* (2014): http://ujamaa.ukzn.ac.za/Libraries/manuals/Ujamaa_CBS_bibl e_study_Manual_part_1_2.sflb.ashx) (last accessed June 2024).
[182] Ibid., p. 8.

to discern a biblical text that will fit the chosen theme. A biblical text that is relevant is chosen, but then organisers of the workshop may include also other biblical texts in order to "read familiar texts in unfamiliar ways (by approaching them differently)", and reading "unfamiliar texts (those texts that are neglected, avoided, or forgotten by the church)".[183]

The third step is about the questions raised. "Contextual Bible Study is based on asking questions about our context and about the biblical text" and so they distinguish between contextual questions and textual questions.[184] The contextual questions are also referred to as community consciousness questions, because they emerge out of the particular community and its resources. These contextual questions "draw on the lived experience and the embodied theologies of the participants themselves", as well as biblical interpretations they are familiar with from church.[185] The textual questions are also known as critical consciousness questions, and draw on the resources of biblical scholarship.[186] Biblical scholarship provides resources for adding knowledge about the socio-historical world that produced the text, the text itself as a literary composition, and the possible worlds the text projects beyond itself towards the active reader.[187]

The fourth step is about articulating and owning the Bible study. "The power of the Contextual Bible Study process is that it allows participants to articulate and own their own interpretation of a particular text in relation to their context".[188] The Bible study should become a safe place for participants so that they are able to articulate their "embodied theologies",[189] that is, theologies formed from participants' theological heritage and their own experiences. "For many marginalised people their embodied theologies are different from the public theologies of the church, so Contextual Bible Study is an important resource in enabling marginalised people to articulate and own their embodied theologies".[190] Finally, the fifth step develops an action plan. Here the aim to not only interpret biblical texts is explicit. It is about change and about action.[191] Contextual Bible Study is in this sense more outcome-oriented than something like SenseLab. The manual

---

[183] Ibid.
[184] Ibid., p. 9.
[185] Ibid.
[186] Ibid.
[187] Ibid.
[188] Ibid., p. 11.
[189] Ibid.
[190] Ibid., pp. 11–12.
[191] Ibid., p. 12.

encourages CBS to be done with a facilitator, but the overall aim is *group collaboration*.[192] The focus is on small groups. Local reading resources are encouraged and ice-breaker exercises can be used to enable participants to get to know one another.

As I already pointed out, much in CBS fits with what I am calling for with BibleLab. Rather than focus on a particular biblical text, though, BibleLab would focus on a major Bible. It would need to be a biblical assemblage that the group collectively recognises as a major assemblage. The War Bible assemblage could, for instance, function as a starting point. As I mentioned in chapter 7, concern with the violence in biblical texts and the violence done that is legitimated by "the Bible" has been taken up by biblical scholars in relation to faith communities for whom a Bible is a sacred text. In a community where the phrase "God is love" is theologically central, it might seem a problem that many biblical texts and much Bible-use does not embody that phrase. Individual biblical texts could then be read and re-read in the group, texts relating to violence but also texts that relate to love. Other elements in the War Bible assemblage should also be addressed, such as discussion of particular people who have used Bibles to do violence; particular attitudes and worldviews that have been assembled with Bibles, such as misogyny, patriarchy, and racism; and any other elements that participants recognise as working *with* a Bible to make it work a particular (violent) way. Of course, not everything can be addressed. The point would be that a facilitator might furnish some materials, examples, and information, but much of what is discussed together as groups could come from participants themselves and their own experiences, knowledge, history, and background. It would be about reflecting on the way a Bible is territorialised and its potential for deterritorialisation.

It is important that BibleLab does not only function as a highly academic-sounding endeavor, as this could quickly become exclusive. Passing around a lengthy bibliography as pre-reading for a group will not always, or even often, work. Other ways of beginning a project around a set of shared readings would be to focus on different biblical texts, like CBS normally does. Or it could involve reading brief examples of violent Bible-use, watching films, reading short stories or novels, reflecting on a piece of art, or sharing stories from participants' lives. N. Lynne Westfield writes about the activities of Bible-reading she was involved in at an urban African American

---

[192] Ibid., p. 13.

congregation in Philadelphia, where the literacy rate was low, and where biblical literacy was also, as she discovered, low.[193] She talks about organising a Bible study and the importance of building a community to get the study to work well. Due to the challenge in literacy, Westfield talks about how the group—which quickly grew—began by talking about events in their lives. Then they would read a biblical story, and then they would act out the story, through mime or performance.[194] They told and retold the story, allowing different people to take on different roles. They sometimes used creative expression, such as paint, collage, clay, or poetry to engage with the story. At the end, they would bring it back to their own lives and society. The communal elements here are what is important, as well as the creativity. What seemed to work for Westfield's approach was the empowering mode of claiming a Bible that was enabled through collective and creative endeavours that revolved around biblical stories.

The main point of the beginning phase is that a theme is identified and is related to a major Bible. This could be a theme like racism or misogyny or violence, and *then* a major biblical assemblage is identified; or it could be a major Bible, and then problems that relate to this Bible might be discussed. It is key for BibleLab that after the theme is identified, project-oriented work is undertaken in which the group shares a set of readings or resources and discussion. In small groups, people could work together on the way perceptions of a particular biblical assemblage have led to violence or have legitimated violence. Liturgical and ritual practices could be created and planned with the use of Bibles or biblical texts. Visual depictions of biblical stories could be created. Again, canons could be experimented with, or the emphasis put on particular biblical texts could be played around with by making some stories quite literally big in scale and others small. These kinds of activities would not need to happen in spite of more "official" theology or the views of faith leaders and central documents of faith communities. But they would have to take place in ways that disrupt the usual power dynamics and hierarchies sedimented by the official, the canonical, the dominant, and the "business-as-usual" practices. The point would be to make something together in ways that emphasise the process and that flip usual positions of power. Afterwards,

---

[193] N. Lynne Westfield, 'Life-Giving Stories: The Bible in a Congregation', in *African Americans and the Bible: Sacred Texts and Social Textures*, edited by Wimbush, pp. 577–578.

[194] These kinds of practices are of course already happening and have at times been captured well by theologians, such as Anthony Reddie, *Dramatizing Theologies: A Participative Approach to Black God-Talk* (London: Routledge, 2006).

the group can reflect on what they have done, what relations emerged, and on what events—if any—were generated by the project. In this sense, BibleLab might depart from Contextual Bible Study by not seeking to articulate a clear-cut action plan at the end, but rather reflect on the process, on relations that have emerged, and on future potential events.

The classroom and Bible study are the most obvious spaces for experimenting with Bibles, though they are by no means the only ones. As I have argued earlier, it is crucial to confront the way Bibles operate in cultural and secular ways, too, and in ways that are less immediately visible. A museum or gallery space could be ideal for bringing together a group of people who want to explore the Civilisation Bible as a particular kind of cultural artefact tightly linked to Western culture. A group of pacifist activists might come together to work on the War Bible, experimenting with the elements that produce a War Bible and those elements that destabilise a Bible that legitimates violence. A kindergarten or playschool could function to bring children together to experiment with a dominant Children's Bible assemblage. Scholars have argued for the immense importance of Children's Bibles in forming peoples' attitudes to, and assumptions about, scripture.[195] What would happen if children themselves were allowed to experiment with biblical stories that are otherwise not accessible to them, or be empowered to represent biblical stories through their own dramatising or drawing of stories?[196] Eco-activists might meet in a BibleLab project to discuss obstacles to dealing with climate change. Here a Bible might not be perceived to be the main problem, but an anthropocentric Bible might form part of a privileging of human domination of the earth that could be experimented with to think and act otherwise. Students, faith groups, children, artists, activists, interfaith groups, atheist or humanist organisations could all perform experimentations with Bibles. Even better, mixtures of these groups might work together on a major Bible that is of concern to the participants, however different they may otherwise be.

It is important to state again that there is no straightforward programme or outcome of BibleLab. The purpose is experimentation, not a fixed agenda.

---

[195] Caroline van de Stichele and Hugh Pyper, eds., *Text, Image, and Otherness in Children's Bibles: What Is in the Picture?* (Leiden: Brill, 2012); Ingunn Aadland, 'Casting Biblical Narratives: Gendered Power Hierarchies and Cultural Imagination in Scandinavian Children's Bibles', *Studia Theologica* 77, no. 1 (2022): pp. 40–61, 10.1080/0039338X.2022.2075461.

[196] A lot has been written about this; see for instance Annemie Dillen, 'Children's Spirituality and Theologising with Children: The Role of "Context"', *International Journal of Children's Spirituality* 25, no. 3–4 (2020): pp. 238–253.

The main point is to address Bible-use in different settings, along different trajectories, and to do something about Bible-use by coming together in project-oriented work in groups.

To be sure, this might seem woefully inadequate as a response to far-right hatred and racism. I am not making the case that my proposal for BibleLab is or should be the only or even main response to far-right terror and far-right ideas and practice. There are many important, creative, and courageous responses to far-right milieus by activists, practitioners, politicians, artists, scholars, and others. My proposal cannot hope to tackle the rise of far-right ideas and far-right practices in any straightforward way. Rather, it proposes indirect ways of tackling the use of Bibles by—amongst others—figures on the far right. Indirectly, tackling territorialised Bibles and experimenting with deterritorialising Bibles in the way I suggest can forge new connections between people, awaken solidarities, challenge assumptions, create new attachments and forego old ones, inspire and provoke different ways of thinking about Bibles, and prompt the emergence of other Bibles. In other words, I am not directing my response to biblical violence at perpetrators of violence first and foremost, as if "bad" people can be easily identified and trained to see a Bible otherwise.

Rather, I am arguing that a more effective way of engaging with Bible-use, particularly major biblical assemblages, is to indirectly target these major Bibles by working with groups who are committed to addressing a problem, creatively and collectively. I am interested in how to "get at" dominant Bibles rather than at "bad people" who foster hate and promote racism. And, to come back to Massumi's notion of affect in the micropolitical, it is crucial to think concretely about what the next experimental step is rather than pretend that it is possible to skip ahead and address the "big picture". The big picture cannot be painted, but as Stephen Moore points out, Deleuze and Guattari's micropolitical thought experiments "do dovetail with many macropolitical liberation movements, if only to further radicalise the concepts of freedom that fuel such struggles".[197] Changing peoples' perceptions, habits, and attachments cannot be done simply or straightforwardly. BibleLab can begin this work in concrete, creative, and collective ways.

---

[197] Moore, *The Bible after Deleuze*, p. 19. Moore's example is racism and the face that comes up in the "Year Zero: Faciality" chapter of *A Thousand Plateaus*. Moore discusses this in his chapter on race. Moore, *The Bible after Deleuze*, pp. 181–232. It would be interesting to explore these ideas of freedom in relation to Christoph Mencke's articulation theory of freedom, in which freedom is a verb rather than a noun: freedoming. Christoph Mencke, *Theorie der Befreiung* (Berlin: Suhrkamp, 2022).

Simply by participating in a BibleLab project, members gain recognition of the way Bibles and biblical texts have an impact on the world. Bible-use is pervasive and can take concrete as well as more diffuse forms. It always operates with other elements. Being able to begin to articulate in what ways Bibles are used for different ends and with what other elements is a key purpose of BibleLab. Coming together in groups to think concretely and creatively about Bible-use makes possible an experimentation with Bibles that opens up for change, but does not dictate particular outcomes. As Adkins points out in relation to Deleuze and Guattari's deterritorialisation, nothing guarantees that "the new that is created will be beneficial, but we also can't know that until we experiment with it".[198] Jessica Ringrose warns that lines of flight are not some kind of magical escape. Lines of flight can be destructive, too.[199] Deleuze and Guattari are "explicit about the need to map whether lines of flight are *destructive or productive (or both)* and to consider what they *enable or affect* in specific space/time configurations".[200]

Is BibleLab, then, a totally relative practice? Could any Bible emerge in a BibleLab, also a violent, fascist Bible? Admittedly, there is risk with experimentation. There is no guarantee that a deterritorialised Bible will be—or remain—good or unproblematic. Of course, I am also not assuming there will be a consensus about what constitutes a "good" or "unproblematic" Bible. As I have already made clear, the commitment to thinking in terms of minor and major Bibles is, as I see it, also a commitment on the side of liberation and critique of systems of oppression. The goal, then, although necessarily open and open-ended, is always with a view to liberation, and to giving voice and agency to those who fall outside dominant systems of power, to minorities. But the fact is that Bibles are, and can always be, territorialised and reterritorialised. Focusing on the becomings of Bibles is a matter of making that fact explicit and acting on it. It is about creating a hospitable environment for experimenting with these territorialisations and deterritorialisations. BibleLab is necessarily ongoing, then, rather than a one-off. It is about seeing the potential for change in territorialised Bibles. It is about, to come back to Deleuze and Guattari, the minor—the emergence of minor Bibles. Change is, of course, not always or by definition good. But deterritorialising Bibles is about challenging any fixed or final notion of ownership of what a Bible is and what it does. In this sense also it is an inherently

---

[198] Adkins, *Deleuze and Guattari's* A Thousand Plateaus, p. 247.
[199] Ringrose, 'Beyond Discourse?', p. 603.
[200] Ibid. Emphasis in the original.

anti-tyrannical or anti-dictatorial, democratic or anarchic practice. BibleLab is about curating spaces for experimenting with dominant major Bibles and for giving these Bibles up to "others". Bibles are openly acknowledged as works in progress.[201] They are books or material artefacts, machines or assemblages, with symbolic value or left to gather dust, with a particular feel and texture, or with a specific significance as they are used and claimed in the public sphere. In this setting, everyone can become an artist and an activist.

I have used the term "curation" to talk about the role of biblical scholars here to avoid the more hierarchically laden terms "teacher", "lecturer", "expert".[202] But "curator" is not perfect, either, with its overtones of control and associations with high culture. Because I have been talking about the creative work that can be done with major biblical assemblages, though, curation is an attractive term. "Facilitator", though (as CBS uses) might be a more down-to-earth and appropriate term in some ways.

BibleLab is a project-driven experimentation with major Bibles to address problematic and dominant Bible-use. BibleLab can be done in classrooms and amongst faith communities. But it can also be done in more secular or non-educational settings, such as amongst activists, artists, children, interfaith groups, or a combination of very different people who share a commitment to addressing a particular problem where Bible-use is one element. There is no fixed agenda as to what should be accomplished or what the outcome should be. Rather, the experimentation itself is the point. The relations that emerge in the work done are the outcome. Attachments to particular Bibles might change in the interaction with other participants, with resources that alter feelings about interpretations and attitudes to biblical texts, as well as attachments to particular structures and set-ups in the world. The process of working with a Bible is itself a way of enacting and embodying change that may or may not be impactful on a bigger scale.

---

[201] Ulrich Schmiedel writes in some ways similarly about the need for churches to be seen as "elasticized" rather than fixed, works in progress rather than essentialised. Ulrich Schmiedel, *Elasticized Ecclesiology: The Concept of Community after Ernst Troeltsch* (London: Palgrave MacMillian, 2017).

[202] Holly Morse uses the term "curation" for her excellent reception-critical study of Eve, in which she presents different exhibitions and galleries. She in turn draws on the work of biblical scholar and cultural theorist Mieke Bal. Holly Morse, *Encountering Eve's Afterlives: A New Reception Critical Approach to Genesis 2–4* (Oxford: Oxford University Press, 2020).

Experimenting with Bibles

In this chapter, I returned to Deleuze and Guattari's concept of mapping to demonstrate the way mapping is not only or primarily descriptive. Mapping indicates the tendency of an assemblage toward statis or change. For Deleuze and Guattari, all assemblages are subject to change. No assemblage can remain static. But some assemblages—major assemblages—tend toward stasis, whereas minor assemblages tend toward change or becoming. They call the processes of change that assemblages undergo territorialisation, deterritorialisation, and reterritorialisation. Deterritorialisation names the lines of flight that are possible when an assemblage is affected by something outside itself and, as a result, undergoes a change that alters the assemblage to become a different assemblage. To name the way assemblages have different tendencies to change or stasis, Deleuze and Guattari talk about major and minor assemblages. I have suggested that Bibles, too, can be thought of in these terms. Mapping biblical assemblages involves identifying major Bibles that tend towards stasis and stabilisation. There is nothing in and of itself that is problematic with a stable biblical assemblage, but a major Bible tends towards tyranny, enforcing its majoritarianess in ways that usually cause harm through the exclusion and eradication of difference and otherness. I mentioned the major biblical assemblages during colonialism and the minor Bibles emerging from the colonised and from minority criticism that challenged and changed these major Bibles.

Biblical scholars, I have suggested, might contribute to the becoming of Bibles through experimentation with biblical assemblages. BibleLab can be a way of articulating a crucial part of mapping biblical assemblages. What BibleLab does is to identify a major biblical assemblage. In other words, its starting point is one way in which a particular kind of Bible-use has gained traction. This might be on a local scale for a particular group of people or on a more global scale. It is key that the majority biblical assemblage that is identified is of concern to the participants—it has to be something they find important to address. It is about naming problematic Bible-use as it relates to problems in the world. What the group shares is a commitment to addressing this problem. This might sound overly problem-focused, turning Bibles into problems. But part of BibleLab is precisely to take account of the fuzzy feelings and complex attachments that stick to Bibles and that are felt by, and arise amongst, participants. These feelings and attachments might include guilt, joy, sadness, exhilaration, shame, love, and anger, as well as heady mixes and changes through the course of a BibleLab project. The purpose of BibleLab is to experiment with the major assemblage and in this way potentially deterritorialise the biblical assemblage through creative and collective work. In this critical and creative collective work, minor Bibles might emerge.

In developing a model for this experimentation, I both gesture towards the limitations of what biblical scholars can accomplish and open up for more expansive possibilities. Previous chapters demonstrated what biblical reception as mapping looks like in terms of analysis: such mapping aims to name emergences, tendencies toward stabilisation, and the traction assemblages enjoy in particular milieus. This chapter has turned to mapping as praxis—mapping as political and pedagogical. The kinds of practices I have discussed involve taking an experimental step from a point at which people already are, taking a biblical assemblage as a focal point, and working collectively and creatively on its tendencies towards stasis and towards change. BibleLab is necessarily local and small-scale. It is without a clear-cut agenda or outcome. But that does not mean it is apolitical. It functions on the scale of the micropolitical. It is about what happens when people come together and open up for affecting each other and being affected in the encounter with others and with a Bible. To map Bibles and be part of the deterritorialisations of biblical assemblages as I have suggested can be done within classroom and other spaces in institutions and amongst faith communities, organisations, and social formations of which biblical scholars may be a part. It can also take place amongst groups and in spaces that biblical scholars are less frequently present in, and part of, such as children's playgroups, eco-activist organisations, NGOs, collections of artists or atheists, interfaith groups, or a mixture of different people who share particular concerns.

In light of the rise of the far right across Europe in recent decades, my call for experimentation with Bibles might seem flippant. I am not suggesting BibleLab is *the* response to the rise of the far right or to all Bible-use in far-right circles. BibleLab could not directly respond to the kinds of Bible-use and Bible-formations I have been discussing. Rather, it is a deliberately *indirect* response to the use and formation of Bibles more generally. It is a concrete proposal for critically and creatively addressing perceptions of Bibles in spaces where such perceptions are formed, sustained, and perpetuated. In other words, BibleLab is concerned with actual and potential Bibles in society, problematic trends of Bible-use, and the dominance of particular versions of "the Bible" that do harm. In this sense it is about getting at the more dominant forms of Bible-use that inform and influence extremist Bibles that turn up in acts of violence. BibleLab, therefore, speaks to the impossibility of cordoning off the extreme from the mainstream, but looks squarely at the complicities and connections between what makes headlines and what takes place in everyday life. What constitutes harm will of course to some extent be a subjective judgement. That is why I have emphasised the importance of bottom-up identifications of themes that would constitute BibleLab projects rather than a top-down lecturing on what needs to be done. But that is not to say that biblical scholars cannot also function as "bottom-up" participants. Biblical scholars do not sit above the fray, disentangled from the messy Bible-use that takes place on the ground. BibleLab takes power dynamics seriously and attempts to think creatively about how to enable different kinds of relations than those constituted by encounters between "teachers" and "students", "peers", "experts", and "laypeople".

BibleLab taps into potential Bibles through collective and creative practice that focuses on the elements that make a biblical assemblage familiar and dominant, where the tendencies to change lie, and experiments with a biblical assemblage to foster potential lines of flight. The Bibles that might be deterritorialised in BibleLab cannot be controlled. It is not a matter of setting particular aims and then ticking boxes as these aims are accomplished. There is no knowing the fallout of experimentations with Bibles. But working with the identification of a biblical assemblage, its emergence, formation, and change, forms a process that is itself valuable for tackling diverse and complex attachments to Bibles and the diverse and complex affects that fuel Bibles and make them what they are.

9
Biblical Lines of Flight

In this book, I have argued that a particular understanding and use of "the Bible" is part of the ideology and practice of the contemporary European far right. I set out to examine why a Bible is part of the worldview of the far-right perpetrator of the 22 July terrorism in Norway, and where this Bible comes from more broadly. The Bible that is part of this worldview is an important artefact and archive for negotiating claims about European identity. I have argued that two biblical assemblages—the War Bible and the Civilisation Bible—are operant not only in the Breivik case, but more broadly in contemporary counterjihadist writings, right-wing movements, and conservative philosophy, as well as having connections and continuities with past Bible-use. Biblical reception as mapping involves analysis of the way Bibles form and reform as assemblages, thus enabling scholars to see connections and disconnections that might otherwise be missed in the way biblical texts are used and Bibles are invoked. Because biblical scholars are not above or set apart from the way Bibles are territorialised and reterritorialised, I suggested that we can be part of deterritorialising major biblical assemblages. In this concluding chapter I start by summarising my analysis before reflecting on the implications for biblical studies.

Far-Right Biblical Assemblages

I began this study by introducing the case of far-right terrorism in Norway on 22 July 2011. I made the case that it is crucial to analyse the attacks of 22 July as part of far-right trends and tendencies across Europe in the last few decades. To understand the case of 22 July, including the wider landscape it is a part of, it is necessary to grapple with the sources that influenced Breivik's thinking and the more mainstream forms it takes—both before and after 2011. While I discussed the difficulties of talking about "the far right" in Europe as if it is a singular phenomenon, I highlighted the intensified anti-immigration and anti-Islam features that characterise extreme-right actors, street-level movements, and populist parties across the continent. What is striking about Breivik's cobbled-together ideology is, as Jean-Yves Camus and Nicolas Lebourg point out, that the central idea of the manifesto "is now the basis of the new political program of European neopopulism".[1] I made a case for why claims to Christianity should be taken seriously, also in Western and Northern European countries, where these claims may look superficial, banal, or cynical. More specifically, I proposed that scholars should look more closely at the Bible-use that can be glimpsed in far-right pamphlets, protests, placards, manifestos, web pages, and social media posts in these contexts.

To do justice to the way Bibles may be important but are not always centre-stage, I have argued that it is crucial to think of Bibles operating as assemblages. Bibles and biblical texts always appear *with* other texts, ideas, practices, histories, materials, institutions, interpreters, and technologies. In the second chapter, then, I discussed how instead of asking about "the Bible" and its meanings, scholars think instead of "the Bible" in terms of the dynamic processes, capacities, connections, and potential activities that make up different Bibles. I suggested that we do not take it for granted that we know what "the Bible" is until we see it in use. Deleuze and Guattari's concept of assemblage is helpful for appreciating the composite and shifting nature of Bibles. They urge a shift from questions such as "What is a thing?", or in this case, "What is a Bible?", to questions such as, "Which Bible?" "How does it work?" "With what else?" As a basic starting point, "the Bible" refers most commonly and least controversially to a collection of texts for Jews and Christians that are considered sacred or of special importance. But what is meant by "the Bible"—what it looks like, who uses it, what difference it makes—is multiple and multifaceted.

Bibles are made up of texts, imagery, and materials we might recognise as "biblical" components—such as the books of Genesis and Jeremiah, Jonah and the Psalms, leather and paper, columns and print—but also of non-biblical components—such as institutions, traditions, persons, groups, markets, bodies, things. This point may seem self-evident. Yet such factors are not always explicitly identified in biblical reception research that tracks histories of interpretation from rabbinical literature and the church fathers, to theologians in the Middle Ages, into the art and culture of modernity and postmodernity. Any Bible is only legible in terms of the relations it bears to

---

[1] Camus and Lebourg, *Far-Right Politics in Europe*, p. 112.

users, markets, material conditions, institutions, rituals, interpretations, practices, and ideas. Velma Love and Barbara Holdrege have emphasised the necessity of thinking of scripture as fundamentally *relational*.[2] This entails, for instance, observing how people engage Bibles relationally in different physical spaces, such as "in the street, in churches, hospitals, clinics, gyms, restaurants, barber shops, beauty shops, prisons, and funeral homes",[3] as well as how a Bible is regarded *as scripture* in a community, and how a set of texts has been meaningful to successive generations of readers.[4]

Outlining my approach to biblical reception, then, I have grappled with the way constructions of "the Bible" and uses of biblical texts in far-right environments are entangled with non-biblical factors, such as political affiliations and milieus, terminologies and vocabularies, civilisational narratives, conspiracy theories, historical events, and contingencies. *Use* of Bibles, then, is crucial for my proposal of how to do biblical reception to include far more than the reading and interpretation of biblical texts. To figure out why and how a Bible works and is put to work in a particular milieu, I argued that it is key to identify the heterogeneous elements that are part and parcel of any idea about, and any interpretation and use of, a Bible. Following Sara Ahmed on stickiness, I have suggested that particular biblical assemblages function like sticky signs: they are repeated and accumulate affective value.[5] Different things stick to a Bible. Bibles emerge and become sticky partly because their material existence makes a difference. In this sense, Bibles do things and people do things with Bibles. Their existence on a bedside table, as a product in a shop, as a gift or beloved possession, as a ritual artefact, as an indifferent piece of decoration gathering dust, or as part of a historical narrative about civilisations, has effects. To take better account of Bibles, I proposed that *mapping biblical assemblages* is a key exercise for biblical scholars, particularly for biblical reception. Identifying where particular biblical assemblages emerge and become stabilised, and where biblical assemblages are changing, is key to analysing rising and falling trends in relating to this multiple thing we call "the Bible".

---

[2] Love, 'The Bible and Contemporary African American Culture I: Hermeneutical Forays, Observations, and Impressions', p. 50; Holdrege, 'Beyond the Guild: Liberating Biblical Studies', p. 140.

[3] Love, 'The Bible and Contemporary African American Culture I', p. 50; Holdrege, 'Beyond the Guild', p. 50.

[4] Holdrege, 'Beyond the Guild', pp. 140–141.

[5] Ahmed, *The Cultural Politics of Emotion*.

A War Bible and a Civilisation Bible

What, then, was a Bible doing in the lengthy copy-and-paste manifesto Breivik produced and shared shortly before his acts of violence? In chapter 3, I mapped the Bible that is assembled in Breivik's manifesto and put to work in the violent ideology he lays bare in this massive text. By examining the references to "the Bible" as well as to individual biblical texts, I argued that these references are arranged in such a way that they play two overarching roles, and therefore I categorise them as two different biblical assemblages. I named these two assemblages the "War Bible" and the "Civilisation Bible". What I called the War Bible assemblage is made up of a number of biblical references in the manifesto. I named this assemblage due to the multiple biblical references that pertain to warfare and violence. These biblical references are arranged in such a way that they undergird the violence executed by Breivik, in deeming God to be on his side and helping him to fight his enemies. This War Bible cannot only be understood from the select biblical verses cited in the manifesto, however. It is combined with the Eurabia and counterjihad conspiracies that fill the manifesto; they work with references to the medieval crusades in the imagined continuation of a battle between Christians and Muslims; and with stories of Muslim persecution of Christians that are cited to justify forms of violence.

The assemblage I called the Civilisation Bible is made up of references to "the Bible" that connect it to the civilisational roots and cultural achievements of Europe. It functions in a substantially different way to the War Bible in terms of the selection, use, and purpose of the bits of Bible-text in the manifesto. In fact, there is not much biblical text to the Civilisation Bible. This Bible is invoked in the manifesto to call for the survival and revival of Europe's Christian culture. The Bible that is referenced functions as a prop to prove Europe's superior and fixed identity—an identity perceived to be under threat, particularly from Muslim immigrants. It is an assemblage that functions alongside other classic Western literature and art, and that is threatened by so-called political correctness, multiculturalism, religious pluralism, and demographic change. A return to this Civilisation Bible is part of the vision of the manifesto in combatting these perceived threats. The two biblical assemblages could be said to come together, though, in the sense that the War Bible assemblage includes the premise that its users are the underdog needing to defend themselves, while the Civilisation Bible assemblage essentially stands for what needs to be defended. In this sense, both Bibles operate in conjunction.

I then went on to clarify in chapter 4 that the biblical assemblages that appear in Breivik's manifesto do not appear out of nowhere. The biblical references cannot be isolated to the "inside" of the manifesto as if this text is singular and closed. Examining key figures in the counterjihad milieu that Breivik cited and was inspired by, I demonstrated how they contribute to the emergence, stabilisation, and acceleration of the Civilisation Bible in their repeated statements about "biblical values" and their core role in Western civilisation. Figures in the counterjihad scene such as Robert Spencer, Bat Ye'or, "Fjordman", Bruce Bawer, and Oriana Fallaci complain about the decline of the West and of the threat of Islam to European countries and culture, and see the loss of a particular Bible as part of this decline. It is the Civilisation Bible assemblage that they lament in these instances. The biblical assemblage I called the War Bible, while prominent in Breivik's manifesto, is less prominent in the key far-right sources he cited. A version of the War Bible is, however, also present in the counterjihad literature I examined. The Eurabia conspiracy and references to the crusades are part of the narrative pedelled by counterjihadists about the battle between Christian Europe and Islam they state is currently taking place. Some references to biblical texts in which violence features can be identified more explicitly in the counterjihad material, too. Particularly highlighted is the image of Jesus as a sword-bearing heroic figure willing to fight and die for a cause. Notions of a prophetic voice speaking up against political correctness and calls for martyrdom are more obliquely biblical. How does an assemblage pick up speed? How does it become stabilised in particular discourses and practices, through uses, repetitions, and reiterations? I found that the biblical assemblages in Breivik's manifesto bore clear resemblances to the Bible figuring in the counterjihad milieu and beyond, and these consistencies indicate the way a particular view of "the Bible" as both civilisational foundation and violent archive has become territorialised.

In chapters 5 and 6 I examined the War Bible and Civilisation Bible assemblages more closely. In the fifth chapter, I argued that Breivik's War Bible assemblage is connected to two American sources mentioned in the manifesto that are less obviously part of the counterjihadist milieu I covered in the previous chapter. Clearly in many ways the biblical texts Breivik cites came from the Bradley brothers' web page and were inspired by Farah's Bible as a radical document to fight the so-called governing elites. The Bradley brothers' Bible-Knowledge web page about biblical battle verses and Farah's Tea Party manifesto promote a Bible of heroic resistance, in which God is on one's side in the battles one faces. This Bible connects both explicitly and more implicitly to Breivik's War Bible assemblage. Notions of masculine heroism, resistance to the government, and invocations of a god who protects you from your enemy are at work in the War Bible of the Bradley brothers, Farah, and Breivik. What is absent from the War Bible assemblage in these US sources is the counterjihadist and Eurabia conspiracies that stick so squarely to Breivik's War Bible.

However, Breivik's War Bible is not a new invention, nor is it particularly innovative. Past Bibles haunt this current War Bible, even if Breivik himself was unaware of Bibles used in warfare in the past. To draw out connections between the far-right War Bible in Breivik's manifesto and past Bible-use that justifies warfare, I briefly discussed Bible-use during the crusades, as well as soldiers' Bibles used in the First World War. The tendencies I aimed to reveal by gesturing towards these past War Bibles were about a Bible that functioned to posit innocent and Christ-like Christian soldiers against Muslims—or an enemy more generally—to provide a sense of comfort in the idea that God is on one's side and to transform violence into sacrifice. In one sense, the War Bible I have analysed in Breivik's manifesto is a reterritorialisation of these past War Bibles. That is not to suggest that it is a conscious or explicit reterritorialisation, but a Bible is territorialised in Breivik's manifesto which reactivates potencies in Bible-use that have previously been activated in very different settings by very different actors.

Two non-biblical elements that stick to Breivik's War Bible assemblage that I explored are the Middle Ages and masculinity. The use of the Middle Ages in far-right circles, such as Breivik's own use, plays upon the idea of a loss of a golden age. This non-biblical component of the War Bible provides an image of a past of white European Christendom when men were brave and valiant crusaders and women knew their place. Masculinity could of course be a biblical element, but anxieties about masculinity in contemporary society more broadly are clearly partly what fuels Breivik's War Bible; they also appear in the American and European sources he cites. Aggrieved entitlement is a key component of the War Bible, because it stokes a sense of loss and nostalgia for a past when everything was better. Anger arises from this loss and is directed against particular groups, who are blamed for the loss, however misdirected this anger is. In Breivik's worldview, the anger is directed at Muslims and particularly Muslim immigrants. The War Bible is fuelled by aggrieved entitlement. It plays into a loss of masculinity and pride, which is then doubled up and played upon to reinforce particular views of masculinity as valour, strength, and honour.

Chapter six takes the Civilisation Bible assemblage as its focus. I argued that Breivik's Civilisation Bible assemblage needs to be understood in connection with forms of Bible-use that emphasise the biblical form and content of European culture and Western civilisation. I examined two figures who are connected to Breivik's worldview through citations and references in his manifesto: the philosophers Rémi Brague and Roger Scruton. I investigated the way these philosophers come up in the manifesto and examined how their writings might support a Civilisation Bible. Brague's and Scruton's arguments about Western civilisation and European culture present a Bible that connects to Breivik's Civilisation Bible and accelerates it beyond extremist far-right milieus. Not much of a War Bible was present in Brague's and Scruton's work (although a gesture towards a Bible of defensive warfare is made by Scruton). What they construe instead is a Bible of Western culture and a Bible that marks the very form and content of Europe. There is nothing particularly controversial about these claims in and of themselves, even if there might be disagreement over the details of their Bible and its relationship to Europe. What is more interesting is the way their emphasis on the uniqueness of a Western Christian scriptural tradition, different from Islam, can feed into the far-right views of a Christian West fighting Islam, even if that is not their intention. Strikingly, both Scruton and Brague do draw fairly strong distinctions between a Western civilisation indebted to Christian scripture and Islam and the Qur'an. In this sense it is not strange to see why contemporary far-right groups turn to these philosophers as validators for their anti-Islamic campaigns.

But neither the counterjihad milieu nor the philosophical traditions of which Brague and Scruton are a part operates in a vacuum when it comes to constructing Bibles. To better understand the Civilisation Bible that comes up in Breivik's manifesto and in the writings of the ideologues he was inspired by, it is useful to draw connections to biblical assemblages of the past that are reactivated today. Particularly, the development of early modern Europe and the colonial era are keys to an emergent Bible that operates as a repository for Western culture. This Bible furnishes particular values and traditions tied to Europe, as both symbolic of European civilisational values and as a violent tool for oppression in Europe's colonial practices around the world. But the Civilisation Bible is not only a biblical assemblage. It is made up of non-biblical components, too. I gestured particularly towards one non-biblical component that is key for the Civilisation Bible to work, namely, the clash of civilisations thesis, which cuts the world up into clearly delineated civilisations operating with starkly separate religiously defined cultures.[6] This worldview sticks to the current-day Civilisation Bible as it is used by figures such as Breivik, but it does so in part because of dominant conceptions of "culture" and "religion". As I discussed, drawing on Seyla Benhabib's work, different peoples are assumed to "have" a culture, and this culture is assumed to be clearly identifiable and fairly homogenous and proper to a group of people.[7] Religion, as I argued by building on Elizabeth Shakman Hurd's analysis, is assumed to be a key marker of belonging, separable from other aspects of identity such as age, gender, class, ethnicity, and political and socio-economic status.[8] With the clash of civilisations thesis, these assumptions about culture and religion are what make the Civilisation Bible effective.

The effects of a Civilisation Bible are that Europe can be invoked as joined to a Bible that gives it a strong religious and cultural identity. The main purpose this serves is to "other" Islam as a different religious and cultural identity that does not belong in Europe. This Civilisation Bible is not a major assemblage in far-right discourse across Europe, but it is there in the background when the Christian culture and heritage of Europe are invoked. It is at work when "values" are talked about, sometimes as national, sometimes European, sometimes more specifically as Christian or biblical. It is at work when the otherness of the Qur'an and of Muslim culture is emphasised. One way in which the glories of European culture, its civilisational triumphs, superiority and specialness, then, are held up and held together is with the help of the Civilisation Bible.

Of course, I am not making the claim that my mapping exercise in this book has exhaustively explained the Bibles that are at work in the counterjihad milieu of which Breivik became a part. There are no doubt other connections and elements that I could have focused on and discussed to make sense of the use of a Bible amongst contemporary figures on the far

---

[6] Huntington's ideas themselves could be traced back to colonialism, as Ulrich Schmiedel indicates in relation to the idea of the Muslim world. See Ulrich Schmiedel, *Terror und Theologie: Der religionstheoretische Diskurs der 9/11-Dekade* (Berlin: Mohr Siebeck, 2021) ; see also Cemil Aydin, *The Idea of the Muslim World: A Global Intellectual History* (Cambridge, MA: Harvard University Press, 2019).
[7] Benhabib, *The Claims of Culture*.
[8] Hurd, *Beyond Religious Freedom*.

right. As I mentioned in chapter 2, it is impossible to be exhaustive in mapping the far-right milieu of which Breivik is a part, with its harder and looser connections. It is not only, however, that no one monograph could hope to exhaustively map a given Bible or interlinking biblical assemblages in a milieu. It would be impossible altogether to produce some final and fixed map. The elements that make up contemporary European far-right milieus are already changing and shifting. That does not mean it is not possible or useful to map particular arrangements and moments of stasis and stability, however. What I have attempted to do in this book is to map key elements in Bible-use that have become—for a time—stabilised as part of a political narrative in which Christian Europe is battling "Islamisation". The Civilisation Bible assemblage and the War Bible assemblage have both played a role in the political pronouncements and practices of people pedelling far-right conspiracies about the decline of Europe and the threat of Islam.

Deterritorialising Bibles

Mapping assemblages as I have described it is an analytical exercise, designed in this case to understand the Bible-use at work in contemporary right-wing circles. More broadly, it is a mode of doing biblical reception that aims to name phenomena that might otherwise be taken to be insignificant, disconnected, and uninteresting. By analysing the way biblical assemblages emerge, gain traction, lose traction, both connecting to past biblical assemblages and determining future assemblages, it is possible to shed light on Bible-use that does not normally gain attention as biblical reception. Biblical reception as mapping identifies tendencies towards stabilisation in Bible-use and tendencies towards change. In this way it can indicate major trends as well as more niche, or minor, claims to biblical texts and biblical canons.

What about engaging with these biblical assemblages and responding to them on a normative level? Broadening the discussion, I sought to reflect more generally on the use of Bibles to legitimate violence. In chapter 7, then, I turned to four responses to biblical violence from biblical scholars who have been concerned with the harm Bibles can and have done: the historicising biblical texts approach, the battling selectivity approach, the challenging authority approach, and the resistant reading approach.

The first of these approaches responds to biblical violence with a demand to historicise biblical texts. Any Bible-use that does not take account of the ancient origins of these texts is ahistorical and anachronistic. The value of this approach is that it defamiliarises biblical texts. They are not our possessions today, in any straightforward way, and they do not "speak" to "us" clearly or literally.[9] These are ancient texts written in ancient languages and in historical circumstances that are enormously different from modern-day societies. Paying attention to the historical dimensions of Bibles is about acknowledging and exploring the temporal and geographical textures of these texts. Biblical assemblages operate across different temporal and geographical dimensions that cut across cultures and are stuck to ontological commitments that might be alien to present-day people. However, even if this knowledge could be made more accessible, the historicising biblical texts approach neglects the affective ties and attachments people have to Bibles. More historical knowledge will not necessarily make an impact on the way many people feel about Bibles and the investments particular communities have in whatever they deem "the Bible" to be and mean.

The battling selectivity approach is critical of the way bits of Bible are picked out to do work that these bits of text could never have done had they been kept in their longer version, broader narrative, balanced by other canonical texts, or read with the help of a theological hermeneutic. This approach makes good sense in that it demonstrates the problem of selectivity. But just as Bibles cannot be seen as isolated entities when it comes to understanding their content, capacities, and features, but must be seen as assembled with multiple different elements, so it must be recognised that small bits of biblical text function alongside other elements rather than always as texts to be read. As I showed in relation particularly to trends in digital culture, but also to the history of Bible-use, texts do not function in only one way, as literary wholes to be read from start to finish, or as texts to be interpreted. Committing to particular theological ways of reading or to canonicity are ways of critiquing selectivity. But a canonical approach is not straightforward. How do you measure the multiple different biblical texts against each other all at once to avoid creating hierarchies? A Christological hermeneutic risks perpetuating the violence Christians have done to Jews and to Jewish texts by imposing a Christian-centric meaning on texts that are not only Christian. Also, biblical texts do not belong to faith communities

---

[9] Of course, what constitutes a "literal" reading is not nearly as clear as some people like to think. Mordechai Z. Cohen and Adele Berlin's *Interpreting Scriptures in Judaism, Christianity and Islam* (Cambridge: Cambridge University Press, 2016), gives fascinating examples of the way notions of "literalism" change amongst different faith communities, over time, and in relation to one another.

alone, where particular theological perspectives and appeals to canonicity might hold sway. Bibles are also secular objects and cultural archives.

The challenging biblical authority approach takes seriously the problematic elements in Bibles and in Bible-use and invites sustained critique of them. Claiming certainty about the meanings of biblical texts and using this certainty to hurt others is explicitly challenged. The authority attached to Bibles should, in this view, be dismantled. Biblical texts are exposed as contradictory, messy, and the result of communities that are flawed rather than the word of God in any straightforward way. Rather than challenge biblical violence by providing historical contextualisation of biblical texts, the challenging biblical authority approach directs its attention to the theological and cultural capital of Bibles. Decanonising and rewriting biblical texts are two suggestions for how to challenge the authority of Bibles and biblical canons. This could be effective in dealing also with problematic individual texts, but its ultimate target is the reverence shown towards Bibles as authoritative canons. The problem with this response, though, is that there is not much reflection on the complex way the authority that is associated with Bibles actually works. This comes back to affective ties and attachments as well as sticky histories of faith communities, interpretative trajectories, and theological traditions. It is not clear how proposals to decanonise biblical texts or add to the biblical canon would actually work in practice.

The resistant reading approach can be explained in contrast to an approach that seeks only to describe, explain, and understand biblical violence. Biblical texts are exposed as the products of patriarchal societies with particular interests to uphold and particular assumptions about gender and sexuality that many in the modern world would not endorse. What I have wanted to capture with the resistant reading approach is the call to actively question, challenge, and resist the violence that abounds in biblical texts, the patriarchal assumptions and misogynistic attitudes that produce this violence, as well as its effects, particularly on women and girls. Resistant reading is a response to biblical violence, then, that is about active commitment to challenging biblical violence in all the forms it takes, grounded in normative judgements of biblical texts, and committed to addressing the real-life repercussions of biblical violence. This can be about more than being sad about biblical violence against women, hoping that the exposure of biblical violence will bring change, but rather is also about interrogating the messiness of these texts, as

Rhiannon Graybill urges.[10] The limitation of the resistant reading approach, though, is that it is focused on fostering alternative interpretations of biblical texts, of performing close readings that prompt sympathy for victims of violence, and therefore mostly on Bible-as-content and Bible-as-text. The focus lies on reading otherwise, or telling biblical stories differently, rather than on Bibles as material and symbolic objects, and on Bibles as components that are used alongside and with other objects to produce particular effects and affects.

These responses all contain valuable proposals that can confront different forms of biblical violence. In evaluating them in relation to my own analysis of how biblical assemblages work, I argued that what is crucial in responding to biblical violence is attention to the affective investments that inform how biblical texts are read and how Bibles are invoked, by examining the fluid and flexible modes of Bible-use on the ground that go beyond reading and interpretation of texts. Returning to my earlier discussion of Deleuze and Guattari's notion of mapping in chapter 8, then, I proposed my own response to biblical violence. I argued that the task of mapping biblical assemblages has a normative edge, whereby mapping contributes to identifying territorialisations of Bibles and of pointing to, or setting in motion, *deterritorialisations* of Bibles. Biblical scholars can map territorialisations of Bibles, help set in motion lines of flight in Bible-use, and actively engage with deterritorialisations of Bibles. Deterritorialisation names the lines of flight that are possible when an assemblage is affected by something outside itself and, as a result, undergoes a change that alters the assemblage to become a different assemblage. To name the way assemblages have different tendencies to change or stasis, Deleuze and Guattari talk about major and minor assemblages. I have suggested that Bibles too can be thought of in these terms. Mapping biblical assemblages involves identifying major Bibles that tend towards stasis and stabilisation. There is nothing in and of itself that is problematic with a stable biblical assemblage, but major Bibles tend towards tyranny, enforcing their majoritarianess in ways that usually threaten difference and otherness. I mentioned the major biblical assemblages during colonialism and the minor Bibles emerging from the colonised that challenged and changed these major Bibles.

Building on the approach to biblical reception that I presented and played through in my mapping of the Bibles of the far right, I shifted to the

---

[10] Graybill, *Texts after Terror*.

pedagogy and politics of biblical studies. Drawing on Brian Massumi and Erin Manning's SenseLab projects, I suggested "BibleLab" as a mode and space for experimenting with Bibles that can take place in, for instance, a classroom, a church, a studio, a playschool, a gym, or a gallery. The idea of BibleLab is not that people can come together and somehow engineer a particular version of the Bible that is benign for ever after. The way biblical assemblages emerge, form, and operate is more complex than that and goes beyond the control and agency of any person, group of people, agenda, or programme. There is no one who can have the power to control and constrain any assemblage to be and act a certain way. But Bibles can be experimented with, and this is what I envisage as happening in any BibleLab project. Through experimentation, different Bibles can emerge. It is about what capacities BibleLab can enable and what encounters can be curated, in bringing together different bodies, things, artefacts, texts, feelings, words, movements, and materials. This comes back to the notion of affect as relating to the powers to affect and be affected, the capacities of any body or thing. Rather than thinking about what agency each of us has to effect change, BibleLab is about the possibilities of experimentation when different bodies and things are brought together and can affect each other and be affected.

BibleLab takes seriously the different kinds of attachment that structure peoples' perceptions of Bibles and the way particular Bibles are perpetuated. In Rita Felski's engagement with artwork and forms of attachment to particular interpretations, she prompts teachers to reflect on how students can grapple with their own attachments and become differently attached to literary texts and artworks.[11] Felski is interested in the question of how we can attend and be otherwise. How can we forge other connections? Forging new connections and attending otherwise can happen in all sorts of venues and environments. "Things drift; they get twisted up, misconstrued, repurposed, compromised, or revised".[12] "Individuals, collectives, and materials come together to make things happen; agency is delegated and distributed; it unfolds fitfully in time and space".[13] Classrooms, museums, Bible groups, nightclubs, kitchens—there is no privileged space for ties to be made or unmade. Can connections and attachments be controlled? No. The same can be said of territorialisations and deterritorialisations of Bibles.

---

[11] Felski, *Hooked*, p. 129.
[12] Ibid., p. 140.
[13] Ibid., p. 141.

300   THE BIBLES OF THE FAR RIGHT

Heterogeneous elements are coming together and forming new assemblages, as previous assemblages dissolve. Biblical scholars are not the sole or even main operators for the territorialisation and deterritorialisation of Bibles. Territorialisations and deterritorialisations of Bibles happen with and without biblical scholars. But biblical scholars can be part of mapping these territorialisations and experimenting with deterritorialisations.

Experimenting with Bibles

This might all seem totally inadequate as a response to the victims of the 22 July terror in Norway. To return to Tonje, a survivor of the terror attacks with which this book began, she writes that "I live, but so many others don't anymore".[14] Much has been said about how societies should and could confront acts of terror and work against the extremism and radicalisation that can be lethal. In her discussion of Norway's public response to the terror, Ida Marie Høeg points out that since the end of the Second World War, no gathering has attracted more people in Norway than the rose march on 25 July 2011.[15] Thousands of people gathered in central Oslo, holding roses, to collect in solidarity and sympathy against the terrorist violence. "The mass mobilization with silent actions and singing triggered strong emotions of solidarity and comfort in the community".[16] These communal acts fostered a "we" feeling that promoted attitudes of unity and inclusiveness.[17] Others confirmed this immediate sense in Norway that things would never be the same.[18] The prime minister at the time, Jens Stoltenberg, famously called for more democracy in a speech only a few days after the terror attacks.[19] This call seemed to strike a chord. At the same time, as Astrid Kolås comments, in the next parliamentary election, the Labour Party–led government was replaced by a right-wing coalition made up of the Conservative Party and the right-wing populist Progress Party, the latter entering government for the first time after capturing an unprecedented 16.3% of votes. By that time, the

---

[14] Tonje S, 'Mitt Utøya', testimony published on the 22 July Centre website, https://www.22julisenteret.no/aktuelt/artikler/tonje-s (last accessed December 2022). My translation.
[15] Høeg, 'Silent Actions', p. 199.
[16] Ibid., p. 210.
[17] Ibid.
[18] Åshild Kolås, 'How Critical Is the Event? Multicultural Norway after 22 July 2011', Social Identities 23, no. 5 (2017): p. 518.
[19] The full speech was printed in Aftenposten, 25 July 2011, https://www.aftenposten.no/norge/i/9vPzw/statsminister-jens-stoltenbergs-tale-paa-raadhusplassen (last accessed November 2023).

Progress Party had long complained about "stealth-Islamization", as if a conscious and concealed process was underway to turn Norway into a Muslim country.[20] As Øyvind Strømmen has demonstrated, this rhetoric is plucked right out of the counterjihad environment that Breivik was inspired by.[21] It did not disappear or dissipate after 2011.

My suggestions might feel provocatively inadequate, an indulgent foray into a zany theoretical discussion about assemblages, territorialisations, and deterritorialisations that does little to address serious issues when it comes to the far right. What can biblical studies and biblical reception really do in the face of the far right and violent terrorism? I am not arguing that BibleLab is or should be the only or even main response to far-right terror and far-right ideas and practice. There are many important, creative, and courageous responses to far-right milieus by activists, practitioners, politicians, artists, NGOs, scholars, and others. As I explained in chapter 8, my proposal does not set out to directly tackle the rise of far-right ideas and far-right practices. Rather, the mapping of biblical assemblages furnishes indirect ways of tackling the use of Bibles by figures on the far-right. Indirectly, territorializing and deterritorialising Bibles in the way I suggest can forge new connections between people, awaken solidarities, challenge assumptions, create new attachments and forego old ones, inspire and provoke different ways of thinking about Bibles, and prompt the emergence of other Bibles. Grey Gundaker writes about the way references to, and uses of, a Bible can function "like electrical relays or transformers". A Bible can serve "as the threshold to multiple forms of rebirth".[22] What is crucial for the biblical assemblages I have argued are at work in contemporary society is precisely that they cannot be contained in the "far right". They transmit intensities or function as thresholds to anti-Islamic ideology and sentiments.

What kind of Bible is desirable or undesirable is of course not a given. I am not suggesting that biblical scholars should be the arbiters of Bibles, like an elite panel passing judgement on which Bibles people should or should not use. My proposal is not that biblical scholars have some special jurisdiction on the goodness or badness of Bibles, their effects and affects. At the same time, drawing on feminist and postcolonial biblical scholarship, it is imperative to recognise the power dynamics in the use of Bibles and biblical texts.

---

[20] Strømmen, *Det mørke nettet*, p. 152.
[21] Ibid.
[22] Gundaker, 'The Bible *as* and *at* a Threshold', p. 770.

Major biblical assemblages do harm. Minorities have, and still do, suffer as a consequence of trends in Bible-use that need to be confronted and challenged. This is less about minority in the sense of numbers and more about questions of power. The stabilisation of major biblical assemblages operates as a result of powerful mechanisms. Minor Bibles can and do disrupt these mechanisms, setting in motion lines of flight. Biblical scholars are in many ways assembled with Major Bibles—such as a Guild Bible. But biblical scholars can—with others, such as students or members of a faith community or artists, activists, and atheists—experiment with Bibles in ways that are potentially transformative.

Expanding Biblical Studies

My suggestions in this book in regard to how biblical scholarship can be done and what responses to biblical violence might look like involve some implications for the field of biblical reception and the discipline of biblical studies more broadly. With a more experimental and expansive view of biblical studies, antiquity would not be the presumed or privileged site of study. This is not a new call.[23] Yvonne Sherwood's 2017 volume on remapping feminist biblical scholarship follows a long line of feminist biblical scholarship calling for more institutional and scholarly attention to how biblical texts are used.[24] Wongi Park's multiracial biblical studies project follows earlier postcolonial biblical scholarship calling for an expansion of biblical studies beyond the focus on antiquity. The "sheer dominance of historical criticism", as Park puts it, has left its mark on the field of biblical studies.[25] Historical criticism continues to characterise biblical scholarship as norm and as normative.[26] As Park has discussed, historical criticism or the historical-critical method—though by no means a monolithic approach or a singular method—functions as the key entry point to biblical studies.[27] It is the "industry standard" at virtually every institution of higher education, at least in the Global North.[28] Historical criticism enjoys a privileged status as "an

---

[23] Biblical studies might increasingly be advertised on university web pages and brochures as exploring sex, violence, and the influence of biblical texts, but this is – in my experience at least – not reflected in job advertisements or institutional spaces dedicated to this work.
[24] Sherwood, 'Introduction: The Bible and Feminism: Remapping the Field', pp. 1–11.
[25] Park, 'Multiracial Biblical Studies', p. 445.
[26] Ibid.
[27] Ibid., p. 446.
[28] Ibid.

invisible norm that renders other approaches as aberration".[29] Getting a degree in biblical studies is "virtually synonymous with learning Western history, tools, and methods and interpretation".[30]

Park argues that there is a connection between the privileging of Eurocentric methods in the discipline of biblical studies and the fact that the discipline is dominated by white scholars, particularly white, male scholars. Biblical studies in the United States and Europe is, he points out, "profoundly monoracial".[31] He undertakes a demographic analysis of the membership of the Society of Biblical Literature, the largest professional biblical studies society, focusing on members in the United States. Racial and ethnic minorities make up only 14.38%, while women make up approximately 25%. Although this gives only a snapshot of a part of the discipline of biblical studies, it nonetheless indicates the way biblical scholarship is "male dominated and, even more so, White dominated".[32] But, as Park argues, whiteness is not only connected to white people; rather, it extends to "the very methods and tools of dominant biblical scholarship".[33] To re-envision the monoracial nature of biblical studies to a multiracial future, Park calls for a turn away from "continuing in a scholarly mode of disinterest and decontextualization", urging rather that "the social, religious, and institutional locations and communities we inhabit can be foregrounded and theorized as an essential part of the interpretive task".[34]

The African American biblical scholar Vincent Wimbush commented ten years ago on his feeling early in his career, in the 1980s, after years of training in biblical studies, that he was "writing more and more about less and less of import".[35] He called for "a larger, more rounded and layered history of scriptures, not the history of the lexical content meanings or the historical backgrounds of those characters and events referenced in the texts, but the psychology, the phenomenology, the sociology, the anthropology, the invention and uses, and the political consequences of the uses of the texts".[36] Wimbush talks about having to "retrain" or "untrain" himself, in order to avoid socialising students into a "narrow professionalisation that had in too

---

[29] Ibid.
[30] Ibid.
[31] Ibid., p. 437.
[32] Ibid., p. 442.
[33] Ibid., pp. 444–445.
[34] Ibid., p. 458.
[35] Wimbush, *White Men's Magic*, p. 5.
[36] Ibid., p. 12.

many instances drained me of passion, socialpolitical engagement, and self-awareness", as well as carve a space for research in order to "find a different discourse, a more radical orientation—or invent one for myself".[37] This orientation meant he became "associated with 'those no longer in the field;' it was considered by many to be 'marginal,' not reflective of what those doing traditional biblical scholarship did, with focus on (the theological and lexical meanings of) 'the text'".[38]

Biblical reception can be a field that extends in multiple directions; it can work on different scales with differing scope, follow a variety of actors, and involve contextual and comparative work. Going forward, it seems to me that it would be valuable to undertake more empirical and ethnographic work to understand where Bibles are at work and in what ways they are at work. Wimbush called for this kind of work already in the African Americans and the Bible project in the late 1990s and early 2000s. Several contributors to the book *African Americans and the Bible* undertake ethnographic projects that yield fascinating results, documenting explicit and implicit engagements with Bibles.[39] This kind of work needs to take place also in biblical scholarship in Europe, as Annemarie Foppen, Anne-Mareike Schol-Wetter, Peter-Ben Smit, and Eva van Urk-Coster have suggested.[40] As I have argued, notions of a "(whitened European) Bible"[41] have taken hold and need to be interrogated. But also, there is diversity and complexity in European Bible-use, too, that should be mapped. "Claiming that a book is a classic (culturally and religiously) without knowing how 'ordinary' people use and appreciate the book and while only focusing on a work's formal status and its use in 'high'

---

[37] Ibid., pp. 5–6.
[38] Ibid., p. 7. To create spaces for himself and others to do the kind of work he argued biblical studies could and should do, Wimbush went on to found the Institute for Signifying Scriptures and the Signifying (On) Scriptures book series: https://www.psupress.org/books/series/book_Series SOS.html and www.signifyingscriptures.org.
[39] See particularly Love, 'The Bible and Contemporary African American Culture I: Hermeneutical Forays, Observations, and Impressions', pp. 49–65; and James M. Shropshire, Ida Rousseau Mukenge, Victoria Erickson, and Hans A. Baer, 'The Bible and Contemporary African American Culture II', in *African Americans and the Bible: Sacred Texts and Social Textures*, edited by Wimbush, pp. 66–80. This latter chapter details the way the researchers went about the project, helpfully pointing to different possibilities as well as limitations and problems.
[40] Foppen, Schol-wetter, Smit, and van Urk-Coster, 'The Most Significant Book of the Netherlands—And its Ordinary Readers', pp. 107–133. Here biblical studies can learn from research done in ecclesiology and ethnography, theologies using qualititative methods, and ordinary theology.
[41] Wimbush, 'Introduction: Reading Darkness, Reading Scriptures', p. 13.

culture is not sufficient to appreciate a work's impact".[42] This kind of research gives insight into what the Bible is "in terms of its use and functioning".[43]

The obvious spaces of biblical reception can be pushed, then, beyond the rabbis, the church fathers, medieval art, scholastic theologians, modern high culture, and postmodern pop culture—to spaces where it is not immediately obvious that a Bible is at work.[44] It is crucial to be open to the multiplicity of ways Bibles function, not only as texts to be interpreted, or as bits of text that become slogans and mottos, but also as icons and symbols. As Gundaker puts it, a Bible can "serve as a source of imagery, a ritual tool, and a threshold of transformation rather than a source of information".[45] New Materialist approaches have foregrounded this necessity more recently in biblical studies, as I mentioned in chapter 2.[46] Bible-use is not only explicit, conscious, and extensive. A Bible can function "as an implied object".[47] It could be just as interesting to note the way a Bible might be operative when it is absent,[48] or when references to a Bible are obscure, unclear, or implicit. Bibles are not only texts, they are also "engaged, experienced, embodied, and performed", as Holdrege posits.[49] Traditional and social media, pop and high culture, politics and law, are all areas that hold enormous potential for biblical reception and for biblical studies more broadly.

Brennan Breed has suggested that biblical scholars could treat biblical scholarship more like ethology—the study of animal behaviour—than exegesis.[50] Reception history, as he envisions it, is invested in "observing the actual activities and capacities of things as they occur 'in the wild' in all of its diverse processual forms and activities".[51] An "ethological perspective would

---

[42] Foppen, Schol-wetter, Smit, and van Urk-Coster, 'The Most Significant Book of the Netherlands—And its Ordinary Readers', p. 130.

[43] Ibid..

[44] England and Lyons also make this point when they invite the embrace of "expansion, diversity and change in the academic study of the Bible". England and Lyons, 'Explorations in the Reception of the Bible', p. 5.

[45] Gundaker, 'The Bible *as* and *at* a Threshold', p. 761.

[46] See the special issue on New Materialism edited by Robert Paul Seesengood and Andrew Wilson in *The Bible and Critical Theory* 16, no. 2 (2020); and Smith, 'The Affordances of *bible* and the Agency of Material in Assemblage', pp. 1–13.

[47] Shropshire, Rousseau, Mukenge, Erickson, and Baer, 'The Bible and Contemporary African American Culture II', p. 73.

[48] Hugh Pyper writes about the significance of absent Bibles in 'The Absent Bible: Oaths of Office in Scotland and the United States', in *Challenging Contextuality: Bibles and Biblical Scholarship in Context*, edited by Louise Lawrence, Peter-Ben Smit, Hannah Strømmen, and Charlene Van der Walt (Oxford: Oxford University Press, 2024).

[49] Holdrege, 'Beyond the Guild: Liberating Biblical Studies', p. 144.

[50] Breed, 'What Can a Text Do?', p. 98.

[51] Ibid., p. 100.

define biblical texts by what they have looked like in all their variants and translations, by what they have actually done, and by what they are capable of doing in the future".[52] Nowhere does the urgency of the task to examine the role played by uses of Bibles in Europe become clearer than when violence is executed and associated with a particular understanding of "the Bible". The Breivik case showcases this. Alastair Hunter has urged that we "ignore at our peril the potential for violence built into the Bible".[53] There is nothing abstract about this potential. As Hunter puts it, this potential occupies a real space rather than some "virtual space in which metaphor and rhetoric are safely confined, like computer viruses imprisoned in an IT lab".[54]

For the discipline of biblical studies, the kind of work I have been foregrounding blurs some of the firmly established internal boundaries of biblical scholarship, such as "the Great Testamentary Divide",[55] as Stephen Moore and Yvonne Sherwood put it. Specialising in either Hebrew Bible or the New Testament (or much narrower on Deutero-Isaiah or Mark, or even narrower still on a chapter or verse of a biblical text) does not work well for thinking about major biblical assemblages. However, biblical studies has always embraced interdisciplinarity, working particularly closely with areas such as archaeology, philology, ancient languages, classics, and ancient history. To undertake the sort of mapping I am proposing, another set of disciplines is useful: cultural studies, anthropology, media studies, sociology, philosophy, theology, and political science. As Emma England and John Lyons propose, this expansion means that some of the methods and areas previously required to study the Bible may need to be supplemented.[56] Further, group facilitation and creative expression could become important skills for biblical scholars to undertake the kind of BibleLab projects I have proposed as a response to biblical violence.

In his response to *African Americans and the Bible*, Efrain Agosto notes that of the over sixty contributors to the volume, "only a handful are actually trained in biblical studies".[57] Despite the immense enrichments these contributors bring to the study of biblical texts and Bibles, he expresses concern about whether "there are enough biblical scholars to be sure that the good news of these authors is carried forth to the traditionalists, such as,

---

[52] Ibid.
[53] Hunter, '(De)Nominating Amalek', p. 107.
[54] Ibid.
[55] Moore and Sherwood, *The Invention of the Biblical Scholar*, p. 84.
[56] England and Lyons, 'Explorations in the Reception of the Bible', p. 6.
[57] Agosto, 'It's Not *Just* a *Black* Thing!', p. 823.

for example, those who participate in the Society for Biblical Literature", to actually change and challenge the discipline of biblical studies.[58] Although there are groups at the Society of Biblical Literature that are dedicated to reception, they are still—twenty years later—very much in the minority. Posts advertised in biblical reception are almost non-existent, at least in Europe. Jobs are still framed according to traditional biblical studies, though sometimes with a note as to modern-day interpretations of the Bible also being welcome, as if this work is added on as an afterthought or is something the traditional biblical scholar can do that supplements their main work, like a hobby.

Sketching biblical reception as I have done, within the discipline of biblical studies, it could be suggested—as has been suggested to me—that you do not need a biblical scholar to do this kind of work. Why not a literary scholar, art historian, anthropologist, political scientist, or media scholar? I am not interested either in a militant gatekeeping of "biblical studies" or in gatecrashing the discipline and squatting there. On the contrary, what seems important to me is that there is room institutionally for doing biblical reception, or more specifically, as I have suggested, for mapping biblical assemblages. A discipline devoted to the set of texts or artefacts gathered together under the ambivalent and polyvalent term "Bible" seems a good place for that kind of mapping. If there is no institutional room for this kind of work, then students might not get taught the history of biblical interpretation, contemporary Bible-use, and constructions and invocations of Bibles and biblical texts. Biblical studies as a discipline can be useful for enabling this kind of work. Also, without the discipline of biblical studies, biblical references and the absence and presence of Bibles might be missed. Literary scholars or art historians *may* be looking out for the ways a Bible functions in the material they are examining, but the majority may in no way be interested, aware, or willing to address these functions in their research and teaching. It could so easily be the case, as Chanta Haywood puts it, of "scholarly discomfort with matters religious".[59]

---

[58] Ibid.
[59] Haywood, 'Prophesying Daughters: Nineteenth-Century Black Religious Women, the Bible, and Black Literary History', p. 357.

The Ethics of Biblical Reception

Questions of power, ethics, and the effects of biblical texts are raised by biblical reception scholars in ways that suggest this is a significant and valuable part of the field. James Harding has suggested that reception history "might, in fact, have a profoundly ethical orientation", due to the demonstration of the effects of biblical texts on people throughout history.[60] Examining the way biblical texts have shaped particular cultures can be, he argues, "of incalculable value in the ongoing moral formation of the societies in which biblical scholars have the luxury of practising their art".[61] Eryl Davies is highly critical of the way academic biblical scholars do not see their primary task as critiquing the Bible: "For some reason, we have convinced ourselves that our business is simply to *understand*, to *interpret*, not to evaluate or critique.[62] As "objective scholars", the overriding norm of the biblical scholar, as Davies describes it, is to "keep hidden our personal preferences and our ethical and religious views about the subject matter of our study".[63]

As I have argued, scholars who are part of groups that have historically—and currently—tended to be most harmed by Bible-use have rarely had the luxury to sit back and describe. I mentioned examples from African-American biblical scholarship as well as feminist and womanist biblical scholarship. Many further examples could be mentioned here, from minoritised biblical scholarship, such as Queer biblical scholarship. The mapping of biblical assemblages is part of this critical work that goes beyond description. Others working in biblical reception have made a similar case. Holly Morse eschews the term "reception history" because this term can "limit the scope for creative engagement with biblical texts and their cultural afterlives, as the term 'reception history', unsurprisingly, usually demarcates a practice which is driven by concern for historical issues surrounding interpretations of biblical texts".[64] Reception history studies can become overly descriptive, and as Morse argues, this means that "opportunities for the augmentation of our understanding of the myths and meanings surrounding the biblical text are lost".[65] Morse proposes instead the term "reception criticism", in her study

---

[60] James E. Harding, 'What Is Reception History, and What Happens to You if You Do It?', in *Reception History and Biblical Studies: Theory and Practice*, edited by England and Lyons, p. 42.
[61] Ibid., p. 44.
[62] Davies, *The Immoral Bible*, p. 123. Emphasis in the original.
[63] Ibid.
[64] Morse, *Encountering Eve's Afterlives*, p. 3.
[65] Ibid., p. 4.

of Eve.[66] Morse aims to critique and challenge dominant perceptions of Eve "in order to demonstrate that Eve, and our cultural memory of her afterlives, should not continue to be determined by the naturalized myth of the first female sinner".[67] Rather, a number of other themes such as knowledge and life are present in the story. Further, for Morse it is about highlighting marginal interpretations that are less known to present-day readers.[68] Morse goes on to emphasise *ideological* reception criticism as a way of tackling Eve's legacies, to outline a way of analysing these legacies in terms of dominant strategies of interpretation.[69] Drawing on feminist criticism, the goal is to "refresh" and "renew" contemporary readers' understanding of Eve that move away from misogynistic and patriarchal framings and determinations of Eve "that have had a damaging effect on the popular understanding of the biblical story".[70]

Drawing on Morse, Hanna Liljefors uses critical discourse analysis to both describe *and* critique discourses about the Hebrew Bible in Swedish newspapers over a thirty-year period, showing in the process the problematic anti-Jewish ideologies that are reproduced in these discourses.[71] For her, the point of reception criticism is not only to describe phenomena, but also to critique and problematise dominant discourses that do harm to people. In their reception history of the figure of Samson, Nyasha Junior and Jeremy Schipper write that they are not interested only in cataloguing "references to Black Samson in American art and literature as a corrective to a gap in the scholarly literature", but rather to investigate "legal documents, narratives by enslaved people, speeches, sermons, periodicals, poetry, fiction, and visual arts" in order to "tell the unlikely story of how a flawed biblical hero became an iconic figure in America's racial history".[72] "In telling the story of Black Samson we are telling a story of race in America".[73] In the epilogue, they comment on writing this book during an era of protest in America, with acts of police brutality against Black people and white supremacists marching in the streets.[74] "The American mythology around Samson's complicated life and tragic death addresses messier and less comfortable stories of race

---

[66] Ibid.
[67] Ibid.
[68] Ibid.
[69] Ibid., p. 8.
[70] Ibid.
[71] Hanna Liljefors, *Hebreiska bibeln debatterad: en receptionskritisk studie av diskurser om "Gamla testamentet" i svenska dagstidningar 1987–2017* (Uppsala: Artos Academic, 2022).
[72] Junior and Schipper, *Black Samson*, pp. 1–2.
[73] Ibid., p. 2.
[74] Ibid., p. 114.

in America—stories as urgent today as at any point in American history".[75] Similarly, in her reception history of Hagar, Junior writes about the way Hagar has been imagined as Black, asking: "How did Hagar become Black?" "What purpose did or does that serve?"[76] Her reception history explores the way "interpretations of biblical Hagar as Black emphasize elements of Hagar's story in order to connect her with or disassociate her from particular groups".[77]

Biblical scholarship in the mode of reception as I have characterised it can tackle the influence of biblical texts with a strong awareness of the harmful effects of Bible-use and the implications of our work. Wimbush laments that all too often "the response of those trained at the highest academic (doctoral) level in the field of biblical studies is to cultivate essentially a mode of silence".[78] Mapping biblical assemblages is a way of doing reception that eschews this silence, naming the varieties of biblical assemblages that are at work, or that cease to be at work. This kind of work is analytical in that it demonstrates what makes particular Bible-use effective and affective. It is also attentive to tendencies towards the stabilisation of major Bibles that can reveal sites of power as well as the vulnerabilities to change and challenge of major biblical assemblages emerging from the margins. As Greg Carey argues, it is a matter of being held "accountable for the ethical implications of our work".[79]

Causing Runoffs

By speaking of different biblical assemblages emerging, is it not the case that I have dissolved any possibility of laying claim to what "the Bible" *really* means? And if so, what are the consequences? Am I making all Bibles equal in a sweeping gesture of relativism, by departing from any notion of "the Bible"? I am, but this is more an empirical fact than a choice. There is no one Bible. Any claim to *the Bible* is a claim to power over the use of a Bible. It functions as a territorialisation of a Bible, one that may be consequential

---

[75] Ibid.
[76] Nyasha Junior, *Reimagining Hagar: Blackness and Bible* (Oxford: Oxford University Press, 2019), p. 1.
[77] Ibid., p. 2.
[78] Wimbush, 'Introduction: Reading Darkness, Reading Scriptures', p. 11.
[79] Greg Carey, *Using Our Outside Voice: Public Biblical Interpretation* (Minneapolis, MN: Fortress Press, 2020), p. 2.

or inconsequential when it comes to the effects of such a Bible in the world. Biblical scholars, with the accolades of titles and salaries and embedded in recognised institutions, have a certain amount of power and authority in steering understandings and uses of Bibles. Faith leaders have a different kind of power and authority. Family members, friends, and lovers may also operate with some power to guide how Bibles are encountered and engaged. But, following Felski, I suggest that rather than attempting to police understandings and uses of Bibles according to some notion of "proper" interpretation, we attend instead to the possibilities that emergences of Bibles and the ties that are forged by and with these Bibles afford.

To do this we need to map biblical assemblages. In other words, biblical scholars can identify the biblical assemblages that are part and parcel of society, past and present, in which society encompasses everything from religious life, political life, art, film, literature, law, architecture, tourism, marketing, technology, and public spaces.[80] Major biblical assemblages can be mapped to demonstrate how a particular version or construction of a Bible operates and has become stabilised in a particular milieu. Biblical scholars, then, can indicate where the tendency to stasis and to change lies in any biblical assemblage. The tendency to change indicates where a minor biblical assemblage might be emerging—where a Bible is becoming.

BibleLab is a project-driven activity that I have suggested can experiment with major biblical assemblages and be part of the minoritarian becoming of Bibles. There is no guarantee that the kind of activity I called BibleLab will be considered good and benign by everyone. This kind of activity could be misunderstood, or it could result in malign outcomes.[81] Any new becomings can be stabilised in ways that exclude and oppress. In this sense, the commitment to liberation is crucial in the work of identifying the stabilisation of major biblical assemblages and their effects, and the creation of minor biblical assemblages. Ultimately, any and all attention to Bibles as assemblages pays heed to the shifting elements that make up a Bible, the conditions under which a Bible is stabilised or destabilised, and the knowledge that for any Bible to have power, it needs people, structures, ideas, practices, repetitions, publications, statements, narratives, and systems to ensure its functioning

---

[80] Examples of this kind of work that could be mentioned here are Edwards, *Admen and Eve: The Bible in Contemporary Advertising*; James S. Bielo and Lieke Wijnia, eds., *The Bible and Global Tourism* (London: T&T Clark, 2021); and David Tollerton, ed., *A New Hollywood Moses: on the Spectacle and Reception of Exodus: Gods and Kings* (London: Bloomsbury, 2017).
[81] Ringrose, 'Beyond Discourse?', p. 603.

and its efficiency. This means that this power can always also be challenged. The hope for change is always there. Experimenting with Bibles collectively—as I suggested would be the task of BibleLab—is all about the capacities for affecting and being affected that are in every body and thing. Massumi explicitly links affect to hope. In fact, he writes that affect is the word he uses for hope.[82] For him, hope is about what directions we might be able to take and what we might be able to do. Who might we become? What Bibles might become? This is precisely what affect is all about: potential. It is about focusing on the next experimental step, in the hope for something better.[83] It is not about grandiose agendas for change or for programmes that operate on a global scale, which often are unrealistic and lead to hopelessness and resignation.

My hope, then, does not lie in some state intervention into how Bibles are produced and propagated. My hope lies in the way the minoritarian, as Deleuze and Guattari put it, can always destabilise assemblages that become staid and static. Becoming—the hope for change—is minoritarian.[84] Deterritorialisations bring about lines of flight. As Deleuze and Guattari explain, lines of flight are not about running away from the world. They are about "causing runoffs, as when you drill a hole in a pipe; there is no social system that does not leak from all directions".[85] Mapping the way Bibles are always the result of particular arrangements, conditions, and selections, it is also possible to point to the potential for change. By working with Bibles as relational compositions, or assemblages, that are always connected to bodies and histories and non-biblical materials, it is possible also to experiment with these Bibles in collective and creative ways, opening up for new ways of relating to biblical texts and new forms of Bible-use that counter far-right Bibles.

---

[82] Massumi, *Politics of Affect*, p. 3.
[83] Ibid.
[84] Deleuze and Guattari, *A Thousand Plateaus*, p. 123.
[85] Ibid., p. 239.

Bibliography

Aadland, Ingunn. 'Casting Biblical Narratives: Gendered Power Hierarchies and Cultural Imagination in Scandinavian Children's Bibles'. *Studia Theologica* 77, no. 1 (2022): pp. 40–61.

Aasland Ravndal, Jacob. 'Right-wing Terrorism and Militancy in the Nordic Countries: A Comparative Case Study'. *Terrorism and Political Violence* 30, no. 5 (2018): pp. 772–792.

Abrahams, Gareth. 'The Building as a Deleuzoguattarian Strata/Machinic Assemblage'. *Architectural Theory Review* 23, no. 3 (2019): pp. 363–379.

Achinger, Christine, and Robert Fine, eds. *Antisemitism, Racism and Islamophobia: Distorted Faces of Modernity* (Abingdon: Routledge, 2015).

Adkins, Brent. *Deleuze and Guattari's* A Thousand Plateaus: *A Critical Introduction and Guide* (Edinburgh: Edinburgh University Press, 2015).

Agosto, Efrain. 'It's Not *Just* a *Black* Thing!' In *African Americans and the Bible: Sacred Texts and Social Textures,* edited by Vincent Wimbush (Eugene, OR: Wipf & Stock, 2000), pp. 823–824.

Ahmed, Sara. *The Cultural Politics of Emotion*, 2nd ed. (Edinburgh: Edinburgh University Press, 2014).

Aichele, George. 'Canon, Ideology, and the Emergence of an Imperial Church'. In *Canon and Canonicity: The Formation and Use of Scripture,* edited by Einar Thomassen (Copenhagen: Museum Tusculanum Press, 2010), pp. 45–65.

Ali, Ayaan Hirsi. 'Why I am Now a Christian: Atheism Can't Equip Us for Civilizational War'. *Unherd*, 11 November 2023, https://unherd.com/2023/11/why-i-am-now-a-christian/.

Anderson, Greg. *The Realness of Things Past: Ancient Greece and Ontological History* (Oxford: Oxford University Press, 2018).

Arceneaux, Kevin, and Stephen P. Nicholson. 'Who Wants to Have a Tea Party? The Who, What, and Why of the Tea Party Movement'. *Political Science and Politics* 45, no. 4 (2012), pp. 700–710.

Asad, Talal. *Formations of the Secular: Christianity, Islam, Modernity* (Stanford, CA: Stanford University Press, 2003).

Avalos, Hector. *Fighting Words: The Origins of Religious Violence* (New York: Prometheus Books, 2005).

Avalos, Hector. 'Explaining Religious Violence: Retrospects and Prospects'. In *The Blackwell Companion to Religion and Violence,* edited by Andrew Murphy (London: Blackwell, 2011), pp. 137–146.

Avalos, Hector. *Slavery, Abolitionism, and the Ethics of Biblical Scholarship* (Sheffield: Sheffield Phoenix Press, 2013).

Avalos, Hector. *The Bad Jesus: The Ethics of New Testament Ethics* (Sheffield: Sheffield Phoenix Press, 2015).

Aydin, Cemil. *The Idea of the Muslim World: A Global Intellectual History* (Cambridge, MA: Harvard University Press, 2019).

Bailey, Michael A., Jonathan Mummolo, and Hans Noel. 'Tea Party Influence: A Story of Activists and Elites'. *American Politics Research* 40, no. 5 (2012): pp. 769–804.

Bailey, Randall C., Tat-siong Benny Liew, and Fernando F. Segovia. 'Toward Minority Criticism: Framework, Contours, Dynamics'. In *They Were All Together in One Place? Toward Minority Biblical Criticism,* edited by Randall C. Bailey, Tat-siong Benny Liew, and Fernando F. Segovia (Atlanta, GA: Society of Biblical Literature, 2009), pp. 3–43.

Bal, Mieke. *Anti-Covenant: Counter-Reading Women's Lives in the Hebrew Bible* (Sheffield: Almond, 1989).
Bal, Mieke. 'Seduction, the Biblical Imagination, and Activating Art'. In *The Bible and Feminism: Remapping the Field*, edited by Yvonne Sherwood with the assistance of Anna Fisk (Oxford: Oxford University Press, 2017), pp. 589–607.
Bangstad, Sindre. *Anders Breivik and the Rise of Islamophobia* (London: Zed Books, 2014).
Bangstad, Sindre. 'Which Populism, Which Christianity?' In *Religion, Populism, and Modernity: Confronting White Christian Nationalism and Racism*, edited by Atalia Omer and Joshua Lupo (Notre Dame, IN: University of Notre Dame Press, 2023), pp. 223–244.
Barad, Karen. *Meeting the Universe Halfway: Quantum Physics and the Entanglement of Matter and Meaning* (Durham, NC: Duke University Press, 2007).
Barton, John. *The Nature of Biblical Criticism* (Louisville, KY: Westminster John Knox Press, 2007).
Bawer, Bruce. *While Europe Slept: How Radical Islam Is Destroying the West from Within* (New York: Anchor Books, 2006).
Bawer, Bruce———. *The New Quislings: How the International Left Used the Oslo Massacre to Silence Debate about Islam* (New York: Broadside e-books, 2012).
Beal, Timothy. 'Reception History and Beyond: Toward the Cultural History of Scriptures'. *Biblical Interpretation* 19 (2011): pp. 357–371.
Beal, Timothy. *The Book of Revelation: A Biography*. (Princeton, NJ: Princeton University Press, 2018).
Benhabib, Seyla. *The Claims of Culture: Equality and Diversity in the Global Era* (Princeton, NJ: Princeton University Press, 2002).
Bennett, Jane. *Vibrant Matter: A Political Ecology of Things* (Durham, NC: Duke University Press, 2010).
Berardi, Franco 'Bifo'. *Heroes: Mass Murder and Suicide* (London: Verso, 2015).
Berlinerblau, Jacques. *Thumpin' it: The Use and Abuse of the Bible in Today's Presidential Politics* (Louisville, KY: John Knox Press, 2007).
Berntzen, Lars Eric, and Sveinung Sandberg. 'The Collective Nature of Lone Wolf Terrorism: Anders Behring Breivik and the Anti-Islamic Social Movement, Terrorism and Political Violence'. *Terrorism and Political Violence* 26, no. 5 (2014): pp. 759–779.
Betz, Hans-Georg. 'Against the "Green Totalitarianism": Anti-Islamic Nativism in Contemporary Radical Right-Wing Populism in Western Europe'. In *Europe for the Europeans: The Foreign and Security Policy of the Populist Radical Right*, edited by Christina Schori Liang (Aldershot: Ashgate, 2007), pp. 33–54.
Bielo, James S. 'Introduction: Encountering Biblicism'. In *The Social Life of Scriptures: Cross-Cultural Perspectives on Biblicism*, edited by James S. Bielo (New Brunswick, NJ: Rutgers University Press, 2009), pp. 1–9.
Bielo, James S., and Lieke Wijnia. *The Bible and Global Tourism* (London: T&T Clark, 2021).
Bishop, Adam M. '#DeusVult'. In *Whose Middle Ages? Teachable Moments for an Ill-Used Past*, edited by Andrew Albin, Mary C. Erler, Thomas O'Donnell, Nicholas L. Paul, and Nina Rowe (New York: Fordham University Press, 2019), pp. 256–264.
Bjørgo, Tore. *Terror from the Extreme Right* (London: Frank Cass, 1995).
Black, Fiona C., and Jennifer L. Koosed. 'Introduction: Some Ways to Read with Feeling'. In *Reading with Feeling: Affect Theory and the Bible*, edited by Fiona C. Black and Jennifer L. Koosed (Atlanta, GA: SBL Press, 2019), pp. 1–12.
Blee, Kathleen M. 'Ethnographies of the Far Right'. *Journal of Contemporary Ethnography* 36, no. 2 (2007), pp. 119–128.
Bogue, Ronald. 'The Minor'. In *Giles Deleuze: Key Concepts*, edited by Charles J. Stivale (Montreal and Kingston: McGill-Queen's University Press, 2005), pp. 110–120.
Borchgrevink, Aage. *A Norwegian Tragedy: Anders Behring Breivik and the Massacre at Utøya*. Tralsted by Guy Puzey (Cambridge: Polity Press, 2013).

Bottici, Chiara, and Benoît Challand. *The Myth of the Clash of Civilizations* (London: Routledge, 2010).
Brague, Rémi. *Eccentric Culture: A Theory of Western Civilization*, Revised ed. Translated by Samuel Lester (South Bend, IN: St. Augustine's Press, 2002).
Braunstein, Ruth, and Malaena Taylor. 'Is the Tea Party a "Religious" Movement? Religiosity in the Tea Party versus the Religious Right'. *Sociology of Religion: A Quarterly Review* 78, no. 1 (2017): pp. 33–59.
Bray, Karen, and Stephen D. Moore. 'Introduction: Mappings and Crossings'. In *Religion, Emotion, Sensation: Affect Theories and Theologies*, edited by Karen Bray and Stephen D. Moore (New York: Fordham University Press, 2020), pp. 1–17.
Breed, Brennan. *Nomadic Text: A Theory of Biblical Reception History* (Bloomington: Indiana University Press, 2014).
Breed, Brennan. 'What Can a Text Do? Reception History as an Ethology of the Biblical Text'. In *Reception History and Biblical Studies: Theory and Practice*, edited by Emma England and Willian John Lyons (London: Bloomsbury T&T Clark, 2015), pp. 95–109.
Briassoulis, Helen. 'Governance as Multiplicity: The Assemblage Thinking Perspective'. *Policy Sciences* 52 (2019): pp. 419–450.
Brown, Andrew. 'Breivik IS Not a Christian but Anti-Islam', *The Guardian*, 24 July 2011, https://www.theguardian.com/commentisfree/andrewbrown/2011/jul/24/norway-anders-behring-breivik-beliefs.
Brubaker, Rogers. 'Between Nationalism and Civilizationism: The European Populist Moment in Comparative Perspective'. *Ethnic and Racial Studies* 40, no. 8 (2017): pp. 1191–1226.
Brubaker, Rogers. 'A New 'Christianist' Secularism in Europe'. *The Immanent Frame*, 11 October 2016, https://tif.ssrc.org/2016/10/11/a-new-christianist-secularism-in-europe/.
Brueggemann, Walter. *David's Truth in Israel's Imagination and Memory* (Minneapolis, MN: Fortress Press, 1985).
Bruin, Tom de. 'Seeing Is Believing: The Digital Bible and Bible Verses Online'. *Spec Christiana* 31, no. 1 (2020): pp. 123–152.
Buchanan, Ian. *Assemblage Theory and Method* (London: Bloomsbury, 2021).
Bulliet, Richard W. *The Case for Islamo-Christian Civilization* (New York: Columbia University Press, 2004).
Burnette-Bletsch, Rhonda. *The Bible in Motion* (Berlin: De Gruyter, 2016).
Burnette-Bletsch, Rhonda, and Jon Morgan. *Noah as Anti-Hero* (New York: Routledge, 2017).
Byrd, James P. *A Holy Baptism of Fire and Blood: The Bible and the American Civil War* (Oxford: Oxford University Press, 2021).
Camus, Jean-Yves, and Nicolas Lebourg. *Far-Right Politics in Europe*. Translated by Jane Marie Todd (Cambridge, MA: Belknap Press, 2017).
Carey, Greg. *Using Our Outside Voice: Public Biblical Interpretation* (Minneapolis, MN: Fortress Press, 2020).
Carr, Matt. 'You Are Now Entering Eurabia'. *Race and Class* 48, no. 1 (2006), pp. 1–22.
Carroll, Robert P. *Wolf in the Sheepfold: The Bible as Problematic for Theology*, 2nd ed. (London: SCM Press, 1997).
Carroll R., M. Daniel, and J. Blair Wilgus. *Wrestling with the Violence of God: Soundings in the Old Testament* (Winona Lake, IN: Eisenbrauns, 2015).
Castelli, Elizabeth A. *Martyrdom and Memory: Early Christian Culture Making* (New York: Columbia University Press, 2004).
Cesari, Jocelyne. *Muslims in the West after 9/11: Religion, Politics and Laws* (London: Routledge, 2009).
Cleland, Jamie, Chris Anderson, and Jack Aldridge-Deacon. 'Islamophobia, War and Non-Muslims as Victims: An Analysis of Online Discourse on an English Defence League Message Board'. *Ethnic and Racial Studies* 41, no. 9 (2018): pp. 1541–1557.
Clough, Patricia Ticineto, with Jean Halley, eds. *The Affective Turn: Theorizing the Social* (Durham, NC: Duke University Press, 2007).

Clough, Patricia Ticineto. 'Introduction'. In *The Affective Turn: Theorizing the Social*, edited by Patricia Ticineto Clough with Jean Halley (Durham, NC: Duke University Press, 2007), pp. 1–33.
Cohen, Mordechai Z., and Adele Berlin, eds. *Interpreting Scriptures in Judaism, Christianity and Islam: Overlapping Inquiries* (Cambridge: Cambridge University Press, 2016).
Collins, John J. 'The Zeal of Phinehas: The Bible and the Legitimation of Violence'. *Journal of Biblical Literature* 122 (2003): pp. 3–21.
Concannon, Cavan W. *Profaning Paul* (Chicago: University of Chicago Press, 2021).
Creach, Jerome F. D. *Violence in Scripture: Resources for the Use of Scripture in the Church* (Louisville, KY: Westminster John Knox Press, 2013).
Crossan, John Dominic. *How to Read the Bible and Still Be a Christian* (New York: Harper Collins, 2015).
Crossley, James G. *Jesus in an Age of Terror, Scholarly Projects for a New American Century* (London: Equinox, 2008).
Crossley, James G. 'The End of Reception History, a Grand Narrative for Biblical Studies and the Neoliberal Bible'. In *Reception History and Biblical Studies: Theory and Practice*, edited by Emma England and John Lyons (London: Bloomsbury T&T Clark, 2015), pp. 45–59.
Crossley, James G. 'What the Bible Really Means: Biblical Literacy in English Political Discourse'. In *Rethinking Biblical Literacy*, edited by Katie Edwards (London: Bloomsbury T&T Clark, 2015), pp. 23–45.
Crossley, James G. *Harnessing Chaos: The Bible in English Political Discourse since 1968*, 2nd ed (London: Bloomsbury T&T Clark, 2016).
Crossley, James G. *Cults, Martyrs and Good Samaritans: Religion in Contemporary English Discourse* (London: Pluto Press, 2018).
Crossley, James G. 'Boris Johnson and the Divisive Bible'. *The Institutem Blog*, March 2019.
Davies, Eryl W. *The Immoral Bible: Approaches to Biblical Ethics* (London: Bloomsbury, 2010).
De Landa, Manuel. *Assemblage Theory* (Edinburgh: Edinburgh University Press, 2016).
De Paola, Jennifer, and Eemeli Hakoköngäs. 'This Must Surely Be the Way to Happiness! Divergent "Bite-Size Wisdoms" about Happiness in Inspirational Internet Memes'. *Culture Unbound: Journal of Current Cultural Research* 12, no. 3 (2020): pp. 590–614.
Deleuze, Gilles, and Félix Guattari. *A Thousand Plateaus: Capitalism and Schizophrenia*. Translated by Brian Massumi (London: Bloomsbury, 2013).
Deleuze, Gilles, and Claire Parnet. *Dialogues* (New York: Columbia University Press, 1987).
Diebold, William J. 'The Nazi Middle Ages'. In *Whose Middle Ages? Teachable Moments for an Ill-Used Past*, edited by Andrew Albin, Mary C. Erler, Thomas O'Donnell, Nicholas L. Paul, and Nina Rowe (New York: Fordham University Press, 2019), pp. 104–115.
Dillen, Annemie. 'Children's Spirituality and Theologising with Children: The Role of "Context"'. *International Journal of Children's Spirituality* 25, no. 3–4 (2020): pp. 238–253.
Dube, Musa. 'Introduction: Silenced, Nights, Bible Translation and the African Contact Zones'. In *Postcoloniality, Translation and the Bible in Africa*, edited by Musa Dube and R. S. Wafula (Eugene, OR: Pickwick, 2017), pp. xiii–xxvii.
Dufour, Lynn Resnick. '"Sifting through Tradition": The Creation of Jewish Feminist Identities'. *Journal for the Scientific Study of Religion* 39, no. 1 (2000): pp. 90–106.
Edwards, Katie B. *Admen and Eve: The Bible in Contemporary Advertising* (Sheffield: Sheffield Phoenix Press, 2012).
Edwards, Katie, ed. *Rethinking Biblical Literacy* (London: Bloomsbury, 2015).
Eggestad, Silje J. 'Gullalder, korstog og apokalypse: Forskeren om høyreekstremismens historieforståelse'. *Filter Nyheter*, 10 July 2021.
Ekman, Mattias. 'Online Islamophobia and the Politics of Fear: Manufacturing the Green Scare'. *Ethnic and Racial Studies* 38, no. 11 (2015): pp. 1986–2002.
Elabdi, Florian. 'Dane Who Wants to Deport Muslims, Ban Islam to Run in Election'. *Aljazeera*, May 16, 2019: https://www.aljazeera.com/indepth/features/rasmus-paludan-danish-islamophobe-rises-political-stardom-190516090301567.html.

Ellinas, Antonis A. *The Media and the Far Right in Western Europe* (Cambridge: Cambridge University Press, 2010).
Elliott, Andrew B. R. *Medievalism, Politics and Mass Media: Appropriating the Middle Ages in the Twenty-First Century* (Cambridge: DS Brewer, 2017).
Ellis, Justine Esta. *The Politics of Religious Literacy: Education and Emotion in a Secular Age* (Leiden: Brill, 2022).
England, Emma, and William John Lyons. 'Explorations in the Reception of the Bible'. In *Reception History and Biblical Studies: Theory and Practice*, edited by Emma England and William John Lyons (London: Bloomsbury T&T Clark, 2015), pp. 3–13.
Erikson, Mia. 'Breivik and I: Affective Encounters with "Failed" Masculinity in Stories about Right-wing Terrorism'. *International Journal for Masculinity Studies* 13, no. 3–4 (2018): pp. 265–278.
Esseveld, Johanna, and Ron Eyerman. 'Which Side Are You On? Reflections on Methodological Issues in the Study of "distasteful" Social Movements'. In *Studying Collective Action*, edited by Mario Diani and Ron Eyerman (London: Sage, 1992), pp. 217–218.
Exum, J. Cheryl. *Fragmented Women: Feminist (Sub)versions of Biblical Narrative* (Valley Forge, PA: Trinity Press International, 1993).
Fallaci, Oriana. *The Force of Reason* (New York: Rizzoli International Publications, 2004).
Farah, Joseph. *The Tea Party Manifesto: A Vision for an American Rebirth* (Washington, DC: WND Books, 2010).
Farah, Joseph, and Rush Limbaugh. *See, I Told You So* (New York: Pocket Books, 1994).
Fekete, Liz. *Europe's Fault Lines: Racism and the Rise of the Right* (London: Verso, 2018).
Felski, Rita. *Hooked: Art and Attachment* (Chicago: University of Chicago Press, 2020).
Fiorenza, Elisabeth Schüssler. *Bread Not Stone: The Challenge of Feminist Biblical Interpretation* (Boston: Beacon Press, 1985).
Fiorenza, Elisabeth Schüssler. *In Memory of Her: A Feminist Theological Reconstruction of Christian Origins* (Chicago: Independent Publishers Group, 1994).
Fiorenza, Elisabeth Schüssler. *But She Said: Feminist Practices of Biblical Interpretation* (Boston: Beacon Press, 1993).
Flannery, Frances, and Rodney Werline. *The Bible in Political Debate* (London: Bloomsbury, 2016).
Fleischer, Rasmus. 'Two Fascisms in Contemporary Europe? Understanding the Ideological Split of the Radical Right'. In *In the Tracks of Breivik: Far Right Networks in Northern and Eastern Europe*, edited by Mats Deland, Michael Minkenberg, and Christin Mays (Münster: Lit Verlag, 2013), pp. 53–70.
Foppen, Annemarie, Anne-Mareike Schol-Wetter, Peter-Ben Smit, and Eva van Urk-Coster. 'The Most Significant Book of the Netherlands—And Its Ordinary Readers'. *Journal of the Bible and Its Reception* 8, no. 1 (2021): pp. 107–133.
Foster, Clare L. E. "Familiarity and Recognition: Towards a New Vocabulary for Classical Reception Studies". In *Framing Classical Reception Studies*, edited by Maarten De Pourcq, Nathalie De Haan, and David Rijser (Leiden: Brill, 2020), pp. 33–69.
Frydenlund, Iselin. 'Global Islamofobi'. *Klassekampen*, 22 July 2021.
Gaffney, Amber M., David E. Rast III, Justin D. Hackett, and Michael A. Hogg. 'Further to the Right: Uncertainty, Political Polarization and the American "Tea Party" Movement'. *Social Influence* 9, no. 4 (2014): pp. 272–288.
Gamble, Harry Y. *Books and Readers in the Early Church: A History of Early Christian Texts* (New Haven, CT: Yale University Press, 1995).
Gardell, Mattias. 'Crusader Dreams: Oslo 22/7, Islamophobia, and the Quest for a Monocultural Europe'. *Terrorism and Political Violence* 26 (2014): pp. 129–155.
Gardell, Mattias. 'Urban Terror: The Case of Lone Wolf Peter Mangs'. *Terrorism and Political Violence* 30, no. 5 (2018): pp. 793–811.

Gattinara, Pietro Castelli. 'Framing Exclusion in the Public Sphere: Far-Right Mobilisation and the Debate on Charlie Hebdo in Italy'. *South European Society and Politics* 22, no. 3 (2017): pp. 345–364.

Gattinara, Pietro Castelli, and Andrea L. P. Pirro. 'The Far Right as Social Movement'. *European Societies* 21, no. 4 (2019): pp. 447–462.

Gilkes, Cheryl Townsend. 'The Virtues of Brotherhood and Sisterhood: African American Fraternal Organizations and their Bibles'. In *African Americans and the Bible: Sacred Texts and Social Textures*, edited by Vincent Wimbush (Eugene, OR: Wipf & Stock, 2000), pp. 389–403.

Goodchild, Phillip. *Deleuze and Guattari: An Introduction to the Politics of Desire* (London: Sage, 1996).

Graybill, Rhiannon. *Texts after Terror: Rape, Sexual Violence, and the Hebrew Bible* (Oxford: Oxford University Press, 2021).

Gregg, Melissa, and Gregory J. Seigworth. 'In Inventory of Shimmers'. In *The Affect Theory Reader*, edited by Melissa Gregg Durham and Gregory J. Seigworth (London: Duke University Press, 2010), pp. 1–25.

Grumke, Thomas. 'Globalized Anti-Globalists—The Ideological Basis of the Internationalization of Right-Wing Extremism'. In *The Extreme Right in Europe: Current Trends and Perspectives*, edited by Uwe Backes and Patrick Moreau (Göttingen: Vandenhoeck & Ruprecht, 2012), pp. 323–332.

Guiora, Amos N. *Tolerating Intolerance: The Price of Protecting Extremism* (Oxford: Oxford University Press, 2014).

Hafez, Farid. 'Shifting Borders: Islamophobia as Common Ground for Building Pan-European Right-Wing Unity'. *Patterns of Prejudice* 48, no. 5 (2014): pp. 479–499.

Hafez, Farid. 'Street-Level and Government-Level Islamophobia in the Visegrád Four Countries'. *Patterns of Prejudice* 52, no. 5 (2018): pp. 436–447.

Hagelia, Hallvard. 'Violence, Judgment and Ethics in the Book of Amos'. In *Encountering Violence in the Bible*, edited by Markus Zehnder and Hallvard Hagelia (Sheffield: Sheffield Phoenix Press, 2013), pp. 128–147.

Hagelia, Hallvard, and Markus Zehnder. 'Introduction'. In *Encountering Violence in the Bible*, edited by Markus Zehnder and Hallvard Hagelia (Sheffield: Sheffield Phoenix Press, 2013), pp. 1–12.

Harding, James E. 'What Is Reception History, and What Happens to You if You Do It?' In *Reception History and Biblical Studies: Theory and Practice*, edited by Emma England and William John Lyons (London: Bloomsbury T&T Clark, 2015), pp. 31–44.

Harding, Vincent. 'The Annointed Ones: Hamer, King, and the Bible in the Southern Freedom Movement'. In *African Americans and the Bible: Sacred Texts and Social Textures*, edited by Vincent Wimbush (Eugene, OR: Wipf & Stock, 2000), pp. 537–545.

Harris, Dana M. 'Understanding Images of Violence in the Book of Revelation'. In *Encountering Violence in the Bible*, edited by Markus Zehnder and Hallvard Hagelia (Sheffield: Sheffield Phoenix Press, 2013), pp. 148–164.

Hawk, L. Daniel. *The Violence of the Biblical God: Canonical Narrative and Christian Faith* (Grand Rapids, MI: William B. Eerdmans, 2019).

Haywood, Chanta M. 'Prophesying Daughters: Nineteenth-Century Black Religious Women, the Bible, and Black Literary History'. In *African Americans and the Bible: Sacred Texts and Social Textures*, edited by Vincent Wimbush (Eugene, OR: Wipf & Stock, 2000), pp. 355–366.

Hoffman, Bruce. *Inside Terrorism* (London: Victor Golliancz, 1998).

Holdrege, Barbara A. 'Beyond the Guild: Liberating Biblical Studies'. In *African Americans and the Bible: Sacred Texts and Social Textures*, edited by Vincent Wimbush (Eugene, OR: Wipf & Stock, 2000), pp. 138–159.

Holland, Eugene W. *Deleuze and Guattari's A Thousand Plateaus* (London: Bloomsbury, 2013).

Hoover, A. J. *God, Germany, and Britain in the Great War* (London: Praeger, 1989).

Hunter, Alastair G. '(De)Nominating Amalek: Racist Stereotyping in the Bible and the Justification of Discrimination'. In *Sanctified Aggression: Legacies of Biblical and Post-Biblical Vocabularies of Violence*, edited by Jonneke Bekkenkamp and Yvonne Sherwood (London: T&T Clark, 2003), pp. 92–108.
Huntington, Samuel P. 'The Clash of Civilizations'. In *The Clash of Civilizations? The Debate, Foreign Affairs* 72, no. 3 (1993): pp. 22–49.
Huntington, Samuel P. *The Clash of Civilizations and the Remaking of World Order*, (New York: Simon and Schuster, 1996).
Hurd, Elizabeth Shakman. *Beyond Religious Freedom: The New Global Politics of Religion* (Princeton, NJ: Princeton University Press, 2015).
Hurtado, Larry W. *The Earliest Christian Artefacts: Manuscripts and Christian Origins* (Grand Rapids, MI: Eerdmans, 2006).
Hverven, Tom Egil, and Sverre Malling. *Terrorens ansikt: skisser fra 22.juli-rettsaken* (Oslo: Flamme Forlag, 2013).
Høeg, Ida Marie. 'Silent Actions: Emotion and Mass Mourning Rituals after the terrorist Attacks in Norway on 22 July 2011'. *Mortality* 20, no. 3 (2015): pp. 197–214.
Jackson, Paul. 'The License to Hate: Peder Jensen's Fascist Rhetoric in Anders Breivik's Manifesto 2083: A European Declaration of Independence'. *Democracy and Security* 9 (2013): pp. 247–269.
Jenkins, Henry, Sam Ford, and Joshua Green. *Spreadable Media: Creating Value and Meaning in a Networked Culture* (New York: New York University Press, 2013).
Johnson, Barbara. *The Barbara Johnson Reader: The Surprise of Otherness*, edited by Melissa Feuerstein, Bill Johnson Gonzáles, Lili Porten, and Keja L. Valens (Durham, NC: Duke University Press, 2014).
Junior, Nyasha. *Reimagining Hagar: Blackness and Bible* (Oxford: Oxford University Press, 2019).
Junior, Nyasha, and Jeremy Schipper. *Black Samson: The Untold Story of an American Icon* (Oxford: Oxford University Press, 2020).
Jurgensmeyer, Mark. 'Sacrifice and Cosmic Warfare'. *Terrorism and Political Violence* 3, no. 3 (1991): pp. 101–117.
Jurgensmeyere, Mark. *Terror in the Mind of God: The Global Rise of Religious Violence*, 3rd ed. (Berkeley: University of California Press, 2003).
Kalmar, Ivan. '"The Battlefield Is in Brussels": Islamophobia in the Visegrád Four in Its Global Context'. *Patterns of Prejudice* 52, no. 5 (2018), pp. 406–419.
Kangas, Sini. 'The Slaughter of the Innocents and the Depiction of Children in Twelfth- and Thirteenth-Century Sources of the Crusades'. In *The Uses of the Bible in Crusader Sources*, edited by Elizabeth Lapina and Nicholas Morton (Leiden: Brill, 2017), pp. 74–101.
Kartzow, Marianne Bjelland, Kasper Bro Larsen, and Outi Lehtipuu, *The Nordic Bible: Bible Reception in Contemporary Nordic Societies* (Berlin: De Gruyter, 2023).
Keith, Chris, Helen Bond, Christine Jacobi, and Jens Schröter, *The Reception of Jesus in the First Three Centuries* (London: Bloomsbury, 2019).
Kennedy, Rachael. 'Denmark's Quran-Burning Politician Gathering Support for Election Candidacy'. *Euronews*, April 25, 2019: https://www.euronews.com/2019/04/25/denmark-s-quran-burning-politician-gathering-support-for-election-candidacy.
Kimmel, Michael. *Angry White Men: American Masculinity at the End of an Era* (New York: Nation Books, 2013).
King-Hammond, Leslie. 'The Bible and the Aesthetics of Sacred Space in Twentieth-Century African American Experience'. In *African Americans and the Bible: Sacred Texts and Social Textures*, edited by Vincent Wimbush (Eugene, OR: Wipf & Stock, 2000), pp. 433–447.
Kinyua, Johnson Kiriaku. 'A Postcolonial Analysis of Bible Translation and its Effectiveness in Shaping and Enhancing the Discourse of Colonialism and the Discourse of Resistance: The Gĩkũyũ New Testament—A Case Study'. In *Postcoloniality, Translation and the Bible in Africa*, edited by Musa Dube and R. S. Wafula (Eugene, OR: Pickwick, 2017), pp. 57–93.

Klungtveit, Harald, and Jonas Skybakmoen. '"Kanskje vi på sikt må slippe ham ut, så vi får ryddet opp": SIAN gjentar Breivik-uttalelser før ny demonstrasjon'. *Filter Nyheter*, 12 September 2020, https://filternyheter.no/kanskje-vi-pa-sikt-ma-slippe-ham-ut-sa-vi-far-ryddet-opp-sian-gjentar-breivik-uttalelser-for-ny-demonstrasjon/.

Knight, Mark. '*Wirkungsgeschichte*, Reception History, Reception Theory'. *Journal for the Study of the New Testament* 33, no. 2 (2010): pp. 137–146.

Koenig, Sara M. *Bathsheba Survives* (London: SCM Press, 2019).

Kolås, Åshild. 'How Critical Is the Event? Multicultural Norway after 22 July 2011'. *Social Identities* 23, no. 5 (2017): pp. 518–532.

Koosed, Jennifer L., and Robert Seesengood. *Jesse's Lineage: The Legendary Lives of David, Jesus and Jesse James* (London: Bloomsbury, 2013).

Köttig, Michaela, Renate Bitzan, and Andrea Pető. *Gender and Far Right Politics in Europe* (London: Palgrave Macmillan, 2017).

Kuhar, Roman, and David Paternotte. *Anti-Gender Campaigns: Mobilizing against Equality in Europe* (London: Rowman and Littlefield, 2017).

Kuhlin, Joel. *A Beautiful Failure: The Event of Death and Rhetorical Disorder in the Gospel According to Mark* (Lund: Mediatryck, 2024).

Laborde, Cécile. *Liberalism's Religion* (Cambridge, MA: Harvard University Press, 2017).

Latour, Bruno. *Reassembling the Social: An Introduction to Actor-Network-Theory* (Oxford: Oxford University Press, 2005).

Lawler, Peter Augustine. 'Roger Scruton's Conservatism: Between Xenophobia and Oikophobia'. *Perspectives on Political Science* 45, no. 4 (2016): pp. 251–260.

Lazaridis, Gabriella, Giovanna Campani, and Anne Benveniste. 'Introduction'. In *The Rise of the Far Right in Europe: Populist Shifts and 'Othering'"*, edited by Gabriella Lazaridis, Giovanna Campani, and Anne Benveniste (New York: Palgrave Macmillan, 2016), pp. 1–23.

L'Estrange, Elin. 'Det vanskelige hatet'. *Klassekampen*, 22 July 2021.

Legaspi, Michael. *The Death of Scripture and the Rise of Biblical Studies* (Oxford: Oxford University Press, 2010).

Lewis, Bernard. 'The Roots of Muslim Rage'. *The Atlantic*, September 1990, pp. 47–54.

Lewis, Thomas A. 'On the Role of Normativity in Religious Studies'. In *The Cambridge Companion to Religious Studies*, edited by Robert Orsi (Cambridge: Cambridge University Press, 2011), pp. 168–185.

Liljefors, Hanna. *Hebreiska bibeln debatterad: en receptionskritisk studie av diskurser om "Gamla testamentet" i svenska dagstidningar 1987–2017* (Uppsala: Artos Academic, 2022).

Lippestad, Geir. *Det Kan Vi Stå For* (Oslo: Aschehoug, 2014).

Lippestad, Geir. 'Vi skal ikke etterlyse en verdikamp med 22. juli som utgangspunkt'. *Aftenposten*, 8 June 2021, https://www.aftenposten.no/meninger/kronikk/i/X8KEbg/vi-skal-ikke-etterlyse-en-verdikamp-med-22-juli-som-utgangspunkt?fbclid=IwAR09mY2XLF4FhdkG2yQfxJuMxVXBc3jsm-i20zi7qyzIYlUPYAyhYVMC0gU.

Listhaug, Sylvi. *Der andre tier* (Oslo: Kagge Forlag, 2018).

Llewellyn, Dawn. '"But I still read the Bible!" Post-Christian Women's Biblicalism'. In *The Bible and Feminism: Remapping the Field*, edited by Yvonne Sherwood with the assistance of Anna Fisk (Oxford: Oxford University Press, 2017), pp. 567–588.

Lodge, Carey. 'Nigel Farage Promises "Muscular Defence" of Christianity in "Christian Manifesto"'. *Christian Today*, 28 April 2015.

Love, Velma. 'The Bible and Contemporary African American Culture I: Hermeneutical Forays, Observations, and Impressions'. In *African Americans and the Bible: Sacred Texts and Social Textures*, edited by Vincent Wimbush (Eugene, OR: Wipf & Stock, 2000), pp. 49–65.

Lundberg, Johanna Gustafsson. 'Christianity in a Post-Christian Context: Immigration, Church Identity, and the Role of Religion in Public Debates'. In *Religion in the European Refugee Crisis*, edited by Ulrich Schmiedel and Graeme Smith (London: Palgrave Macmillan, 2018), pp. 123–143.

Løland, Ole Jakob. 'The Norwegian 9/11: In the Church without a Bible'. *Political Theology* 18, no. 7 (2017): pp. 628–642.
Lövheim, Mia, and Linnea Jensdotter. 'Banal Religion and National Identity in Hybrid Media: "Heating" the Debate on Values and Veiling in Sweden'. *Nordic Journal of Religion and Society* 36, no. 2 (2023): pp. 95–108.
Macklin, Graham, and Tore Bjørgo. 'Breivik's Long Shadow? The Impact of the July 22, 2011 Attacks on the *Modus Operandi* of Extreme-right Lone Actor Terrorists'. *Perspectives on Terrorism* 15, no. 3 (2021): pp. 14–36.
Madden, Thomas F. *The Crusades Controversy: Setting the Record Straight* (North Palm Beach, FL: Wellspring, 2017).
Malkki, Leena, Mats Fridlund, and Daniel Sallamaa. 'Terrorism and Political Violence in the Nordic Countries'. *Terrorism and Political Violence* 30, no. 5 (2018): pp. 761–771.
Mammone, Andrew, Emmanuel Godin, and Brian Jenkins. 'Introduction: Mapping the "right of the mainstream right" in Contemporary Europe'. In *Mapping the Extreme Right in Contemporary Europe*, edited by Andrea Mammone, Emmanuel Godin, and Brian Jenkins (London: Routledge, 2012), pp. 1–14.
Manning, Erin, and Brian Massumi. *Thought in the Act: Passages in the Ecology of Experiences* (Minneapolis: University of Minnesota Press, 2014).
Martinson, Mattias. 'Towards a "Theology" of Christian Monumentality: Post-Christian Reflections on Grace and Nature'. In *Monument and Memory*, edited by Jonna Bornemark, Mattias Martinson, and Jayne Svenungsson (Berlin: Lit Verlag, 2015), pp. 21–42.
Martinson, Mattias. *Sekularism, populism, xenofobi: En essä om religionsdebatten* (Malmö: Eskaton, 2017).
Marzouki, Nadia, and Duncan McDonnell. 'Populism and Religion'. In *Saving the People: How Populists Hijack Religion*, edited by Nadia Marzouki, Duncan McDonnell, and Olivier Roy (London: Hurst & Co, 2016), pp. 1–11.
Massumi, Brian. *Politics of Affect* (Cambridge: Polity Press, 2015).
Masuzawa, Tomoko. *The Invention of World Religions: Or, How European Universalism Was Preserved in the Language of Pluralism* (Chicago: University of Chicago Press, 2005).
McLean, Bradley Hudson. *Deleuze, Guattari and the Machine in Early Christianity: Schizoanalysis, Affect and Multiplicity* (London: Bloomsbury, 2022).
Meer, Nasar. 'Racialization and Religion: Race, Culture and Difference in the Study of Antisemitism and Islamophobia'. In *Racialization and Religion: Race, Culture and Difference in the Study of Antisemitism and Islamophobia*, edited by Nasar Meer (London: Routledge, 2014), pp. 1–14.
Mencke, Christoph. *Theorie der Befreiung* (Berlin: Suhrkamp, 2022).
Miller, Seumas, Adam Henschke, and Jonas Feltes, eds. *Counter-Terrorism: The Ethical Issues* (Cheltenham: Edgar Elgar, 2021).
Minkenberg, Michael, Mats Deland, and Christin Mays. 'Introduction'. In *In the Tracks of Breivik: Far Right Networks in Northern and Eastern Europe*, edited by Mats Deland, Michael Minkenberg, and Christin Mays (Münster: Lit Verlag, 2013), pp. 9–18.
Moon, Sung-Jae, and Kyeong-Hwa Lee. 'Deleuzian Actualizations of the Multiplicative Concept: A Study of Perceptual Flows and the Transformation of Learning Assemblages'. *Educational Studies in Mathematics* 104 (2020): pp. 221–237.
Moore, Stephen D. 'A Bible That Expresses Everything While Communicating Nothing: Deleuze and Guattari's Cure for Interpretosis'. In *Biblical Exegesis without Authorial Intention? Interdisciplinary Approaches to Authorship and Meaning*, edited by Clarissa Breu (Leiden: Brill, 2019), pp. 108–125.
Moore, Stephen D. *The Bible after Deleuze: Affects, Assemblages, Bodies without Organs* (Oxford: Oxford University Press, 2022).
Moore, Stephen D., and Yvonne Sherwood. *The Invention of the Biblical Scholar: A Critical Manifesto* (Minneapolis, MN: Fortress, 2011).

Morey, Peter, and Amina Yaqin. *Framing Muslims: Stereotyping and Representation after 9/11* (Cambridge, MA: Harvard University Press, 2011).

Morse, Holly. *Encountering Eve's Afterlives: A New Reception Critical Approach to Genesis 2–4* (Oxford: Oxford University Press, 2020).

Moslener, Sara. 'Material World: Gender and the Bible in Evangelical Purity Culture'. In *The Bible and Feminism: Remapping the Field*, edited by Yvonne Sherwood with the assistance of Anna Fisk (Oxford: Oxford University Press, 2017), pp. 608–621.

Mudde, Cas. 'The Populist Zeitgeist'. *Government and Opposition* 39, no. 4 (2004): pp. 541–563.

Mudde, Cas. *Populist Radical Right Parties in Europe* (Cambridge: Cambridge University Press, 2007).

Myles, Robert. 'Biblical Literacy and *The Simpsons*'. In *Rethinking Biblical Literacy*, edited by Katie Edwards (London: Bloomsbury T&T Clark, 2015), pp. 143–162.

Naas, Michael. 'Introduction: For Example'. In Jacques Derrida, *The Other Heading: Reflections on Today's Europe*. Translated by Pascale-Anne Brault and Michael B. Naas (Bloomington: Indiana University Press, 1992), pp. vii–lix.

Nail, Thomas. 'What Is an Assemblage?' *SubStance* 46, no. 1 (2017): pp. 21–37.

Noort, Ed. 'Biblical Violence and the Task of the Exegete'. In *The Present State of Old Testament Studies in the Low Countries*, edited by Klaas Spronk (Leiden: Brill, 2016), pp. 180–191.

Nygaard, Axel Geard. 'Ti år'. *Klassekampen*, 22 July 2021.

Nykvist, Kato. 'Ti år etter terroren er vi flere som bør reflektere litt'. *Adresseavisen*, 22 July 2011.

O'Donnell, S. Jonathan. 'Islamophobic Conspiracism and Neoliberal Subjectivity: The Inassimilable Society'. *Patterns of Prejudice* 52, no. 1 (2019): pp. 1–23.

Oliphant, Elayne. *The Privilege of Being Banal: Art, Secularism and Catholicism in Paris* (Chicago: University of Chicago Press, 2021).

Omer, Atalia, and Jason A. Springs. *Religious Nationalism* (Santa Barbara, CA: ABC-CLIO, 2013).

Omer, Atalia, and Joshua Lupo. 'Introduction: The Cultural Logic of White Christian Nationalisms'. In *Religion, Populism, and Modernity: Confronting White Christian Nationalism and Racism*, edited by Atalia Omer and Joshua Lupo (Notre Dame, IN: University of Notre Dame Press, 2023), pp. 1–20.

Önnerfors, Andreas. 'Between Breivik and PEGIDA: The Absence of Ideologues and Leaders on the Contemporary European Far Right'. *Patterns of Prejudice* 51, no. 2 (2017): pp. 159–175.

Orsi, Robert A. *Between Heaven and Earth: The Religious Worlds People Make and the Scholars Who Study Them* (Princeton, NJ: Princeton University Press, 2005).

Pancevski, Bojan. 'Loser Who Lived with His Mum: The Pathetic Life of Mass Killer Anders Breivik'. *The Sunday Times*, 22 April 2012.

Park, Wongi. 'Multiracial Biblical Studies'. *Journal of Biblical Literature* 140, no. 3 (2021): pp. 435–459.

Paynter, Helen. *Blessed are the Peacemakers: A Biblical Theology of Human Violence* (Grand Rapids, MI: Zondervan, 2023).

Paynter, Helen, and Trevor Laurence. Eds. *Violent Biblical Texts: New Approaches* (Sheffield: Sheffield Phoenix Press, 2022).

Peace, Timothy. 'Religion and Populism in Britain: An Infertile Breeding Ground?' In *Saving the People: How Populists Hijack Religion*, edited by Nadia Marzouki, Duncan McDonnell, and Olivier Roy (London: Hurst & Co, 2016), pp. 95–108.

Pearson, Elizabeth. 'Extremism and Toxic Masculinity: The Man Wuestion Re-posed'. *International Affairs* 95, no. 6 (2019): pp. 1251–1270.

Pengelly, Martin. 'A Photo Op as Protests Swirled: How Trump Came to Walk to the Church'. *The Guardian*, 2 June, 2020. https://www.theguardian.com/us-news/2020/jun/02/trump-washington-walk-to-the-church-photo-op.

Perreau, Randi Johansen. 'Vi fikk sorgen og gleden rett i fanget'. *Adresseavisen*, 22 July 2011.

Perry, David. 'Introduction'. In *Whose Middle Ages? Teachable Moments for an Ill-Used Past*, edited by Andrew Albin, Mary C. Erler, Thomas O'Donnell, Nicholas L. Paul, and Nina Rowe (New York: Fordham University Press, 2019), pp. 1–8.

Phillips, Peter. 'The Pixelated Text: Reading the Bible within Digital Culture'. *Theology* 121, no. 6 (2018): pp. 403–412.

Phillips, Peter. *The Bible, Social Media, and Digital Culture* (London: Routledge, 2019).

Pidd, Helen, and Declan Lloyd. 'Police Investigate Far Right "Invasions" of Bradford and Glasgow Mosques', *The Guardian*, 13 May 2014, https://www.theguardian.com/world/2014/may/13/police-far-right-invasions-bradford-glasgow-mosques-britain-first.

Prior, Michael. *The Bible and Colonialism: A Moral Critique* (Sheffield: Sheffield Academic Press, 1997).

Pyper, Hugh. 'The Battle of the Books: The Bible versus the Vedas'. In *In the Name of God: The Bible in the Colonial Discourse of Empire*, edited by Carly Crouch and Jonathan Stökl (Leiden: Brill, 2013), pp. 169–187.

Pyper, Hugh. 'The Absent Bible: Oaths of Office in Scotland and the United States'. In *Challenging Contextuality: Bibles and Biblical Scholarship in Context*, edited by Louise Lawrence, Peter-Ben Smit, Hannah M. Strømmen, and Charlene Van der Walt (Oxford: Oxford University Press, forthcoming 2024).

Rane, Halim, Jacqui Ewart, and John Martinkus. *Media Framing of the Muslim World: Conflicts, Crises and Contexts* (Basingstoke: Palgrave Macmillan, 2014).

Rasmussen, Tarald. 'The Biblical Canon of the Lutheran Reformation'. In *Canon and Canonicity: The Formation and Use of Scripture*, edited by Einar Thomassen (Copenhagen: Museum Tusculanum Press, 2010), pp. 143–158.

Ravndal, Jacob Aasland. 'Anders Behring Breivik's Use of the Internet and Social Media'. *Journal Exit-Deutschland. Zeitschrift für Deradikalisierung Und Demokratische Kultur* 2 (2013): pp. 172–185.

Ravndal, Jacob Aasland. 'From Bombs to Books, and Back Again? Mapping Strategies of Right-Wing Revolutionary Resistance'. *Studies in Conflict and Terrorism* 46, no. 11 (2021): pp. 1–29.

Reddie, Anthony. *Dramatizing Theologies: A Participative Approach to Black God-Talk* (London: Routledge, 2006).

Reinhartz, Adele. *Bible and Cinema: An Introduction* (London: Routledge, 2013).

Renton, James, and Ben Gidley. *Antisemitism and Islamophobia in Europe: A Shared Story?* (London: Palgrave Macmillan, 2017).

Rindge, Matthew S. *Bible and Film: The Basics* (Abingdon: Routledge, 2022).

Ringrose, Jessica. 'Beyond Discourse? Using Deleuze and Guattari's Schizoanalysis to Explore Affective Assemblages, Heterosexually Striated Space, and Lines of Flight Online and at School'. *Educational Philosophy and Theory* 43, no. 6 (2011): pp. 598–618.

Roberts, Colin H., and T. C. Skeat. *The Birth of the Codex* (London: Oxford University Press, 1987).

Robinson, Gnana. *1 and 2 Samuel* (Grand Rapids, MI: W.B Eerdmans, 1993).

Rogerson, J. W. *Introduction to the Bible* (London: Routledge, 2006).

Roy, Eleanor Ainge, Harriet Sherwood, and Nazia Parveen. 'Christchurch Attack: Suspect Had White Supremacist Symbols on Weapons'. *The Guardian*, 15 March 2019, https://www.theguardian.com/world/2019/mar/15/christchurch-shooting-new-zealand-suspect-white-supremacist-symbols-weapons.

Roy, Olivier. 'Beyond Populism: The Conservative Right, the Courts, the Churches and the Concept of a Christian Europe'. In *Saving the People: How Populists Hijack Religion*, edited by Nadia Marzouki, Duncan McDonnell, and Olivier Roy (London: Hurst & Co, 2016), pp. 185–201.

Roy, Oliver. 'The French National Front: From Christian Identity to Laïcité'. In *Saving the People: How Populists Hijack Religion*, edited by Nadia Marzouki, Duncan McDonnell, and Olivier Roy (London: Hurst & Co, 2016), pp. 79–93.

Runions, Erin. *The Babylon Complex: Theopolitical Fantasies of War, Sex and Sovereignty* (New York: Fordham University Press, 2014).

S, Tonje. 'Mitt Utøya'. Testimony published on the 22 July Centre website, 2016, https://www.22julisenteret.no/aktuelt/artikler/tonje-s.

Salomonsen, Jone. 'Kristendom, paganisme og kvinnefiendskap'. In *Akademiske Perspektiver På 22. Juli*, edited by Anders Ravik Jupskås (Bergen: Fagbokforlaget, 2012), pp. 74–89.

Salomonsen, Jone. 'Graced Life After All? Terrorism and Theology on July 22, 2011'. *Dialog: A Journal of Theology* 54, no.3 (2015), 249–259.

Sanders, Cheryl J. 'African Americans, the Bible, and Spiritual Formation'. In *African Americans and the Bible: Sacred Texts and Social Textures*, edited by Vincent Wimbush (Eugene, OR: Wipf & Stock, 2000), pp. 588–602.

Sauer, Birgit, and Edma Ajanovic. 'Hegemonic Discourses of Difference and Inequality: Right-Wing Organisations in Austria'. In *The Rise of the Far Right in Europe: Populist Shifts and 'Othering'*, edited by Gabriella Lazaridis, Giovanna Campani, and Anne Benveniste (New York: Palgrave Macmillan, 2016), pp. 81–108.

Saul, Ben. *Defining Terrorism in International Law* (Oxford: Oxford University Press, 2008).

Schmiedel, Ulrich. *Elasticized Ecclesiology: The Concept of Community after Ernst Troeltsch* (London: Palgrave MacMillian, 2017).

Schmiedel, Ulrich. '"We Can Do This!" Tackling the Political Theology of Populism'. In *Religion in the European Refugee Crisis*, edited by Ulrich Schmiedel and Graeme Smith (New York: Palgrave Macmillan, 2018), pp. 205–224.

Schmiedel, Ulrich. '"Take Up Your Cross": Public Theology between Populism and Pluralism in the Post-Migrant Context'. *International Journal of Public Theology* 13, no. 2 (2019): pp. 140–162.

Schmiedel, Ulrich. 'Introduction: Political Theology in the Spirit of Populism—Methods and Metaphors'. In *The Spirit of Populism: Political Theologies in Polarized Times*, edited by Ulrich Schmiedel and Joshua Ralston (Leiden: Brill, 2021), pp. 1–22.

Schmiedel, Ulrich. 'The Cracks in the Category of Christianism: A Call for Ambiguity in the Conceptualization of Christianity'. In *Contemporary Christian-Cultural Values: Migration Encounters in the Nordic Region*, edited by Cecilia Nahnfeldt and Kaia S. Rønsdal (London: Routledge, 2021), pp. 164–182.

Schmiedel, Ulrich. *Terror und Theologie: Der religionstheoretische Diskurs der 9/11-Dekade* (Tübingen: Mohr Siebeck, 2021).

Scholz, Susanne. 'Introduction: The Past, the Present, and the Future of Feminist Hebrew Bible Interpretation'. In *Feminist Interpretation of the Hebrew Bible in Retrospect, Volume I: Biblical Books*, edited by Susanne Scholz (Sheffield: Sheffield Phoenix Press, 2017), pp. 1–10.

Schwartz, Regina. *The Curse of Cain: The Violent Legacy of Monotheism* (Chicago: University of Chicago Press, 1997).

Scruton, Roger. *The West and the Rest: Globalization and the Terrorist Threat* (London: Continuum, 2002).

Scruton, Roger. *Modern Culture*, 4th ed. (London: Bloomsbury, 2018).

Seesengood, Robert Paul. 'Bespoke Words: The Bible, Fashion, and the Mechanism(s) of Things'. *The Bible and Critical Theory* 16, no. 2 (2020): pp. 50–58.

Seesengood, Robert Paul, and Andrew Wilson. 'Biblical Stuff: (Re)reading the Bible as/with/through/by Materiality'. *The Bible and Critical Theory* 16, no. 2 (2020), pp. 1–6.

Segovia, Fernando F. 'Minority Biblical Criticism: Reading Texts Together as Critical Project'. In *Reading Biblical Texts Together: Pursuing Minoritized Biblical Criticism*, edited by Tat-siong Benny Liew and Fernando F. Segovia (Atlanta, GA: SBL Press, 2022), pp. 3–43.

Seibert, Eric. *Disturbing Divine Behaviour: Troubling Old Testament Images of God* (Minneapolis, MN: Fortress, 2009).

Seibert, Eric. *The Violence of Scripture: Overcoming the Old Testament's Troubling Legacy* (Minneapolis, MN: Fortress Press, 2012).

Semati, Mehdi. 'Islamophobia, Culture and Race in the Age of Empire'. *Cultural Studies* 24, no. 2 (2010): pp. 256–275.
Sheehan, Jonathan. *The Enlightenment Bible: Translation, Scholarship, Culture* (Princeton, NJ: Princeton University Press, 2013).
Sherwood, Yvonne. *A Biblical Text and its Afterlives: The Survival of Jonah in Western Culture* (Cambridge: Cambridge University Press, 2001).
Sherwood, Yvonne. 'Feminist Scholarship'. In *The Oxford Illustrated History of the Bible*, edited by John Rogerson (Oxford: Oxford University Press, 2001), pp. 296–329.
Sherwood, Yvonne. *Biblical Blaspheming: Trials of the Sacred for a Secular Age* (Cambridge: Cambridge University Press, 2012).
Sherwood, Yvonne. 'Comparing the "Telegraph Bible" of the Late British Empire to the Chaotic Bible of the Sixteenth Century Spanish Empire: Beyond the Canaan Mandate into Anxious Parables of the Land'. In *In the Name of God: The Bible in the Colonial Discourse of Empire*, edited by C. L. Crouch and Jonathan Stökl (Leiden: Brill, 2014), pp. 5–62.
Sherwood, Yvonne. 'Introduction: The Bible and Feminism: Remapping the Field'. In *The Bible and Feminism: Remapping the Field*, edited by Yvonne Sherwood with the assistance of Anna Fisk (Oxford: Oxford University Press, 2017), pp. 1–11.
Sherwood, Yvonne, and Jonneke Bekkenkamp. 'Introduction: The Thin Blade of Difference between Real Swords and Words about "Sharp-edged Iron Things"—Reflections on How People Use the Word'. In *Sanctified Aggression: Legacies of Biblical and Post-Biblical Vocabularies of Violence*, edited by Jonneke Bekkenkamp and Yvonne Sherwood (London: T&T Clark, 2003), pp. 1–9.
Shin, SuJung. 'A "Vital Materiality" of the Ark in Its Relativity to the Body of David in 2 Sam 6'. *The Bible and Critical Theory* 16, no. 2 (2020): pp. 7–22.
Shropshire, James M., Ida Rousseau Mukenge, Victoria Erickson, and Hans A. Baer. 'The Bible and Contemporary African American Culture II'. In *African Americans and the Bible: Sacred Texts and Social Textures*, edited by Vincent Wimbush (Eugene, OR: Wipf & Stock, 2000), pp. 66–80.
Siker, Jeffrey S. *Liquid Scripture: The Bible in a Digital World* (Minneapolis, MN: Fortress Press, 2017).
Simpson, Patricia Anne. 'Mobilizing Meanings: Translocal Identities of the Far Right Web'. *German Politics and Society* 34, no. 4 (2016): pp. 34–53.
Skottki, Kristin. 'The Dead, the Revived and the Recreated Pasts: "Structural Amnesia" in Representations of Crusade History'. In *Perceptions of the Crusades from the Nineteenth to the Twenty-First Century, Engaging the Crusades Vol. 1*, edited by Mike Horswell and Jonathan Phillips (London: Routledge, 2018), pp. 107–132.
Smith, Abraham. 'Aaron Douglas, the Harlem Renaissance, and Biblical Art: Toward a Radical Politics of Identity'. In *African Americans and the Bible: Sacred Texts and Social Textures*, edited by Vincent Wimbush (Eugene, OR: Wipf & Stock, 2000), pp. 682–695.
Smith, Eric C. 'The Affordances of bible and the Agency of Material in Assemblage'. *The Bible and Critical Theory* 18, no. 1 (2022): pp. 1–13.
Smith, Katherine Allen. 'The Crusader Conquest of Jerusalem and Christ's Cleansing of the Temple'. In *The Uses of the Bible in Crusader Sources*, edited by Elizabeth Lapina and Nicholas Morton (Leiden: Brill, 2017), pp. 19–41.
Snape, Michael. *God and the British Soldier: Religion and the British Army in the First and Second World Wars* (London: Routledge, 2005).
Soper, J. Christopher, and Joel S. Fetzer. *Religion and Nationalism in Global Perspective*. (Cambridge: Cambridge University Press, 2018).
Sparks, Kenton L. *Sacred Word, Broken Word: Biblical Authority and the Dark Side of Scripture* (Grand Rapids, MI: Eerdmans, 2012).
Spencer, Robert. *Religion of Peace? Why Christianity Is and Islam Isn't* (Washington, DC: Regnery Publishing, 2007).

Spencer, Robert. *Not Peace but a Sword: The Great Chasm between Christianity and Islam* (San Diego, CA: Catholic Answers, 2013).
Spinoza, Baruch. *Ethics* (London: Penguin, 1994).
Stalsberg, Linn. 'Det enkle er ofte det verste'. *Agenda*, 21 July 2021.
Stanley, Brian. *The Bible and the Flag: Protestant Missions and British Imperialism in the Nineteenth and Twentieth Centuries* (Leicester: Apollos, 1990).
Steussy, Marti J. *David* (Columbia: University of South Carolina Press, 1999).
Stichele, Caroline van de, and Hugh Pyper. *Text, Image, and Otherness in Children's Bibles: What Is in the Picture?* (Leiden: Brill, 2012).
Storch, Beatrix von. 'Grußwort'. In *Warum Christen AfD wählen*, edited by Joachim Kuhs (Eßbach: Arnshaugh Verlag, 2018), pp. 11–13.
Stordalen, Terje. 'Canon and Canonical Commentary: Comparative Perspectives on Canonical Ecologies'. In *The Formative Past and the Formation of the Future: Collective Remembering and Identity Formation*, edited by Terje Stordalen and Saphinaz Naguib (Oslo: Novus, 2015), pp. 133–160.
Stordalen, Terje. 'The Production of Authority in Levantine Scriptural Ecologies: An Example of Accumulative Cultural Production'. In *Levantine Entanglements: Cultural Productions, Long-Term Changes and Globalizations in the Eastern Mediterranean*, edited by Terje Stordalen and Øystein S. LaBianca (Sheffield: Equinox, 2021), pp. 322–372.
Stordalen, Terje, and Saphinaz Naguib. 'Time, Media, Space: Perspectives on the Ecology of Collective Remembering'. In *The Formative Past and the Formation of the Future: Collective Remembering and Identity Formation*, edited by Terje Stordalen and Saphinaz Naguib (Oslo: Novus, 2015), pp. 17–37.
Stratton, Beverly J. 'Consider, Take Counsel, and Speak: Re(Membering) Women in the Book of Joshua and Judges'. In *Feminist Interpretation of the Hebrew Bible in Retrospect: Volume 1: Biblical Books*, edited by Susanne Scholz (Sheffield: Sheffield Phoenix Press, 2017), pp. 80–109.
Strømmen, Hannah M. 'Christian Terror in Europe? The Bible in Anders Behring Breivik's Manifesto'. *The Journal of the Bible and its Reception* 4, no. 1 (2017): pp. 147–169.
Strømmen, Hannah M. 'Goliatmyten: Bibelbruk i høyrepopulistiske og høyreekstreme miljøer'. In *Populisme og kristendom*, edited by Sturla Stålseth, Kristin Graff Kallevåg, and Sven Thore Kloster (Oslo: Cappelen Damm, 2021), pp. 86–101.
Strømmen, Hannah M. 'Scripts and Scriptures of Populism: On Populist Reading Practices'. In *The Spirit of Populism: Political Theologies in Polarized Times*, edited by Ulrich Schmiedel and Joshua Ralston (Leiden: Brill, 2022), pp. 85–100.
Strømmen, Hannah M. 'A Nordic Far Right Bible? Right-wing Biblical Assemblages and the Role of Reception History'. In *The Nordic Bible: Bible Reception in Contemporary Nordic Societies*, edited by Marianne Bjelland Kartzow, Outi Lehtipuu, and Kasper Bro Larsen (Berlin: De Gruyter, 2023), pp. 39–59.
Strømmen, Hannah M. 'Crusades, Christ and Christmas: Islamophobia and the Bible in the European Far-Right after 9/11'. *Zeitschrift für Religion, Gesellschaft und Politik* 7, no. 2 (2023): pp. 711–728, https://doi.org/10.1007/s41682-023-00148-1.
Strømmen, Hannah, and Ulrich Schmiedel. *The Claim to Christianity: Responding to the Far Right* (London: SCM Press, 2021).
Strømmen, Øyvind. *Det Mørke Nettet: Om Høyreekstremisme, kontrajihadisme og terror i Europa* (Oslo: Cappelen Damm, 2012).
Strømmen, Øyvind. *I Hatets Fotspor* (Oslo: Cappelen Damm, 2014).
Stuckey, Sterling. '"My Burden Lightened": Frederick Douglass, the Bible, and Slave Culture'. In *African Americans and the Bible: Sacred Texts and Social Textures*, edited by Vincent Wimbush (Eugene, OR: Wipf & Stock, 2000), pp. 251–265.
Svenungsson, Jayne. 'Christian Europe: Borders and Boundaries of a Mythological Conception'. In *Transcending Europe: Beyond Universalism and Particularism*, edited by

Susanna Lingberg, Mika Ojakangas, and Sergei Prozorov (New York: Palgrave Macmillan, 2014), pp. 120–134.
Svenungsson, Jayne. 'Religion and Secularity as Supersessionist Categories'. *Zeitschrift für Religion, Gesellschaft und Politik* 7, no. 2 (2023): pp. 751–763, https://doi.org/10.1007/s41682-023-00156-1
Swami, Praveen. 'Norwegian Mass Killer's Manifesto Hails Hindutva'. *The Hindu*, 26 July 2011, https://www.thehindu.com/news/national/norwegian-mass-killers-manifesto-hails-hindutva/article2293829.ece.
Sørensen, Øystein. 'En totalitær mentalitet: det ideologiske tankegodset i Anders Behring Breiviks manifest'. In *Akademiske Perspektiver På 22. Juli*, edited by Anders Ravik Jupskås (Bergen: Fagbokforlaget, 2012), pp. 103–114.
Taras, Raymond. '"Islamophobia Never Stands Still": Race, Religion, and Culture'. In *Racialization and Religion: Race, Culture and Difference in the Study of Antisemitism and Islamophobia*, edited by Nasar Meer (London: Routledge, 2014), pp. 33–49.
Thomassen, Einar. 'Some Notes on the Development of Christian Ideas about a Canon'. In *Canon and Canonicity: The Formation and Use of Scripture*, edited by Einar Thomassen (Copenhagen: Museum Tusculanum Press, 2010), pp. 9–28.
Tollerton, David. *A New Hollywood Moses: on the Spectacle and Reception of Exodus: Gods and Kings* (London: Bloomsbury, 2017).
Topolski, Anya. 'A Genealogy of the "Judeo-Christian" Signifier: A Tale of Europe's Identity Crisis'. In *Is there a Judeo-Christian Tradition? A European Perspective*, edited by Emmanuel Nathan and Anya Topolski (Berlin: De Gruyter, 2016), pp. 267–283.
Toscano, Alberto. *Fanaticism: On the Uses of an Idea* (London: Verso, 2010).
Trible, Phyllis. *Texts of Terror: Literary-Feminist Readings of Biblical Narratives* (Philadelphia: Fortress Press, 1984).
Turner, Bryan S. *Religion and Modern Society: Citizenship, Secularisation and the State* (Cambridge: Cambridge University Press, 2011).
Turner, Eric G. *Typology of the Early Codex* (Philadelphia: University of Pennsylvania Press, 1977).
Ujamaa Centre for Community Development & Research, *Doing Contextual Bible Study: A Resource Manual* (2014), (http://ujamaa.ukzn.ac.za/Libraries/manuals/Ujamaa_CBS_bible_study_Manual_part_1_2.sflb.ashx.
Vetlesen, Arne Johan. 'Ondskap som perspektiv på hendelsene 22. juli'. In *Akademiske Perspektiver På 22. Juli*, edited by Anders Ravik Jupskås (Bergen: Fagbokforlaget, 2012), pp. 93–101.
Vries, Hent de. *Philosophy and the Turn to Religion* (Baltimore, MD: Johns Hopkins University Press, 1999).
Walsh, Richard. *Reading the Gospels in the Dark: Portrayals of Jesus in Film* (San Antonio, TX: Trinity Press, 2003).
Walsh, Richard. *T&T Clark Companion to the Bible and Film* (London: T&T Clark, 2018).
Walton, Stephen J. 'Anti-feminism and Misogyny in Breivik's "Manifesto"'. *Nordic Journal of Feminist and Gender Research* 20, no. 1 (2012): pp. 4–11.
Westfield, N. Lynne. 'Life-Giving Stories: The Bible in a Congregation'. In *African Americans and the Bible: Sacred Texts and Social Textures*, edited by Vincent Wimbush (Eugene, OR: Wipf & Stock, 2000), pp. 577–587.
Whitehouse, Ginny. 'The Murderer's Salute: News Images of Breivik's Defiance after Killing 77 in Oslo'. *Journal of Mass Media Ethics* 28, no. 1 (2013): pp. 57–59.
Wiederer, Ralf. 'Mapping the Right-Wing Extremist Movement on the Internet—Structural Patterns 2006–2011'. In *In the Tracks of Breivik: Far Right Networks in Northern and Eastern Europe*, edited by Mats Deland, Michael Minkenberg, and Christin Mays (Münster: Lit Verlag, 2013), pp. 19–51.
Williams, Maggie M. '"Celtic" Crosses and the Myth of Whiteness'. In *Whose Middle Ages? Teachable Moments for an Ill-Used Past*, edited by Andrew Albin, Mary C. Erler, Thomas

O'Donnell, Nicholas L. Paul, and Nina Rowe (New York: Fordham University Press, 2019), pp. 220–232.

Williams, Maggie M. 'Mobilizing Religion in Twenty-First-Century Nativism in the United States'. In *Religion in Rebellions, Revolutions, and Social Movements*, edited by Warren S. Goldstein and Jean-Pierre Reed (London: Routledge, 2022), pp. 199–218.

Williams, Rhys H. 'Civil Religion and the Cultural Politics of Immigration in Obama's America'. *Journal for the Scientific Study of Religion* 52, no. 2 (2013): pp. 239–257.

Willis, Ika. *Reception* (London: Routledge, 2017).

Wilson, Angelia R., and Cynthia Burack. '"Where Liberty Reigns and God Is Supreme": The Christian Right and the Tea Party Movement'. *New Political Science* 34, no. 2 (2012), pp. 172–190.

Wimbush, Vincent. Ed. *African Americans and the Bible: Sacred Texts and Social Textures* (Eugene, OR: Wipf & Stock, 2000).

Wimbush, Vincent. 'Introduction: Reading Darkness, Reading Scriptures'. In *African Americans and the Bible: Sacred Texts and Social Textures*, edited by Vincent Wimbush (Eugene, OR: Wipf & Stock, 2000), pp. 1–43.

Wimbush, Vincent. *White Men's Magic: Scripturalization as Slavery* (Oxford: Oxford University Press, 2012).

Wise, J. Macgregor. 'Assemblage'. In *Giles Deleuze: Key Concepts*, edited by Charles J. Stivale (Montreal and Kingston: McGill-Queen's University Press, 2005), pp. 77–87.

Wodak, Ruth. *The Politics of Fear: What Right-Wing Populist Discourses Mean* (London: Sage, 2015).

Wooden, R. Glenn. 'The Role of "the Septuagint" in the Formation of the Biblical Canon'. In *Exploring the Origins of the Bible: Canon Formation in Historical, Literary, and Theological Perspective*, edited by Craig A. Evans and Emmanuel Tov (Grand Rapids, MI: Baker Academic, 2008), pp. 129–146.

Yancy, George. *Look, a White! Philosophical Essays on Whiteness* (Philadelphia: Temple University Press, 2012).

Ye'or, Bat. *Understanding Dhimmitude: Twenty-One Lectures and Talks on the Position of Non-Muslims in Islamic Societies* (New York: RVP Press, 2013).

Økland, Jorunn. 'Feminismen, tradisjonen og forventning'. In *Akademiske Perspektiver På 22. Juli*, edited by Anders Ravik Jupskås (Bergen: Fagbokforlaget, 2012), pp. 115–128.

Økland, Jorunn. 'Manifestos, Gender, Self-Canonization, and Violence'. In *The Bible and Feminism: Remapping the Field*, edited by Yvonne Sherwood, with the assistance of Anna Fisk (Oxford: Oxford University Press, 2017), pp. 15–44.

Index

For the benefit of digital users, indexed terms that span two pages (e.g., 52–53) may, on occasion, appear on only one of those pages.

9/11, 3, 8, 15–16, 89, 120–21, 166–67, 188–89, 206–7

abolition, 229–30, 255–56
actor network theory, 71–72
affect, 34, 41–42, 51–52, 53–54, 72–75, 76–77, 78, 79–80, 89–90, 100–1, 102–3, 142–43, 157–58, 163, 174–75, 198, 202–3, 207–8, 209–10, 211, 218–22, 226–27, 232–33, 236–38, 239–42, 243–44, 248, 253, 257–58, 259–60, 264, 265–66, 269, 271–73, 276, 281–82, 284, 285, 286, 289, 295–96, 297–99, 301–2, 310, 311–12
agency, 41–42, 69–75, 80, 172–74, 200–1, 249–50, 258, 282–83, 298–300
aggrieved entitlement, 170–74, 292–93
Ahmed, Sara, 52–53, 72–74, 141, 218, 220–21, 289
anti-abortion, 263–64
antifeminism, 2–3, 170. *See also* misogyny
anti-immigration, 2–3, 17–18, 39–40, 149–50, 203–4, 209
antisemitism, 2–3, 118–20, 212–13
Assemblage Theory, 55–59
atheist, atheism, 89–90, 122, 127, 132–33, 156–57, 180, 209, 280
attachment, 1, 70–72, 219–20, 244, 259–60, 262–64, 267–68, 271, 272–73, 274–76, 281, 283, 284–85, 286, 295–96, 297, 299–300, 301
AUF, vii, 5–6
authority
    biblical/scriptural, 27, 31, 33–34, 35, 37, 65–66, 92, 194–97, 209, 223–24, 228–34, 235, 236–37, 240–41, 243–44, 262–63, 297
    canonical, 62, 65–66
    cultural, 196–98
    divine, 138, 143–44, 188, 210
    religious, 189–90, 310–11
    removing, 94–95
    theological, 194, 196–98

banal, 33–34, 41–42, 49–52, 80, 167–68, 211, 287–88
Bathsheba, 45–46
becoming, 53–54, 65–66, 75, 160–61, 246–47, 249–51, 253, 258–59, 260–62, 273, 282–83, 284, 311–12
Bernard of Clairvaux, 160–61
BibleLab, 244, 264, 271–83, 284–86, 298–300, 301, 306, 311–12
biblical
    criticism/scholars/scholarship
        African-American, 212, 244–45, 308–9
        Asian, 244–45
        contextual, 212, 272, 276–79, 283
        feminist, 73, 209, 212, 301–3, 308–9
        historical-critical, 209, 235
        Latinx, 244–45
        minority, 244, 257–59
        modern, 42–43, 240
        postcolonial, 244, 245, 252, 259–60, 274, 301–3
        Queer, 73, 244–45, 252n.37, 308–9
        traditional, 42–43, 303–4, 306–7
        womanist, 209, 212, 234, 236–37, 244–45, 308–9
    literacy, 33–34, 223–24, 278–79
    values, 51–52, 111, 115–16, 122–29, 138–39, 197–98, 291
biblical reception
    criticism, 283n.202, 308–10
    history, 33n.207, 34, 35, 40, 41–45, 75–76, 214, 305–6, 308–10
bibliocentrism, 41–42, 45–49, 76–77
Black, Blackness, 82, 99–100, 164–65, 236–37, 254–57, 309–10
Brague, Rémi, 36, 176–85, 187–88, 193, 197–98, 207–8, 293–94
Britain First, 15–16, 39–40, 141, 176
Brundtland, Gro Harlem, 6n.23, 170
Bush, George W., 66

Catholic, 17–18, 26–27, 31–32, 62, 67, 89–90, 104–5, 108, 122, 124, 127, 129–30, 132, 135, 199–200
Christendom, 24–25, 103–4, 106–7, 109, 111, 125–26, 136–37, 164–66, 174, 292–93
Christian
 canon, 62, 69
 conservative, 25–27, 150–51
 Europe, 1, 5–6, 12–13, 20, 22, 23–24, 26–27, 37–38, 87, 88, 99–100, 104–5, 108, 111, 114–15, 123, 147–48, 164, 165–67, 169–70, 181–83, 195, 291, 294–95
 heritage, 21–22
 nationalism, 23n.139, 149–50
Christology, Christological, 225–27, 296–97
class, 171, 174, 205–6, 210, 245, 274, 293–94
classroom, 219–20, 263–64, 271–74, 280, 283, 285, 298–300
colonial
 Bible/Bible-use, 177, 198–99, 200, 201–2, 207–8, 252–53, 254–55, 259–60, 274–75
 era, 36, 193, 198–200, 202, 293–94
 missions, 201–2, 254, 274
colonialism, 200, 252, 284, 294n.6, 298
conservative
 anti-Marxist, 103–4, 110
 British, 51–52, 184–85
 Catholic, 17–18 (*see also* Christian: conservative)
 Church, 90–91
 cultural, 86–87, 92–93, 95–96
 movements, 14–15
 national, 26–27
 neo-, 118–19
 party, 184–85, 300–1
 philosophy, 184–85, 287
 Republican, 150–51
 right, 92
 vision of the family, 156
conspiracy, 1, 2, 11–12, 18–19, 35–36, 46, 84, 86–89, 91–92, 97–98, 102–3, 111, 115, 117, 118–20, 138–40, 142, 143–44, 147–48, 150, 157–58, 171, 289–90, 291–92, 294–95
Constitution
 Christian, 21–22
 US, 150, 152–54, 155
counterjihadist/m, 11–15, 36, 69, 84, 86–88, 89–90, 97–100, 102–3, 104, 107, 109, 111, 114–15, 116–20, 122–23, 125–26, 137–40, 143–44, 147–48, 150, 153, 157–58, 161, 167–69, 176–77, 178–79, 183–84, 203–4, 207–8, 287, 290, 291–92, 293–95, 300–1

crusades, crusader, 5–6, 27, 31–32, 36, 87, 90, 92–93, 98–101, 102–3, 106–7, 111, 113, 125–26, 130, 142–44, 158–69, 170–71, 172–74, 290–93
cultural
 Bible, 67–68, 186–87, 195–99, 201–3
 heritage, 58–59, 90–91n.64, 177, 180–81, 194, 198–99, 252
 identity, 89, 204–5, 252, 274–75, 294
culture
 Christian, 5–6, 19–20, 23, 127, 164–65, 200–1, 290–91, 294
 common, 89, 185, 186–88, 195
 high, 50, 185–87, 283, 304–5
 Judeo-Christian, 21–22, 123, 128–29
 modern, 185, 186, 188–89, 191–92
 popular, 50, 67–68
curation, curator, 259–60, 282–83, 283n.202

Daniel, 43–44, 90, 154
David and Goliath, 99–100, 112, 146–47
decanonization, 230, 232–33, 243–44, 297
demythologizing, 229
Deus vult, 163–64, 165–67
Douglass, Frederick, 255–56

eco-activist, 280, 285
emotion, 73–75, 74n.192, 186–87, 218–21, 226–27, 238, 243–44, 260–61, 263, 300–1
empire
 Assyrian, 215–16
 British, 199–201
 Byzantine, 165
 Roman, 127, 187–88, 200
 Spanish, 199–200
Enlightenment, the, 45–46, 117, 188, 194–202
ethics, 229–30, 308. *See also* normative/normativity
ethnocentrism, 17–18, 21, 86–87, 210–11
ethology, 305–6
Eurabia, 11–12, 36, 86–88, 97–98, 102–3, 111, 115, 117–26, 130–31, 138–40, 143–44, 147–48, 157–58, 161, 172, 176–77, 178–79, 203–4, 290–92. *See also* conspiracy; counterjihadist/m
Europe, Western, 17, 19–20, 21, 23–24, 33–35, 86–87, 105–6, 116, 121, 165, 203–4
European
 culture, 16, 21–22, 86–87, 96, 105–6, 111–12, 120–21, 124, 128, 139, 172, 176–80, 183, 193–95, 199–200, 207–8, 252, 293–94
 identity, vii–viii, 1, 104–5, 287
Evangelical
 American, 64–65, 91–92, 142, 150–51

British, 254–55
Protestants, 149–50, 200–1
White, 255
Exodus, 51–52, 90, 94–95, 161–62, 186–87
extremism, 3, 7–8, 10–11, 25–26, 87, 115, 167–68, 203–4, 285–86, 293, 300–1

fanaticism, 3
Felski, Rita, 41, 70–72, 221, 241–42, 263, 272–, 73–, 310–11
fiction, 169–70, 238, 309–10
film, 34, 42–43, 51–52, 62–63, 67–68, 132, 134–35, 238, 263, 272–73, 274n.179, 278–79, 311
First World War, 36, 142–43, 158, 161–63, 292
Fremskrittspartiet (The Progress Party), 14, 51–52, 300–1

gender
  equality, 170–71
  hierarchy, 87
  ideology, 64–65
  neutral, 106–8
  See also masculinity
Good Samaritan, the, 32, 39–40

Hagar, 234, 309–10
Herder, Johann Gottfried, 124, 204–5
Herod, 94, 160–61
Hinduism, 26–27
hope, 311–12
Huntington, Samuel P., 88–89, 190–91, 197–98, 202–7

Jesus
  Christ, 39–40, 51–52, 64–65, 67–68, 95, 103–4, 127, 141, 158–61, 180, 191–93, 226–27, 229–30
  soldiers of, 98–100
  sword-bearing, 32, 115–16, 122–23, 129–34, 138–40, 161, 172–74, 291
Jihad, 14–15, 89–90, 100–1, 108–9, 117–18, 124–26, 131, 135–37, 167
Joan of Arc, 39–40, 141
Johnson, Boris, 51–52, 184–85
Judaism, 2–3, 61, 117, 119–21, 123, 180–83, 187
Judeo-Christian, 21–22, 104–5, 108–9, 117–18, 122–27, 139, 153, 207. *See also* Judeo-Christian culture

King James Bible, 63–64, 66, 90–91, 98–99, 106–7, 109, 198n.129
King Jr, Martin Luther, 257
Knights Templar, 12–13n.69, 87, 99–100, 161

Latour, Bruno, 41, 70–76
Lone Wolf terrorism, 8–11, 10n.52
Luther, Martin, 62–63, 69, 127–28

Manning, Erin, 244, 264–74, 298–99
Martyr/martyrdom, 32, 87, 92–93, 96, 100–1, 129–30, 131, 133–40, 150, 153–54, 291
Mary, mother of Jesus, 67–68, 107
masculinity, 36, 98, 141–43, 163–74, 292–93
Massumi, Brian, 41, 77–78, 260–81, 298–99, 311–12
materiality, 41–42, 48, 65–66, 72–73
medievalism, 49–52, 167–68. *See also* Middle Ages
micropolitics/micropolitical, 270–71, 281, 285
Middle Ages, 45–46, 49–52, 102–3, 141–43, 160–61, 163–69. *See also* medievalism
misogyny, 46, 98, 170–71, 172–74, 233–34, 236–40, 279–80, 297–98, 308–9
mission/missionaries, 136–37, 152, 200–2, 228, 252–54, 274
Moses, 51–52, 128–29, 154, 186–87
multiculturalism, 16, 22–23, 84–85, 86–87, 92–93, 95–98, 110, 117, 130–31, 134–35, 171–72
multiplicity, 55–56, 59–60, 230–31, 246–47, 305

nationalism, 3–5, 10–11, 17–18, 23–24, 26–27, 39–40, 86–87, 102, 104, 141, 149–50, 164–65, 198–99. *See also* Christian: nationalism
nativism/nativist, 17–18, 149–50, 156–57, 178–79
Nestle-Aland Novum Testamentum Graece, 61, 63–64, 66
Noah, 62–63, 67–68
normative/normativity, 1, 28–29, 32, 37, 196–98, 214, 233–34, 238, 239–40, 244–47, 252, 295, 297–303
Norse/Pagan mythology, 26–27, 46, 101–2. *See also* pagan
nostalgia, 50, 77–78, 107, 171–75, 292–93

occidental, 104
ontology, ontological, 44, 122, 216–22, 295–96

pagan/paganism, 26–27, 31–32, 89–90, 101–3, 170–71, 196–97. *See also* Norse myth
paranoid/paranoia, 168, 171, 218–19, 237–38
patriarchy, 31–32, 73, 84, 86–87, 99–100, 107–10, 169–74, 220–21, 233–37, 238–40, 243–44, 258–59, 278, 297–98, 308–9
Paul, the Apostle, 62, 127, 129–30, 131–32, 154, 162, 180–81, 187–88, 191–93, 210, 215–16, 219–20, 229–30n.88, 255–57, 262–63

pedagogy, 47–48, 58–59, 195–98, 264–65, 285, 298–99
persecution, 27, 39–40, 100–1, 102–4, 111, 130–31, 141, 143–44, 200, 207, 210, 290
political correctness, 86–87, 105, 106–7, 111, 188–89, 290–91
populist/populism
  distinctions, 193
  religion of, 24–25, 33–34
  right-wing, 14–17, 21, 24–25, 28–29, 99–100, 104–5, 109–10, 116–21, 287–88
  traits, 152
propaganda, 19–20, 82, 89, 106–7, 168, 207
prophet, prophetic, 115–16, 122–23, 134–40, 142, 155–56, 179–80, 191–92, 199–200, 234, 291
Protestant, 26–27, 32n.204, 33–34, 62, 67, 89, 108, 130, 149–50, 200–2
purity, purification, 64–65, 85, 109–10, 142–43, 159–61, 167, 178–79, 193

Qur'an (Koran), 13, 39–40, 100–1, 123, 124–26, 129–31, 135–36, 183, 189–92, 293, 294

race, 3–5, 10–11, 20–21, 119–20, 205, 210, 245, 256–57, 274–75, 309–10
racism, 3–5, 13, 16, 18–19, 20–21, 82–83, 114–15, 137, 168, 255–56, 274–75, 278–81
Reformation, the, 45–46, 61, 194, 195
Republican Party, 149–53

sacrifice, 98–99, 134–35, 142–43, 150, 153–54, 155–63, 174–75, 192–93, 200, 234, 292
Scruton, Roger, 36, 176–77, 184–98, 207–8, 293–94
secularisation, 27, 30–33, 196–97. *See also* secularism

secularism, 23, 29–30, 127, 156, 193. *See also* secularisation
SenseLab, 244, 264–72, 277–78, 298–99
slavery, 55, 69, 125–26, 133, 212–13, 219–21, 228, 255–60, 274
social media, 3, 50–51, 141, 165, 167, 176, 215, 223–24, 241–42, 287–88, 305
Spinoza, Baruch, 70, 73–74, 194, 260–61
stickiness, 50–51, 73, 220–21, 289. *See also* sticky
sticky
  affect, 237–38
  histories, 81, 231, 248–49, 252, 297
  signs, 289
  See also stickiness

Tamar, 210, 234
Tea Party, the, 36, 142, 150–58, 174–75, 291–92
transnational, 2, 17, 23–24, 23n.139, 121
Trump, Donald, 46–47, 149–50, 228

Ujamaa Centre, 272, 276–77
Utøya, vii, 1, 3, 6n.23, 7–8, 21–22, 25–26, 170–71

Vulgate, 5–6, 40, 106–7, 109

Western
  civilization, 117–18, 197–98, 200–1
  culture, 122–29, 139, 185, 186, 190, 193, 194, 196–98, 205

xenophobia, 13, 16, 18–19, 114–16, 157–58, 178–79, 183, 187–88, 249–50

Zionist/m, 10–11, 119–20, 228

Biblical References

For the benefit of digital users, indexed terms that span two pages (e.g., 52–53) may, on occasion, appear on only one of those pages.

Genesis, 62–63, 90, 288–89
Genesis 1:27, 135–36
Genesis 2–3, 215–16
Genesis 4, 210
Genesis 7, 210
Genesis 9:25–27, 255–56, 274
Exodus, 51–52, 90, 154, 186–87
Exodus 14:14, 161–62
Exodus 15:3, 94–95
Exodus 15:6, 94–95
Exodus 22:2–3, 95
Leviticus, 90
Leviticus 18:24–25, 199n.132
Leviticus 19:34, 96
Leviticus 26:3, 146–47
Numbers, 90
Deuteronomy, 90, 210, 215–16
Deuteronomy 9:5, 199n.132
Deuteronomy 10:19, 96
Deuteronomy 18:9–14, 199n.132
Joshua, 210, 235–36
Judges, 90, 235–36
Judges 3, 154
Judges 19–20, 209–10, 235
Ruth, 235
1 Samuel, 90, 93–94, 180, 235
1 Samuel 25:13, 93–94
2 Samuel 13, 210
2 Kings, 90
1 Chronicles, 90
2 Chronicles, 90
Nehemiah, 90, 149–50
Nehemiah 4:17–18, 95n.99, 149–50
Job 19:25–27, 44–46
Psalms, 62, 90, 288–89
Psalms 18:34, 5–6, 93–94
Psalms 18:37–39, 93–94
Psalms 67, 93–94
Psalms 68:31, 256–57
Psalms 119:46, 136–37
Psalms 144:1, 147n.31

Psalms 149:5–9, 154
Proverbs, 90
Proverbs 3:3, 176
Proverbs 24:10, 94
Proverbs 24:17, 148
Proverbs 25:21, 148
Isaiah, 90, 235, 306
Isaiah 41:13, 94–95
Isaiah 42:13, 94–95, 146–47
Isaiah 54:17, 147n.31
Isaiah 65:17, 199–200
Jeremiah, 288–89
Jeremiah 29:11, 223–24
Ezekiel, 90
Ezekiel 33:11, 135–36
Daniel, 43–44, 90, 154
Daniel 6, 154
Daniel 11:32, 93–94, 147n.31
Jonah, 288–89
Habakkuk, 90
Maccabees, 90
Matthew, 90
Matthew 2:16–18, 160–61
Matthew 5:38–40, 108–9
Matthew 5:43–47, 96, 108–9
Matthew 10:34–35, 39–40, 129–30, 132, 141
Matthew 21:12–14, 100–1
Matthew 22:15–22, 127n.98
Matthew 22:17, 180
Matthew 26:52–54, 95
Matthew 27:54, 162n.132
Mark, 306
Mark 6:17–20, 200
Mark 11:15–18, 158–59
Mark 12:1317, 127n.98
Luke, 90
Luke 6:31, 104–5
Luke 10:25–37, 39–40
Luke 19:45–47, 158–59
Luke 20:20–26, 127n.98
Luke 22:36, 95, 131–32

John 2:13–16, 158–59
John 3:16, 52–53, 76–77, 223–24
John 6:15, 180
John 15:13, 98–99, 162–63
John 15:20, 39–40, 141
Acts 5:29, 94–95
Acts 12:23, 94
Romans, 90
Romans 11:24, 180–81
Romans 13:1–7, 154, 154n.86
1 Corinthians, 90
1 Corinthians 1:20, 147n.31

1 Corinthians 4:20, 94
1 Corinthians 13, 219n.48
2 Corinthians, 90
2 Corinthians 7:14, 153–54
Galatians 15:12, 210
Ephesians, 90
Ephesians 6:17, 129–30
2 Timothy 2:3, 141
James, 90
Revelation, 9n.43, 68, 170
Revelation 19, 210
Revelation 21:1, 199–200